Continued on back

ECOLOGICAL APPROACHES
TO CLINICAL AND
COMMUNITY PSYCHOLOGY

ECOLOGICAL APPROACHES TO CLINICAL AND COMMUNITY PSYCHOLOGY

Edited by

WILLIAM A. O'CONNOR

Department of Psychology
University of Kansas
Lawrence, Kansas

BERNARD LUBIN

Department of Psychology
University of Missouri
Kansas City, Missouri

A WILEY-INTERSCIENCE PUBLICATION

JOHN WILEY & SONS

New York • Chichester • Brisbane • Toronto • Singapore

Library of Congress Cataloging in Publication Data:

Main entry under title:

Ecological approaches to clinical and community psychology.

(Wiley series on personality processes)
"A Wiley-Interscience publication."
Includes indexes.
1. Community psychology. 2. Psychotherapy—Social
aspects. 3. Social systems—Therapeutic use. 4. Family
psychotherapy. I. O'Connor, William A., 1939– .
II. Lubin, Bernard, 1923– . III. Series.
RA790.E35 1984   616.89′144   83-23420
ISBN 0-471-87669-0

Printed in the United States of America

10 9 8 7 6 5 4 3 2 1

For
Kris, Matt, Bill and Sharon.
W.O'C.

For Alice.
B.L.

Contributors

ROBERT B. BECHTEL, PH.D.
Professor, Department of Psychology
University of Arizona
Tucson, Arizona

STEVEN L. BRIGGS, PH.D.
Private Practice Family Therapist
Shawnee Mission, Kansas

RUTH C. CRONKITE, PH.D.
Research Associate
Social Ecology Laboratory
Department of Psychiatry and
    Behavioral Sciences
Veterans Administration and
    Stanford University Medical Center
Palo Alto, California

STACEY DANIELS, M.A.
Senior Research Associate
Greater Kansas City Mental Health
    Foundation
Kansas City, Missouri

JOHN W. FINNEY, PH.D.
Research Associate
Social Ecology Laboratory
Veterans Administration and
    Stanford University Medical Center
Palo Alto, California

ROBERT FUHR, PH.D.
Research Associate
Department of Psychology
Stanford University
Palo Alto, California

DARLENE E. GOODHART, PH.D.
Visiting Assistant Professor
Department of Psychology
University of Illinois
Champaign, Illinois

PAUL GUMP, PH.D.
Professor, Department of Psychology
University of Kansas
Lawrence, Kansas

SUSANNA A. HAYES, PH.D.
Program Administrator
Department of Psychology
Western Washington University
Bellingham, Washington

OLGA HERVIS, M.S.W.
Adjunct Assistant Professor
Department of Psychiatry
University of Miami
School of Medicine
Miami, Florida

GARY S. HURD, PH.D.
Assistant Professor of Psychiatry
    (Anthropology)
Medical College of Georgia
Augusta, Georgia

MARY L. JASNOSKI, PH.D.
Postdoctoral Fellow
Department of Psychology
Northwestern University
Evanston, Illinois

BRADFORD P. KEENEY, PH.D.
Director of Research
Ackerman Institute for Family
  Therapy
New York, New York

WILLIAM M. KURTINES, PH.D.
Associate Professor
Department of Psychology
Florida International University
Miami, Florida

FORTUNE V. MANNINO, PH.D.
Scientist Director, USPHS and
  Assistant Chief, Mental Health
  Study Center
Intramural Research Program
National Institute of Mental Health
Adelphi, Maryland

ANTHONY J. MARSELLA, PH.D.
Director, WHO/NIMH Schizo-
  phrenia Research Program and
  Professor, Department of
  Psychology
University of Hawaii
Honolulu, Hawaii

RUDOLPH H. MOOS, PH.D.
Professor and Research Career
  Scientist
Social Ecology Laboratory
Veterans Administration and
  Stanford University Medical Center
Palo Alto, California

WILLIAM A. O'CONNOR, PH.D.
Graduate Faculty
Psychology Department
University of Kansas
Lawrence, Kansas

E. MANSELL PATTISON, M.D.
Professor and Chairman
Department of Psychiatry

Medical College of Georgia
Augusta, Georgia

MILTON F. SHORE, PH.D.
Chief, Mental Health Study Center
Intramural Research Program
National Institute of Mental Health
Adelphi, Maryland

FRANK SPENCER, PH.D.
School Psychologist
Strafford Learning Center
Somersworth, New Hampshire

JAMES STACHOWIAK, PH.D.
Private Practice of Psychotherapy
Shawnee Mission, Kansas

SUSAN M. SWAP, PH.D.
Associate Professor
Department of Professional Studies
Wheelock College
Boston, Massachusetts

JOSE SZAPOCZNIK, PH.D.
Director, Spanish Family Guidance
  Center
Department of Psychiatry
University of Miami
Coral Gables, Florida

JOSEPH E. TRIMBLE, PH.D.
Department of Psychology
Western Washington University
Bellingham, Washington

CHARLES B. WILKINSON, M.D.
Executive Director
Greater Kansas Mental Health
  Foundation
Kansas City, Missouri

ALEX ZAUTRA, PH.D.
Associate Professor
Department of Psychology
Arizona State University
Tucson, Arizona

Series Preface

This series of books is addressed to behavioral scientists interested in the nature of human personality. Its scope should prove pertinent to personality theorists and researchers as well as to clinicians concerned with applying an understanding of personality processes to the amelioration of emotional difficulties in living. To this end, the series provides a scholarly integration of theoretical formulations, empirical data, and practical recommendations.

Six major aspects of studying and learning about human personality can be designated: personality theory, personality structure and dynamics, personality development, personality assessment, personality change, and personality adjustment. In exploring these aspects of personality, the books in the series discuss a number of distinct but related subject areas: the nature and implications of various theories of personality; personality characteristics that account for consistencies and variations in human behavior; the emergence of personality processes in children and adolescents; the use of interviewing and testing procedures to evaluate individual differences in personality; efforts to modify personality styles through psychotherapy, counseling, behavior therapy, and other methods of influence; and patterns of abnormal personality functioning that impair individual competence.

IRVING B. WEINER

University of Denver
Denver, Colorado

ix

Preface

Few of our friends and colleagues failed to tell us on at least one occasion that it is easier to write a book than to edit one. Although the truth of their admonitions is undeniable, we remain convinced that this book should have been done as it was. What we have chosen to call ecological models have been proposed as the most appropriate and effective approach to the area of mental health for decades. But the current state of the art of clinical and community practice has not applied such a perspective as fully as is possible. Particular individuals, using various terms implying systems or ecological perspectives, have made landmark contributions; often their applications have targeted selected populations or have been published for a specific audience. The singular advantage of an edited work is that it can present a careful selection of cutting-edge contributions written by those who are developing the area rather than by a single author who reviews and restates the work of others.

Our most fundamental intent in this volume is the clear, organized presentation of ecological or systems approaches. We demonstrate how the current state of the art allows the application of such an approach across the broadest range of clinical endeavors—from individual assessment and therapy to community intervention and prevention. It is an approach whose time has come, and an edited work is essentially an announcement of that fact.

WILLIAM A. O'CONNOR
BERNARD LUBIN

Kansas City, Missouri
February 1984

Contents

ECOLOGICAL APPROACHES
TO CLINICAL AND
COMMUNITY PSYCHOLOGY

Introduction

The term *ecosystem* originated in biology almost a century ago, referring to any organizational unit or interactive system composed of populations and their related environments. The size and characteristics of biological ecosystems may vary widely, from the entire earth (ecosphere) to complex microscopic organizations. But it is only recently that human organizations of intermediate size, ranging from family systems to communities, have been considered from the ecological perspective.

Psychosocial ecology is generally traced to the work of Park and Burgess, who established a center for ecological research at the University of Chicago in 1921. Their early studies involved a direct transfer of concepts from general ecology to human behavior; Burgess' urban zones are based on the concepts of competition and succession in a biological ecosystem. But the ecological paradigm was never fully applied to practical mental health issues. Similarly, organismic and field theories in psychology were initially recognized as providing a more comprehensive model in which the individual and the context are seen as part of the naturally occurring system; but applications to clinical and community psychology were limited until recently.

The current resurgence of interest in human ecosystems parallels the growth of community mental health centers and public sector funding over the last two decades. The development of community mental health centers may have forced us to look at the effects of the service delivery system itself on therapeutic outcome. The obvious differences in organizational structure and service delivery between state hospitals and community mental health centers provided clear data on the effects of variables beyond the therapist-client dyad as determinants of treatment outcome. At the same time, new populations of clients were presented to the mental health practitioner: As we began to deal with geriatric mental health, substance abuse, sexual assault, and child abuse, it was no longer possible to conceptualize and implement treatment as if a clearly identified client could be labeled as pathologic as the basis for a simple treatment of choice delivered by the practitioner to the patient.

With these events a second awareness is unavoidable: We can no longer separate clinical and community intervention. Both treatment and prevention occur within the same population, the same organization, the same catchment area, and with the same staff participating in each process. When both clinical and community activities are intermeshed, it becomes conceptually absurd to use two separate models of behavior, and to separate pathology from normalcy,

1

therapeutic techniques from institutional and community context, treatment from prevention, and the development of "psychopathology" from the area of human development in general. This of course leads to the realization that we have been using one set of techniques for what we term *diagnosis,* another for the evaluation of treatment outcome, another for program evaluation, and another for what we term *research.* Unless we are dealing with the behavior of unrelated organisms, then clients, consumers, community members, and subjects are all human beings who interact with an external context. The growth of family therapy and family systems approaches has also generated an awareness of the ecosystemic perspective. The family is the most obvious and immediately accessible ongoing system which presents the clinician with evidence that behavior cannot be adequately understood by isolating individual and context. If, then, a systems approach is relevant to understanding an individual in a family context, it becomes clearly relevant as well to the relationship between individuals and other systems and to the relationship between the family and the multiple social contexts in which it is embedded.

Viewing the individual in an interactive context is not, however, an easy task. The complexity of the total system has tended to focus research on persons and populations to the exclusion of environments and person-environment interactions. The clinician is presented with a similar problem: The therapist can come to understand the patient, but may lack the effective means to understand the life events occurring before, during, and after the therapeutic process. At a practical level, the patient is accessible to the therapist's direct intervention; the community as a whole is not. It is therefore tempting to treat the patient and in the process fail to understand the essential functions that the community has ascribed to the therapeutic process.

The difficulty in organizing such complex perspectives is reflected in the organization of this volume as well. We have chosen to divide this volume into four parts. The first focuses on the relationship of the individual to context. However, it is difficult to separate the contributions in Part 1 in a clear fashion from those in the following sections that may relate the functioning of the individual to family context, social network, or sociocultural systems. Similarly, Part 2 focuses on the relationship of the family system to its multiple contexts; any one of the chapters, however, could also have been placed in Part 1. The relationship of the individual to the family system is not isolated from individual and context interactions with other systems. Part 3 focuses on the relationship of individuals to larger and more complex social organizations; it tends to be more applicable to community and preventive mental health efforts than are preceding chapters but is not clearly and absolutely distinct from the contributions in preceding sections. Marsella's chapter, for example, could have easily been allocated to Part 1, focusing on aspects of psychopathology in a general interactional model of human behavior. Part 4, the final section of this volume, is intended to focus awareness and raise issues with respect to broad cross-cultural processes. By this point in the volume, having extended our perspective to the diverse cultures of the communities of our kind that inhabit this planet, it becomes impossible to be either comprehensive or representative in the selection of topics and chapters. We have, therefore, included chapters of some practical significance to black American, Hispanic, and Native American populations as well as to the phenomenon of spirit possession which is noted in subpopulations within the United States and noted cross-culturally as well.

The intent of this volume, therefore, could not be to represent all possible ecological perspectives or to provide a comprehensive casebook by which ecological techniques could be implemented. It was, however, intended to represent major contributors and points of view that could be conceptualized within an ecological perspective. Many of the contributors have not identified themselves or their work as "ecological" or ecosystemic. It does, nevertheless, represent an approach that is consistent with three basic assumptions. First, that clinical and community processes related to mental health occur in a context. Second, that these clinical and community processes are a function of interaction between persons and larger systems. And third, that the outcome of clinical and community interventions is a function of person, environment, and the interactive process with larger surrounding systems.

If the individual is viewed as a system within a system, then each behavioral act is a change of state of matter/energy or its movement over space from one point to another. Such an ecosystemic perspective would view health as a relationship between person and system that maximizes the functioning of both. The mentally healthy person interacts with an environment in which the requirements and resources of that system are congruent with the needs and abilities of the person.

From such a perspective, psychopathology exists when group structure lacks sufficient resources to meet the needs of all inhabitants or does not distribute resources in a fashion that allows all members of the ecosystem to meet their needs within the limits of expected behaviors. In this sense, psychopathology may be viewed as a function of normality; when individual roles do not allow effective and conventional behavior, deviant roles and behaviors emerge. The individual, on the other hand, can be assessed in terms of capacity to implement effectively those behaviors or performances that produce positive outcomes. Psychotherapy then becomes a mechanism by which both the individual and the system can correct the imbalance between system and occupant needs. The role of the healer or therapist emerges, in a sense, so that the system can treat itself by the same process with which the therapist treats the clients.

An ecosystemic perspective does not, therefore, contradict the autonomy and responsibility of the individual in determining behavior. It does not, further, confuse the healing process with that of social control; the therapist is not the agent of the environment or social system, enforcing norms and limits. Some theorists have suggested that the motivation of the actor is internal with the environment as mere background; others have suggested that the performer can express only what the role demands and the setting allows. From an ecosystemic perspective, however, both the individual and the environment can exert powerful influences, but they are always interactive.

PART ONE

Ecological Models: Applications at the Individual Level

The task of the editor in organizing contributions by part and in a particular order produces its own learning. From a conceptual standpoint, the original intent of the organization of the volume seemed relatively straightforward. Because complex ecosystems may be viewed as having levels of organization, Part 1 would focus primarily on the individual as a level of organization in relation to the multiple contexts in which he or she is embedded. Part 2 would then focus on the family system, Part 3 on larger social networks and organizations within the community, and Part 4 on the total community or sociocultural level of organization. Within each chapter, the individual contributor was asked to specify assumptions or the conceptual framework from which he or she proceeded, to identify key concepts or the theoretical model presented, and then to provide the most applicable and practical assessment and intervention techniques with which a mental health practitioner could implement clinical practice from an ecosystemic perspective. But between the initial conceptual plan for organization of the volume and its final execution, it became clear that the ecosystemic perspective raises difficult and fundamental issues with respect to clinical and community practice. To "focus" a chapter at the individual level conceptually while operating from a framework in which the individual is seen as interactive with all the contexts—physical and psychosocial—that constitute the individual life experience, presents a paradox. The conceptual organization of the volume as a whole appears to contradict its underlying assumptions; if the ecosystem of which the individual is a part operates as a unitary and multilevel system, then every chapter should focus on all levels of the system from complex events at the level of the cell or physiological subsystems within the individual to the most molar cultural process. In fact, such a perspective is valid: We do know that specific events at the level of the cell, as in the case of genetic anomalies, may impact on the behavior or "psychology" of the individual in a powerful fashion, and that such events as the economy or international politics (i.e., war or peace) impact the incidence of specific individual diagnosis such as depression.

What became clear as the individual chapters were reviewed was that the organization of the volume is not so much conceptually valid as it is practical from the standpoint of service delivery. That is, from whatever perspective the therapist operates, the service delivery system and the organization of mental health services treat the individual as a distinct level of organization. By tradition and in practice it is the individual who presents himself or herself to the clinician for assessment and for "treatment" in a setting isolated from the usual life environment of the client and unaccompanied by the physical presence of family, significant others in the social network, organizations, and the culture as a whole. We do not deliver service most typically by accompanying the client throughout his or her day and week in all of those settings and interactions which in aggregate constitute the individual's life experience. We traditionally sit with the individual in an office and define the process as assessment and intervention.

The chapters selected for Part 1 are therefore intended to provide the clinician or practitioner with an ecosystemic perspective that may be utilized most effectively when an individual client initially seeks help and presents self alone.

The intitial chapter by Stachowiak and Briggs is an excellent example of the dilemma and resolution of the conceptual paradox presented to both contributor and editor. Ecosystemic therapy is presented in relation to anorexia nervosa; the anorectic client is typically presented to the practitioner as if the "problem" were eating, and clearly eating is an individual act. The consequences or impact of anorectic behavior are seen at the level of the physical, biological self; the anorectic may die of starvation. Stachowiak and Briggs therefore begin with an ecosystemic perspective, the reality of the clinical setting, and proceed to describe the process of assessment and intervention which extends through family and organizational contexts.

The chapter by Keeney approaches the dilemma in a somewhat different fashion. Keeney's prior work, like that of Bateson and many of the "Palo Alto" family system group, has focused primarily on family system and family therapy areas. But the perspective initially proposed by Bateson is successfully and clearly presented in relation to the individual.

Jasnowski's contribution focuses most directly on the clinical assessment and intervention process, but from a cybernetic model applied to living, complex, and multilevel systems. Assessment techniques are presented at the intra-individual and extra-individual levels, as are intervention techniques. It becomes clear, then, that the central task of the clinician or practitioner is to select the appropriate level at which assessment and intervention can be effectively implemented in contrast to approaches that predefine the level and focus of diagnostic and therapeutic techniques.

The final chapter in Part I resolves the conceptual paradox represented by this volume in the most straightforward way possible: Where a conceptual paradox exists because we conceptualize paradoxically, it can be utterly ignored. The seemingly impossible then becomes remarkably clear and simple; Gump has represented the area of ecological psychology, a major area of contemporary psychological theory which is both complex and massive in its scope, by presenting straightforward clinical/anecdotal material from the standpoint of an ecological psychologist. In the process, the perspective simply makes itself clear.

CHAPTER 1

Ecosystemic Therapy:
"A Treatment Perspective"

JAMES STACHOWIAK AND STEVEN L. BRIGGS

CONCEPTUAL FRAMEWORK

The conceptual framework from which a therapist operates determines such crucial factors as who is seen in therapy, how the problem is formulated, and what intervention is made. This frame of reference, called an epistemology, is the conceptual grid or filter through which the therapist interprets the behavior presented during the session.

Ecosystemic therapy is founded on the principles of human ecology and systems theory. It is a multiple level treatment perspective focused on the context of interaction among individuals and their environment. In this paradigm, diagnosis and treatment are based on an interactive description of the problem situation followed by systems intervention.

Ecosystemic therapy emphasizes diagnosis and treatment focused on the most inclusive system context relevant to the problem situation. The unit of treatment is the person-environment context, taken as a whole. This context is in turn composed of a series of interlocking system levels. Physiological and intrapsychic processes interact with dyadic and family dynamics all within a network of social relationships, role responsibilities, and community-cultural influences. From this matrix of interaction, the therapist selects relevant elements from each system level to compose a system context suitable for intervention.

Underlying the contextual basis of ecosystemic therapy is a fundamental assumption regarding the process of problem formulation. As Bateson (1971) states, the shift from a single to a multiple person treatment unit "brings with it a new epistemology and ontology, i.e., a new way of thinking..." (p. 242). The fundamental change is from interpreting behavior in terms of linear cause-and-effect sequences to conceptualizing the same behavior as resulting from a reciprocally causal system of interaction.

In his training workshops, Haley (1981) extends this view, emphasizing that each unit (individual, dyad, triad, etc.) requires a different theory and approach to treatment. Each more inclusive system provides both additional information and a broader context from which to formulate a diagnosis and treatment plan.

When the individual is the focus of treatment, emphasis is placed on the intrapsychic domain of thoughts, feelings, attitudes, and so on, as the means to accomplish behavior change. With systems of two or more individuals, the focus shifts to the identification of cyclic patterns of reciprocally causal behavior underlying such relationship dynamics as the process of communication, the balance of power, and the interplay of reward and punishment.

In a reciprocal causal cycle, each person's behavior both influences, and is influenced by, the behavior of others in the system. Within this cycle, a person's thoughts, feelings, attitudes, communication patterns, and behavior are reflexive, organized by the system, often without the participant's awareness. For example, the stress of negative family or social interaction can result in fatigue and irritability which in turn provokes more negative interaction in an increasing cycle of negative behavior.

Ecosystemic intervention utilizes the systemic properties of the person-environment context as a catalyst for change. Intervention is strategic and additive, focused on the alteration or replacement of negative behavior cycles. Symptoms are viewed as functional for the system in which they occur. By changing the process of interaction, symptomatic behavior can be altered, then redirected into a positive cycle serving the same maintenance function for the system. The treatment context spans the full range of system levels from physiological to community-cultural. Interventions are directed toward those elements of the system context relevant to the problem situation.

Ecosystemic therapy represents a developing treatment perspective uniting the concepts of system intervention with a multisystem view of the treatment context. Since the 1940s, the socially sanctioned unit of treatment has undergone a progressive development toward more inclusive levels of social organization. The practice of psychotherapy has expanded from the biochemical domain, to include intrapsychic processes, dyadic interaction, then family and extended family dynamics, and most recently, social and community systems. The next logical step in this progression is intervention from a systems perspective, not restricted to a single systems level, but incorporating the interactive qualities of multiple systems into a contextual framework for diagnosis and treatment.

THE ENVIRONMENTAL SYSTEM

In human ecology, the person-environment context constitutes the totality of relationships among individuals and their environment. Each person-to-person and person-to-environment interaction forms a linkage in an intricate network of interconnections. Viewed over time, this network of interactions establishes a dynamic equilibrium as each individual strives to adapt to changing social and environmental conditions.

In its totality, the environmental context forms what Keeney (1979) terms a "unitary interactive system." A system functions as a single unit due to the property of synergy. In a synergetic system, the interaction of the system components taken together have a greater total effect than the sum of their individual effects. The key is interaction. Each person within a system is functionally and reciprocally related to every other person and environmental factor. Thus the behavior of any individual must be understood within the total context formed by the interrelationships of the other individuals and elements of the system.

The person-environment system is also organized in a series of increasingly inclusive system levels. Each system level is delineated by a boundary separating the functional interaction of one set of system components from those of the next higher level of organization. Typically, system levels are identified by a qualitative difference in either the system components or the norms governing system interaction. For example, on the physiological level, the circulatory, pulmonary, and endocrine systems consist of separate organs and perform different functions, yet work synergetically to maintain the next higher order system, the human body.

Theoretically, system levels can be identified from the smallest subatomic particles to the interaction of galaxies. In human services, the focus extends from the level of physiological functioning to that of social and cultural influences. Given this range, selection of the system levels relevant to a specific problem is a crucial first step in the process of diagnosis and treatment. This selection will, in turn, be influenced by the conceptual model employed and the therapists' degree of access to each system.

Theories of interaction tend to be directed at a single system level; physiological, intrapsychic, and so on, often ignoring the coupling or the connection of that system level to those above and below. Consistent with this is the tendency of therapists to treat the system level typically available to them in their work setting. This frequently results in the implicit dismissal of the effects of such factors as a physical condition, home environment, extended family, work, school, neighborhood, and culture. In contrast, ecological therapy offers a model incorporating the interactive effects of a range of system levels in conceptualizing and intervening in human systems.

SYSTEM LEVELS

Treatment begins with an assessment phase which involves the examination of each system level to determine both its function and contribution to the problem situation. This process consists of (1) a review of each system level, (2) a determination of the relevance of each system level to the problem situation, and (3) conceptualization of the interactive or systems effects operating initially to create and then maintain the problem situation. This approach to assessment counters the tendency to dismiss relevant information by formulating one's assessment and treatment plan based on information from a single system level.

The authors have found consideration of the following system levels particularly useful in conceptualizing system interaction.

Physiological

A human being is an organism whose physical integrity as a functioning system depends on the effective operation of pulmonary, circulatory, digestive, and other subsystems. Each subsystem must operate within an effective range for the organism as a whole to exist and function effectively. Feedback mechanisms within the body maintain the synergetic function of these subsystems and attempt to restore homeostatic balance if the effective range is exceeded. When balance cannot be restored, the effective function of the body is impaired. This impairment in turn affects the person's behavior and interaction on other system levels.

Individual Psychology

This system level consists of a set of internal constructs; perceptions, images, cognitions, feelings, motivations, whose interaction is seen as mediating behavior. Within this frame of reference, an individual's competence in relating to changing environmental conditions is dependent upon his or her ability to: (1) accurately perceive surrounding conditions; (2) give meaning to these perceptions by relating them to an internal conceptual scheme; (3) decide on an appropriate action; (4) carry out this action over time; and (5) elevate its effectiveness, reinitiating the cycle as necessary. A developmental deficit or breakdown in any of these skill areas is likely to result in the formation of a problem situation.

Individual/Physical Environment

An individual lives in a dynamic interchange with his or her environment. This exchange characterizes an open system, one in which energy and information are exchanged across permeable system boundaries. On the physiological level, the organism must exchange air, food, water, and heat to maintain itself. Physical health is thus an interaction between the function of the body's physiological subsystems and the conditions in the physical environment (Cheroskin & Ringsdorf, 1971).

Perception and behavior form a similar person-environment circuit. As Bateson (1971) points out, the unit is the completed circuit:

Consider the case of a man felling a tree with an ax. Each stroke of the ax must be corrected for the state of the cut face of the tree after each chip flies. In other words, the system which shows mental characteristics is the whole circuit from the tree to the man's sense organs, through his brain to his muscles and the ax, and back to the tree. (p. 244)

The fundamental shift is from a linear cause-and-effect sequence to a systems model of completed person-environment circuits.

Bandler, Grinder, and Satir (1976) have developed an approach based on linguistic analysis to assist therapists in shifting from a static linear conception of behavior to this completed circuit model. Their focus has been to convert such static phrases as "I don't know," "I'm confused," or "I've just lost touch," into the active circuits "what don't you know?," "what specifically are you confused about?," and "what have you lost touch with?" The effect is to shift the attribution of cause and the focus of intervention from a static description of symptoms to an active description of the relationship.

Dyadic Relationship

Paired interaction between two individuals introduces reciprocally causal behavior patterns. In a reciprocal relationship pattern, each person's behavior is mutually and circularly influenced by that of the other. These reciprocal behavioral cycles in turn mediate such basic relationship processes as closeness-distance, communication, dominance-submission, and reward-punishment. Each of these factors interacts with the others forming a complex system of interaction. Thus a distant couple may engage in a periodic bicker to reestablish contact. Or a spouse may use vague, tangential communication to nullify the decisions of an overcontrolling partner. The challenge to the therapist is to discern the underlying reciprocal pattern through the haze of superficial transactions.

Family System

The family system extends mutually reciprocal behavior to patterns involving three or more individuals. As a system the family unit seeks to balance its need for internal organization and stability with outside demands for adaptation and change. A dynamic equilibrium is maintained through the operation of negative and positive feedback loops. Negative feedback is used to maintain family functioning within acceptable limits by countering deviation from normal or expected behavior. Positive feedback promotes change in the family system by encouraging new behavior. Positive feedback is essential to the family's ability to adapt to new situations and conditions.

In a healthy family, positive and negative feedback loops work in conjunction to maintain both family stability and the ability to respond flexibly to changing conditions. There is a balance between the resources available in the family and family members' needs, both physical and emotional. Communication is clear and direct, with norms supporting both fair distribution of resources and the responsibility of family members to ask for what they need. Family goals and values are explicit and provide sufficient rewards to maintain family cohesion.

Also, in a healthy family, the rules and procedures necessary to carry out such family functions as child rearing, preparing meals, coordinating activities, are consistent and reviewed with changing circumstances. Norms governing acceptable behavior are flexible and clearly understood, allowing each family member several degrees of freedom to accommodate individual differences. When the accepted range of behavior is exceeded, verbal feedback and an opportunity to learn new behavior precedes the introduction of negative consequences or withdrawal of freedom and resources. Finally, the healthy family displays both creativity and resilience in adapting to changing conditions, crises, or periods of stress in which resources are diminished.

The breakdown of any of these functions produces a state of imbalance or disequilibrium in the family system. When one function fails, other family functions compensate in an attempt to maintain the stability of the imbalanced family system. Thus in a family where resources, such as attention or affection, are unfairly distributed among the children, rigid rules and punishments will be developed to combat the visible symptoms of bickering and sibling rivalry. The stability thus gained must in turn be supported by norms preventing the open discussion of what constitutes a "fair share" in this family, as this would reopen the conflict and the risk of instability.

As a family system becomes increasingly dysfunctional, symptomatic or irrational patterns of behavior may be employed by family members in a last-ditch attempt to maintain the marginal stability of the imbalanced system. The behavior generally appears at a point when the family system is under stress and serves a change-resistant or homeostatic function. Such symptomatic behavior is interactive, maintained by reciprocal behavior sequences played out among family members. Each time the family's stability is threatened, the symptomatic behavior is offered as a solution by the "problem" family member in an unacknowledged program of reciprocal behavior designed to reduce the stress on the family system. The power of the cycle appears to lie in its programmed, reciprocal nature and the goal of insuring the survival of the family system.

The irrational quality of symptomatic behavior stems from its sacrificial basis. To maintain stability within a failing system, family members will enact behavior sequences that are destructive to either another family member or themselves. In an attempt to reduce stress, families frequently create a scapegoat (Bell & Vogel, 1960) by labeling one family member as the "problem" followed by increasing efforts to control and then expel the person from the family system.

Barker (1968), in his environmental study of behavior settings, described this process in terms of deviation countering and vetoing circuits. When a person's behavior exceeds the allowed degrees of freedom for the system, deviation-countering circuits are imposed to check the behavior. These circuits generally take the form of placing obstacles in the person's way or offering reminders of the loss of rewards and opportunities that will result if the deviant behavior continues. If these are not successful, vetoing circuits are invoked to expel the individual, denying his or her membership and participation in the supportive interpersonal context of the behavior setting. Similarly, Kantor and Lehr (1975) note the potential for "serious emotional disorder" when an individual is relegated to what they describe as the social intraspace, the zone within the family perimeter but outside of the closed interpersonal system of the family.

Self-sacrifice arises most frequently with children, whose personal survival is closely identified with that of the family system. Repeated conflict between the parents represents a serious imbalance in the family system which intrinsically threatens the child's survival. Sensing the initiation of conflict between his parents, the child invokes a reciprocal behavior sequence with himself as the target. By misbehaving, the child can use his behavior as a buffer, disrupting his parents' conflict cycle while forcing them to unite for the same behavior he is invoking to deal with his behavior.

The child's symptomatic behavior is thus functional within a dysfunctional family system. Although the child cannot correct the source of the conflict between his parents, he can disrupt the cycle each time it occurs. The child, however, pays a high price by taking onto himself the stress of family imbalance in order to maintain the stability and thus the survival of the family system. Unfortunately, this survival-oriented altruistic act is rarely perceived as such by the child or parents, and both come to believe that the child's misbehavior is the source of marital and family problems. Deviation countering and vetoing circuits are then invoked to control the misbehavior, placing the child in the untenable position of risking exclusion from the family system in order to maintain its stability by preventing his parents' conflict cycle.

External demands for adaptation and change also place stress on the family system. Changes in the national economy may have a pronounced effect on the availability of resources to family members. Periods of stress at work or school divert energy and time from family interaction. Changes in activities and schedules disrupt accepted family routines, placing a demand on the family to adapt to the new situation. Similarly, the growth of children necessitates review of the continued appropriateness of rules and expected behavior.

Families adhere to routines and normative behavior because they are safe, well-tried procedures, which have been found to maximize success with a minimum of risk (Nadel, 1968). Faced with the prospect of change the family may respond with self-limitation, denial, or reorganization. Self-limitation involves the choice to avoid the environmental demand by limiting one's activities or potential. This occurs, for example, when a husband or wife turns down a promotion that would require relocation, or when a child declines an offer to join the swim team rather than ask his parents to disrupt the family schedule by taking him to an evening practice. Second, the family may deny the existence of the demand. This involves establishing a consensus of unreality by convincing the affected family member that he really doesn't have a problem and that no change is necessary (Chin, 1961). Finally, the family could acknowledge the demand and enter into a process of communication and negotiation to reorganize the system, establishing new routines geared to the demands of the new environmental situation.

Extended Family and Social Network

Beyond the boundary of the family system there exists an intricate network of extended family and social relationships. Extended family relationships include blood relatives; uncles, aunts, and cousins, as well as those by marriage; stepparents, stepchildren, and in-laws. An individual's social network is comprised of his or her friends, neighbors, and associates from work, school, or social organizations. The interrelationships among all the individuals in the extended family and each family member's social network form an extensive social system surrounding the family. The family system is thus embedded within an interactive system of relationships to the extent that events occurring in each relationship reciprocally influence those in other relationships.

Sociological studies of the family present the extended family and social network as a supportive context, sustaining the family through provision of both affective and instrumental resources. Affective resources include shared involvement, emotional support, and advice/problem solving. Instrumental resources involve direct financial assistance, food, clothing, help in finding work, or accomplishing required tasks such as child care for a young working couple. Pattison et al. (1975) found that the size and positive/negative quality of the relationships in a person's social network were associated with psychological health or dysfunction. Psychologically healthy people were found to maintain social networks of 20 to 30 people, neurotics 10 to 12, and psychotics 4 to 5, generally composed of ambivalent relationships in a closed family system.

Assessment of the extended family and social networks for the purpose of effecting systems intervention includes the interactive influence of: (1) generational patterns, (2) system effects, (3) network dynamics, and (4) system balance. Generational patterns are sequences of behavior that are handed down from generation to generation within the extended family system. System effects include such factors as a parent who has not successfully separated from his or her family of origin, a child caught in a triangle between a parent and grandparent, or exclusion of a family member from the extended family resource network. Recognition of the effects (both positive and negative) of social network dynamics opens up new possibilities for system intervention. The therapist may activate a healthy social system to help a family cope during a time of crisis or work to open the closed negative social system of the psychotic (Pattison et al., 1975). Finally, both the balance and interconnectedness of relationships serve an important role in family function. Dysfunction is typically associated with the extremes of isolation versus fusion, intensity versus distance, and sparsity of behavior settings versus overstimulation.

In the following case presentation many of the ideas and concepts contained in this chapter will be highlighted and discussed.

THE PRESENTING PROBLEM

Annie was a 16-year-old daughter of parents who were in their middle forties; Mr. C. had been employed for the past several years at an upper-level executive position in industrial management, and, for most of the 24-year marriage, Mrs. C.'s major family role was as a housewife-mother. Three older siblings (2 males and 1 female), no longer regularly living at home, completed the family composition.*

*Names and details have been modified to preserve the anonymity of the family.

At the time of admission, the family's primary concern was focused on Annie's long-term habit of proceeding through alternate phases of "gorging" food and vomiting, and "starvation" dieting. Her condition had been previously diagnosed as anorexia nervosa, and she had been hospitalized twice during the past three years. Over a period of eight years, the family had moved to different states several times due to Mr. C.'s job changes, and Annie's previous hospitalizations occurred in institutions in two different states. Her clinical records indicated a recurrent pattern of stabilization (of eating and weight gain) during the hospital stays, with a return to the dysfunctional anorexic states shortly after discharge to the home situation. The treatment programs in both institutions emphasized medical management and individual psychotherapy with relatively little involvement of the family.

Anorexia Nervosa: Initial Assessment

Much has been written about the importance of family involvement in the treatment of anorexia nervosa. Most clinicians and researchers would agree, however, that not all anorexic families fit into the same descriptive picture. In general, anorexic patients and their families fall into three categories:

1. Families who seek out help and become so distressed at the prospect of hospitalization of their child that they terminate further contacts (Stern et al., p. 406).
2. Families who accept and follow the prescription of Minuchin et al. (1978), that is, an abbreviated hospital stay for the patient, with a longer period of follow-up psychotherapy; individual, family, or a combination of the two.
3. Families who comprise the most seriously disturbed group and require long-term treatment of the patient with repeated hospital admissions.

Clinicians who are experienced in working with anorexics and their families generally subscribe to the proposition that "all members of the anorexic family are developmentally arrested in the area of separation-individualization" (Stern et al., p. 406). In a very real sense, the patient requires a program of reparenting and resocialization, and successful intervention frequently requires that the therapist (and treatment team) provide such services for the parents of the patient as well.

In Annie's case, it was obvious that planning for treatment would require viewing the family as falling into category 3. Both parents had experienced strong conflicts in separating from their families of origin. These conflicts were manifested, in part, by the frequent moves occasioned by Mr. C.'s job changes, with the result that their family lifestyle involved little or no direct contact with extended family members. Shortly before Annie's admission, Mr. C. had lost his job due to a company reorganization and spent several months trying to secure a similar position with other companies. A considerable effort was made to keep members of the extended family from becoming aware of Mr. C.'s jobless status. Thus, when Mr. C.'s mother came to stay for a week's visit, Mr. C. left the home each morning in a suit and tie, and carrying his briefcase, as if he were leaving for work. As one might imagine, Annie's "illness" was treated as strictly a "medical problem" and was not discussed outside the nuclear family. Similarly, Mrs. C. took a position as a secretary in a large firm as a result of Mr. C. having lost his job, but this was explained to extended family members as being based on her "need for change."

It was determined that Annie's rigid insistence on maintaining her eating habits represented an abortive attempt to establish her own personal identity through an extreme commitment to controlling this one area of her life. Of equal importance for the formulation of a treatment plan, however, was the realization that the arena she chose for acting out her adolescent rebellion had seriously limited the frequency and number of contacts she had with other persons in her psychosocial network.

Assessment of the Social Network

From initial interviews and appraisal of the clinical records from Annie's previous hospitalizations, the treatment team focused its attention on four interrelated areas that comprised the C. family's social network: (1) school setting, (2) peer relationships, (3) intra-family relationships, and (4) parents' work settings.

Although test results and teacher reports depicted Annie as possessing superior intellectual capacity, her grade averages were about C+ over a period of 3–4 years. In large part, this was attributed to irregular school attendance, the frequent moves occasioned by the father's job changes, and the disruption of regular school attendance by her previous hospitalizations. Her peer relationships were characterized as sparse and there had been little opportunity for developing long-term continuous contacts with friends. It had been noted in previous hospital reports, however, that she demonstrated a capacity for entering into close relationships with one or two fellow patients. These relationships were not continued following hospitalization.

With respect to intra-family relationships, the C. family can best be described as a set of six "loners." Contacts between any combination of dyads and triads were extremely infrequent, and seldom did the entire family share an activity, except for eating an occasional meal together. It should be noted that Annie frequently refused to eat at family meals, even though both parents insisted that she be present at the table. One significant deviation from the family pattern of individuality was the father's tendency to regularly attend, and be supportive toward, both of his sons' athletic activities. This was the source of considerable bitterness and resentment on Annie's part, because she felt he was unwilling to pay attention to, and be supportive of, her attempts to excel at tennis and track. It is interesting to note that Annie's older female sibling elected to develop her sense of competence and skill by excelling in dramatics and cheerleading—activities that were clearly approved of by Mrs. C.

For most of the 24-year marriage, the relationship between Mr. and Mrs. C. could best be described as being designed in a traditional manner. Thus, Mr. C., in an upper-level sales management position, traveled extensively during each week. Mrs. C., the traditional housewife, kept "the home fires burning," taking care of the house and raising the children. Since Mr. C.'s business travel was on an individual basis and involved most of his working hours, he had relatively little contact with business colleagues, except for business meetings. As is so often the case with husbands whose work involves considerable travel, Mr. C. preferred to spend his "free time" on weekends at home. Although the family usually attended church services on Sundays as a group, they did not become involved in any church social functions, nor did they establish social relationships with other church members.

The Treatment Plan

Because of the extreme constriction of physical and emotional contacts in both the intra- and extra-family sphere of relationships, a treatment plan was designed to focus on four areas:

1. A monitored program of diet and exercise for Annie during her stay at an Inpatient Center.
2. A combined program of individual and group therapy for Annie, and weekly family therapy meetings to include both parents, Annie, and her siblings (when they were home from college).
3. A closely monitored school program designed to provide Annie with the opportunity to experience greater success in academic pursuits.
4. Providing Annie with the opportunity to increase the sphere of her peer relationships through participation in recreational group activities.

It was believed that the achievement of the treatment goals would require a period of from four to six months in residence at the Center for Annie.

Evaluation of Results and Outcome

The treatment plan was judged to be effective within the originally projected six-month hospitalization period. At the end of six months:

1. Annie's weight level had remained stable for the last two months, and the frequency of her vomiting had decreased from an initial base rate of 18–20 times per day (on the average) to 2–3 times per week during the sixth month.
2. The combination of individual, group, and family therapy sessions was considered to be quite successful in assisting family members in working toward the resolution of the separateness-attached issue, and to recognize how their pattern of isolation and restricted social contacts had contributed to a dysfunctional organization for family members. The members reported experiencing increasingly more satisfying interactions within the family when Annie returned home for weekend passes. One area of concern to the treatment team,

however, was the parents' resistance to being included in multifamily group therapy meetings, because it paralleled their continuing tendency to restrict contacts with persons outside their family.

3.   Under the closely supervised and highly structured school program at the Center, Annie's grade average had improved to a B+ during her six-month residence.

4.   From the staff's daily records, it was clear that Annie had become much more willing and interested in initiating and maintaining peer relationships. In addition to having established several friendships with other residents, she was described as having maintained a continuing, close relationship with another adolescent female with whom she shared a room for most of her six-month stay.

It would be gratifying to consider the outcome as successful for Annie and her family. Such was not the case, however. In the original treatment plan, it had been proposed that Annie would enter a group home for adolescent females following her dismissal from the center, as a means of assisting in the transition from hospitalization to a return to the family and community. Having completed high school, she was to seek out a part-time job and to enroll in one or two courses at the local community college. Unfortunately, the parents balked at the idea of the group home placement, and Annie convinced them that she was "ready to leave home" to attend college on a full-time basis. Members of the treatment team held the opinion that the working through of Annie's separation and dependency conflicts in relation to her family would require a follow-up program of therapy on an outpatient basis.

Because the college that Annie attended was located at a considerable distance from the family home, follow-up therapy sessions were not pursued. Also, Annie declined to seek out further help for herself in the mental health clinic at the college. Attempts were made by the treatment team at the center to maintain contact with the parents in an effort to determine whether the treatment gains were being maintained. As had been expected, Annie's attempt to undertake a full-time academic program was unsuccessful at this time. Within a month after arriving at the college, Annie had a "falling out" with her dormitory roommate and was given permission to reside in a room by herself. She later revealed that she had soon regressed to her previously dysfunctional eating patterns, and during the third month of the semester, she became ill with what was diagnosed as "mononucleosis." Due to her lack of energy and poor attendance, she found herself to be failing in most of her courses and withdrew before the end of the first semester. She returned to live with her parents, who, "out of desperation," are again seeking psychological assistance. This case has been described as an illustration of the necessity of focusing attention on the community resource network, in addition to a treatment program focused on the individual and his/her family, if therapeutic gains are to be maintained. The next section will discuss the Community Resource Network as a system level for assessment and intervention.

Community Resource Network

Ecologically, the community may be viewed as an interactive network of social institutions, each with its attendant behavior settings and boundary of operations. Thus, physicians are charged with physical health care which takes place in clinics and hospitals. Police apprehend individuals who break laws and confine them in jails and prisons. Lawyers present cases in courtrooms before judges who arbitrate conflicts through a formal procedure set by legal precedent. Psychiatrists confine individuals to mental hospitals and inpatient units when they are disturbing to others (i.e., act outside of community norms for socially expected behavior) or fail to care for themselves (i.e., are suicidal or out of contact with reality).

Each social institution plays an important role in maintaining the stability and function of the community as a whole. Ecologically, these institutions perform functions on a community level that were not adequately performed at the lower system levels of the extended social network. This is illustrated in the case of the child who sacrifices himself to disrupt his parents' conflict cycle. The family initially counters the deviant behavior with negative feedback. If this strategy fails, the family begins the process of excluding the child from the family system. This procedure generally involves seeking suppport and advice from the extended family and social network. The child may then be removed from the home and passed from relative to relative until the social network concurs in the judgment that the child is disturbed and professional help must be sought.

Ecological assessment of the problem situation at the point of contact with the community care giver can make the difference between perpetuating the problem and effective intervention. In seeking help, the family and social networks are admitting failure in their attempt to control the child's behavior (Mendell et al., 1968). The next step in the sequence is to transfer responsibility for the control and care of the child to the professional or social institution. As Haley (1980) points out, "By placing the young person in a mental hospital or other social control institution, or by arranging that a doctor heavily medicate the offspring, the parents keep the family stable" (p. 31). Then, as long as the child continues to evidence disturbing behavior, the functional role can be maintained, "without the inconvenience of actually living with and taking care of him or her" (p. 31).

The professional and institution can thus become unknowingly enlisted as a participant in a reciprocal behavior cycle designed to maintain the stability of a family system. Ineffective intervention in this reciprocal cycle would "institutionalize" the problem by maintaining control at the community level through medicating or institutionalizing the child. Effective intervention would return control to the family system by involving the family and extended social network in treatment to effect a system change at the source of the disruption, the triangulation of the child to maintain stability in an imbalanced family system.

Social Role and Cultural Influences

Systems' intervention is made possible by the existence in society of a recognized social role: that of therapist as social change agent. On the social/cultural system level, the context of therapy is sanctioned as the socially recognized medium for behavior change (O'Connor, 1977). Therapists are licensed and credentialed to ensure that only appropriate change, toward socially acceptable behavior, will take place in this setting. Thus, when the client enters treatment, a three-way contract is formed: between the community and therapist, between the therapist and client, and between the client and his or her social network. The importance of this contract is that it allows the individual or family to reject dysfunctional attitudes and behavior while at the same time sanctioning the process of change in the eyes of the community and social network. Without this sanction, the function of the social system would be to maintain system stability by returning the person to his or her previous function. Ecosystemic therapy seeks to invoke this social sanction to enable the therapist to involve the family and social network in the treatment process. The goal is to effect an intervention that rebalances the family system while redirecting the efforts of the community and social network to return control to the family as it restabilizes.

TREATMENT PROGRAMS: PLANNED REORGANIZATION

From what has been presented so far it seems clear that a reorganization of treatment institutions presently in operation will be required for the efficacy of treatment methods to be improved. We would now like to describe an ongoing reorganization of the treatment program at a center for adolescents, located in a large midwestern city.* The reorganization has been planned to design a program that is more in keeping with the principles discussed in this chapter.

In the spring of 1979, the Executive Director of the Center contacted the first author about the possibility of directing a training program for the therapists and counselors, with the primary aim of changing the focus of treatment from advocacy for the adolescent patient to a family-oriented approach. The multifaceted treatment situations that were available in the Center's facilities provided an ideal opportunity for introducing a systems' orientation and evaluating the results. The recently completed building complex had provided the Center with the facilities for offering a four-level entry into the treatment program: () a long-term residential treatment center for 42 adolescent females; (2) a short-term (crisis) hospital program for 25 boys and girls, aged 5–18; (3) a day-school treatment program for 90 boys and girls, which includes providing education for the residents; and (4) three group homes, each housing 9–10 adolescent females.

The training program in family therapy was initiated with a two-day workshop for all professional personnel, and included the therapists, youth

*The Crittenton Center, Kansas City, Missouri.

counselors, and teachers. The purpose of the workshop was to familiarize the staff with a family systems' approach to clinical intervention, as well as to outline the directions we planned to take during the next year in implementing the training program. A secondary goal was to promote acquaintanceship and cohesion among the staff. Some were new staff members and many had little or no contact with staff who worked in departments other than their own.

For the first three months of the training program staff members were assigned to four teams composed of 6–8 staff members. Each team included therapists, youth counselors, and teachers, in an effort to maintain the closeness and cohesion which had been initially established during the workshop. Within each team, one of the staff members served as cotherapist with the first author in working with families while the other team members sat in and observed. The one-hour family sessions were followed by a one-hour processing session attended by the Director of Training and the team members.

Following the initial three-month training period, an "apprentice model" of training was initiated, with each of the therapists "sitting in" as cotherapist with the Director in individual and multifamily therapy meetings. In addition, weekly meetings were held to provide supervision and consultation for therapists with their ongoing cases. Finally, weekly sessions were held to provide didactic training lectures on family systems, theory, and therapy for all staff members.

The major focus of the first year of the training program included the following aims and goals:

1. To have provided sufficient knowledge, experience, and skill training for all staff therapists to consider themselves as comfortable and competent in conducting therapy with individual families and multifamily groups.

2. To have increased the availability of family therapy experiences for all patients and their families who are accessible to such experience.

3. To have provided sufficient information and an increased sense of awareness of the reciprocal impact of the family system and the patient for all staff members, including youth counselors, nursing staff, teachers, and so on.

4. To encourage a greater degree of family involvement in the patient's treatment from the outset of applying for admission to the Center. This includes planning for initial waiting list and/or multifamily group sessions.

5. To increase the degree of attention that is focused on planning for transition from the Center to the home and community, and for follow-up and aftercare.

After 18 months of training the following results can be reported:

1. The availability of family therapy services for hospital and residential patients and their families increased from 50% to 80%.

2. The length of stay for residential (long-term) patients decreased significantly.

3. Over 75% are now being reintegrated with their families and community settings which compares with a national success average of 50%.

The initial success of the training program provides guidelines for establishing and maintaining a treatment program based on ecological concepts.

The clinical assessment phase includes: (1) an evaluation of the individual's social network and extended family system, (2) an evaluation of system dynamics both within and across system levels, (3) the rigidity or flexibility of system contexts, (4) the richness and degree of participation in interaction settings, and (5) the capacity for recognition of, and adaptation to, normative behavioral values in different behavior settings. The treatment plan would include consideration to planning for density and/or restriction of interaction settings for the individual and his/her family. Finally, the return of the individual patient to his/her family and community requires identification and replacement of dysfunctional behavior patterns, systems intervention, transitional planning, interagency coordination, and follow-up care.

REFERENCES

Bandler, R., Grinder, J., & Satir, V. (1980) *Changing with families.* Palo Alto, Calif.: Science and Behavior Books.

Barker, R.G. (1968) *Ecological psychology.* Stanford, Calif.: Stanford University Press.

Bateson, G. (1971) A Systems Approach. *International Journal of Psychiatry,* **9**, 242–244.

Bell, N.W., & Vogel, E.F. (1960) The emotionally disturbed child as a family scapegoat. *Psychoanal. Psychoanal. Review,* **47** (2), 21–42.

Cheroskin, E. & Ringsdorf, W.M. (1971) Predictive medicine: An ecologic approach. *Journal of American Geriatric Society,* **19**, 505–510.

Chin, R. (1961) The utility of system models and developmental models for practitioners. In W.G. Bennis, K.D. Benne, & R. Chin (Eds.), *The Planning of change: Readings in the applied behavioral sciences.* New York: Holt, Rinehart, and Winston.

Haley, J. (1980) *Leaving home.* New York: McGraw-Hill.

Haley, J. & Madanes, C. (1981) Opening remarks on the development of family therapy at their workshop on strategic therapy. Kansas City, Missouri, June 19–20.

Kantor, D., & Lehr, W. (1975) *Inside the family.* New York: Harper & Row.

Keeney, B.P. (1979) Ecosystemic epistemology: Critical implications for family therapy. Unpublished manuscript.

Mendell, D., Cleveland, S.E., & Fisher, S. (1968). A five-generation family theme. *Family Process,* **7**, 126–132.

Minuchin, S., Rosman, B.L., & Baker, L. (1978) *Psychosomatic Families: Anorexia Nervosa in Context.* Cambridge, Mass.: Harvard University Press.

Nadel, S.F. (1968) Social Control and Self-Regulation. In W.T. Buckley (Ed.), *Modern Systems Research for the Behavioral Scientist.* Chicago: Aldine, 401–408.

O'Connor, W.A. (1977) Ecosystems theory and clinical mental health. *Psychiatric Annals,* **7** (7), 363–372.

Pattison, E.M., DeFrancisco, D., Wood, P., Frazier, H., & Crowder, J. (1975) A psychosocial kinship model for family therapy. *American Journal of Psychiatry,* **132** (12), 1246–1251.

Stern, S., Whitaker, C., Hagemann, N., Anderson, R., & Borgman, G. (1981) Anorexia nervosa: The hospitals' role in family treatment. *Family Process,* **20,** 395–408.

CHAPTER 2

An Ecological Epistemology for Therapy*

BRADFORD P. KEENEY

Therapists are not accustomed to thinking beyond the immediate pragmatic effects of their work. Even outcome research typically focuses on whether the presenting problem was solved or what the success of the solution was. The latter consideration may be in terms of the degree of improvement (or relapse) or evaluating whether other problems have arisen in the client's social context. All of these inquiries are on the level of examining the effect of the therapist's intervention within a small slice of a total ecosystem. The effect of altered subsystems on higher order systems is usually not approached. Just as in studying the effects of DDT, the time periods involved in higher order systemic change make it difficult to assess whole ecologies.

The idea that systems which comprise a whole ecology are connected in complex ways is demonstrated by Charles Elton (in Hardin, 1978, p. 169):

Some keen gardener, intent upon making Hawaii even more beautiful than before, introduced a plant called *Lantana camara,* which in its native home of Mexico causes no trouble to anybody. Meanwhile, someone else had also improved the amenities of the place by introducing turtledoves from China, which, unlike any of the native birds, fed eagerly upon the berries of *Lantana.* The combined effects of the vegetative powers of the plant and the spreading of seeds by the turtle doves were to make the *Lantana* multiply exceedingly and become a serious pest on the grazing country. Indian mynah birds were also introduced, and they too fed upon *Lantana* berries. After a few years the birds of both species had increased enormously in numbers. But there is another side to the story. Formerly the grasslands and young sugarcane plantations had been ravaged by vast numbers of army-worm caterpillars, but the mynahs also fed upon these caterpillars and succeeded to a large extent in keeping them in check, so that the outbreaks became less severe. About this time certain insects were introduced in order to try and check the spread of *Lantana* and several of them (in particular a species of Agromyzid fly) did actually

---

Bradford P. Keeney, Ph.D., is Director of Family Therapy Research, Texas Tech University and Co-Director, Project for Human Cybernetics.

*The ideas in this chapter are more fully developed in the author's book, *Aesthetics of Change* (1983).

destroy so much seed that the *Lantana* began to decrease. As a result of this, the mynahs also began to decrease in numbers to such an extent that there began to occur again severe outbreaks of army-worm caterpillars. It was then found that when the *Lantana* had been removed in many places, other introduced shrubs came in, some of which are even more difficult to eradicate than the original *Lantana*.

In the world of therapy, Gregory Bateson has consistently called for attention to higher levels of pragmatics. He has suggested that therapists take their interventions as seriously as we do for coal miners, petroleum engineers, insecticide chemists, and so forth. Bateson has repeatedly argued that clinicians view the world through the lens of an ecological way of knowing—an ecological epistemology (see Keeney, 1979; Keeney, 1983; Keeney & Sprenkle, 1981). His seriousness in this proposal is indicated as follows (G. Bateson, 1972, p. 462):

If I am right, the whole of our thinking about what we are and what other people are has got to be restructured. This is not funny, and I do not know how long we have to do it. If we continue to operate on the premises that were fashionable in the precybernetic era, and which were especially underlined and strengthened during the Industrial Revolution, which seemed to validate the Darwinian unit of survival, we may have twenty or thirty years before the logical *reductio ad absurdum* of our old positions destroys us....The most important task today is, perhaps, to learn to think in the new way.

Accordingly, the purpose of this chapter is to help connect ecological epistemology to therapeutic work. The reader should be warned that thinking "ecologically" is radically different from the way we traditionally and habitually encounter the world. The movement toward a congruent ecological understanding of our world signifies a dramatic change in paradigm. To help the clinician in this transition a discussion of "pathology," "health," "therapist," and "ecology" will be delineated. In this way, steps toward an ecological understanding of therapy may be initiated.

PATHOLOGY AND HEALTH

Therapists have different beliefs about what symptoms signify. Symptoms are often regarded by therapists as a troublesome problem and a nuisance to be immediately alleviated. This is also typically characteristic of the way in which clients view their trouble. Clients often come to therapists with a complaint hoping the therapist will cure them like a dentist cures their toothache. The medicalization of the therapeutic context perpetuates this form of expectation.

In contrast, other therapists believe symptoms to be natural signals of change or "motors for growth." These therapists are more inclined to let the body-mind system heal itself and sometimes attempt to "protect" the client from outside intervention. This latter approach may involve blocking "solution behavior" of the client and his social partners. Others may even attempt to provide a refuge center to protect the client from "outside" intervention. Note, however, that this is a "solution behavior" and an "outside intervention" that may also perpetuate the systemic organization containing the symptom.

Some clinicians do not attempt to understand what a symptom "means." The strict pragmatist, for example, may only attempt to place symptoms within the context of a patterned organization of events. This strict focus on seeing *how* the symptomatic behavior is maintained exemplifies the position of Watzlawick, Weakland, and Fisch (1974). Ecology, however, also provides a way of understanding symptoms and pathology. To understand this view requires that we recognize that all systems, whether individuals or families, are organized through processes of change.

This means that an individual's behaviors and a family's sequences of interaction must always be changing. Let us begin by examining the individual level of organization. From the ecological perspective, the healthy individual is characterized by complex sets of diverse behaviors and emotions. There are several ways in which these behaviors and emotions can change. For example, someone may shift between feelings of despair, hope, hate, love, and so forth. An ecology of emotions that juxtaposes many different emotions over time may be said to characterize a balanced emotional life. Such a balanced process of changing emotions leads to stability or autonomy of the personality system.

Another way in which the individual may achieve systemic organization is to escalate a particular emotion or behavior. For example, an initial discouragement may escalate into meta-discouragement or what is called "clinical depression." In this way, change of an emotion through escalation maintains the individual's organization of a psychological system. Or there may even be an oscillation between escalated emotions, for example, manic-depressive episodes. This view suggests that pathology or symptomology represent one way in which stability is achieved through change, namely, the escalation (or oscillation of escalations) of behavior and emotion. We might say that symptoms represent "escalating sameness." What changes is the intensity of a particular emotion or the extremeness of a behavior.

This view of symptomology requires that any other similar process also be seen as pathological. Along these lines, Keith (1980) has proposed in the case of clinical depression that other family members who are not depressed are equally pathological. Following Whitaker, he suggests that there are pathologies of "always smiling," "always being rational," "always having good behavior" (Whitaker's category of psychopathology called "the white knight").

The observation that each member of such a family may have different forms of escalating behavior and experience suggests that the whole family organism balances the escalations of each member. Not only does the family maintain its identity this way, but each member's pattern of behavior and experience is as pathological as any other member's. This is the view that enables Whitaker and Keith to call the whole family their patient and to engage in the technique called "moving the symptom" from one member to another.

On the interactional level it is highly probable that a "depressed" person's escalating depression is in sync with another person's escalating "call for hope" or "rationality." In this way, the two complementary sets of emotions and behavior create a whole interactive system. Thus helping the "white knight" be less perfect becomes as therapeutic as alleviating the problem behavior—an automatic operative for the family therapist, Carl Whitaker.

It is important to realize that the systemic organization maintaining the symptom does not necessarily include the whole family nor is it limited to that social group. For example, Watzlawick and Coyne (1980, p. 13) have created therapeutic interventions in treating "depression" by "interdicting the self-defeating efforts of family members to be supportive and encouraging." Their view, like Whitaker's, suggests that "successful therapeutic interventions often involve changing the behavior of persons other than the identified patient." Their view, however, is as parsimonious as possible, attempting to attend only to those individuals who are part of the immediately relevant systemic organization.

A symptom can be defined as a particular class of change. In other words, symptoms represent redundant cycles of escalated behavior and experience for individuals, and these cycles are organized into a whole complementary system in the social context. From the level of social interaction, an individual's symptomatic behavior marks a particular kind of choreographed relationship with others. As we've discussed, "clinical depression" can be seen as a marker for sequences of social interaction wherein there is another individual(s) involved in a spiral of emotions and behavior complementary to the runaway depression. In this way, an individual's symptoms may be taken as a metaphor about interpersonal relationships. More broadly, symptoms are indicators for an ecology of relationships.

Because symptomatic behavior and experience occur in sync with the escalating patterns of other individuals, it is incorrect to presuppose that the DSM-III has named all forms of symptomology. More correctly, as Whitaker and Keith's work demonstrates, any social setting wherein someone can identify "pathology" indicates that other connected members may be sites of pathology. Other labels for the diagnostician might include "psychotic normality," "involutional happiness," "delusions of dualisms," and "punctuation paranoia." The organized sequences of interaction are pathological; or more accurately, there is only a particular type of change process maintaining individual and social organizations.

The ecological view does not suggest that families instead of individuals be considered "disturbed." Rather it identifies a particular way in which individuals and families maintain their systemic organization through redundant patterns of change. The shift toward an ecological epistemology involves not blaming etiological factors, identified patients, or their families for their idiosyncrasies. Seeing symptoms as metaphors for the ecology of relationship systems leads one to a stage of awareness that Bateson (1958) depicts as "humility and loneliness." According to Watts (1961) this "loneliness of liberation" arises when there is no longer any person, group, or etiological factor to blame and feel anger toward.

Individuals and families may maintain themselves through other processes of change that are not strictly characterized by escalating sameness. In ecological science, when the interactions of a large number of diverse species are held in balance, it is called "ecological climax." This balance of complexity in an ecosystem indicates a way of talking about health. The alternative to health is characterized by the maximization (or minimization) of any variable in an ecosystem. Organisms that outbreed other species are necessarily the most flexible and if uncontrolled lead to an ecosystem of weeds. Bateson (in Brand, 1974, p. 18) connects with this discussion as follows:

The idea of sanity or health or whatever has got to be somehow related to the whole concept of climax. The definition of pathology then is: those things which destroy climax. They destroy it to the point, where 50 species lived you can now have only five. These pathologies leave a dull world...the more you make these sudden changes...the more you fractionate down to only accept the plants we call weeds. The same is true of human society.

Thus, health in individual ecosystems refers to a "vital balance" of diverse forms of experience and behavior. There is no maximization of any particular behavior or experience. To engage in an effort of maximization leads to the escalating sameness we have defined as pathology. In contrast, Maslow's (1970) studies of the "growing tip" of healthy individuals indicate that these people escape simplistic, dichotomous forms of description. For example, they may be seen (Maslow, 1970, p. 179) as simultaneously very spiritual and very pagan, where the "age -old opposition between heart and head, reason and instinct or cognition and conation is seen to disappear in healthy people where they become synergic rather than antagonists."[1]

This idea, which is at the root of many theories of individual psychotherapy, characterizes the healthy individual as an integrated, whole unity. This suggests that a "whole, integrated personality" is not necessarily one which can be traditionally called "symptom free." Following Maslow's terminology, the dichotomy between adjustment and maladjustment is transcended. Thus a whole, integrated, healthy personality system at times appears a bit symptomatic (e.g., depressed, manic, psychotic) and at other times symptom free. What is pathological is to be symptomatic *or* symptom free consistently.

On the level of social interaction, the whole social group may be stabilized by sequences of interaction that either escalate (escalating sameness) or permutate. The latter does not imply that healthy ecosystems do not have repeating

---

[1] Maslow (1970, p. 179) also described healthy individuals as escaping the dichotomies of "kindness-ruthlessness, concreteness-abstractiveness, acceptance-rebellion, self-society, adjustment-maladjustment, detachment from others-identification with others, serious-humorous, Dionysian-Apollonian, introverted-extroverted, intense-casual, serious-frivolous, conventional-unconventional, mystic-realistic, active-passive, masculine-feminine, lust-love, and Eros-Agape."

sequences. Instead, there are many species of these redundant cycles, some of which contradict other sequences. Stability arises here in the way these diverse sequences are juxtaposed or patterned. In other words, the arrangement of the sequences provides a "vital balance." Thus, a "healthy conversation" is an alternation of listening and speaking between interactants, a "healthy emotional life" alternates between hate and love (among other emotions), and a "healthy family context" alternates between providing its members individuation and togetherness.

It is at the level of meta-patterning or meta-sequencing that health and pathology become distinguished. Health and pathology do not reside so much in the sequence as they do in the sequencing of an ecosystem's sequences. Consistent repetition (i.e., escalation) of the same form of sequenced experience, behavior, and interaction characterizes pathology. On the other hand, alternating diverse sequences, which are integrated (i.e., "in balance"), exemplify a healthy ecosystem. The task of therapy must therefore include both initiating novel sequences of experience, behavior and interaction, as well as integrating these forms of diversity into a whole gestalt.

In family therapy, Whitaker has described healthy families as contexts where role positions constantly shift, enabling the scapegoat to rotate. As he writes (Whitaker, 1979, p. 112):

I think if the family is healthy that scapegoat-role can move around so that on one day they can razz Sonny-boy for being childish, the next day they can razz Dad for being pompous, the next day they can razz Mom for being over-anxious, and next day they can razz Sister for playing sexy games with Daddy when she should be doing the dishes. That way the scapegoat function—the "cut-em-down-to-size" function—moves throughout the family. Nobody is stuck with the horror of carrying all of the family's anxiety all the time.

This suggests that a study of healthy families might indicate that they, like Maslow's self-actualizers, escape dichotomous forms of description. A healthy family, like a healthy individual, will then alternate between appearing "symptomatic" and "symptom-free" in the conventional (i.e., nonecological) meaning of those terms.

In sum, health refers to a balance of complexity, a balance or integration of sequences of behavior and experience as well as a balance of the sequencing of those sequences. Therefore, descriptions of health and pathology become ways of identifying how systems maintain stability through change of lower order subsystems. The lack of complexity or balance implies pathology. In these systems stability will be achieved through escalated sameness, that is, the maximization or minimization of some variable. Health and pathology of human relationship systems are therefore comparable with ecological relations we see in our biosphere.

THERAPIST

The work of Rosenthal (1966) has repeatedly demonstrated the obtrusiveness of the human investigator and observer. A dramatic example of the effect of intervening into a system is provided by Halberg (cited in Luce, 1971, p. 298), who found that a single drop of blood taken from a mouse's tail disturbs the animal's circadian rhythm of certain blood cells for several days. It follows that therapists affect the systems they are treating whether they intend to or not. On the other side of the relationship, it is likely that the systems treated always affect the therapist. As Bateson (in Lipset, 1980, p. 214) stated, "when the investigator starts to probe unknown areas of the universe, the back end of the probe is always driven into his own vital parts."

This Heisenberg-like hook[2] between the observer and the observed has led Rollo May (in Gilbert, 1975, p. 6) to state: "We don't study nature, we investigate the investigator's relationship to nature." These ideas support Sullivan's (1953) notion that the therapist is always a part of the field being observed in diagnosis. In view of this, Haley (1973, p. 161) has insisted that the "therapist include himself in the description of a family."

The way in which a therapist views himself as part of the system he treats is largely determined by his epistemology. For example, the therapist's presence in the system he treats is sometimes described by therapists in terms of metaphors of "power." Haley, in particular, speaks of power and control when describing the relationship of therapist and client. This view looks on therapists as "power brokers" who control the ways in which power is distributed and used in the therapeutic system. This form of description overlooks the admonition from Bateson (1974, p. 26) that "all metaphors derived from a physical world of impacts, forces, energy, etc., are unacceptable in explanations" of therapy. Furthermore, he argued that the "'power' metaphor...must be looked at, as a functioning falsehood or error, causing what pathologies?"

Bateson has long viewed Haley's use of the metaphor of power as an epistemological error that is self-validating and potentially pathological. He recently stated (1976, p. 106), "Haley slides too lightly over the real epistemological differences between himself and me....I believed then—and today—that the *myth* of power always corrupts because it proposes always a false (though conventional) epistemology."

Therapists who base their theories on metaphors of power are necessarily embodying an epistemology of billiard balls. The whole crux of the paradigmatic change offered by an ecological view involves a change from watts to information, from substance to pattern. To speak of "power" is to remain part and parcel of an epistemology that has characterized medieval psychotheologies.

---

[2]Heisenberg's famous "Uncertainty Principle" states that the observer constantly alters what he observes by the obtrusive act of observation.

It is important to realize that Bateson was not playing a game of intellectual semantics in his criticism of "power." As he stated (1972, p. 486):

What is true is that the *idea of power* corrupts. Power corrupts most rapidly those who believe in it, and it is they who will want it most...

Perhaps there is no thing as unilateral power. After all, the man "in power" depends on receiving information just as much as he "causes" things to happen. It is not possible for Goebbels to control the public opinion of Germany because in order to do so he must have spies or legmen or public opinion polls to tell him what the Germans are thinking. He must then trim what he says to this information: and then again find out how they are responding. It is an interaction, and not a lineal situation.

But the *myth* of power is, of course, a very powerful myth and probably most people in the world more or less believe in it. It is a myth which, if everybody believes in it, becomes to that extent self-validating. But it is still epistemological lunacy and leads inevitably to various sorts of disaster.

Part of Bateson's criticism of "power" involves the matter of transitivity. The metaphor of power suggests transitivity—that more power will always be more powerful. However, this idea is antiecological. Ecological goods are often intransitive so that goods become toxic if they become greater than some optimum (e.g., population, oxygen, protein, money). Anyone suggesting that the therapist is solely responsible for change is implying a transitive and lineal relationship. It may then be assumed that the more skilled the therapist, the more "power" the therapist has to achieve change. Such an idea is potentially toxic and after a certain point may lead the therapist to become less flexible, less open-minded, less creative, less effective as a therapist, teacher, and student.

We now suspect that our planet faces certain "points of no return" owing to social policy created through an epistemology containing "power" metaphors. What ecological pathologies are being caused by therapists who implement strategic action on relationship systems through an epistemology containing metaphors of "power" and "control"? Bateson has continuoutly issued prophetic warnings in this regard.

Belief in the myth of power is self-verifying since it is a habit of punctuation. The myth of power will lead to a world where power is always seen. This is demonstrated by Madanes' (1981, pp. 217–218) remarks:

It has even been suggested that power may be a myth, a dangerous metaphor to be mistrusted. Yet the influence of one nation over another or the power of the rich over the poor cannot be ignored....However, power is an important factor in human relations.... It is difficult to imagine how the relevance of power can be denied when people lock each other up, murder each other, or devote their lives to helping one another...

The ecologist's argument is not about whether "power" exists. That is a question which is epistemologically questionable due to its assumption that there can be an objective proof of its existence. What is being criticized and objected to is not the "reality" of power, but the consequences of a habit of punctuating the world in terms of power. Bateson's work clearly demonstrates how such punctuation reinforces greed and corruption in all those who believe in the "reality" of "social power." To avoid such pathology, the alternative is to not punctuate the world of human relationship in terms of power.

Rabkin (1978, p. 45) writes that "the Bateson-Haley controversy is for me the epistemological core of family therapy." His definition is stated figuratively by the medieval question: "Who plays the pipes and who dances?" This controversy relates to issues concerning "control." Early cybernetics, associated with the black-box method, presupposes that an outsider can manipulate a system and change its rules of interaction. This emphasis on control engineering is useful in the creation of trivial machines where a particular invariant relationship among component parts is established in order to create a predictable machine. When nontrivial machines are treated as trivial machines, however, one risks "trivialization." This is what occurs in some contexts of learning and psychotherapy.

When therapists assume that the system before them can be fed particular inputs that result in particular outputs, they punctuate their context in a way which may lead to trivialization. Like an experimenter punctuating a laboratory context, a therapist may also punctuate therapy in order to generate self-verifying outcomes. Of course, therapists' punctuations are always offerings to the client who may accept or reject them. If rejected, the client (or therapist) is often said to be "resisting" or engaged in a "power struggle." Incidentally, both "explanations" are of the same logical type and as punctuation habits, will lead the observer to seeing nothing but "resistance" or "power struggles."

Bateson suggests that the metaphors of power and control be replaced by the ecological metaphor, "part in an ecosystem." A crucial individual in a system (e.g., therapist) is always a *part* of that system and "is therefore subject to all the constraints and necessities of the particular part-whole relationship in which he exists" (Bateson, 1974, p. 27). This terminology describes the therapist's presence in the ecosystem he treats as "part in" or "part of" rather than outside spectator, manipulator, or power broker.

Ecological epistemology suggests that the system of which a therapist is a part is a cybernetic loop having feedback structure. When a therapist is seen as being part of such a circuit, what becomes critical is identifying the nature of the emergent feedback relations. The therapist's presence in that circuit which includes the symptom will help determine whether the circuit will become stable, oscillate, or run away. As anyone can observe, a therapist may join a family (or part of a family) without noticeable change, or the therapist's interventions may coincide with events of apparent change. Although a therapist's presence in a system does appear to have an effect, it is important to realize that "control" refers to the whole circuit, not the unilineal influence or the therapist of any other member. The way in which a therapist is part of a control circuit will lead to particular ways in which other members organize their behaviors around him. Their reactions, however, lead to the therapist organizing his or her behavior around them, and vice versa.

Punctuating therapy in terms of "power" or "black-box cybernetics" leads to what McCulloch called lineal "command systems." In these systems the therapist, or commander, is in charge. Such a position leads to treating a nontrivial machine (i.e., one capable of dialogue and learning) as a trivial machine. A skilled therapist, like a skilled commander, may then trivialize his or her troops to behave according to the punctuation rules imposed. This may also include the punctuation of symptom alleviation. However, trivialization is not higher order learning. The context of that learning requires a cybernetic circuit where all participants are processes of correction, oscillation, and runaway.

In such a circuit the most a therapist can do is vary his behavior, recognize the consequences in the behavior of those in the social field surrounding him and modify his reactions to their reactions. If the effects of his behavior on others is used to change the therapist's consequent behavior, a feedback loop has been established. The therapist is not controlling their behavior, but is recognizing the response of their behavior to his and the response of his behavior to theirs. Even the training of an earthworm does not imply that the human teacher is controlling the "taught." The system of learning is a cybernetic circuit wherein information is in-formed; that is, information is created within the closed loop with all participants sharing in the creative process.

This follows Pask's (1969) theory where he sees the learning situation as one where both teacher and taught are learning. Similarly, Bateson (1972) proposes that the circuit encompassing organism and environment is the unit of evolution. The unit of therapy is a cybernetic circuit where both therapist and client are aiming to be parts of learning and evolution. What learns and evolves is the circuit of which they are both parts.

Once again, to become an "effective" part of this circuit, therapists must be able to vary their behavior and recognize the effects of all action—theirs as well as other participants. Varying one's behavior corresponds to what is traditionally called "intervention," whereas recognizing the effects of these interventions may be called "diagnosis." Along these lines, Haley (1971, p. 282) suggests that the family therapist is "interested in diagnosing how the family responds to his therapeutic interventions." This view of intervention and diagnosis as parts of cybernetic circuits suggests that they are actually inseparable.

The way in which the therapist is part of the therapeutic circuit should include more than the conscious part of his or her mind. Bateson argues that conscious, purposeful mind uninfluenced by unconscious process will lead to distortions and pathology. As he (1972, pp. 444–445) states:

...the cybernetic nature of self and the world tends to be imperceptible to consciousness, insofar as the contents of the "screen" of consciousness are determined by considerations of purpose...The argument of purpose tends to take the form "D is desirable; B leads to C; C leads to D; so D can be achieved by way of B and C." But, if the total mind and the outer world do not, in general, have this lineal structure, then by forcing this structure upon them, we become blind to the cybernetic circularities of the self and the external world. Our conscious sampling of data will not disclose whole circuits but only arcs of circuits, cut off from their matrix by our selective attention.

Bateson further argues that the role of unconscious parts of mind involves correcting the errors of "purposeful consciousness." Therapists who ignore the levels of aesthetics and unconscious mentation fall susceptible to a form of pathology that can be called "the pathology of uncorrected purposiveness." The whole circuit of a therapist's work requires both unconscious and conscious processes of mind.

Whenever a therapist is part of a cybernetic circuit of social interactions, it must be assumed that his or her actions are part of a feedback process. Thus, the therapist's actions and the actions of others will be organized by the feedback circuit of which they are all parts. When therapy is considered as a whole circuit, it is impossible to distinguish what is contributed by whom. This is comparable with the findings of Linde and Goguen's (cited in Varela, 1979) study of the discourse structure of a planning session. Varela (1979, p. 269) summarizes their work as follows:

In their careful descriptions of the structure of the discourse, they found no evidence that the text, as a coherent entity, could be attributed to separate speakers, but it was an alloy of their participation, and exhibited rules and laws that are not reducible to the separate contributions.

In therapy, the cybernetic circuit is the unit of treatment that emerges from the interweaving of two major relational fields whose nodal points are represented by the "identified patient" and "identified therapist." The term *identified therapist* implies that the role of therapist is as flexible and indeterminate as the role of identified patient. Both are only punctuations of the circuit.

The experience of being part of the circuit one wishes to know is what Maslow (1969, p. 50) describes as "becoming and *being* what is to be known." This view is a Taoist approach that is experienced as nonpurposeful, noncontrolling, and process-oriented. Bateson (1972, p. 146) refers to this "sense or recognition of the fact of circuitry" as "wisdom." Although experiential therapists point to this level of awareness, there have been few efforts to understand this from the perspective of ecological epistemology. That is territory open for exploration.

ECOLOGY

The broadest view for looking at all possible systems, levels of systems, and interrelations among systems is defined as ecology. Following Roszak (1977, p. 30), we can see ecology as the fundamental doctrine that all things in nature are complexly but systematically interrelated. As he comments, if you "extend this idea as far as it will go you can imagine the Earth at large, including ourselves and our culture as a single, evolving system of life."

Because all description arises from acts of epistemology, the systems we choose to see are, in part, arbitrary punctuations. This view reminds us that perception of "individuals" and "families" is also constructed and that one could alternatively choose to focus on more holistic metaphors which dissolve any particular person, place, or nodal point. The metaphors of American Indians (see Boyd, 1974), for example, see the whole earth as a single organism, with the rivers as veins and the soil as flesh. From the more technical side, Lovelock (1979) has similarly suggested that the science of ecology adopt the term *Gaia,* a metaphor for considering the planet and its interlocking systems as a whole system.

Although the identity of "individuals" and "families" can be seen as arbitrary punctuations, it must also be remembered that these identities do refer to particular cyclical patterns or sequences in the whole ecology. In other words, an individual more accurately refers to a particular form of redundancy or patterning in the ecosystem. Thus, perhaps individuals (and families) should be seen more as nodal points, similar to waves that punctuate an ever-connected ocean. This ecological view would include both the notion that autonomous redundant patterns could be identified, as well as suggest that on a larger scale each is a nodal point in an ever-connected ecosystem.

The various systems that emerge in the punctuations of a therapist can, from the perspective of ecology, be built up to construct a Supra-System, that is, a whole ecology called Earth. On a smaller level, systems that correspond to the boundaries of individuals can be seen as organized in the social context of families; that organization corresponds to the whole family system. Then, the coupling of those systems creates higher order systemic organizations. In this way, complexity within ecosystems can be approached.

The pragmatics of therapy typically focuses on evaluating how the therapist's actions affect the immediate systemic organization surrounding symptoms. As has been previously noted, this pragmatic view does not deal with how those altered systems may affect the higher order systems that embody them. There are also oversights concerning the coupling of a therapist's organization of self to other forms of system organization.

One of the major issues of therapy concerns the systemic organization of the therapist. Experiential and growth-oriented therapists propose that it is important to attend to the growing edge of the therapist. Other more strategic orientations argue against any focus on the therapist as a person and imply that therapy be problem-oriented with an emphasis on technique and performance.

Ecological epistemology suggests that the idea of a therapist separate from a client is a false dualism which overshadows the therapist-client supra-system. This implies that it is important to attend to the systemic organization of both therapist and client in the context of therapy. This broader view further suggests that the way in which a therapist is organized as a whole personality ecology becomes critical when that therapist relates to another individual.

The way in which this relationship is critical is at least twofold. First, an "unintegrated or unbalanced personality ecology" may be coupled with another unintegrated personality such that the two subsystems will achieve stability through the union of their interactions. In this way, therapists may stabilize their client's problems in order to stabilize their own systemic organization (and vice versa). On the other hand, a therapist can be "integrated" so that the context of therapy facilitates his or her own growing edge. Existential approaches to therapy accentuate this view and demonstrate that the course of therapy may be a shared pilgrimage between therapist and client.

Another issue of therapy concerns whether a therapist can heal himself. Watzlawick, Weakland, and Fisch (1974) seem to argue that a change agent must be meta to the system requesting change. From this perspective, it would not be possible for a "physician to heal thyself." Nevertheless, the history of psychotherapy includes several profound cases where individuals have conducted their own "therapy." Psychoanalysis, for the most part, was based on Freud's own self-analysis. Similarly, Jung's (1963) "confrontation of his unconscious" is another example of a self-directed odyssey. In family therapy, the explorations of Bowen (1974) are exemplary.

Beyond these self-directed approaches to therapy, there are a large number of "transpersonal" approaches to personal change which include a history of self-journeys. Pearce (1974), Lilly (1967), Castaneda (1974), and Merrell-Wolff (1976) are among the individuals whose personal evolutions have included gurus and/or therapists arising from their own fantasies or unconscious. It should also be noted that Jung had a "teacher," Philemon, who arose from his own unconscious mind. All these examples bear testimony that it may be possible for individuals to effect their own change of systemic organization.

The voyage called "schizophrenia" may also be seen as a way of evolving. As Bateson (personal communication) put it, "with luck, people who go into schizophrenia come out deeply and humanly wiser than when they went in." The accounts of Perceval, Mary Barnes, O'Brien, and Greenburg are examples. More recently, Bateson (1976a, p. XVI) proposed that "schizophrenia should be thought of as a response to epistemological transition, or to threat of transition."

These processes of change which sometimes occur unaided by a professional change agent may suggest the Taoist position that organisms and ecologies heal themselves if uninterfered with. This connects to Bateson's argument that the world is circuit-structured and hence self-corrective if we leave it alone. For example, if you reduce one of the species in a forest by a certain percentage, 10 years later it will have adjusted itself to the original level (assuming no other interventions took place). The Taoist position (one compatible with the ecology of cybernetic circuits) suggests that the problem of family therapy is how to let an individual, a family, a system, achieve its own adjustments. As Bateson puts it, "letting the wisdom of the family find the things they need."

One way of understanding how individuals heal themselves is to follow the old explanation that they dissociate their personality system. In other words, the ecology of their personality is split between a teacher and a student, or unconscious and conscious, or nagual and tonal (to use Castaneda's metaphor). Given this split, a dialectical process between the two parts is enacted, similar in form to the process between therapist and client systems in the course of therapy. Through this dialectic, the two parts evolve into an integrated, balanced whole personality system—the personality becomes individuated, in Jung's terms.

Viewing this process from a reverse angle, therapy could be described as analogous to the dialectic between conscious and unconscious process that occurs in self-directed healing journeys. In the therapeutic situation, the client speaks the part of the client's conscious mind, while the therapist "mirrors" or speaks the client's unconscious mind. In this way, the therapist role plays the unconscious part of the client. This view suggests again that the role of a therapist is noncontrolling in the sense that a therapist is part of a feedback loop coupling him or her with the client's own communication processes. Of course, the client may also speak the therapist's unconscious mind, helping the therapist to learn, change, grow, and evolve.

It could be argued that family therapy is actually a way in which the unintegrated and unbalanced components of individuals' personality systems attempt to become balanced, integrated, or reach ecological climax. There is a gestalt technique used by Satir (see Grinder and Bandler, 1976) in which she has a client choose other people to enact parts of themselves. The client thus has a group of people that symbolically represents the unintegrated components of that client's personality ecology. The task of the therapist in this technique is to get the clients to integrate (i.e., make whole) the group. Through making the group whole the client unconsciously achieves an integration of his or her own personality.

This gestalt technique provides an alternative way of viewing family therapy. In family therapy all the members of a family represent the unintegrated parts of each family member. When the therapist evolves the whole family toward integration, the therapist enables each personality ecology to become integrated as in gestalt work. It must be remembered, however, that such a view proposes that every member of the family is a client (although each is unintegrated in a different and complementary way). Thus, through having the whole family integrated, each member becomes integrated.

At this time it is important to suggest that a consideration for an individual's family and social niche should always be part of therapy. Any strict limitation to treating individuals is ecologically unwise. The idea that one should help mobilize "healthy individuals" is itself an attempt to maximize only one variable—health. Health is not transitive. After a certain limit, health is unhealthy. This is demonstrated by the great forests that died out in central China because each individual tree was so healthy it impinged on its neighbors.

The limits of individual growth, evolution, or health are constrained by the health of their immediate contexts—their families. Families in turn must help to maintain the health of the contexts which embody them; and so on, until we can conceive of a healthy planet. This view suggests a new form of "totemism" where the general systemic structure of the natural world around us is taken as "an appropriate source of metaphor to enable man to understand himself in his social organization" (M. Bateson, 1972, p. 484).

A metaphor for ecology is provided by the "Jewel of Indra" described in Hua-yen Buddhism (in Cook, 1977, p. 2):

Far away in the heavenly abode of the great god Indra, there is a wonderful net which has been hung by some cunning artificer in such a manner that it stretches out infinitely in all directions. In accordance with the extravagant tastes of deities, the artificer has hung a single glittering jewel in each "eye" of the net, and since the net itself is infinite in dimension, the jewels are infinite in number. There hang the jewels, glittering like stars of the first magnitude, a wonderful sight to behold. If we now arbitrarily select one of these jewels for inspection and look closely at it, we will discover that in its polished surface there are reflected *all* the other jewels in the net, infinite in number. Not only that but each of the jewels reflected in this one jewel is also reflecting all the other jewels, so that there is an infinite reflecting process occurring.

An awareness of the complexity of complexity provided by an ecological view enables us to remind ourselves that all drawn systems are necessarily parts of other systems. The broadest view suggests that as we are reflections of our families, or "'knots' of recycled biography" (Roszak, 1977, p. 168), our families are also reflections of us. On the level of ecology, the parts and wholes become one and the same.

Denial or destruction of parts of ourselves will be reenacted in our environment. Similarly, what we do to that which we assume is outside ourselves will be reflected within. When we understand the world through ecological epistemology, we find that it is a complex of systems or "mind." Seeing "mind" in nature gives us the alternative and necessary view. As Mary Catherine Bateson (1977, p. 65) summarizes this:

Then "mind" becomes a property not just of single organisms, but of relations between them, including systems consisting of man and man, or a man and a horse, a man and a garden, or a beetle and a plant. Some mind-like properties seem very simple when they occur by themselves, but together they suggest a way of thinking which neither reduces mind to a model of billiard balls, nor sets it off in contrast to matter, but allows for a search through all orders of material complexity for forms of organization comparable to our own. This is perhaps a basis for a new kind of respect for the structures of the world in which we live.

REFERENCES

Bateson, G. (1958) Language and psychotherapy--Frieda Fromm-Reichmann's last project. *Psychiatry,* **21,** 96–100.

Bateson, G. (1972) *Steps to an ecology of mind.* New York: Ballantine.

Bateson, G. (1974) Draft: Scattered thoughts for a conference on "broken power." *CoEvolution Quarterly,* **4,** 26–27.

Bateson, G. (1976a) Foreword: A formal approach to explicit, implicit and embodied ideas and to their forms of interaction. In C. Sluzki & D. Ransom (Eds.), *Double bind: The foundation of the communicational approach to the family.* New York: Grune & Stratton, 1976.

Bateson, G. (1976b) Comments on Haley's history. In C. Sluzki & D. Ransom (Eds.), *Double bind: The foundation of the communicational approach to the family.* New York: Grune & Stratton, 1976.

Bateson, M. (1972) *Our own metaphor: A personal account of a conference on the effects of conscious purpose on human adaptation.* New York: Knopf.

Bateson, M. (1977) Daddy, can a scientist be wise? In J. Brockman (Ed.), *About Bateson.* New York: Dutton.

Bowen, M. (1974) Toward the differentiation of self in one's family of origin. In F. Andres & J. Lorio (Eds.), *Georgetown family symposium papers, I.* Washington, D.C.: Georgetown University Press.

Boyd, D. (1974) *Rolling thunder.* New York: Dell.

Brand, S. (1974) *Two cybernetic frontiers.* New York: Random House.

Castaneda, C. (1974) *Tales of power.* New York: Simon & Schuster.

Cook, F. H. (1977) *Hua-yen buddhism.* University Park, Pa.: The Pennsylvania State University Press.

Gilbert, R. (1975) *Edited transcript of AHP theory conference.* San Francisco: Association for Humanistic Psychology.

Grinder, J., & Bandler, R. (1976) *The structure of magic* (Vol. 2). Palo Alto; Science and Behavior Books.

Haley, J. (1971) Family therapy: A radical change. In J. Haley (Ed.), *Changing families.* New York: Grune & Stratton.

Haley, J. (1973) Beginning and experienced family therapists. In A. Ferber, M. Mendelsohn, & A. Napier (Eds.), *The book of family therapy.* Boston: Houghton Mifflin.

Hardin, G. (1978) *Stalking the wild taboo* (2d ed.). Los Altos, Calif.: William Kaufmann.

Jung, C. (1963) *Memories, dreams, reflections.* A. Jaffe (Ed.), New York: Vintage Books.

Keeney, B.P. (1979) Ecosystemic epistemology: An alternative paradigm for diagnosis. *Family Process,* **18**, 117–129.

Keeney, B.P. (1983) *Aesthetics of change.* New York: The Guilford Press.

Keeney, B.P., & Sprenkle, D.H. (1982) Ecosystemic epistemology: Critical implications for the aesthetics and pragmatics of family therapy. *Family Process* **21**, 1–19.

Keith, D.V. (1980) Family therapy and lithium deficiency. *Journal of Marital and Family Therapy,* **6**, 49–53.

Lilly, J. *Programming and metaprogramming in the human biocomputer.* New York: Julian Press, 1967.

Lipset, D. (1980) *Gregory Bateson: The legacy of a scientist.* Englewood Cliffs, N.J.: Prentice-Hall.

Lovelock, J. (1979) *Gaia: A new look at life on earth.* Oxford: Oxford University Press.

Luce, G. (1971) *Body time.* New York: Bantam Books.

Madanes, C. (1981) *Strategic family therapy.* San Francisco: Jossey-Bass.

Maslow, A. (1969) *The psychology of science.* Chicago: Regnery.

Maslow, A. (1970) *Motivation and personality* (2d ed.). New York: Harper & Row, 1970.

Merrell-Wolff, F. (1976) *Pathways through to space.* New York: Warner.

Pask, G. (1969) The meaning of cybernetics in the behavioral sciences. In J. Rose (Ed.), *Progress of cybernetics.* New York: Gordon & Breach.

Pearce, J. (1974) *The crack in the cosmic egg: Challenging constructs of mind and reality.* New York: Pocket Books.

Rabkin, R. (1978) Who plays the pipes? *Family Process,* **17,** 485–488.

Rosenthal, R. (1966) *Experimenter effects in behavioral research.* New York: Appleton-Century-Crofts.

Roszak, T. (1977) *Person/planet.* New York: Anchor Press.

Sullivan, H.S. (1953) *The interpersonal theory of psychiatry.* New York: Norton.

Varela, F.J. (1979) *Principles of biological autonomy.* New York: Elsevier-North Holland.

Watts, A. (1961) *Psychotherapy east and west.* New York: Ballantine.

Watzlawick, P., & Coyne, J. (1980) Depression following stroke: Brief, problem-focused treatment. *Family Process,* **19,** 13–18.

Watzlawick, P., Weakland, J., & Fisch, R. (1974) *Change: Principles of problem formation and problem resolution.* New York: Norton.

Whitaker, C. (1979) On family therapy (Interview with Bruce Howe). *Pilgrimage: The Journal of Existential Psychology,* **7,** 107–114.

CHAPTER 3

The Ecosystemic Perspective in Clinical Assessment and Intervention

MARY L. JASNOSKI

The ecosystemic perspective is a new way of viewing human lives. It offers the working clinician a comprehensive conceptual framework for processing and utilizing a vast amount of information. Ecosystemic thinking is relational in focus and complex, approaching the complexity inherent in human lives. As such, this clinical method evolved from past theoretical trends. A brief historical review of psychological thought will epistemologically ground ecosystems theory. After this conceptual background has been sketched, the ecosystemic perspective itself will become the focus and then the backdrop for a later discussion on clinical assessment and intervention.

CONCEPTUAL DEVELOPMENT OF ECOSYSTEMS THEORY

Mental health workers have historically favored a conceptual orientation predominantly based on either individual *or* situational factors. Ekehammar (1974) termed these disparate orientations personologism and situationism, respectively. The clinician either saw the person or the environment as the primary cause of human events and experiences. Trait theories (e.g., Cattell, 1973) and psychoanalysis (Freud, 1955) typify personologism. Behaviorism (e.g., Skinner, 1938) and social learning theories (e.g., Mischel, 1973) exemplify the situationist perspective. In their extremes, personologism and situationism were antithetical positions, ready for a theoretical synthesis in a dialectical development of psychological thought.

The dialectical synthesis of these disparate positions resulted in interactionism (see Lewin, 1935; Kantor, 1924). This new conceptual position considered the mutual contributions of person and situation in addition to an important third factor, their relationship or interaction. In order to understand and affect humans more fully, the clinician now viewed the separate effects of the person and the environment, *and* their interrelationship. This synthesis allowed full use of both bodies of previous knowledge instead of, for example, necessitating dismissal of knowledge concerning situational influences if a person-oriented explanation was utilized. The two positions complemented and supported each other in interactionism, plus new vistas opened when considering interactionism's addition: relational dynamics.

In relational dynamics, the interplay between person and situation came to be viewed as a process of reciprocal causation or interaction. The interactionist synthesis transformed the simple linear, unidirectional cause-and-effect models of "personologism" and "situationism" into a multiple causation, bidirectional model. This metatheoretical approach in interactionism marked a conceptual leap in psychological thought. In other words, instead of focusing on a single cause of human behavior—either the individual or the environment—the clinician now considered both personal and situational factors and how they worked together; three potential causal influences instead of one. In addition, the direction of influence was now considered mutual. This reciprocal, multiple-causation model expanded psychologists' conceptual focus to the larger scope of relational analysis. The amount, complexity, and content of information the clinician now considered in assessment and intervention encompassed a wider range of information on a more abstract level. This relational conception of interactionism set the stage for the next two epistemological developments that resulted in the ecosystemic perspective.

These two conceptual changes concern general systems theory (Laszlo, 1972) and human ecology (Theodorson, 1961). First, let us discuss general systems theory. Simply stated, general systems theory examines the functioning and structure of a group of interacting components in which the whole group, working together, has greater import than the sum of the independent parts. This synergistic whole has a functional structure composed of interactive connections of communication. Although the functional structure (i.e., the way these parts are organized) cannot be altered without disturbing the overall system's functioning, the components themselves can be replaced with similar parts with little disruption to the system. What the component *does* for the overall arrangement is more important than what the component *is*. This functional analysis is based upon the organismic principle that the whole determines the function of the individual parts.

Two types of systems have been delineated: closed and open systems. If interactions occur only within the system itself, then it is a closed system. No factors external to the system can affect its functioning. On the other hand, a system that may be influenced by external factors is called an open system. Living systems are all open; in other words, active exchange with its surroundings characterizes any living organization of interacting components. Thus, the ecosystemic perspective is concerned with open systems.

The open system in the ecosystemic perspective is a human life. To understand this particular open system, the last step is taken conceptually to the ecosystemic perspective—ecological thought concerning humans provides the content for the abstract form supplied by general systems theory. General ecology utilizes systems theory to understand the relationship between living organisms and their home ranges or environment. Human ecology specifically focuses on the human ecosystem, which is the basic unit of analysis (Evans, 1956). A human ecosystem functions as an open system; that is, active exchange of matter, information, or energy with the environment characterizes the live human. A simple illustration of open systemic functioning is eating, in which the human incorporates items from the environment in order to sustain its functioning.

The human ecosystem functions in terms of change and stability. Central to human ecology and the ecosystemic perspective are the ways in which humans maintain themselves in continually changing, yet restricted surroundings. The human ecosystem always changes in order to maintain stability. Understanding this seeming paradox requires a multilevel model of the functioning and structure in the human ecosystem (O'Connor & Daniels, 1979). Mental health and illness particularly address the type of functioning in the human ecosystem. Therefore, a further analysis of ecosystemic structure and functioning will prepare the foundation necessary to utilize the ecosystemic perspective in clinical work.

THE HUMAN ECOSYSTEM

The human ecosystem functions within a structural framework. A number of different schema have been proposed to conceptualize the structure of a human life (see Lewin, 1935; Murray, 1938). The schematic presented here is an amalgamation of aspects of the works of O'Connor (e.g., O'Connor, W.A., 1977; O'Connor, W.A. & Ramchandani, 1970; O'Connor, W.A., Klassen, & O'Connor, K.S., 1979), Bronfenbrenner (e.g., Bronfenbrenner, 1977), and Barker (e.g., Barker, 1968; Barker & Gump, 1968), as well as original contributions. As can be seen in Figure 3.1 the individual occupies the most central role in the ecosystem. All events and experiences are ultimately interpreted as to their impact on the individual human.

Structurally, the human ecosystem can be represented as a set of concentric circles, each representing a level of functioning within the overall system. Each level forms a boundary that is useful for functional analysis of the entire ecosystem. Boundaries or dividing lines between parts are characteristic of systems in general, but in open living systems these boundaries are semi-permeable, allowing exchange to occur among levels, and between the system and its environment.

The environment, in the ecosystemic perspective, forms a part of the overall human ecosystem, and is defined as the surrounding or context of the individual human's experience and behavior. Psychosocial and physical components can be delineated in the environment for analysis sake. Within the psychosocial environment different levels or fields of functioning can be the focus of inquiry or intervention, that is, the interpersonal, the family or small group, the community,

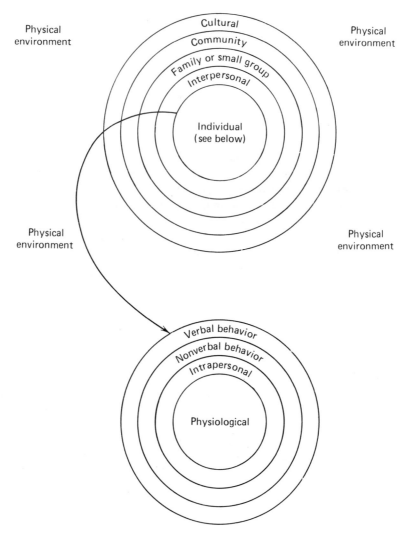

Figure 3.1. The Human Ecosystem.
  (*a*) Ecosystemic view: A human life—Extra-individual factors.
  (*b*) Ecosystemic view: A human life—Intra-individual factors.

and the cultural levels. In the physical environment both built and natural environments need consideration (Stokols, 1978). Psychologists often fail to consider the influence of the physical environment upon the individual (Mannino & Shore, 1980). The individual can be viewed on multiple levels of analysis, that is, internal physiological functioning, verbal and nonverbal behavior, in addition to intrapersonal dynamics. After this analysis, information from all these different levels needs to be synthesized into a total ecosystemic picture if a fuller understanding of the individual human life is to be reached.

The human ecosystem is more complex than the schematic suggests. In this two-dimensional representation only adjacent levels appear to connect with each other, but noncontiguous levels are also interconnected. For example, the cultural level can interact directly with the individual, such as when sex roles change and a middle-aged person is caught in the transition between different cultural expectations. Still, the schematic provided does serve the heuristic purpose of depicting the increasing complexity and abstractness of the levels the farther they are from the individual.

In the human ecosystem all levels interchange with each other, and each level can be viewed as an open system in and of itself. The ecosystemic perspective allows the clinician flexibility to telescope in on any level or subsystem within the overall ecosystem, as well as telescoping back out to understand the ecosystem in its entirety and how the subsystem of particular interest is embedded in the larger ecosystem. Because the ecosystem functions synergistically, that is, the whole ecosystem has an impact greater than the simple sum of its components levels, not only does each level need consideration, but the manner in which they fit together must also be considered. This is why synthesis is the necessary final step in understanding all the "partial" information gained from analysis of each level.

In the human ecosystem, this fit or congruence can be analyzed according to the function of each component in the overall working of the ecosystem. Moreover, the individual parts of a particular level (e.g., members of a family) can also be analyzed according to their function in maintaining that level's systemic processing and, thus, their contribution to the overall ecosystem. Therefore, a congruence model of functioning is proposed in the ecosystemic perspective in which the relationships between the various aspects of a human life are the main emphasis.

The relationships between parts of the human ecosystem are not static, but are in a constant state of flux. A dynamic equilibrium most closely describes the workings of a system (Boughey, 1974). Instead of a static, stable state, a system evolves in its attempts to maintain its preferred state. Equifinality is the concept developed to describe this evolutionary process (Lancaster, 1980). In other words, for each human ecosystem, there is a typical or preferred state toward which it moves. This autotelic conceptualization of the human ecosystem depends upon two fundamental regulatory processes underlying the concept of equifinality: stability and growth.

A system's stabilizing and growth functions can be explained readily using cybernetics. Cybernetic functions refer to those automatic control or feedback mechanisms that regulate a system, usually through exchange of information, energy, or matter. These control processes have been termed *feedback loops*. The idea of loops depicts the continuous, self-reflexive patterns of action in a system. Systems analysis is, again, more complex than simple interactionism. Similar to interactionism, though, the patterns of action are reciprocal; that is, any change will at some point return to influence itself indirectly via its direct influence on other parts of the feedback loop (Keeney, 1979).

Feedback loops come in two varieties, negative and positive, which correspond to the system functions of stabilization and growth, resepctively. Negative loops negate any changes in the system's favored state. To put it another way, these negative processes stabilize the system by minimizing any deviations from the system's typical or preferred balance. Negative loops maintain the functional integrity of the system. On the other hand, when a deviation is amplified so that the system's status quo changes, a positive loop has occurred. These positive growth functions allow the system flexibility in its responses to internal or external input.

Positive and negative loops work together in the human ecosystem to preserve the functional integrity of the system as environmental and internal conditions change. In the past, this interplay of stability and change has popularly been termed adaptation (Dubos, 1965). People have been observed to adapt or cope with existing or changing environmental conditions. In its strictest sense, adaptation is only a situationist concept; the effects of the person upon the situation or environment are not represented in the concept of adaptation. Thus, a new idea was needed to represent the system of person and situation transactions. The idea of *optimization* does just that.

Optimization is the cyclical, feedback process whereby people seek optimal environments for themselves (Stokols, 1978). Optimal environments are those that maximize fulfillment, meet needs, or accomplish goals the individual has. Not only do individuals adapt or cope with their milieu, but they also arrange or modify it to better suit themselves. In optimization, humans actively orient to, operate on, and evaluate the quality and conduciveness of the environment as a context for future goals and activity. Consistent with the teleological ecosystems view presented thus far, optimization is a goal-directed view of human–environment transactions.

An open system has an exchange of input between itself and its surroundings. This input serves as the system's resources and may be information, energy, or matter (Jasnoski, 1980). Resources enter the system, undergo a transformation of some sort, and then leave the system as output. The feedback controls of negative and positive loops affect this transformation, regulating systemic response to input as well as reintroducing some of the output back into the system as input. This processing supplies the dynamic optimizing movement to the system. In systems theory, events are viewed at the most basic level not in terms of structure but in terms of this optimizing process (Odum, 1972). The structural levels delineated in Figure 3.1 are heuristic conventions that facilitate analysis and synthesis of information pertaining to this dynamic process. More will be said about ecosystem input in the section on assessment and intervention.

All of these abstract notions about system functioning become more concrete and clinically relevant when applied to the human ecosystem. Specifically, telescoping in on the family level will provide an illustration of the interplay of the two feedback functions of stability and change. The family is a level of organization composed of individuals and is embedded in a network of relationships, institutions, social processes, and cultural context. Negative loops are found in the stabilizing forces that maintain the family's organization and function in the larger ecosystem. For example, in our culture, child-rearing responsibilities typically are assigned to families. Meeting these responsibilities on a consistent basis requires stable, effective family and cultural interfunctioning. In other words, negative feedback loops or patterns of action need to reorient the family and culture continually so that child-rearing resonsibilities can be optimally and realistically met. For example, cultural tolerance of divorce may hamper family stability and necessitate reestablishment of the cultural value of marital, and, thus, family cohesion, as is currently apparent in the trends of our culture. On the family level, as children develop, changes in division of labor and in parental expectations of children also need to evolve so that the family unit can maintain stability. These negative loops all help maintain the overall ecosystem's functioning in terms of child rearing, but when child-rearing years end for a particular family, a transformation is necessary between cultural and family levels that will also reestablish congruence in the overall ecosystem. A positive loop can change the overall ecosystemic functioning by changing what has become less than optimal functioning, or the cultural/family incongruence. Change could be initiated on either a cultural or family level, and it would then permeate to other levels. On the cultural level, a different cultural assignment for remaining family members, such as becoming a member of the labor force or leaders in community activities may be needed. On the family level, an increased importance of the companionate bond of the marital relationship could occur. Thus change in the ecosystemic perspective results from positive loop actions and stability comes with negative loop patterns. Congruence between components and their environment is the goal of the optimization process inherent in the interplay of positive and negative feedback loops.

In summary, the fundamentals of the human ecosystem refer to its functioning and its structure. Its functioning concerns the process level of analysis, whereas its structure refers to the content level of analysis. General systems theory describes the human ecosystem's process whereas general ecology grounds the abstract form of systems analysis within the concrete content area of human/environment transactions. Within the broad areas of functioning and structure, different aspects, such as growth and stabilizing functions, and family and cultural levels of structure have been delineated.

In terms of functioning, three major principles of systems theory have been applied here to the human ecosystem. These are the notions that it is an open, synergistic system aspiring toward equifinality. First, as an open system the human ecosystem represents various functioning units that interact with external influences as well as interacting among themselves. Input comes from both external and internal sources to affect the system. Next, because the human ecosystem is synergistic, the simple sum of the independent effects of these various functioning units is less than their combined systemic, synergistic effect. In a synergistic system the function of the part is determined by its purpose in the overall system. Therefore, synthetic understanding of components in terms of their place in the larger system is necessary in order to understand totally their individual functioning. Finally, equifinality is a teleological concept referring to the preferred state toward which a system functions. Thus, the human ecosystem has a final goal or state that draws its action onward. This final state in the human ecosystem is one of congruence or optimization between individual and environment. In order to achieve optimization, the cybernetic functioning of negative and positive feedback loops regulates the processes of the ecosystem. The negative loops stabilize the system when it is congruent and the positive loops change the system when it needs to move from incongruence to a more congruent state. Hence, a human ecosystem functions as an open, synergistic pattern of action that continually moves toward a state of congruence of optimal functioning.

In terms of structure, an ecological model has been developed which centers on individual/environment transactions. Moving outward from the individual are fields of systemic influence concerning interpersonal relationships, the family or small groups, the immediately surrounding community and the overall cultural context. A backdrop to this psychosocial environment is the physical environment, both natural and built, which can affect the individual. Internal to the individual are systemic levels of physiological functioning and phenomenological experiencing. Verbal and nonverbal behaviors are the "skin," or targets for explanation and prediction in the ecosystemic perspective. Analysis of all these divisional levels ultimately demands a synthesis to complete the method by which the ecosystemic perspective explains and predicts human behavior and experience.

CLINICAL ASSESSMENT AND INTERVENTION FROM THE ECOSYSTEMIC PERSPECTIVE

Now that the ecosystemic perspective has been elaborated as a conceptual viewpoint, its use in clinical assessment and intervention can be examined. Assessment and intervention in this perspective involve the entire ecosystem of a human's life. Every level of functioning and its interrelationship can enter into an ecosystemic conceptualization and treatment strategy. The ecosystemic perspective offers some unique assessment techniques and a new conceptual framework for planning therapeutic interventions. These assessment techniques do not replace existent methods, however, but rather they assess the new variable of ecosystemic functioning that this perspective provides. In addition, this viewpoint provides a synthetic conceptualization and predictive framework for utilizing existent therapeutic techniques where appropriate. As such, the ecosystemic perspective capitalizes on the eclectism already so prevalent in clinical work. A brief overview of different assessment and therapeutic techniques that could be applicable to each specific level within the ecosystem will follow a more elaborate discourse on assessment of ecosystemic functioning.

What has been presented thus far in systems theory can be termed intrasystem functioning. Negative and positive loops regulate the internal processes of the system as it moves toward optimal functioning of the overall system. The cybernetic optimization described previously delineated the exchange patterns not only among the components of the system itself, but also the exchange between the system and its surrounding. Remember, some of the complexity of systems theory comes from the intricate intertwinings of components, some comes from the telescoping capabilities and ubiquitous applicability of systems theory, and much comes from the complexity reflected from human lives. Regarding the second source of complexity, that is, the wide-ranging applicability of systems theory, almost every unit within the system can be viewed as a system itself if finer delineations within the smaller unit are made. Then this smaller subsystem has as its surroundings the rest of the system and the surroundings of that encompassing system. This regression and progression could go on endlessly, but some bounds must be placed on it. In mental health we are usually concerned with an intermediate level of the human ecosystem, such as the family or interpersonal relationships.

Pattison (1977) has cogently stated that the social mandate of psychology has historically been the individual, and that consideration of any other levels of functioning, such as the family or community levels, must, in the final analysis, implicate these levels' effects upon the individual. Because the environment acts upon the individual as well as being acted upon by the individual, mental health workers are justified in examining other levels besides the individual. Then, we must conscientiously and scrupulously direct our attention back to the individual. Consistent with this social mandate of psychology, the ecosystemic perspective ultimately aims to explain and affect the individual's experience as well as verbal and nonverbal behavior. Yet, ecosystemic methods do not focus exclusively on the individual; assessment and intervention extend beyond the individual to the relationship, or fit between the individual and his or her environment.

The ecosystemic relational definition of mental health and illness emphasizes the fit between levels in the ecosystem. In other words, the focus is the relationship between each level's demands and available resources, with the resources available and demands made from other levels. Illness is neither simply reduced to pathology, which is a personologist concept, nor health simply reduced to restructuring an aversive environment, a situationist concept. Rather, health in the ecosystemic sense is the promotion of congruence between the individual and other levels in his or her life or ecosystem. This view is a positive model of healthy functioning; it emphasizes achieving health, which is not synonymous to the absence of illness.

Optimal functioning and congruence within an ecosystem has been defined by Bateson's (1979) climax optimal ecosystem. Here, the mature ecosystem is viewed as one of high stability, diversity, and richness, with multiple pathways and a maximum conservation of energy. This climax model provides a standard by which to judge the functional efficacy of an ecosystem. In the mature human ecosystem all relationships, by their congruence, maximize each other's functioning. When the mature system is environmentally challenged, the individual's solution and response to modifying the environment (i.e., optimization) leaves the ecosystem at a higher level of functioning rather than returning it to the customary equilibrium or to a lower level (Dubos, 1965). This spiral of growth characterizes development in the congruent human life.

Health must be understood as a value-laden concept. As such, it is only one possible goal or value for a human life. Other goals, such as ideologies, may be the highest organizing principle in a person's life, and directly result in incongruence perpetually occurring in this person's life; examples would be people such as Susan B. Anthony, Mahatma Ghandi, Martin Luther King, Jr., and Ralph Nader. Persons such as these retain personal ecosystemic incongruence in order to bring about change at the extra-individual levels, which will result in better congruence between the larger, more pervasive levels and the smaller levels in other people's ecosystem. In essence, they take a stand on the individual level, which reverberates out to the extra-individual levels, as well as maintaining a level of stress on the individual level, because the extra-individual levels try to maintain stability by pressuring these individuals to conform to the demands of these extra-individual levels.

Growth, from the ecosystemic perspective, is not always an easy process and must be defined for each individual life, given the values, goals, limitations, and potentials of a person. In addition, a realistic assessment can be made of the cost or stress incurred by choices made on the individual level, thereby minimizing the actual stress by preparing the individual for the cost of incongruence. Much research has documented that predictability of stress can attenuate somewhat its effect on the individual (e.g., Badia & Culbertson, 1972). So, health is ecosystemic specific and requires a clinical judgment based upon the functional integrity of each unique individual life that we term an ecosystem. For a more general example, individuals vary in their temperaments and sensitivities to the environment and in their rate of personal development. At the community level, these social units have varying resources to offer the individual and different demands to make upon individuals in order to maintain societal functioning. All these level variations illustrate the necessity of making an assessment of the unique human life, that is, the ecosystem of interest, before intervening.

The source of incongruity, or stress, in a human life can occur on any level of the ecosystem, or between levels, both adjacent and nonadjacent. The dysfunctional effects of an incongruity can permeate to many levels because of the interconnectedness of the human ecosystem. Because of systemic negative functioning, an incongruent state may stabilize within the system; often a clinician is sought when this has occurred. Therefore, disease in the ecosystemic perspective is not a discrete entity, but rather a pattern of action which may be termed stress, that may be multiply caused in terms of the conditions currently contributing to its maintenance. A clinician needs to delineate the following about an incongruent human life:

1. Where the stress shows itself, that is, the symptoms.
2. Where the ecosystem is most affected (this is not necessarily where symptoms occur).

Table 3.1. Assessment Techniques

Ecosystem Level	Assessment Techniques
A. Intra-Individual Factors	
1. Physiological	1. Halstead-Reitan; physical exams
2. Intra-personal	2. Rorschach; free association; MMPI; Q-sort; Kelly's Role Construct Repertory Test
3. Nonverbal behaviors	3. Behavioral rating techniques; Structured Interview for Type A's; Facial Affect Coding System; Goal Attainment Scheduling
4. Verbal Behaviors	4. Interview techniques; linguistic techniques
B. Extra-Individual Factors	
5. Interpersonal	5. TAT; Interpersonal Behavior Inventory; Duncan's Reputation Test; Marital Conflict and Accord
6. Family or small group	6. Organizational Climate; Chart of Social Behavior; Allred Interaction Analysis for Counselors
7. Community	7. Needs assessments; ecological techniques
8. Cultural	8. Kluckhon's Value Scale
9. Physical environment	9. Psychophysical Scaling Procedure for Noise, Temperature, Air quality Landscape Value; Behavioral Mapping; Sociophysical Assessment of Neighborhoods and Housing Quality; Perceived Environmental Quality Indices; Behavioral Analysis of Environmental/Ecological Problems

3. What environmental demand contributed to the development of the problem.
4. What personal aspect contributed to the development of the problem.
5. Where a therapeutic disruption (intervention) might be most effective.
6. What potential resistances (i.e., negative loops) may occur as the ecosystem tries to maintain stability.
7. What reverberating and countering effects a therapeutic intervention might have.

The signs and symptoms of dysfunction often represent the weakest point in the human life where the disruption could surface without being counteracted by cybernetic functioning. For example, a dysfunctional family community level could have the symptoms of juvenile delinquency in the child, but the source of difficulty could be the job demands of parents which interfere with child-rearing responsibilities and attention.

Assessment should encompass all levels of the ecosystem of interest (see Table 3.1). Such an intricate understanding is necessary to pinpoint systemic forces that currently sustain the dysfunctional state and to plan for possible system counteractions that might offset the effects of the disruption caused by therapeutic intervention. The assessment information can be client supplied or may come from other sources of knowledge about certain groups or cultures. Each level of the ecosystem has certain assessment techniques that could be utilized, as Table 3.1 illustrates.

Assessment is the first step to treatment in the ecosystemic perspective. Both the weaknesses and strengths in the ecosystem should be assessed in terms of past and present functioning. The strengths of the ecosystem are what has and is currently functioning congruently in the person's life; these aspects will buoy the individual during the instability inherent in the change being sought. Strengths should be pointed out to the person, and should be reinforced to provide the most solid stability possible. Weaknesses in an ecosystem come in two varieties, that is, what is happening that should not be, and what is *not* happening that should be. By focusing on past functioning, both functional and dysfunctional patterns

Table 3.2.   Intervention Techniques

Ecosystem Level	Assessment Techniques
A. Intra-Individual Factors	
1. Physiological	1. Drug therapies; exercise therapies; desensitization
2. Intra-personal	2. Cognitive restructuring; gestalt; psychoanalysis; hypnosis
3. Nonverbal behaviors	3. Behavioral rehearsal; sculpting
4. Verbal Behaviors	4. Communication techniques; use of metaphor
B. Extra-Individual Factors	
5. Interpersonal	5. Couple therapy; relationship therapy (i.e., using therapeutic relationship)
6. Family or small group	6. Family therapy; T-group; group therapy
7. Community	7. Social network; community education
8. Cultural	8. Political activism; setting mental health and professional standards (e.g., redefining child abuse, rape, or homosexuality)
9. Physical environment	9. Political activism; architectural interventions; reward and prompting strategies

should emerge. Present functioning will highlight which aspects of the ecosystem are presently maintaining the overall dysfunctional process. The key question asked is *what systemic purpose the incongruity might serve.* This systemic purpose relates to the stabilizing of incongruent functioning within the human ecosystem. Because the incongruence is usually stabilized or habitual by the time mental health workers observe it, this dysfunctional processing can be extremely difficult to change; hence, resistance to change is often encountered.

Therapeutic intervention can then be designed to maximize the chances to restore the ecosystem's functional integrity. Depending upon which level is targeted for intervention, any number of techniques may be used, as briefly sketched in Table 3.2. The ecosystemic perspective offers a theoretical super-structure for the eclecticism so prevalent in mental health today.

CONCLUSION

In summary, the ecosystemic perspective views human life as a complex dynamic process. This viewpoint offers a new way of conceptualizing, assessing, and evaluating human living. Some new assessment techniques and a theoretical justification for assessing and intervening on levels other than the individual are provided by this conceptual framework. The theoretical underpinnings and implications for assessment and intervention have been presented in this chapter. The conceptual base of ecosystems theory relies upon both systems theory and ecological thought. Systems theory describes systemic functioning (which is the process level of understanding an ecosystem) and utilizes such concepts as synergism, cybernetics, and the open system characteristic of a human life. With the form or context of systems theory, ecological thought focuses the substance of the systemic processes on the content of human–environment relationships. Moreover, the physical environment serves as a backdrop for the psychosocial, intrapersonal, and physiological areas of input and functioning within the human ecosystem. Hopefully, the reader understands that the bounds placed on the ecosystemic perspective are not the traditional psychological boundaries of the individual, but rather the organizational structure that includes and encompasses the individual.

GENERAL REFERENCES

Allred, G.H., & Kersey, F.L. (1977) The Allred Interaction Analysis for counselors: A design for systematically analyzing marriage and family counseling. *Journal of Marriage and Family Counseling,* **3**, 17–25.

Anatasi, A. (1961) *Psychological testing.* New York: Macmillan.

Becker, W.C., Madsen, C.H., Jr., Arnold, C.R., & Thomas, D.R. (1967) The contingent use of teacher attention and praise in reducing classroom behavior problems. *Journal of Special Education,* **1**, 287–307.

Benjamin, L.S. (1977) Structural analysis of a family in therapy. *Journal of Consulting and Clinical Psychology,* **45**, 391–406.

Bergin, A.E., & Lambert, M.J. (1978) The evaluation of therapeutic outcome. In S.L. Garfield, & A.E. Bergin (Eds.), *Handbook of psychotherapy and behavior change. An empirical analysis.* New York: Wiley.

Buros, O.C. (Ed.) *The ace mental measurement yearbook.* Highland Park, N.J.: Gryphon Press, 1978.

Butler, J.M., & Haigh, G. (1954) Changes in the relation between self-concepts and ideal concepts consequent upon client-centered counseling. In C. Rogers, & R. Dymond (Eds.), *Psychotherapy and personality change.* Chicago: University of Chicago Press.

Ciminero, A.R., Calhoun, K.S., & Adams, H.E. (Eds.) 1977 *Handbook of behavioral assessment.* New York: Wiley.

Duncan, C.B. (1966) A reputation test of personality integration. *Journal of Personality and Social Psychology,* **3**, 516–524.

Gurman, A.S., & Kniskem, D.P. (1981) *Handbook of family therapy.* New York: Brunner/Mazel.

Kelly, G.A. (1955) *The psychology of personal constructs.* New York: Norton.

Kiresuk, T.J., & Sherman, R.E. (1968) Goal attainment scaling: A general method for evaluating comprehensive community mental health programs. *Community Mental Health Journal,* **4**, 443–453.

Kluckhohn, F.R., & Strodtbeck, F.L. (1961) *Variations in value orientations.* New York: Harper & Row.

Rosenman, R.H. (1978) The interview method of assessment of the coronary-prone behavior pattern. In T.M. Dembroski, S.M. Weiss, J.L. Shields, S.G. Haynes, & M. Feinleib (Eds.), *Coronary-prone behavior.* New York: Springer-Verlag.

Rychlak, J.F. (1981) *Personality and psychotherapy.* Boston: Houghton Mifflin.

Stokols, D. (1978) Environmental psychology. *Annual Review of Psychology,* **29**, 253–295.

Strupp, H.H. (1978) Psychotherapy research and practice: An overview. In S.L. Garfield, & A.E. Bergin (Eds.), *Handbook of psychotherapy and behavior change. An empirical analysis.* New York: Wiley.

Weiss, R.L., & Margolin, G. (1977) Assessment of marital conflict and accord. In A.R. Ciminero, K.S. Calhoun, & H.E. Adams (Eds.), *Handbook of behavioral assessment.* New York: Wiley.

Yalom, I.D. (1975) *The theory and practice of group psychotherapy.* New York: Basic Books.

REFERENCES

Badia, P., & Culbertson, S. (1972) The relative aversiveness of signaled vs. unsignaled escapable and inescapable shock. *Journal of Experimental Analysis of Behavior.* **17**, 463–471.

Bandler, R., & Grinder, J. (1975) *The structure of magic: A book about language and therapy.* Palo Alto, Calif.: Science and Behavior Books

Barker, R. (1968) *Ecological psychology*. Stanford, Calif.: Stanford University Press.

Barker, R., & Gump, P. (1968) *Big school, small school.* Stanford: Stanford University Press.

Bateson, G. (1979) Size and shape in mental health: A symposium sponsored by the Menninger Foundation, Topeka, Kansas (September). Participants: G. Bateson, W. Berry, L. Wynne, J.W. Perry, M.C. Bateson, & R. Rabkin.

Boughey, A.S. (1974) Human ecology. *Man-environemnt Themes,* **1,** 1–16.

Bronfenbrenner, U. (1977) Toward an experimental ecology of human development. *American Psychologist,* July, 513–531.

Cattell, R.B. (1973) Personality pinned down. *Psychology Today,* **7,** 40–46.

Dubos, R. (1965) *Man adapting.* New Haven, Conn.: Yale University Press.

Ekehammar, B. (1974) Interactionism in personality from a historical perspective. *Psychological Bulletin,* **31,** 1026–1043.

Evans, F.C. (1956) Ecosystem as the basic unit in ecology. *Science,* **123,** 1127–1128.

Freud, S. (1955) *Standard edition of the complete psychological works of Sigmund Freud* (Vol. 1). London: Hogarth Press.

Jasnoski, M.L. (1980) Ecotherapies: Interventions with family and context interactions. Paper presented at the American Psychological Association Convention in Montreal, Quebec, Canada.

Kantor, J.R. (1924) *Principles of psychology* (Vol 1). Bloomington, Ind.: Principia Press.

Keeney, B. (1979) Ecosystemic epistemology: An alternative paradigm for diagnosis. *Family Process,* **18,** 117–129.

Lancaster, J. (Ed.). *Community mental health nursing: An ecological perspective.* St. Louis, Mo.: Mosby, 1980.

Lazlo, E. (1972) *A systems view of the world.* New York: Braziller.

Lewin, K. (1935) *A dynamic theory of personality: Selected papers.* New York: McGraw-Hill.

Mannino, F.V., & Shore, M.F. (1980) Ecologically-oriented family interventions. Paper presented at the American Psycological Association Convention in Montreal, Quebec, Canada.

Mischel, W. (1973) Toward a cognitive social learning reconceptualization of personality. *Psychological Review,* **80,** 252–283.

Murray, H.A. (1938) *Explorations in personality.* New York: Oxford University Press.

Odum, E. (1972) Ecosystem theory in relation to man. In J. Weins (Ed.), *Ecosystem structure and function.* Corvalis, Ore.: Oregon State University Press.

O'Connor, W.A. (1977) Ecosystems theory and clinical mental health. *Psychiatric Annals,* **7,** 63–71.

O'Connor, W.A., & Ramchandani, K. (1970) Community mental health: Training for innovation. *International Journal of Social Psychiatry,* **16,** 194–200.

O'Connor, W.A., & Daniels, S. (1979) Psychosocial ecosystems: A multi-level model. Paper presented at the American Psychological ssociation Convention in New York City.

O'Connor, W.A., Klassen, D., & O'Connor, K.S. (1979) Evaluating human service programs: Psychosocial methods. In P. Ahmed, & G. Coelho (Eds.), *Toward a new definition of health.* New York: Plenum Press.

Pattison, E.M. (1977) A theoretical-empirical base for social systems therapy. In E.P. Foulks, R.M. Wintrob, J. Westmeyer, et al. (Eds.), *Current perspectives in cultural psychiatry*. New York: Spectrum.

Skinner, B.K. (1938) *The behavior of organisms*. New York: Appleton-Century Crofts.

Stokols, D. (1978) Environmental psychology. *Annual Review of Psychology,* **29,** 253–295.

Theodorson, G.A. (Ed.) (1961) *Studies in human ecology*. New York: Harper & Row.

CHAPTER 4

Ecological Psychology and
Clinical Mental Health

PAUL V. GUMP

Some years ago, an experience in the assessment of a young woman outpatient helped me realize more clearly how the approaches and findings of ecological psychology were relevant to clinical practice. A group of young psychiatrists and clinical psychologists interested in a variety of popular diagnostic tools asked each member to describe the patient using only one diagnostic technique. Among the assessment procedures were the Rorschach, the Thematic Apperception Technique, and a standard psychiatric interview. My own chosen approach was an interview to obtain the patient's activity on the most recent weekend. The task was to describe, not the patient's symptoms or personality, but her living. The "test" then was a record of two days of activity described in sequence and in considerable detail in response to open-ended and interested queries from the interviewer.

The cooperating patient, Lucy, presented a situational and symptom picture not uncommon in Detroit at that time. This young wife and mother had recently moved from rural Tennessee so that her husband could take an assembly-line job with Ford. Lucy complained of "attacks"—periodic trouble in breathing, temporary feeling of choking, with rapid pulse. The "attacks" seldom persisted very long, but they frightened the patient.

The three traditional diagnostic techniques showed reasonable agreement about Lucy's difficulties and personality deficiencies. She was, according to classical Rorschach interpretation, impulsive with loose ego, control, and exhibited other signs compatible with a hysterical reaction. The TAT indicated fear of adult male figures and of heterosexual actvity; "immaturity" in response to stress was likely. The psychiatric interview found similar personality elements and provided material from which the interviewer inferred a psychosomatic aspect to the "attacks."

The picture of Lucy and her situation generated by the account of weekend activities was not in conflict with the other diagnostic findings, but it was quite different.

Saturday began with Lucy dressing herself and her 2-year old daughter who was eager to be up and ready for activity. After breakfast, Lucy washed dishes and then cleaned the apartment. Her husband still slept. The daughter was eager to "help," and part of Lucy's time was spent finding little tasks at which the daughter could keep busy. Other events of Saturday included: preparation and consumption of lunch for her husband and child, two visits with an elderly woman who lived in an apartment down the hall, supper, putting the daughter to bed (which required both a bath and a story), and a period of TV watching with her husband before retiring.

Sunday started off the same as Saturday: Lucy dressing herself and her daughter and then getting breakfast (again her husband slept). Lucy made lunch preparations and at the same time started the roast and the pie that would be for company coming that afternoon. In the early afternoon, her husband worked on the car while Lucy had little to do except respond to the chatter and enterprises of her toddler daughter.

Late in the afternoon, after all had washed and dressed up, the company came—a young couple their own age. They stayed through supper and early evening. Lucy excused herself after supper to put her daughter to bed, then rejoined the group for further visiting. After the couple left, clean-up took considerable time and Lucy did most of it. In bed on Sunday night, Lucy suffered a short but annoying "attack." She fell asleep about midnight.

Some of Lucy's reactions to the events of the weekend describe her and her situation more fully. Although many categories could be used to describe two days of living, I would like to consider the two broad aspects of *activity* and *sociality*.

With regard to activity, as Lucy described her work for the household, it was clear that she carried it out willingly and without much difficulty. If anything, there was too little to do at times; and much of the work that was done was routine, not challenging. The idle times were used for resting and, as the day wore on, partially desultory attention to her daughter's play and "talk." Hobbies, special household projects, or reading were not a part of Lucy's weekend. No activities outside the apartment house occurred.

In the *sociality* arena, Lucy's interactions with her husband were not rewarding. She volunteered the information that he was often restless at home and she thought part of the problem related to sex. "He thinks about it all the time and yet never seems satisfied."

During the weekend spent with other people, Lucy experienced much better social interaction. She enjoyed her daughter's enthusiasm in starting the day, for eating, for "helping." Lucy took considerable time to give her daughter support and pleasurable activity. The daughter was an enterprising person who rewarded her mother's generous attention by seeking even more of it. Lucy easily absorbed most of the 2-year-old's demands, although it was clear that late in the day it was becoming wearisome and other activity might have been preferred.

Lucy described the two visits with the elderly neighbor in positive terms. Mutual affection was apparent. As Lucy expressed it, "We can really talk." On one visit, the older woman came to Lucy's apartment during the daughter's nap. The two women talked mostly about family: the older woman's children and grandchildren, Lucy's mother and sisters back in Tennessee. On the second visit, Lucy and her daughter went to the woman's apartment and helped her braid her hair. As usual, the daughter wanted to help but was diverted into using an extra brush on her mother's hair. The older woman clearly enjoyed the child's bounce and vigor. Lucy enjoyed the woman's pleasure.

The account of the Sunday evening visit with the other couple contained several incidents showing easy talk and frequent pleasure. Lucy liked the other wife and she said the husband was "a good guy." Being a hostess for the couple included a chance to cook for a different audience. Lucy expressed a bit of pride in reporting that they liked her roast beef and lemon pie.

Lucy's weekend interview did not reveal the cause of her symptoms; it did portray a woman and her context more positively than the classical diagnostic procedures.

In terms of *activity,* Lucy could manage what was asked of her; however, the activity undertaken lacked variety and challenge. In terms of *sociality,* Lucy's relationship with her husband clearly was not optimum, but her interactions with other associates during the weekend were quite positive.

Most of the time she enjoyed and was proud of, her young daughter. She looked for ways to help the child join in mutual activity. The visits with the older woman also showed that Lucy was capable of giving and of receiving affection. Her capacity to have a good time entertaining the visiting couple indicated an important aspect of mental health. In spite of the marital difficulties, it was quite clear that Lucy could make positive emotional contact with the very young, with peers, and with the older generation. It may be inferred that the context in which Lucy operated, although perhaps too restrictive, did offer opportunities for social belonging and social significance. Lucy capitalized on these opportunities.

All in all, Lucy, the individual living the weekend, seemed a more developed and fully functioning person than Lucy, the patient, diagnosed by the projective tests and psychiatric interview.

The appreciation of Lucy, derived from a self-report of her days, encouraged me to ask what might be learned about individuals and their situations if the record of their days was more exact and detailed. What might be learned from a "specimen record," taken by observers, of an individual's behavior from awakening in the morning to going to sleep at night? An opportunity for such an investigation arose when a group of ecological psychologists investigated the impact of summer camp upon children. As a part of this research, we recorded full-day accounts of a 9-year-old boy, Wally, at camp and then another of Wally at home in his suburban neighborhood (Gump, Schoggen, & Redl, 1963). Not only did these records provide more objective and much more detailed accounts than the interview-assisted recall, but they offered a contrast of environments which, we hoped, would illustrate for us something of the impact of the total camp situation. We also wondered what these kinds of data would tell us about Wally—the camper and subject of the investigation.

Wally had been an outpatient at a family service agency for diagnosis and psychotherapy for several periods since he was five. Although he performed moderately well at school and was seen as a reliable boy, he experienced significant problems. His mother reported that he was unable to "hold his own" in conflict with other children; he suffered from excessive fears which his caseworker related to repressed hostility to his parents, particularly his father. He was very rivalrous with his brothers and sisters. Wally occasionally wet his bed. The basic psychiatric label was "adjustment difficulties in a neurotic pattern."

The description of Wally's day at camp, especially when compared with his day at home, might answer an interesting question: Was Wally's "neurotic pattern" so fixed that he would live a camp day in much the same way he lived at home or would he respond to the camp encouragements for different behavior and experience?

University Boy's Camp was designed to give boys with adjustment difficulties an opportunity to spend a beneficial month away from home. In most ways this camp was like other summer camps. For example, the provision of thick woods with trails, and of a lake for swimming and boating, was intended to support outdoor fun and adventure. Other arrangements were designed to assist in adjustment. Boys were assigned to cabin groups so that rough equality in social power among campers was obtained. This meant more than placing together boys of similar ages; it meant clustering boys who were at the same interval along the "social toughness" dimension. This arrangement meant that Wally would spend most of his camp day with potential associates who were, like himself, not very "tough." Wally's ecological situation would provide true peers, not weaker children or significantly stronger youngsters.

The camp also downplayed structured competition; although there were spacious fields where baseball and soccer games might occur, such activities were infrequent.

Two counselors served each cabin group; by training (which continued during camp) and by organizational arrangements, these counselors were likely to give their young charges considerable attention and support.

Wally's home situation involved four younger siblings and a busy mother and father. The family lived in a modest frame three-bedroom house in a lower-middle class suburb. Recreation was supported by a home TV set, two city parks within walking distance, and street and yard areas used by a large number of neighborhood children.

Five trained observers, rotating in half-hour periods, took the camp and home specimen records. Analysis of the record required a unit. The *episode*, a segment of behavior, well defined and bounded by previous ecological research (Wright, 1967), was employed. The major feature of an episode in a person's behavior stream is continuity of direction. Episodes vary in length according to the continuity of direction. For Wally to watch a counselor urge a camper to do his share of cleanup required only a little time, perhaps 30 seconds. For Wally to carry out his own cleanup chores required longer—perhaps 20 minutes. Both the number of episodes devoted to particular kinds of behavior and the total time spent in such episodes became quantifications of Wally's living during the recorded two days.

As with Lucy, it is possible to learn about Wally's *activity* and *sociality*. A full sequential record of all that a child does for an entire day yields an impressive number of episodes. Wally's day at camp produced 1054 episodes, the day at home 1016. These constituted the basic pool of units for a quantitative description of Wally's living on these two occasions. A brief account of the major activities on the two days will help in understanding the numerical description to follow:

Officially, the camp day began with a brief flag-raising ceremony followed by breakfast with campers, sitting as cabin groups, in the dining hall. On this day Wally's cabin was scheduled for a cleanup period in the craft shop; action here gradually faded from work orientation to an impromptu hike in the woods. After a late-morning swim, the cabin had their own midday cookout in the woods near a popular tree hut. Another swimming session in midafternoon was followed by a session of bracelet making at the craft shop. A flag-lowering ceremony and supper in the dining hall came next. The major evening event was an "Indian Council Fire," and then bedtime.

At home, Wally had breakfast soon after arising (seven poeple in a small kitchen) and then played with his next-youngest sibling, Gene. Wally's mother started card games with the two boys, but household events for which she was responsible kept pulling her away. During the morning Wally made two visits to the park where he climbed about in a tree, but he spent more time watching games between other children. After lunch, Wally was given the job of cleaning the bird cage and he interspersed this with long sessions of TV watching. Wally played some baseball in the street, did a few outside chores, had one more stint of play with neighborhood children, and after a rather prolonged and "recreational bath" with his brother, went to bed.

One major difference in the support for activity on the two days refers to settings. Wally entered 17 quite discrete behavior settings at camp, 6 at home. The variety of places entered at camp supported stimulation and adventure. Whether these actually affected Wally is the first question.

One measure of activity is play form. Examples of play forms include: Watching (for sake of interest, not for necessary orientation or work); Investigation and Exploration (breaking up a rotting log to see what is inside); Sportiveness (out of exuberance, Wally runs up one side of a pile of lumber and down the other); Sedentary and Active Formal Games; Construction (of objects, of earth works, of hideouts, etc.); Drama (making like Superman); Teasing (trying to "get a rise" out of an associate); and Manipulative Amusement ("fiddling" with a string—stretching it, wrapping it around a finger, etc.).

Findings show that Wally's pattern of play episodes at camp was substantially correlated to the pattern at home ($r = +.49$). It is roughly accurate to say that the boy somewhat attempted similar play activity in the two environments. In terms of *time* spent in various play forms, however, there was *no* significant correlation between the camp and home days ($r = -.16$).

Wally may have started similar play actions in both environments, but ecological support to these actions differed in the environments and thus changed the play pattern as measured by time. One fairly obvious example: The

Watching play form was very frequent at camp, 67 episodes; somewhat fewer episodes occurred at home, 41 episodes. Yet the time spanned by Watching episodes reversed the camp–home relation: 86 minutes at camp and 328 minutes at home. However, both comparisons are correct and both are meaningful. To explain: Wally, probably out of his fears and hostility, was a "conflict voyeur." He avidly watched any bit of conflict or trouble between campers and especially between campers and camp staff. At home, there were fewer incidents to watch but there were hours of aggression and violence on TV: cowboy pursuits and fights, war stories, and the like. These presentations resulted in a few very prolonged watching episodes. Thus the home situation supported the desire to watch trouble more continuously than the camp (where there was no TV).

Wally played much more actively at camp:

Exploration 62 minutes (5 minutes at home)

Sportiveness 85 minutes (19 minutes at home)

Construction 51 minutes (0 at home)

Drama 84 minutes (32 at home)

At home, besides this passive watching, Wally's play was characterized by much Manipulative Amusement and by Formal Games. As described by play forms, Wally's activity for the two environments was quite different. The sites and the programs of camp achieved for Wally the more adventurous exuberant, and expressive experience for which they were intended. Wally, to a significant extent, started many of the same kinds of play in camp and home, but the environments dominated the *extent* to which these starts could be maintained.

Wally's social activity and experience at camp and home could be described by an analysis of the episodes in which he and another person interacted. Wally may have had adjustment difficulties but these did not mean he was reclusive or withdrawn. He was involved with an associate during 366 episodes at camp and 362 at home.

These units were analyzed in terms of "modes" of interaction (Wright, 1967). For example, Wally, or an associate, might express a dominant mode ("Now, you do it."), an aggressive mode ("Do it or I'll hit you!"), a resistant mode ("Don't push me.") Other modes included submission, nurturance, appeal, and avoidance. Some social episodes contained no modes—neither subject nor associate was doing to, or for, the other—or counteractng the other's action. Many of these interactions were conversational *sharing* of feelings or ideas ("Say, look at that speedboat go!" "Yeah!").

Summary of the total social episodes at camp and home showed several differences. At camp, as compared with home, Wally was significantly less frequently aggressive toward others and more frequently nurturant. Wally's experience of social action from others also differed. At camp, associates were less frequently aggressive, or resistant and more often nurturant and sharing. Wally received a substantially different "social diet" at camp than at home.

This overall contrast masks social qualities in relation to kinds of associates: Adults, Child Peers, and Child Non-Peers. Camp provided many accessible adults; Wally, a first-born child, made the most of this opportunity, interacting with 22 of them (home, 5). At camp, he engaged in 188 episodes with an adult associate (home, 90). Examination of these adult episodes showed two important aspects. Because these are adult-child relationships with wide differences in social power, a basic similarity exists between camp and home: Adults often dominated Wally, he did not dominate them; they more often nurtured him than the other way around. However, there was a significant difference within this basic similarity. Camp adults significantly more often dealt with Wally in a sharing or comradely fashion; home adults were more exclusively "parental." Much of the benign aspect of Wally's overall sociality at camp was a result of a much heavier interaction with adults at camp, where adults behaved somewhat more acceptingly than those at home.

One of Wally's major problems socially was reported to be his inability to "hold his own" with peers. The camp attempted to provide associates of similar social power. The question arises: Was Wally able to "hold his own" in these situations or would he still be dominated or aggressed against without sufficient counteractions?

All of Wally's child associate relationships were investigated for "power discrepancies." A power discrepancy exists when one person in a social episode aggresses against or dominates another who submits without counteraggression or domination.

Wally's associates at camp had power discrepancies over him in 15 episodes; at home, in 28 episodes. An analysis of the camp discrepancy episodes showed that nine of these were received from his best friend, Ernest. However, these power discrepancies almost evened out for the two boys; that is, Ernest was dominant over Wally in nine episodes, but Wally was dominant over Ernest in seven. The boys took turns "leaning on" one another. This was in contrast to the home situation where a frequent associate, Sid, dominated or aggressed against Wally 14 times with Wally showing no Sid-dominating episodes of his own.

Clearly, Wally could "hold his own" with camp children but had difficulty doing so with some children at home.

Wally's situation at home presented two worlds of child associates: his siblings over whom he was persistently dominant and the neighborhood boys who dominated him. At camp, no campers clearly dominated Wally and he dominated two fat boys who were somewhat bullied by other campers as well.

A final note must be added regarding relations between Wally and camp peers. Although aggressive reactions by others to Wally were significantly less frequent at camp, those encounters with peers that did involve aggression often yielded more intense aggression than occurred with children of unequal power at home. Our impression from this and other observational studies of children is that competition and aggression between social peers are likely to be considerably more intensive than between associates of unequal social power.

A final aspect of Wally's camp experience is how he felt about what was happening to him in the two environments. One measure of feeling is that of "emotionality." As episodes develop, individuals can experience positive, negative, or ambivalent feelings. Some of these reactions show in the facial and bodily expressions and in speech. Most of Wally's episodes on both days did not yield cues showing clear emotionality and were coded neutral. However, camp did show more highly positive, highly negative, and ambivalent episodes. (Ambivalence was coded when strong positive and strong negative appeared in the same episodes.) Time of the strongly emotional episodes amounted to 171 minutes at camp and 70 minutes at home. One could say that Wally's emotional life was more labile at camp.

These emotional contrasts were related to environmental differences. For example, the negative reactions (anger and frustration) derived mostly from aggressive encounters with cabin peers.

Negative emotions (fear) were also connected with the dark swampy area of the woods where Wally and his cabin mates went exploring. However, a more frequent emotion in the woods—especially in response to decaying wood and scurrying insects—was "horrible fascination." Wally was simultaneously repelled and attracted; he was ambivalent.

Away from the swamp and near the tree hut Wally experienced happy excitement in war games. He also had pleasing success in a group toad hunt. Playful teasing and diving episodes in swimming provided other highly positive emotional experiences.

WALLY AS A PERSON AND WALLY AS RESPONSIVE TO SITUATIONS

The records of camp and home days provided information about the stable adjustment qualities of Wally as a person and also about his response to contrasts in ecological situations.

The clinically reported "neurotic pattern" was in operation in respect to aggression on both days. The compulsive "trouble watching" was extremely frequent at camp, frequent and very prolonged at home. Although most boys are interested in aggressive encounters, Wally's need here was more persistently intrusive; he would sometimes leave his own interesting activity to be sure and "take in" conflicts between others.

Watching hostilities (and defeats and victories in the game play of others) was, of course, a way of being involved in aggression without risk. Other aggressive behaviors were also indirect: The dramatics of play were dramatics of war and conflict—but then it was only play. The most frequent direct aggressions, again relatively safe, were the many bossings and bickerings in relation to younger siblings.

The persistent need for adult or parental love showed in the large number of different adults Wally contacted and in the number of nurturant and sharing responses he managed to obtain from them. Examination of the concrete events in the records showed that he possessed a variety of moves to "pull" desired adult attention. He could: tease provocatively, then ease off if the response was unfavorable; develop minor aches or injuries; support the adult in the adult's efforts to have campers behave; become solicitous of the adult's welfare; act openingly dependent and childish if the situation in any way permitted it (as in bedtime rituals at camp).

Although Wally showed some fixity in his adjustment pattern across the camp and home situation, there were important differences in his behavior and experience on the two days; these showed an encouraging potential to take advantage of favorable environmental possibilities.

At camp, Wally was clearly more physically and psychologically active, more persistently socially involved. At camp, Wally took one modest retreat from others as he lazed alone in the sun on a kind of "swinging barrel horse." This lasted about 15 minutes; Wally's retreat at home was centered on TV watching and lasted several hours. During this retreat family members came and went and he sometimes interacted with them—but he remained tethered to the TV set.

Camp experience showed that Wally, given primary association with true peers, did not, in balance, suffer from "power discrepancies"; he could "hold his own." This social success at camp does not indicate that there is no problem in peer give-and-take; it demonstrates, though, that there is in Wally a potential for better adjustment in this regard. Matters would not have had to turn out this way; Wally could have been bullied as were the two fat boys in his cabin. Wally had the capacity to change his social action and the reactions of others to him when the group composition was optimum.

One reservation about the findings of camp-induced improvements in Wally's living might be that only one day in this milieu is reported here. Of course, the amount of behavioral data employed is considerable so the "sample" is sufficiently large. It might not be "representative," however. Although there is insufficient space to detail the findings here, we did gather shorter records on Wally and his cabin mates for two swim, two cookouts, and one dining hall occasion. Again, Wally held his own fairly well, and was active and involved in the events of these settings.

These camp–home comparisons, then, illustrate two opposing truths. They show the extent to which certain well-internalized adjustments can persist. Just as surely they also demonstrate how situational factors can produce a significant difference in the quality of living that individuals diagnosed as maladjusted will experience. The objective quantifications of data and our own intuitive response to the thousands of concrete events on the two days lead us to say that Wally, at camp, "had a good day." Further, the good qualities of that day were related to characteristics of the camp environment.

PSYCHOLOGICAL VERSUS ECOLOGICAL CONTEXTS

Records of behavior, such as those of Lucy or Wally, contain not only descriptions of *actions* but also of *situations* in which these actions occur. Lucy's entertainment of the visiting couple put her in a very different situation than the earlier Sunday afternoon period when she was in the apartment with little to do. Wally's relaxed solo play on the barrel horse provided a situation in contrast to the sociality and the stress of his cabin group's hike in the woods. These situations are much tied to the moment-by-moment behavior, to the episodes of the individual; they also "coerce" the individual's behavior and experience. Lucy having visitors determined what she did (entertained, conversed) and what she experienced (some pride in their compliments on her cooking). The word *situation* has a variety of meanings. Of interest here is the relation between situation and environment. The situations described in records have been labeled psychological situations; they contain elements of the objective environment but in a very subject-determined fashion.

First, these situations are often described in terms of their meaning for the subject. "It was a pleasant situation." Second, these situations in the records are generated at the interface of a subject's action and the external environment. They are limited to that interface. If we consider one of Wally's environments to be the cookout setting at camp, the parts of that environment which were present but which did not cross that interface were not represented. (For example, some setting important events occurred during the fire building but during much of this phase, Wally was in the woods collecting firewood and the events were not entered in the record.) The psychological situation then contains fragments of external environments. If our aim is to understand persons in ongoing situations, a record containing the environment as psychological situation can be very useful, as we have tried to illustrate with Lucy and Wally.

One limitation of psychological situations to describe external environments is the selection the subject makes in reacting to the world. This selection should not imply an autonomy from the unselected section of the world. Events from the external world, selected or not, have their own persisting reality, often their own insistence upon entering the subject's psychological situation.

When one insists upon the importance of this external world in determining behavior and experience, the easy rejoinder usually is: "It's clearly not a matter of person variables or environmental variables determining action but an integration of the two." When the concepts used to describe this interaction are examined, however, the person variables almost always preempt the environmental ones. Environments are described as if they simply are people: Some environments are nurturant, others are stressful, and so on.

Environments as understood by ecological psychologists are coupled to the behavior of individuals, but are outside their skin and follow laws very different from those of individual (or even group) behavior (Barker, 1968).

A recitation of all events, stimuli, objects, and so on, that are in any modest environmental span could present a veritable chaos. Fortunately, this chaos is only a possibility in the mind of the psychologist; matters "out there" usually are quite well structured. The human environment manifests concrete, bounded, functioning units of various spans. There are, for example: cities, neighborhoods within cities, schools within neighborhoods, classrooms within schools and "mini-settings" within classrooms. An external unit of modest span is the *behavior setting* (Barker, 1968). During Wally's day he inhabited such settings as Flag Ceremony, Dining Hall Meals, Cabin Cookout, Indian Council Fire, and so on.

The behavior-setting unit is central to much that ecological psychology has done, so a brief explanation of the unit is desirable. The major constituents of behavior settings are a physical milieu, a standing pattern of behavior (sometimes referred to as a program), and a fit between milieu and behavior pattern. For the behavior-setting Dining Hall Meals, the physical milieu includes the enclosing hall, the tables, benches, cooking and eating utensils, food, and so on. The standing pattern of behavior includes the meshing behaviors of cooking, serving, eating, and cleanup. Milieu factors are so placed and shaped that the behavior pattern is facilitated. There is even a clear geographical fit between the shape of sitting behavior of campers and the arrangement of benches to tables.

One importance of behavior settings is the likelihood that they will persistently and insistently affect the psychological situations of their inhabitants. Settings "call for" and get certain behaviors and not others. The setting effects are not limited to such obvious matters as swim settings encouraging swimming, and craft shops encouraging making things. The setting also produces situations that yield more subtle behavioral outcomes. Settings like swimming at camp produced the gross motor activity of water play which, in turn, yielded robust peer interaction. Challenging and countering behavior, play aggressions, and "show-off" interactions were common in swims and very limited in the craft shop; boys in swims used counselors for audiences to their exertions; used them in crafts as supporters and technical helpers when projects became difficult (see Gump & Sutton-Smith, 1955). Truly hostile behavior (not playful aggression) was not common in the swim settings, but when the same boys (with the same counselors) went to cookouts, hostile interactions rose significantly; they rose even higher when these inhabitants were in the dining-hall setting (Gump & Kounin, 1959). Furthermore, in the latter study and in others carried out by ecological psychologists, prediction of behavior was more successful using the question: "In what setting—or setting cluster—is the subject?" then by asking "Who is the subject?"

Over the years, ecological psychologists have produced considerable data showing that ecological situations, as represented by qualities of behavior settings, influence the psychological situations and the behavior of inhabitants in a variety of important directions (Barker & Associates, 1978). For example, on-task behavior of children in school is partially dependent upon learning format (an educational term for the standing pattern of behavior). Seat work sessions ordinarily produce more deviancy and off-task behavior than small reading circle lessons (Kounin, 1966; Gump, 1969).

The influence of settings upon the lives of individuals is particularly impressive when a cluster of settings, which makes up the individuals' environment, present some identical quality throughout its array. (One reason for Wally's active play and emotional lability at camp was the numerous settings that were manifestly child- or play-centered; crafts, swimming, cookouts, tree hut, Indian Council Fire, and so on.)

The setting arrays that constitute small towns are significantly different than those of large towns. Small towns have many fewer settings and duplicates of settings: one variety store, one drugstore, one set of 4-H meetings, one third-grade classroom. As a result, small-town children repeat visits to the same settings much more frequently than do large-town children (Wright, 1969). Further, small-town children are likely to experience the visited settings differently because they more often visit their community settings unescorted by parents. (The closeness of the settings to the child's home and street safety in small towns contribute to this unescorted condition.) Over time, the qualities of the small-town settings repeatedly create psychological situations that affect the child's behavior and the child's psychological world (Gump & Adelberg, 1978; Wright, 1969). For example, various methods of direct and projective testing will show that the small-town child knows more about the community than the large-town youngster. He or she knows more neighbors' names, jobs, children, and more town settings. This difference is not just that the small-town child knows a larger proportion of a smaller arena; the difference is absolute. The "community in the head" of the small child is substantially larger and richer than that of the large-town child.

The preceding capsule statement hardly does justice to the careful and productive study by Wright and his colleagues. An inspection of the references will reveal other differences between large and small communities which create important variations in childrens' lives. One more example of a persisting quality through an array of settings and its effect upon the behavior and experience of persons should be described briefly.

As high schools increase in attendance size, their ecological environments, as represented by their settings clusters, enlarge also. However, population increases at a much faster rate than settings. In one comparison of small and large schools, populations increased by a factor of 65; settings by a factor of 8. The results of the differential rates indicates that large schools have many more students available per setting than do small schools. For the extracurricular array of small-school settings there was less than one-half of one student available per setting; in the large school the rating was four students (Barker & Gump, 1964). The larger schools have many more students to "man" the operations of their settings than do the small schools. The small-school shortage has some very decisive and beneficial effects. All small-school students are likely to be needed; many will be pressed to become functionaries or leaders in the school affairs. Actual research data will show that the small-school students are much more likely to hold responsible positions in setting affairs than are large-school students. The difference in positions held changes the experience in the settings. For example, small-school students report more active, competence-building, group-involved satisfactions; large-school students remember more vicarious excitements and more pleasure in being part of large crowds supporting the school at atheletic events.

Small-school students report substantially more sense of obligation to their school affairs than do large-school students (Willems, 1967). Of particular interest to persons involved in helping maladjusted individuals are the findings relating to the academically marginal students in small and large schools. In the small schools, these marginal youths reported that just as many felt obligations to their school affairs as did their more adequate associates. But in the large school, the marginals reported almost no obligation reactions. Other evidence showed that the small-school marginal students had often been involved in their school's extracurricular operations, whereas such students in the large school had not been included. The large-school marginal students have rejected the school that first rejected them. Sadly, when the large-school marginal youth says, "I'm not needed here!" he's right.

SUMMATION

The stance and the findings of ecological psychology have implications for mental health in a number of directions; several have already been stated.

First, ecological psychologists have methods and concepts for getting at the "round of life." Retrospective and directly observed specimen records can offer an enriched picture of what the client is like as a person, of how the referral problems are revealed in the ordinary and repeated circumstances of life. The capacity of the individual to relate effectively to others, to have a good time, to work with satisfaction, are examples of dimensions that can appear in the specimen records. Because the daily round operates across a number of settings, the individual's capacity to respond appropriately and flexibly is also discernible. The standardized stimuli and situations by which clients are usually diagnosed or treated are very restricted, even peculiar, situations. Accuracy and depth of assessment might significantly improve if assessors obtained data from the "real-life" situations.

Second, a description of daily situations tells us what kind of life our client is leading. It is possible to consider the "health" of this life-style as well as the health of the individual. One can learn what situations seem to invigorate or comfort the client, which are stressful or dispiriting. One might sometimes conclude that the person was not "sick" as much as was his or her life-style.

Third, what actually appears in the episodes and situations of an individual's day depends both on the nature of that individual and upon the nature of the external world contacted. I have encouraged here, more explicit attention to factors in this external (nonpsychological) context. The external human environment exhibits a structure that can be described by use of behavior settings. We all spend our lives in one setting or another. The quality of these settings and our ecological position in them shapes our actions and experiences. The coercivity of individual settings upon important aspects of living has been demonstrated. The coercivity of settings when an array of them share a common quality and operate over substantial time periods is even more marked. (The marginal student in the small high school did not experience being needed in one setting at one time but in several settings on repeated occasions. The result was a vigorous sense of obligation to the affairs of his school.) Attention should be paid to the nature of the settings and other external events with which clients are involved. According to this view, the helping person should sometimes avoid hastily determining "how the client experiences matters" but learn what "matters really are." This orientation assumes that regardless of how the client sees matters, in time these matters will exert their influence, will affect the client.

A FINAL SPECULATION ABOUT ECOLOGICAL REALITIES AND MENTAL HEALTH

To clearly communicate the importance placed upon environmental control of behavior and experience, let us propose this hypothesis: Improvements in mental health will often not *hold* if the same ecological context is maintained after the improvements as existed before. This hypothesis proposes that for a new "outlook" or a healthier adjustment to persist, a changed round of life is required. Therapeutic changes will erode if subjected to the same old sets of behavior settings and their objective events.

One implication of this view is that psychotherapy would establish, or help clients establish, new objective contexts for their living. This view would not deny the likelihood that some clients' problems are the main cause of poor choices of external contexts. The view is simply that optimal therapy does not just change perceptions or feelings or even behaviors but insures change in the real world inhabited by the client.

REFERENCES

Barker, R.G. (1968) *Ecological psychology: Concepts and methods for studying the environment of human behavior.* Stanford, Calif.: Stanford University Press.

Barker, R.G., & Associates (1978) *Habitats, environments, and human behavior: Studies in ecological psychology and eco-behavioral science from the Midwest Psychological Field Station, 1947–1972.* San Francisco: Jossey-Bass.

Barker, R.G., & Gump, P.V. (1964) *Big school, little school.* Stanford, Calif.: Stanford University Press.

Gump, P.V. (1969) Intra-setting analysis: The third grade classroom as a special but instructive case. In E. Willems, & H. Raush (Eds.), *Naturalistic viewpoints in psychological research.* New York: Holt, pp. 200–220.

Gump, P.V., & Adelberg, Bettina. (1978) Urbanism from the perspective of ecological psychologists. *Environment and Behavior,* **10,** 171–191.

Gump, P.V., & Kounin, J. (1959) Issues raised in "classical" research efforts. *Merrill-Palmer Quarterly of Behavior and Development,* **6,** 145–152.

Gump, P.V., Schoggen, P., & Redl, F. (1963) The behavior of the same child in different milieus. In R. Barker (Ed.), *The stream of behavior.* New York: Appleton-Century-Crofts.

Gump, P.V., & Sutton-Smith, B. (1955) Activity and social interaction. *American Journal of Orthopsychiatry,* **25,** 755–760.

Kounin, J. (1966) Managing emotionally disturbed children in regular classrooms. *Journal of Educational Psychology,* **57,** 1–13.

Willems, E.P. (1967) Sense of obligation to high school activities as related to school size and marginality of student. *Child Development,* **38,** 1247/091260.

Wright, H.F. (1967) *Recording and analyzing child behavior.* New York: Harper & Row.

Wright, H.F. (1969) *Children's behavior in communities differing in size.* Report of Project Grant MH01098 (NIMH). Department of Psychology, University of Kansas.

PART TWO

Ecological Models: Applications at the Family System Level

As noted in the introduction to Part 1, the execution of this volume produced its own organization, recycling an initially impossible conceptual task, so that the final product no longer represented a theoretical focus on levels of organization but rather an ecosystemic perspective from the practical service delivery frame of reference. Within this part, each of the authors has selected the "situation" in which a family is presented as the unit with which assessment and intervention is to be conducted. The greatest potential difficulty with this part of the volume has then been avoided; family system approaches are well known, and do not represent a "new" approach that should simply be relabeled as ecosystemic. The transition from the usual limits of family system or family therapy models to a broader conceptual framework is well represented in the chapter by Mannino and Shore. The authors are intimately acquainted with the development and growth of the family system area and have identified the critical areas in which that approach can be extended in both clinical practice and preventive mental health.

The formidable body of research produced by Moos and his associates at Stanford is brought to bear in the second chapter of this part in a specific case study that illustrates the clinical use of social-ecological concepts; the process integrates clinical research and a field theoretical model with contemporary clinical practice.

The chapter by Swap represents yet another perspective on what might otherwise have been viewed a traditional individual-child or family therapy assessment and intervention. Beginning with the critical distinction between "disturbed" children whose dysfunction occurs across settings, and "disturbing" children whose dysfunction occurs across settings, and "disturbing" children whose relationship to a specific setting is disruptive, Swap clarifies not only the basic assumptions but implications for practice from an ecological perspective.

The final chapter by Pattison and Hurd was selected for this part of the volume specifically because it presents the social network paradigm as a basis for intervention. From a traditional perspective, the social network approach would be distinct from practice with families; it is most typically viewed as falling within the province of community psychology or as involving broad social-organizational processes. But the application presented by Pattison and Hurd occurs within the clinical setting and with a "case" that might typically be presented to a family therapist. The placement of this chapter is consistent with the intent of the volume: to integrate diverse approaches that are consistent with an ecological or ecosystemic model in a manner which allows implementation in clinical and community mental health settings.

CHAPTER 5

An Ecological Perspective on Family Intervention

FORTUNE V. MANNINO AND MILTON F. SHORE

In what may be seen as a Lewinian revival, there has, in recent years, been an increased concern with the relationship between individual behavior and the total life space. The model is no longer a Gestalt model based on physics with forces and vectors. We now have a model based on a general systems communications perspective, that is, one that refers to a relationship between a set of units, such as family members, members of an organization, and so on.

Although a systems model has close ties to ecological approaches to human services and mental health, it is important to recognize that thinking "system" and thinking "ecology" are not one and the same. The term *ecology* is broader and includes the concept of system; on the other hand, the concept of system does not necessarily include the concept of ecology. For example, from a systems perspective one can view the family as a group of individuals interacting within the context of the family. Here, an individual's problem is seen as related to a position of functioning in the family relationship system. An ecological perspective broadens the context to include other relationship systems beyond the family, for example, school, workplace, hospital. Here an individual's problem may not be restricted to the family context, but extends to other physical and social contexts within which he or she interacts. Moreover, the ecological perspective forces one to deal with the real problems of social living by placing emphasis upon the environmental context in which one performs roles and creates and interacts with institutions in order to obtain such basic life necessities as food, clothing, medical care, and housing (Freilich, 1967; Minuchin, 1969).

Thus, an ecological systems model may be defined as a set of units with relationships among them operating in an environmental context. The latter includes physical and biological dimensions, social structures, and the psychological dimension of personality dynamics, each with its own unique boundary. From a family systems perspective it is the relationship of family members within the family's ecological context that is emphasized. Concern here is with understanding the reciprocal relationship of family behavior and environment as components of the ecological system for purposes of planning intervention strategies.

Since the emergence of the family movement in the 1950s, a number of theories have evolved which relate to intervention and treatment of families within a systems perspective. A number of treatment strategies and techniques often associated with particular theoretical approaches have also been developed. These have been reviewed in the literature and will not be repeated here. The purpose of this chapter is to focus on four particular areas of intervention in family systems which, in our opinion, have not yet been adequately considered in terms of an ecological framework:

1. Family based interventions and ecologically based family interventions.
2. The relationship of social class to an ecological framework in terms of family intervention.
3. The utilization of the inanimate environment in ecologically oriented family interventions.
4. The implications of ecologically oriented family interventions for prevention.

FAMILY BASED INTERVENTIONS AND ECOLOGICALLY BASED FAMILY INTERVENTIONS

Recent writings on the family, especially in the area of family therapy, place great emphasis upon systems theory and the importance of interactions, communications, and patterns of relationships. Too often, however, family therapists tend to concentrate their efforts entirely on "family," to the neglect of the individual personality systems and/or the environmental context of the family's activities. There is often little or no concern with an individual's feelings of sorrow, pain, happiness, or distress. In fact, in the course of criticizing the traditional psychological approaches, some family therapists, such as Andolfi (1979), throw out the individual, arguing that intrapersonal dynamics and structures are irrelevant to what goes on between the units that compose the system. Others who utilize a family systems approach become very skilled and competent technicians and are able to get in and make changes quickly, for example, unbalance a family, create boundaries, and so on. Minuchin, who ironically has been involved in much of this type of training, recently expressed concern that many of these people are therapeutically illiterate, and are presenting themselves as family therapists even though they have not acquired the necessary wisdom to be effective change agents (Simon, 1980). These are good examples of "family therapists" who are trained to think systems, to see systems, and to change systems. Unfortunately, they do not deal with the people who comprise the system, nor do they deal with the environmental context within which the family and its members function.

One of the subtle dangers of the family orientation as described above is that it can disguise a shift back to the cause-and-effect thinking or the reductionist approach to explanation, to which the systems approach was originally a reaction (Nichols, 1978). Psychopathology is now seen as having a family systems orientation; various relationship patterns become associated with particular pathologies. Therapists talk about their schizophrenic family, their runaway family, or their "encopretic" family.

Thus, it appears that we may have moved (not in a sense of growth) from the boundaries of the individual personality structure unrelated to the environment, to the boundaries of the family unrelated to the environment. In the former, individual orientations led us to seek indications of problems inside the person, and when found there, treatment was directed at the person as the intervention target. This is the familiar medical model of diagnosis. Interest in persons other than the patient was based on concern about genetic history and infectious contamination (Aponte, 1979). The latter substitutes a family orientation for the individual. Thus, we look to the family system for indications of the problem and, when found, direct treatment on this relationship system as the intervention target. In both of these approaches the ecological context is ignored and either the individual or the family, depending upon the orientation, is viewed as the only level necessary to focus upon for diagnosis and intervention. Disregarded in these approaches is the concept that the problem could lie at the level of the ecological system, of which both the individual and the family are component parts (Willems & Stuart, 1980).

From a historical context, what is happening appears not dissimilar to what happened in the field of social psychology in the 1940s and 1950s. At that time social psychologists were highly critical of the "narrow" view of the traditional fields of experimental psychologists and saw their own field as holistic with a foundation in the study of human problems in the real world. In time, however, it became apparent that although the concepts, the words, and the problems differed, social psychology was going in the same direction as the experimental fields of which it had earlier been so critical. What they actually did and said was quite different from their espoused views regarding the organization of human behavior (Proshansky, 1976).

Fortunately, not all family therapists function within such narrow frames of reference. A number have shown in their writings an active interest and involvement in contextual *ecological diagnosis* and intervention. It is their lead that we must follow in developing new forms of diagnoses and interventions. One family therapist who writes about such an ecological approach to diagnosis is Aponte (1979):

To diagnose in family therapy is to understand a module of human behavior the ecological context of which this behavior is a product. It is to see how all the forces in that context converge to produce a specific action at a particular moment in time. In this consideration the physical-biological dimension would need to be accounted for along with dynamics ranging from the broadest social considerations to the psychological structure of the individual personality.

We need to cease trying to deal with behavior in bits and pieces as though it is somehow separate from the larger contextual interdependencies in which it occurs. We must recognize that contexts produce behavior and that our interventions must be based on an understanding of the complexity and interdependency of the ecological systems in which it is embedded. The use of contextual diagnosis and treatment is well expressed in the following statement by Auerswald (1969):

A whole new technology of prevention, diagnosis, and treatment is taking shape. For example, labels which describe syndrome, the etiology of which is multidetermined and may vary from case to case, need no longer be the focus of diagnosis, which will consist instead of identification in the total ecological field of the various etiological vectors in each case. Treatment, following this form of diagnosis, will consist of the production of change through an attack on these vectors in vivo. Treatment effort, confined to work in one location during fixed segments of time called appointments will, as time goes on, be used much more selectively. The agent of change will need to be mobile, to move freely from system to system in the pursuit of his goals. Thus the impact of his skills, though primarily applied to alleviation of an identified problem in an individual, will be felt in a much broader arena. He becomes an ongoing agent of community enhancement.

SOCIAL CLASS AS A VARIABLE IN ECOLOGICALLY BASED FAMILY INTERVENTIONS

Those efforts which go beyond the boundaries of relationships within the family as a unit have occurred when therapists have had to intervene with lower socioeconomic classes. Much of the family therapy literature has been confined to middle and upper classes and focuses for the most part on traditional family structures. Because of their social position, lower-class families have been forced to interact with agencies within the community, particularly public agencies. Because lower-class families have multiple needs, they may require welfare services, employment services, special health services, public housing, and may even be involved with the correctional system. A great deal has been written about the abuse and exploitation that lower-class families have experienced in their dealings with bureaucratic agencies. But the dependence of middle- and upper-social classes on the environment and the impact of ecological structure on the behavior of the middle- and upper-class families have been underestimated.

An example is an upper middle-class family living in an expensive home in a suburban section of a large metropolitan community in an eastern state (Mannino & Shore, 1972). The mother was in psychotherapy for an acute depressive episode and, with her husband, was also receiving marriage counseling from a minister. Their 11-year-old son had been expelled from school because of repeated truancy and disruptive behavior. School officials were making plans to send him to a nearby residential treatment facility. Although all of this was taking place concurrently, there was no communication among any of the helping sources. Crucial factors that came to light later were all but ignored. Briefly, they were as follows.

The family had moved to the area eight months earlier from a small rural community in the South. Father was a professional, advancing rapidly with a firm whose policy was to move employees at regular intervals to positions of greater responsibility and pay. Although he had made three moves in a six-year period, each was to a relatively small southern community where the company had a plant. The son had always attended elementary schools quite small in size, and had experienced no problems. The recent move, which coincided with his elevation to junior high school, however, was complicated by the fact that the junior high school was much larger than other schools he had attended, and the academic standards were considerably higher. As a result, he began falling behind in his work, which eventually resulted in truancy and expulsion.

Mother, who had always been able to adjust to previous moves, found suburban living unlike anything she had experienced before, and when father was sent away for a few weeks to take a management training course, she became depressed. The church, which in the past had been of great support to her, now offered little; it, too, was large and contacts tended to be transient and impersonal. Father was having his own problems. He was locked into a job situation with increasing pressures, and although he disliked management, he felt that he had come too far to turn back. He knew that to refuse a transfer meant no further promotions, and he did not want to risk that. Hence, he found himself working longer and harder and spending less time at home with his family.

This illustration is an example of fragmentation of helping sources, all of which were oriented to psychological issues to the neglect of crucial reality factors, which could have been utilized for more effective work with this family. Why are lower classes treated differently than middle and upper classes? With the poor there is clearly a lack of balance between help with reality issues and intrapersonal and family issues with a greater emphasis given to reality considerations. With other groups there is also a lack of balance, but the distribution of weight is reversed. Attention is given almost entirely to psychological and/or family relationship issues. The manner in which reality intervenes in intrapsychic and interpersonal functioning in the middle and upper classes is seemingly ignored.

One explanation for this phenomenon is that ecological approaches are more relevant for the poor. Many of the problems of the poor stem from and are perpetrated by the inadequacies of the social institutions that allegedly are designed to meet their needs. Because of this, intervention strategies must deal with these social institutions that are contributing so heavily to the problems of this group. One *must* become involved contextually with the lower-class family to have any impact.

But as we have pointed out in the case example above, middle and upper classes also experience situational or reality problems that impinge on intra-personal and interpersonal functioning. Yet little attention is given to such factors when working with these groups.

It is important to recognize that going beyond the boundaries of intrafamily relationships in dealing with social organizations such as welfare, health, or housing services, is not necessarily indicative of an ecological approach. Just as one can focus exclusively on individual dynamics or a system of family relationships, one can also focus exclusively on changing community agencies to serve the family better. In other words, an exclusive preoccupation with any particular level, whether it is the individual, the family or one of its subsystems, or some aspect of the environmental context, narrows one's understanding of the problem, thus limiting approaches for adequate intervention (Mannino, 1974). By failing to deal with the relatedness of the parts, that is, relationships between the individual and the family, between the family members, and between the family and the community, we often just patch a system that can only break down again later.

In the case illustration above, each of the "helpers" was trying to work with one part out of context. None had any awareness of how they were contributing to the conditions that were producing problems for the family (fragmentation, isolation, alienation) because each was dealing with a very limited aspect of the family's reality. Moreover, each probably viewed his or her level of focus as central, oblivious to the circularity of the larger field of influence forces that needed to be considered (Gronfein, 1966).

One can, of course, intervene at any number of levels, separately or concurrently, and produce some change. Indeed, change may be effected at one level of focus or on another level. That is, one can focus on an individual level and effect change at the family system level and vice versa; or one can focus on a teacher and principal in a day school and effect change in a student. The important point is that the level at which one chooses to focus his or her intervention must be determined by a contextual assessment.

THE PHYSICAL ENVIRONMENT AND ITS RELATIONSHIP TO FAMILY INTERVENTIONS

Although an increasing number of family therapists are becoming aware of the importance of environmental considerations in their work with families, their focus has been chiefly on the social environment, that is, the influence of extended family members, friendships, neighbors, or other social systems. Few have as yet become aware of the influence of the physical or inanimate environment on family behavior and family activities. Thus, architecture and environmental design tends to be ignored as an important variable in behavior. Indeed, it is only recently that architects have become a part of the mental health team; but much of their work has been concerned primarily with psychiatric settings. Recently, important contributions have been made in showing how the physical properties of the environment influence social behavior and communication (S. Lennard & H. Lennard, 1977).

Studies have shown that the physical design of high-rise apartment buildings influences social interaction and tends to exert an atomizing effect on informal relationships (Holahan, 1980). Similarly, in student residential environments, students' perception of social support and cohesiveness, cooperation and pro-social behavior is at a lower level in high-rise as opposed to low-rise student housing (Holahan, 1980). Quilitch and Risley (1973) have demonstrated how the type of toys used by children dramatically influences their rate of social interactive play, probably even more than the types of children or differences between children. Brody, Stoneman, and Sanders (1980) have shown that family TV viewing results in parents having less association with and influence on their children. A rather surprising finding, however, was that the amount of touching increased among family members when television was being viewed, suggesting a sensitivity among the family members to maintain personal contact when they decrease their talking and relating to one another.

At the community level, Festinger, Schacter, and Back (1950) showed how the physical layout of a housing project affected the selection of neighbors and the duration of neighborly contact. Whyte (1956) showed that physical settings support enduring patterns of suburban social relationships even after the original residents had moved. Newman (1972) found a relationship between variations in physical designs of housing projects and variations in patterns of criminal behavior. Thus, there is increased evidence which shows that physical contexts influence behavior and produce outcomes that can be useful in planning family interventions.

No doubt many family therapists (especially those who work within an ecological framework) would be sympathetic to incorporating methods to utilize the physical environment as a part of their change strategies, if they were able to see how such change related to therapeutic goals and outcome. However, knowledge of the psychological consequences of changing the physical environment is only beginning to develop. But the art and science of such change is confined more to institutional settings than to family life.

Nevertheless, there are a few examples of producing change in families through altering aspects of the physical environment. One of the best known, perhaps, is what Minuchin calls "manipulating space." He makes use of the way a family geographically arranges itself in chairs to get clues about alliances and coalitions. He also shifts or geographically rearranges chairs as a technique for making the family enact family descriptions. In treatment he relates the changing location of the chairs directly to therapeutic goals; for example, he increases distance (a therapeutic goal) between a parent and a child by separating them in such a manner that the child cannot catch the parent's eye. He also changes the position of chairs to provide support to a particular family member, to create or strengthen a boundary, to increase closeness or distance, and so forth (Minuchin, 1974).

Another example of changing the physical environment as part of family therapy is contained in Bell's (1980) "Family Context Therapy," which, incidentally, he views as a corrective to the "constriction of family-centered thought." A great deal of Bell's work has been with institutions, particularly hospitals, where he works at changing contexts for patients. Efforts to change the physical environment are often related to family access and include the removal of physical barriers, for example, opening locked doors, easing parking problems. Interventions are based on the identification of features of the hospital or patient programs that have actual or potential impact on families and are related directly to therapeutic goals and outcome.

Another ecological dimension, not unrelated to the manipulation of space, is the purposeful use of time as a part of the structure of therapy. All therapy, of course, is structured to some extent around time, that is, setting a time limit on sessions and determining how frequently sessions will be held, and so on, and even though there have been some significant departures from the traditional "50-minute" hour in the practice of psychotherapy, with some approaches using full days, half-days, and weekends, this is not the same as using time as a dynamic in therapy. A good example of the latter is found in the practice of "functional casework" where the worker, usually after an assessment period, sets the frequency of interviews and a time limit for the treatment (e.g., three months, six months, four weeks), so that time becomes an actual part of the treatment structure. It is seen as having a psychological and a practical effect in activating the client to use the treatment relationship: It serves as an incentive to use the time productively but also provides, through the casework treatment, an experience where the mechanism of separation and union could be worked out (Kasius, 1950).

One further example of using the physical environment (together with aspects of the social environment) to promote change at the level of therapy is the fairly widespread use of video playback. According to Alger (1976), video playback changes the actual course of the therapy session. It changes the role relationship of therapist and family members in that during the replay both family and therapist move to a different position (that of "data researchers") and are equally engaged in reviewing and reacting to the recorded material. Alger points out how this shift can be used to alter the usual hierarchical relationships between family members, to aid in shifting alliances or in promoting distance or closeness.

Therapists and others who work with families can, no doubt, find many examples of the ways family members use the physical environment in a destructive manner to deal with feelings and emotions. How, for instance, rage and anger that are interpersonally engendered are vented by the child stomping on the floor, slamming doors, and throwing toys; by an adolescent driving a car in a reckless manner or at excessive speeds; by a man crushing and destroying small appliances or pieces of furniture; by a woman throwing dishes or other small objects. More constructive ways of accomplishing similar goals have been suggested, such as substituting safer and unbreakable objects, for example, punching at pillows, hammering wooden planks or beating on pots, taking long walks or exercising. There are also therapeutic techniques that relate to solitude and meditation which may be useful, for example, resting on a bed in a dark room with no noise, or being submerged in warm water in a large tub.

Similarly, one can think of examples of how families attribute their problems to aspects of the physical environment. A frequent complaint by wives is that husbands who sit in comfortable lounge chairs to watch TV after dinner fall asleep for the rest of the evening. Another is by husbands who complain that their wives save the vacuuming for when they are trying to watch TV or relax. In one family a wife blamed the distance that had developed between her and her husband to the replacement of their double bed with a king-size bed. A typical complaint by parents about children is their failure to clean or straighten their bedrooms, which are strewn with every kind of inanimate object.

The above examples are not meant to suggest that social–psychological problems are caused by the physical environment or that changing the physical environment can necessarily correct social–psychological problems. They are presented to point to the importance and significance of the physical environment in working with families in context, and the need to devote more attention to our understanding of it in both our intervention and research.

As we intervene in physical settings to effect changes in behavior and social activity, it is also important that we be concerned with the interaction between the individual and the environment, and not think simplistically about change in one while neglecting the other. We know, for example, from work with developing community support programs and living arrangements for former mental patients, that the geographical location of such programs is very important. That is, the individual must live in an area where connections to a network of supports are possible. However, we also know that it does little good to make such connections if the individual involved has not been taught the necessary social skills to initiate and maintain them (Holman & Shore, 1978).

THE FOCUS ON INTERVENTION AND TREATMENT WITH LITTLE ATTENTION BEING GIVEN TO THE AREA OF PREVENTION

A fourth area that has not been given adequate ecological exploration is that of prevention. Because a great deal of family anxiety and family dysfunction is an ecologic phenomenon, that is, a consequence of discordant patterns of relations between families and nonfamily systems, there is a need for intervention directed toward improving such relations so that a more harmonious pattern prevails. Several types of problems of this nature have been described previously (Mannino & Shore, 1972).

One deals with the family's relations with primary institutions—school, work, recreation, health, government, church, and so on. These are primary in the sense that they deal directly with growth and development and as such are the main systems through which families strive to attain their goals and satisfy their needs. In general, these family/institution relationships tend to favor the nonfamily institutions (Mannino, 1974). Their greater power enables them to pressure the families to accommodate to their needs and requirements, particularly if there are any conflicts of interest or goals.

A second type of problem occurs in situations in which intended goals of nonfamily systems are subverted so that negative rather than positive effects result (Auerswald, 1969a). An example is the "suitable home" policy (man in the house rule) contained in the early regulations of Aid to Families with Dependent Children. Although this policy was designed to encourage marriage and conformity to community standards, one author points out that "it was destined to accomplish the opposite functions of discouraging marriage, maintaining high illegitimacy rates in families denied public aid, simultaneously reinforcing the caste system" (Mandell, 1971). Similarly, Reissman (1969) discusses the ways in which the welfare system functions to maintain people in the cycle of poverty. Other examples include iatrogenic maladies which are known to any practitioner in the health or mental health field. An abundance of such examples dealing with sexual and marriage problems are discussed in Masters and Johnson's study on *Human Sexual Inadequacy* (1970).

Related to this problem area are unintended and latent effects of policies that impact negatively on the family, such as the "Marriage Penalty" tax that makes it cheaper for dual-income couples not to get married or to get divorced, or provisions of the Social Security Act that make it advantageous for elderly couples to live together without marriage.

Another problem area occurs when a family relates to two or more systems, or to two or more subparts of one system, in which conflicting standards or regulations combine in such a way as to frustrate the activities of all, at best, or create further damage and conflict for the family, at worst. An excellent example of this type of situation was discussed in an article by Hoffman and Long (1969a) in which a family is caught in a paradoxical situation within two nonfamily systems designed to help—a housing authority and a health care system. There are many similar types of situations. One recently brought to the writers' attention involved a black family consisting of a young mother and a small child (Nover, 1979). The family lived in a model cities' neighborhood in a very dilapidated apartment soon to be razed for urban renewal. The child was attending an excellent model cities' day-care center while the mother undertook training through the Work Incentive Program. Upon completion of the training program, the mother was able to obtain employment and shortly thereafter realized a long-awaited goal—that of obtaining a reasonably neat and attractive apartment. However, when she gave her new address to the officials at the day-care center, she was notified that her child could no longer attend the center because the family now resided outside of the service area. Because the mother could not afford the costs of a baby sitter, she was unable to keep her job unless the child could attend the day-care center. Because she could not find suitable housing within the model cities' service area, the only alternative seemed to be to quit her job and reapply for welfare assistance.

In all of the areas described, the common denominator would seem to be the discordant patterns of relations between the family and the nonfamily systems with which it interacts. Dealing in a therapeutic way with families already interlocked with a variety of such nonfamily systems is an important task. We also need to consider ways to deal with such problem situations at the preventive level, however, in order to avoid the kinds of inequities that are currently so prevalent.

One example of intervening at the preventive level to produce a positive effect on family living is that of consulting about the planning of a new town. Lemkau (1969) has written about his experiences as one of a group of consultants to the new town of Columbia, Maryland, during its planning stage. As he put it, "The province of the consultants was the area of human interrelationships and how the physical structure of the community could lead to health in the area of living— health in its broadest definition." The consultants became involved with a number of questions and issues.

One issue was that of creating a feeling of community. The consultants were aware that in large cities a sense of a local feeling of belonging was becoming increasingly difficult to maintain. Recognizing that such a feeling was difficult to develop and/or maintain when the area and the number of people became too large, the consultants concluded that the new town of Columbia should be laid out in such a way as to promote more local primary identification, rather than to attempt to foster a more central citywide identification.

Another question was how large such local groups should be. Here, practical considerations came into play. The optimum population necessary to support a small shopping center and also supply enough pupils for junior high schools was believed to be from 10,000 to 15,000. Hence these two factors determined the size of the local community unit, around which recreation areas, churches, and professional offices could be developed. Spatial considerations also became important. Local health services, for instance, were seen as stemming from professional buildings constructed in advance to foster group practice without dictating that it should exist. Local public health units were conceived as being housed as an expansion of the school health suites in school buildings, with the local physicians' offices nearby, so that part-time and emergency services would be convenient.

Another planning goal was that all students should be able to walk to school, so that each neighborhood would have several elementary schools. Each school would form a center for a smaller commercial development consisting of community rooms, swimming pool, and a small food store for emergency needs.

To further encourage a friendly community climate, traffic safety was also considered an extremely significant planning issue by the mental health consultants. They worked to avoid traffic barriers and wide auto expressways. These considerations led to the grade separation of walkways and roadways at crossings and to a local small-bus transportation system traveling on its exclusive roads to connect the 10 to 12 smaller villages that were envisioned as making up the larger city.

There were many other issues in addition to fostering a sense of community to which the consultants attended. They were concerned with housing for those who preferred to live in a downtown area rather than a suburban area, and with those whose mobility was reduced by reason of disability or advancing age. They were concerned with the demands and needs of a city of 100,000 beyond those that could be satisfied at the local level of 10,000 to 15,000 people. They were very concerned about the context within which the new city of Columbia was being planned, with manpower needs and industrial development. Together with the above were concerns about creating an educational structure that would be capable of retraining workers periodically to meet the anticipated changing demands and needs of industry.

Although we could elaborate further on this example, the above seems sufficient to illustrate how the consultants focused on the interrelationships between the physical environment and family life in their planning efforts geared to creating a socially and physically healthful environment.

INTERVENTION ROLES

In using an ecological systems view, intervention occurs when there is an imbalance within a system or a dysfunctional relationship between two or more systems. The intervener may enter the ecological system structure at the level of the individual, family subsystem, nuclear family, extended family, network group, organization, community or society. Unlike the traditional approach where one has an identified patient with symptoms, who becomes the focus of help, using an ecological framework one might intervene with the strongest and most symptom-free member of the system, assuming that such an intervention will serve to realign the forces toward improving the functioning of the symptomatic member. Thus, unlike the classical medical/doctor relationship, wherein the same role is played over and over, irrespective of the nature of the problem, the intervener must be prepared to play a number of roles and to perform whatever activity or task is appropriate to deal with the problem situation. Minuchin (1974) addresses this when he indicates that a therapist's interventions are determined by his assessment of the family. If his assessment shows that the family is basically sound but that one member is having difficulty with an extra-familial agency, then the intervention may be directed at that member, but within the context of the involved agency. Or, if the assessment reveals a sound family that is overloaded by the impingement of many uncoordinated agencies, the focus is on the family's interactions with the agencies. Or, when in a sound family, broad economic and/or social issues are impinging on the family with one member showing special reactions to the stress, a more broadly based intervention may be needed. These are all examples of case-generated interventions; that is, interventions developed as a part of therapy.

There are also family oriented interventions that are not generated by therapy. They are based on our general awareness and sensitivity of contextual situations impacting adversely on the family and include the types of concerns described above in the section on prevention. When dealt with from a preventative framework, the goal is to effect broad social change that will benefit groups of families rather than one particular family (Bronfenbrenner, 1975). Some examples of roles can be delineated. These roles differ along the dimensions of level, specific task activity, and goals.

Educational Counselor

The educational counselor uses rational and cognitive means to enhance skills in a person or a family with regard to dealing with the environment. The purpose is to increase the competence and ability of the family to negotiate the system, and is done through education and knowledge. This role, however, assumes there is little resistance within an individual or a family and that they are able to accept and utilize material given to them. To determine the appropriateness of this role requires diagnostic skills that can answer the question: "Is knowledge and education enough to obtain necessary skills?"

An interesting example of this role involves a program at the Family Service Agency in Prince George's County, Maryland, where a counselor works with families in purchasing their own homes in collaboration with FHA. Counseling is provided regarding the structure of the house, real and projected expenses, and mortgage information, with an emphasis upon improving the competence of the family around home buying (Family Service Forum, 1981).

Another example involved the training of teenage mothers in job interview skills to increase their competence and competitiveness in the job market. Skills taught were based in part on an assessment of the needs of the teenage mothers, and included presenting succinct summaries of past employment, highlighting specific strengths of academic experiences, and answering questions clearly, concisely, and pleasantly. Training techniques utilized included role playing, positive reinforcement, verbal coaching, and demonstrations (Schinke, Gilchrist, Smith & Wong, 1978).

Case Manager

One image of the case manager is as an individual who acts as a central switchboard through the bureaucratic maze so that families are able to get the care that is available and accessible to them. They do not themselves get involved in the dispensing of the care but keep track of what is being done, seeing that appointments are kept, and that agencies are contacted. The purpose is to make sure that contacts are maintained and that there is interchange between agencies where multiple needs have to be met. Thus, they make contacts between systems and keep track of the family.

It has been suggested, however, that case management also includes responsibility for multiple contacts as an integral part of therapeutic work with individuals or families (Lamb, 1980). Thus, case management becomes a part of the normal duties of a conscientious intervener, where needs are assessed and all aspects of the interchange with institutions and settings become part of the therapeutic program (Massimo & Shore, 1967). The advantages here are that contacts with community agencies can be used as opportunities to intervene into the communicational, organizational, and affective processes of families. It also assures that the contacts are focused upon real needs of the family or individual so that the efficiency of the case management in itself does not become the primary goal.

The major feature of the case manager's job is that it incorporates more than teaching and knowledge. It is a role where either with or without involvement various parts of the helping system are put together and monitored.

Catalyst

The catalyst uses leadership skills and knowledge of the community service structure to stimulate agencies to mobilize their own resources in finding ways to help the multiproblem family. Thus, the goal is to foster more coordination among the members of the service delivery network. One of the techniques is to organize all of the helping agencies involved with a particular family and have them work together in developing a common program plan, delineating responsibilities in attempting to effect change in families. The idea is not to alter the responsibilities of the agencies, but to ensure that these responsibilities are carried out in association with the other agencies with whom the family is in contact.

In an example of this role, Auerswald and Notkin (1969), realizing that trying to coordinate the activities of agencies with disparate vantage points was futile from the viewpoint of the family involved, developed a plan to bring together all agencies working with a family together with the family for a conference, so that agreement on a comprehensive plan within a common vantage point could be developed. This conference technique was not only beneficial in providing needed services to the families involved, but it also played a significant role in changing the structure and operations of the helping systems to make them more responsive to the needs of the community. A similar situation was reported by Nover (1980) where a family was involved with 16 social agencies, most of which worked with individual members in a competing rather than cooperative manner. By bringing all 16 agencies together around a natural family crisis, the agencies began to consolidate around the needs of the family and began working cooperatively, rather than at cross-purposes. It was as though a chain reaction was set off, as one agency after another began to view the family as a unit with overall needs, rather than focusing exclusively on the needs of individual members.

Organizational Consultant

In this role the consultant operates to change a dysfunctional relationship between the family and a community organization by identifying the factors contributing to the dysfunction, then initiating change in the organization necessary for the creation of an alternate, more functional family/organization arrangement. Emphasis is on organizational change and meaningful participation of the family, with a goal of more humane service.

An example of this role is the Family Focus Program at the Stanford University Medical Center, where physical and social aspects of the hospital environment were modified to encourage continuity with normal life. The family was involved as an important change agent in helping the patient adjust to illness (Shapiro, 1980). The patient was seen as an equal member of the family rather than as a passive recipient. Educational efforts were focused on the patient and the family to provide them with skills for adopting their new health care roles and on the staff to ensure their understanding and support of the program. Thus, new strategies and structures within the organization responsible for delivering service are the goals of the organization consultant. The aim is to produce more humane and efficient delivery within a particular organizational setting.

Social Support Systems Consultant

This role involves mobilizing various formal and informal community and family resources to provide help required by families and individuals to cope more effectively. Three intervention approaches can be described here. One involves consultation with existing natural networks in order to expand its sphere of influence. An example is the consultation provided by Collins (1973) to a natural service delivery system. Assistance was given to natural neighbor helpers to increase the scope of the service and the numbers of people served, in no way changing their functioning or position in the neighborhood. The significance of this role is related to the fact that individuals served in natural delivery systems are likely to be those most in need of preventive mental health and least likely to make use of the formal health and agency service structure.

A second approach is to create new networks by organizing the natural care-giving system in a community. Applying family therapy concepts to a wider community system dysfunction, Simpkinson and Anderson (1978) worked to improve the effectiveness of a community's natural relationship resources. Entering the community system structure through its care-giving system, they worked toward establishing links between the formal and informal care-giving systems by breaking the rigidity of the boundaries that existed. The community eventually formed its own organization (Family Life Center) that combined features of both formal and informal systems. The long-range goal of the intervention was to help this organization function as a part of the natural care-giving system that could provide enough family support and stability to lessen the need for more formal helping resources, such as therapists and counselors.

A third approach involves the formation of self-help groups (which can take place with or without a consultant) designed to provide emotional and social support, but also to undertake some political action to influence policies that affect their problem situation. An example of this was the coalition of families of American men who were prisoners of war or who were unaccounted for in

Vietnam. Members of this coalition developed close relationships and acted to confront and challenge the organizations that were capable of resolving their problem. Their efforts influenced the U.S. Congress and developed policies that ultimately helped them by ensuring their financial stability, and providing a guaranteed college education for their children (McCubbin, 1979).

The major feature in this role is focusing directly on natural helpers in neighborhoods and the larger community. The aim is to tap into an extremely efficient and effective helping resource generated in the community.

Advocate

The advocate, by definition, assumes an adversarial role. There is a commitment to the family. The advocate may use a number of techniques, from individual case advocacy to class action advocacy, thus sometimes even using legal means to demand the services that are necessary for the family. Social change is the focus of the role of the advocate, and the belief is that the total organization and structure of the system of service delivery needs to be altered and that this is best done by challenge, confrontation, and pleading the clients' cause.

As Knitzer says in a 1980 article:

advocacy assumes an interrelationship between individuals and the social, political, economic and legal forces which determine both the public perception of a problem and the underlying structural factors that shape its boundaries. Thus, methodologically and substantively, advocacy relies upon an ecological perspective to trace the manifestations of a particular issue through different levels of social processes, to generate a range of remedies responsive to the problem at these different levels, and to try to anticipate the consequences of a corrective action on other parts by the system. (p. 297).

In one example of case advocacy, the advocate applied sufficient social and political pressure to force a local housing authority to combine two apartments by knocking down a wall to accommodate a large family. As a result of the advocate's work, the city was threatened with lawsuits for discriminating against large families, and began to purchase two-family housing for large families. Thus, in this instance, effective social change to benefit one family led to larger change benefiting groups of families (Grosser, 1979).

It is important in delineating these roles to clarify what the implications of each are: the determination of the needs in a given situation; the particular strategy at a given time; and the effect on an ecological framework. There is no doubt that one alters roles. But the important question currently is, rather than adapting individuals to particular kinds of service delivery systems, how does one determine the particular roles in terms of family needs? We do not know, for example, if there is a particular progression in roles for certain groups. Is one capable of changing from one role to the other without creating confusion in the system? Is special training necessary to assume many of these particular roles? How does one orchestrate these roles in terms of particular kinds of family needs at a given time?

CONCLUSION

An ecological approach to family intervention is necessary and appropriate for families, irrespective of social class. It is not limited to treatment but is relevant for prevention as well. It encompasses the animate and inanimate environment. It embraces more than the interactions within the family but includes the broad context of family functioning within a society, culture, and physical world. It is necessary that our interventions be conceptualized along this broad dimension. But such intervention requires learning a number of new roles. What remains are questions of how to assess the most appropriate interventions, how to train for the new roles of intervener, and how to develop ecologically oriented techniques for evaluation. But despite the complexity of this task, we need to be reminded repeatedly of the remark by Hoffman and Long (1969b):

Perhaps the most obvious difference between traditional work and the type of activity described here is this: The more traditional model does not see the persons who are helpers of a given individual or family (and this includes the social worker himself) as part of the problem to be attacked. If reducing inequities of power within all the interlocking systems inhabited by a distressed person is the therapeutic task, the role of the helper is going to have to be recast. It will be increasingly harder to separate the specialist in "emotional" problems from the specialist in "community" problems. In fact, if these practitioners do not combine to produce a new type of helper, they may find themselves atrophied stubs on a form which has developed very different limbs.

The challenge is before us.

REFERENCES

Alger, I. (1976) Integrating immediate video playback in family therapy. In P. Guerin (Ed.), *Family therapy.* New York: Gardner Press.

Andolfi, M. (1979) *Family therapy: An interactional approach.* New York: Plenum.

Aponte, H.J. (1979) Diagnosis in family therapy. In C. Germain (Ed.), *Social work practice: People and environments.* New York: Columbia University Press.

Auerswald, E.H. (1969a) A systems dilemma, introduction. *Family Process, 8,* 211–212.

Auerswald, E.H. (1969b) Changing concepts and changing models of residential treatment. In G. Caplan & S. Lebovici (Eds.), *Adolescence: Psychosocial perspectives.* New York: Basic Books.

Auerswald, E.H., & Notkin, H. (1969c) *Psycho-social services in a comprehensive health program.* Unpublished paper.

Bell, J.E. (1980) Family context therapy. In R. Hernik (Ed.), *The psychotherapy handbook.* New York: New American Library.

Brody, G.H., Stoneman, Z., & Sanders, A.K. (1980) Effects of television viewing on family interactions: An observational study. *Family Relations, 29*(2), 216–220.

Bronfenbrenner, U. (1975) Is early intervention effective? Some studies of early education in familial and extra-familial settings. In A. Montagu (Ed.), *Race and I.Q.* London: Oxford University Press.

Collins, A. (1973) Natural delivery systems: Accessible sources of power for mental health. *American Journal of Orthopsychiatry,* **43**(1), 46–52.

Family Service Forum. (1981) *Pre-purchase housing counseling.* Family Service of Prince George's County, Inc., Lanham, Md. Jan.–March, No. 4, p. 4.

Festinger, L., Schacter, S. & Back, K. (1950) *Social pressures in informal groups.* Stanford, Calif: Stanford University Press.

Freilich, M. (1967) Ecology and culture: Environmental determinism and the ecological approach in anthropology. *Anthropological Quarterly,* **40**(1), 26–43.

Gronfein, B. (1966) Should casework be on the defensive? *Social Casework,* **47,** 650–656.

Grosser, C. (1979) Participation in practice. In C. Germain (Ed.), *Social work practice: People and environments.* New York: Columbia University Press.

Hoffman, L., & Long, L. (1969a) A systems dilemma. *Family Process,* **8,** 211–234.

Hoffman, L., & Long, L. (1969b) A systems dilemma. *Family Process,* **8,** 231.

Holahan, C.J. (1980) Action research in the built environment. In R.H. Price, & P.E. Politser (Eds.), *Evaluation and action in the social environment.* New York: Academic Press.

Holman, T., & Shore, M.F. (1978) Halfway house and family involvement as related to community adjustment for ex-residents of a psychiatric halfway house. *Journal of Community Psychology,* **6,** 123–129.

Kasius, C. (1950) *A comparison of diagnostic and functional casework concepts.* New York: Family Service Association of America.

Knitzer, J. (1980) Advocacy and community psychology. In M. Gibbs, J. Lachenmeyer, & J. Sigal (Eds.), *Community Psychology.* New York: Gardner Press.

Lamb, H.R. (1980) Therapist-case managers: More than brokers of services. *Hospital and Community Psychiatry,* **31**(11), 762–764.

Lemkau, P.V. (1969) The planning project for Columbia. In M. Shore, & F. Mannino (Eds.), *Mental health and the community: Problems, programs, and strategies.* New York: Behavioral Publications.

Lennard, S., & Lennard, H. (1977) Architecture: Effect of territory, boundary, and orientation on family functioning. *Family Process,* **16**(1), 49–66.

McCubbin, H. (1979) Integrating coping behavior in family stress therapy. *Journal of Marriage and the Family,* **41**(2), 237–244.

Mandell, B. (1971) Welfare and totalitarianism: Part I. Theoretical issues. *Social Work,* **16,** 17–26.

Mannino, F.V., & Shore, M.F. (1972) Ecologically oriented family intervention. *Family Process,* **11**(4), 499–505.

Mannino, F.V. (1974) An ecological approach to understanding family and community relationships. *Journal of Home Economics.* **66**(3), 9–13.

Massimo, J.L., & Shore, M.F. (1967) Comprehensive vocationally oriented psychotherapy: A new treatment technique for lower-class adolescent delinquent boys. *Psychiatry,* **30,** 229–236.

Masters, W.H., & Johnson, V.E. (1970) *Human sexual inadequacy.* Boston: Little, Brown.

Minuchin, S. (1969) Technique or theory? In: J. Masserman (Ed.), *Science and Psychoanalysis, XIV: Childhood and Adolescence.* New York: Grune & Stratton, 179–187.

Minuchin, S. (1974) *Families and family therapy*. Cambridge: Harvard University Press.

Newman, O. (1972) *Defensible space*. New York: Macmillan.

Nichols, W.C. (1978) The marriage relationship. *The Family Coordinator*, **27**(2), 185–191.

Nover, R. (1979) Personal communication.

Nover, R. (1980) *Clinical preventive intervention with high-risk infants*. Mental Health Study Center, Adelphi, Md.

Proshansky, H.M. (1976) Environmental psychology and the real world. *American Psychologist*, **31**(4), 303–310.

Quilitch, H.R., & Risley, T.R. (1973) The effects of play materials on social play. *Journal of Applied Behavior Analysis*, **6**, 573–578.

Riessman, F. (1969) *Strategies against poverty*. New York: Random House.

Schinke, S., Gilchrist, L., Smith, T., & Wong, S. (1978) Improving teenage mothers' ability to compete for jobs. *Social Work Research and Abstracts*, **14**(1), 25–29.

Shapiro, J. (1980) Changing dysfunctional relationships between family and hospital. *Journal of Operational Psychiatry*, **11**(1), 18–26.

Simon, R. (1980) A therapy of challenge. Conclusion of an interview with Salvador Minuchin. *Family Therapy Practice Network Newsletter*, **4**(3), 5–10.

Simpkinson, C., & Anderson, K. (1978) Help for the expanded family network: Integrating the formal and informal caregiving systems in a community. In *1978 Synopsis of Family Therapy Practice*. Olney, Md.: The Family Therapy Practice Network.

Whyte, W. (1956) *The organization man*. New York: Simon and Shuster.

Willems, E.P., & Stuart, D.G. (1980) Behavioral ecology as a perspective on marriage and families. In J. Vincent (Ed.), *Advances in Family Intervention, Assessment and Theory*. Greenwich, Conn: Jai Press.

CHAPTER 6

The Clinical Use of Social-Ecological Concepts: The Case of an Adolescent Girl

RUDOLF H. MOOS AND ROBERT FUHR

During the last decade, researchers have noted the limitations of person-oriented assessment procedures and the tendency of clinicians who use these procedures to attribute the causes of behavior primarily to the enduring dispositions of individuals, while minimizing the contribution of environmental factors (Endler & Magnusson, 1976; Mischel, 1979; Moos, 1976). Such person-oriented causal attributions have resulted in assessment techniques, intervention strategies, and program evaluation criteria that focus on person-centered variables to the relative exclusion of environmental variables (Caplan & Nelson, 1973). These facts have led several investigators to underscore the need for clinicians and social researchers to systematically consider social-ecological factors and to explore their relationships to individual mood and behavior (Barker et al., 1978; Holahan, 1978).

Three interrelated issues must be considered to address this need adequately. Most important, alternative theoretical frameworks and concepts must be developed to guide the search for relevant environmental domains of environmental factors and to conceptualize their interrelationships. The next issue is to construct environmental assessment procedures to measure the dimensions identified by such frameworks. Finally, to evaluate the clinical utility of the concepts and procedures, they must be applied to clinical case descriptions and the formulation of intervention strategies. We address these three issues here.

CONCEPTUAL FRAMEWORK

Bronfrenbrenner (1979) has recently proposed a conceptual framework that can serve as a guide to the basic components of social-ecological systems. He

The work was supported by NIAAA Grant AA02863 and by Veterans Administration Medical Research funds. We thank Andy Billings and Josh Holahan for their helpful comments on earlier identifies four such components: (1) The *microsystem* is composed of the interpersonal relationships, goal-directed molar activities, and system-defined roles and role expectations a person experiences in a given setting, such as the school or family. (2) The *mesosystem* comprises the interrelations between two or more microsystems in which an individual participates, such as the relationships between the school and family or the family and work. (3) The *exosystem* is composed of settings that do not involve the individual as an active participant, but in which events occur that can affect what happens in the setting containing the individual (such as the effects of the parents' work settings on the family environment they establish for their children).

Finally, (4) the *macrosystem* refers to cultural consistencies in the other three systems and in their interrelationships, and to the social values and beliefs that underlie such consistencies. For instance, the prevailing belief that the formative years are primarily for formal school education and recreation, has led to a cultural pattern in which adolescent children in America do not participate actively in their parents' work settings.

MEASUREMENT PROCEDURES

One difficulty in focusing on these issues is the lack of available methods by which to measure the salient features of the social settings that comprise the microsystem. Although there are a number of procedures to assess certain limited aspects of an individual's environment, such as life stressors (Dohrenwend & Dohrenwend, 1974) and social supports, (Hirsch, 1979; McKinlay, 1973) these procedures do not provide the breadth and depth of focus that are needed to appreciate the complex nature of the microsettings in which people are embedded. Cowen (1977) has suggested that one recently developed set of Social Climate Scales may hold some promise in this regard.

The Social Climate Scales are a group of measurement procedures, that focuses on family, work, and social group settings, as well as on educational, psychiatric, and correctional milieus (Moos, 1974a). They measure people's perceptions of three underlying domains that characterize these settings: the way in which people relate to each other (*relationship* domain), the personal growth goals toward which the setting is oriented (*personal growth or goal orientation* domain), and the setting's basic structure and degree of openness to change (*system maintenance and change* domain). In general, these domains are comparable to Bronfenbrenner's (1979) concepts of interpersonal relationships, goal-directed molar activities, and system-defined roles and role expectations.

The Social Climate Scales have been used primarily in a research context to compare and contrast settings, to develop empirical typologies and evaluate the differential impacts of settings, to test theoretical propositions about the interrelationships between personal and environmental factors, and to help

drafts of the manuscript. Reprinted, with permission, from the *American Journal of Orthopsychiatry,* copyright 1982 by the American Orthopsychiatric Association, Inc.

construct integrated models by which to conceptualize factors related to the outcome of psychiatric treatment (Moos, 1974b, 1979a; Moos et al., 1979). An effort has been made to develop practical uses of these scales for facilitating consultation and change (Moos, 1979b), but this effort has focused primarily on social systems rather than individuals [but see Eichel (1978) and Waters (1979)]. We attempt here to extend the potential utility of these scales by exploring their use in developing a clinical case description and formulating intervention strategies.

APPLICATION TO A CLINICAL CASE

In this chapter we combine Bronfenbrenner's (1979) concepts and the Social Climate Scales to illustrate how information about the four environmental systems he describes can help to develop a social-ecological perspective of the personal and social problems faced by an adolescent girl and her family. We show how such a perspective can provide clinicians with a useful conceptual framework and sensitize them to environmental factors that tend to remain unrecognized even though they often may have an important influence. Four interrelated issues are addressed: (1) How can information about the social settings in which a client participates (the microsystem) help to formulate a clinical case description, identify problem areas, and suggest intervention strategies? (2) How can data on client perceptions of ideal settings facilitate this process? (3) How can the dynamic interrelationships between the settings in which people participate, such as school and family or family and work (the mesosystem), affect their morale and well-being? (4) How can a setting in which an individual does not participate directly (the exosystem) influence the development of a problem that appears to be primarily intrapersonal?

The Presenting Problem

Beth was a 15-year-old only child whose parents were in their late 40s. Mr. B. had a managerial job in an aerospace firm and Mrs. B. was a medical social worker in a large hospital setting.* Beth entered individual counseling on her parents' insistence after her academic performance had deteriorated markedly and she had dropped out of school and subsequently became moody and depressed. She stated that she disliked the other students and her teachers, and was unable to concentrate on her lessons, was afraid of being ridiculed in class, and consequently felt lonely and isolated. The therapist found it difficult to develop a relationship and to talk with Beth. Furthermore, Beth provided ambiguous information about her school experiences and about the extent to which her problems were academic or social. What precisely had caused her to drop out? What changes did she want at school? The therapist wanted to know more about

---

*These names and details have been altered to protect the anonymity of the family.

her life outside the classroom. How did she spend her time? What type of family environment did she live in? Were her parents contributing to the problem?

GATHERING THE SOCIAL-ECOLOGICAL DATA

In two 2-hour sessions with the family at their home, we employed semistructured interviews and four structured questionnaires to obtain answers to these questions. Three of the questionnaires (the Classroom, Family, and Work Environment Scales) were selected from the Social Climate Scales (1974a), whereas the fourth (the Health and Daily Living Questionnaire) obtained information about the physical, social, and occupational functioning of each member of the family. Details about the psychometric characteristics, the normative samples, and the research applications of these scales are available elsewhere (Moos, 1979a, 1979b; Moos et al., 1979).

Because Beth's presenting problems seemed to center around her experiences at school, we obtained her perceptions of the learning environment of her classrooms with the Real Form (Form R) of the Classroom Environment Scale (CES; Moos & Trickett, 1974). The CES is a 90-item true-false questionnaire consisting of nine subscales that measure three domains of social-environmental dimensions: relationship dimensions (involvement, affiliation, teacher support), personal growth or goal orientation dimensions (task orientation, competition), and system maintenance and change dimensions (organization, clarity, teacher control, innovation). Beth was also asked to complete the Ideal Form (Form I) of the CES to provide an understanding of the type of classroom environment she preferred.

A comparable procedure was used to assess the family social climate. Beth and her parents each independently expressed their opinions about the actual and ideal family environment on the Real (Form R) and the Ideal (Form I) Forms of the Family Environment Scale (FES) (Moos & Moos, 1983). The FES is a 90-item true-false questionnaire consisting of 10 subscales that measure relationship dimensions (cohesion, expressiveness, conflict), personal growth or goal orientation dimensions (independence, achievement orientation, moral-religious emphasis, and intellectual-cultural and active-recreational orientation), and system maintenance and change dimensions (organization, control).

Because the information we obtained on the family environment left some questions unanswered, we decided to inquire about Mr. and Mrs. B's work settings. Accordingly, we asked each of them to complete the Real Form (Form R) of the Work Environment Scale (WES) (Moos, 1981). The WES consists of 10 subscales that measure relationship (involvement, peer cohesion, supervisor support), personal growth or goal orientation (autonomy, task orientation, work pressure), and system maintenance and change dimensions (clarity, control, innovation, physical comfort).

The semistructured interview procedure explored the manner in which Beth actually spent her time—how she "used" her environment. We asked about her participation in more than 50 representative activities, including social and recreational pursuits as well as solitary pursuits such as reading and watching television (see Chapin, 1974). Beth indicated how much time she spent in each activity during a typical week, whether she spent it alone or with someone else, and the extent to which she enjoyed it. To allow for weekly variations, she was asked about her usual activities that were not carried out in the week chosen. We also used the Health and Daily Living Questionnaire (HDL) to obtain information about other relevant personal and environmental factors, such as the family's social activities, stressful life events, social support system, and areas of disagreement.

Social Climate Scale Results

Beth's Classrooms

What caused Beth to drop out of school? To focus on this question, we compared Beth's description of her favorite class, history, to her concept of an ideal class. Figure 6.1 shows Beth's perception in comparison to a national normative sample of 382 classrooms (Moos & Trickett, 1974). The profiles are plotted in standard scores with a mean of 50 (the mean of the normative sample) and a standard deviation of 10. Although Beth named history as her favorite subject, she felt that students disliked the class and tended to ignore the teacher (lack of involvement), that they were unfriendly to each other and especially to her (low affiliation), and that class activities were confused and disorganized (low order and organization). She reported that students had almost no say about how class time was spent and that there was little emphasis on innovative teaching methods or unusual class projects (low innovation). The discrepancies between Beth's perceptions of this class and her concepts of an ideal history class (see Figure 6.1) illustrate the extent of her dissatisfaction.

The results suggested that the primary problem for Beth was her lack of

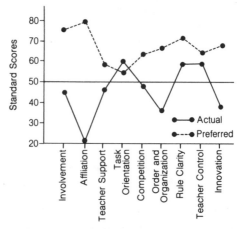

Figure 6.1.   Beth B's perceptions of her actual and preferred classroom environments (compared with a normative sample of 382 classrooms).

interaction with her peers (low affiliation) rather than an inability to relate to the teacher (her perceptions of teacher support and teacher control were quite close to her ideal) or a lack of academic orientation in the class (she felt that the emphasis on task orientation was about right). We also found this pattern of results (especially perceptions of little or no affiliation) in Beth's other classes. In conjunction with the fact that Beth previously had shown above-average academic performance, this informataion indicated that her problems lay more in the interpersonal and social than in the academic arena.

A basic deficit in Beth's interpersonal and social life was highlighted by the finding that she spent a considerable amount of time alone. We learned that Beth generally ate dinner by herself because her parents both worked overtime regularly and came home late. She rarely engaged in social telephone calls, had no close friends, and did both her homework and her part of the housework alone. Beth spent a considerable amount of time in solitary activities (such as reading, photography, and playing the piano) and passive pursuits (such as watching TV, listening to the radio, and listening to music). She did not engage in such activities as playing games, attending parties, going to plays or museums, going on trips, or even walking, hiking, or bicycling. Why did Beth spend so much time alone? We thought that information on the social milieu of her family would help to provide an answer.

The Social Environment of the Family

Beth and her parents independently evaluated the family social climate on the 10 dimensions of the Family Environment Scale (FES). Figure 6.2 plots their perceptions in comparison with a normative sample of 1125 families (Moos, 1981). Beth gave a moderately but consistently more negative assessment. She described her family as very low on cohesion, answering only one of nine questions on the cohesion subscale in a positive direction. Beth felt that there was

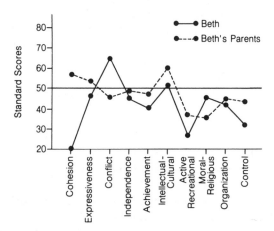

Figure 6.2.   Actual family environment as perceived by Beth B, and her parents (compared with a normative sample of 1125 families).

no feeling of togetherness or belonging, that she did not get along well with her parents, and that she was often just killing time at home. In contrast, Beth's parents perceived a moderate amount of cohesion. Furthermore, although Beth's parents felt that there were few disagreements or open expressions of anger and aggression, Beth thought that family members fought a lot, lost their tempers, and often criticized each other (conflict).

Beth gave the family a very low score on recreational orientation. She reported that most weekends and evenings were spent at home watching TV or listening to the radio, that nobody was active in sports, that friends did not visit often, and that famiy members rarely attended movies or plays. Beth's parents generally agreed with her appraisal, although their rating was somewhat higher. In addition, on the HDL they reported an almost total lack of participation in joint social and recreational activities during the past month. These results suggested that Beth's lack of involvement in social activities with her peers might reflect the fact that she had not learned appropriate social and interpersonal skills from her parents.

Beth also felt that the degree of control in the family was quite low. For example, she stated: "We can do whatever we want to in our family" (true), "There are very few rules to follow in our family"(true), and "You can't get away with much in our family" (false). In conjunction with her perceptions of low family cohesion, this indicates that Beth felt that her parents neither supported nor controlled her adequately. With respect to the other areas, Beth and her parents tended to agree on the amount of family concern with intellectual pursuits (slightly above average), independence (above average), and achievement and religious issues (slightly below average).

In order to identify the extent to which Beth and her parents agreed about the type of family setting they wanted, we asked them to complete the Ideal Form (Form I) of the FES. Figure 6.3 shows that their perceptions of an ideal family milieu were congruent in most areas. For example, Beth and her parents wanted a close-knit expressive family unit with relatively little conflict and considerable emphasis on independence and intellectual and recreational pursuits. However, Beth's parents wanted to emphasize achievement much more strongly than Beth did. A comparison of Beth's perceptions of her actual (Figure 6.2) and preferred (Figure 6.3) family milieu helps to clarify the extent and focus of her dissatisfaction. She wanted to see substantial increases in cohesion, expressiveness, independence, and both cultural and recreational orientation.

Mr. and Mrs. B's Work Settings

The FES results left us with some questions. Beth and her parents both wanted a more cohesive, recreationally oriented family milieu. Why were they not able to create such a setting? Because Beth's parents were employed in demanding professional jobs, we wondered whether factors in their work milieu might be implicated. We therefore asked Mr. and Mrs. B. to use the Work Environment Scale (WES) to describe their work settings. Mr. B was a manager in an aerospace firm. He was responsible for most of the financial transactions, and

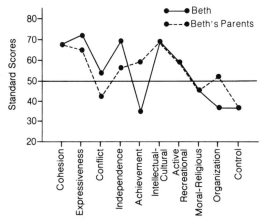

Figure 6.3. Preferred family environment as perceived by Beth B. and her parents.

supervised data collection, personnel, accounting, customer relations, and plant security. There were about 450 people in the firm, of which Mr. B. supervised 6 directly and 150 indirectly. Mr. B. felt that he had considerable influence on the course of activity at work. He believed that his input was essential and that his work would not get done if he did not show up; in fact, he had not taken a day of sick leave in three years.

Mrs. B. was employed as a medical social worker in a large hospital setting, together with several other women in similar positions. On a typical day, she interacted with between 20 and 40 patients. Her job entailed helping new patients, answering their questions, giving them advice, and making referrals to appropriate agencies when necessary. Mrs. B. worked quite independently and almost always made important decisions on her own. She cared about her patients and felt considerable responsibility for their welfare. She almost never missed work, because she felt that no one else would take care of her patients adequately while she was gone.

Figure 6.4, which compares Mr. and Mrs. B.'s perceptions of their work environments with a normative sample of 1442 employees from a wide range of work settings (Moos, 1981) shows that Mr. B. rated his work milieu as high in co-workers' friendliness, in the extent to which management was supportive of employees, and in the opportunity for variety and change. He also felt that task orientation was above average and that there was considerable time urgency and pressure to work hard and meet deadlines (work pressure). Mr. B. rated the physical features of the work setting very positively, perceiving them as cheerful, clean, airy, and comfortable. Mr. B. liked and was very committed to his job, primarily because of his positive relationships with his co-workers and the excitement of daily challenges and problems.

Mrs. B. rated her job setting very positively in all areas but innovation (see Figure 6.4). She perceived a considerable degree of friendliness and support from her fellow employees and her supervisor and a strong emphasis on completing

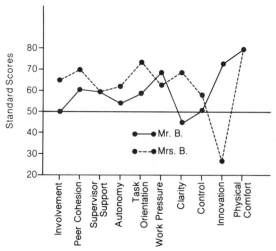

Figure 6.4.   Mr. and Mrs. B's perceptions of their work settings (compared with a normative sample of 1442 employees).

tasks efficiently. She felt that she and her colleagues were enthusiastic and committed to their jobs and were encouraged to make their own decisions. The clarity of rules and policies was seen as high, as was the amount of help provided by her supervisor. However, Mrs. B. also perceived a considerable amount of time urgency and work pressure and noted that very few changes or new approaches to the job were permitted. Overall, Mrs. B. greatly enjoyed her work, the daily interaction with people, and the personal gratification of being able to help some patients successfully.

A Social-Ecological Interpretation

A relatively clear picture of Beth's situation emerges from the foregoing information. Mr. and Mrs. B. were highly committed to and satisfied with their jobs and described their relationship to each other quite favorably. They both worked hard, enjoyed considerable responsibility, and were interested in pursuing their professional careers and obtaining higher-level managerial positions. In contrast, Beth was very critical of both home and school. Although the family status quo was satisfactory for Mr. and Mrs. B. in view of their demanding and rewarding work environments, it did not meet Beth's needs for parental warmth and support, expression of feelings, or the sense of belonging that emerges from shared participation in family activities. Considering that Beth enjoyed reading for pleasure and liked to engage in intellectual and cultural pursuits, and recalling that the major differences between her real and ideal class descriptions involved affiliation, we concluded that her school problems derived primarily from interpersonal and social rather than academic factors.

Beth's "school problems" seemed to have their roots in her relationship to her parents. Beth's parents worked long and demanding hours, were physically and emotionally drained at the end of each day, and did not take sufficient time to understand or fulfill her emotional needs adequately. Furthermore, Beth's parents were dedicated to achievement in their own careers and strongly pressured their daughter to do well academically and to make plans for college and a career. Although Beth also desired these goals, she harbored deep anger toward her parents for valuing their professional activities more than her emotional needs. The mixture of resentment and rejection aroused by this situation had a detrimental influence on Beth's motivation and performance in school. Beth felt that her parents had rejected her in favor of their careers; she retaliated by rejecting school as a means of hurting her parents and gaining their attention. These problems were exacerbated by the fact that Beth's parents had never shown her how to relate comfortably and warmly with others, nor how to plan and enjoy casual social activities with her peers.

Most important, neither Beth nor her therapist, who tended to view the problem in person-centered terms, had been able to "diagnose" the situation. Beth had not conceptualized her problem as rooted in her family relationships, primarily because she felt guilty about placing her needs above those of her parents. Beth's parents did not realize that her problems were due in part to their abiding commitment to their respective careers. The therapist had focused attention on Beth's feelings about school and academic performance and neglected to explore contributing environmental factors. The new information we developed led the therapist to discover that a series of recent events had upset a previously workable equilibrium which Beth's parents had established between the pressures of family and work activities.

Due to her career aspirations, Beth's mother had delayed having a child until she felt compelled to make a decision because of her advancing age. Mr. B. had wanted a child and provided considerable emotional support, but little practical help in housework or child care. After Beth's preschool years, Mr. B. supported his wife's wish to resume her career and they agreed on a plan whereby each of them would temporarily curtail their work activities to spend time with Beth. This plan had worked reasonably well for several years, but was upset by a series of events originating in exosystem and macrosystem factors. Due to financial problems in his firm and pressures from contract negotiation deadlines, Mr. B. became totally immersed in his work. Similarly, hospital budget cuts and resulting layoffs increased work pressure on Mrs. B. At the same time, school system funding problems resulted in the elimination of the school music and drama program, which was Beth's most valued extracurricular activity. In this way, uncontrollable exo- and macrosystem forces combined to upset a family's previously successful homeostasis between school, home, and occupational factors.

Although Beth and her parents had moderately serious problems, it was clear that they did care about each other and were amenable to making necessary changes. Our formulation of the situation pointed to the need for family therapy due to the family-related nature of the problem. Furthermore, we thought that family therapy probably would be effective because joint meetings could help to mitigate Beth's feelings of rejection and enhance family cohesion and expressiveness, because Beth and her parents basically agreed about the features of their ideal family milieu. In addition, because Beth's parents were unaware of the depth of her feelings, it seemed that feedback of the FES results jointly to all three family members would serve to define the problem more clearly and initiate discussions about potential changes. The desire of all three family members to engage in intellectual and recreational pursuits could then be used to encourage their joint participation in some highly valued activities and provide an important step toward increasing family cohesion and togetherness. The therapist initiated joint family sessions and was able to use these ideas to effect positive changes in the family environment and subsequently in Beth's mood and academic performance. Detailed examples of how feedback of FES results to family members can be used in ongoing family therapy are given elsewhere (Fuhr, Moos, & Dishotsky, 1981).

CLINICAL APPLICATIONS OF SOCIAL-ECOLOGICAL CONCEPTS

The clinical utility of the environmental assessment techniques presented here merits further consideration. These techniques can help to gather useful data about social settings and to provide a broader understanding about the current environmental factors that influence clients. The semistructured, easily understandable format makes it possible to collect a great deal of information very quickly. Also, although it may be preferable in some instances, the clinician need not be present for all phases of the assessment; a paraprofessional can be trained to obtain the information and to answer typical questions.

The procedures provide a conceptual framework of three underlying domains of social-environmental variables that can be used to clarify the important dimensions of social settings and to help train clinical and community psychologists, as well as other professionals. For instance, the FES can sensitize nurses to the salient features of their patients' family contexts (Eichel, 1978) and serve as an instructional aid in sociology courses by providing students with concepts by which to understand family environments (Waters, 1979).

Environmental assessment procedures encourage the development of an explicit, practical focus in relation to the client's present environment. Because the emphasis is on the identification and description of currently relevant situational factors, the potential of interventions aimed at changing existing conditions is highlighted. By gaining an awareness of some of the powerful but possibly controllable influences of the physical and social environment, clients learn that they are not necessarily the victims of fixed neurotic traits. Such procedures also provide a means by which clients and clinicians can enhance their understanding of the exosystem factors that affect family functioning. For instance, parents can learn about their children's school and classroom settings and children can begin to develop a perspective on the work pressures that confront their parents. In fact, one of the most intriguing findings about Beth was that her parents' pressured work settings indirectly influenced her morale by affecting the family milieu. This is consistent with other evidence that conditions at work can affect family functioning and an individual's total life situation (Handy, 1979; Kohn, 1977; Wetzel, 1978).

Furthermore, these procedures can be used to organize the discussion of issues of treatment. By using dimensions of the Social Climate Scales as an outline, counselors can understand the client's difficulties in terms of manageable units. They can teach the client to discuss problems in an organized manner. With problems broken down into small, clearly defined units, the client is less likely to feel overwhelmed and to ramble from topic to topic. In working with Beth and her parents, for instance, the FES results pointed to the value of focusing on the concrete goal of increasing specific types of joint family activities.

Through information about their preferred settings, clients can take an active part in shaping the nature of their goals. For example, use of the Ideal Form of the FES, in conjunction with the Real Form, can help to pinpoint both the degree of congruence in family members' perceptions of the current environment and differences in the goals of individual family members. The process of paying equal attention to each member's perceptions and opinions discourages "scapegoating" and helps participants realize that they are discussing individual values rather than "the way things ought to be."

Most important, information derived from environmental assessment procedures can sensitize clinicians to the relevant factors and interrelationships in the micro-, meso-, and exosystems in which their clients function. This can lead to an exploration of macrosystem influences and to the subtle ways in which such influences can disrupt a workable equilibrium among the other environmental systems. Knowledge about the social-ecological system can be applied to individual casework and can clarify the extent to which a client's problems stem from personal or environmental factors or their dynamic interconnections. Such knowledge should help clinicians avoid the attributional error of underestimating the relative importance of environmental as compared with dispositional determinants of behavior.

REFERENCES

Barker, R. & Associates (1978) *Habitats, environments, and human behavior.* San Francisco, Calif.: Jossey-Bass.

Bronfenbrenner, U. (1979) *The ecology of human development: Experiments by nature and design.* Cambridge, Mass.: Harvard University Press.

Caplan, N., & Nelson, S. (1973) On being useful: The nature and consequences of psychological research on social problems. *American Psychologist,* **28,** 199–211.

Chapin, F. (1974) *Human activity patterns in the city.* New York: Wiley.

Cowen, E. (1977) Baby steps toward primary prevention. *American Journal of Community Psychology,* **5,** 1–22.

Dohrenwend, B.S., & Dohrenwend, B.P. (1974) *Stressful life events: Their nature and effects.* New York: Wiley.

Eichel, E. (1978) Assessment with a family focus. *Journal of Psychiatric Nursing and Mental Health Services,* **16,** 11–15.

Endler, N., & Magnusson, D. (1976) *Interactional psychology and personality.* New York: Hemisphere Press.

Fuhr, R., Moos, R., & Dishotsky, N. (1981) The use of family assessment and feedback in ongoing family therapy. *American Journal of Family Therapy,* **9,** 24–36.

Handy, C. (1979) The family: Help or hindrance. In C. Cooper & R. Payne (Eds.), *Stress at work,* New York: Wiley.

Hirsch, B. (1979) Psychological dimensions of social networks: A multi-method analysis. *American Journal of Community Psychology,* **7,** 263–277.

Holahan, J. (1978) *Environment and behavior: A synthesis.* Plenum, New York.

Kohn, M. (Ed.) (1977) *Class and conformity: A study of values (2d ed.).* Chicago: University of Chicago Press.

McKinlay, J. (1973) Social networks, lay consultation, and helpseeking behavior. *Social Forces,* **51,** 275–292.

Mischel, W. (1979) On the interface of cognition and personality: Beyond the person-situation debate. *American Psychologist,* **34,** 740–754.

Moos, R. (1974a) *The social climate scales: An overview.* Palo Alto, Calif.: Consulting Psychologists Press.

Moos, R. (1974b). *Evaluating treatment environments: A social-ecological approach.* New York: Wiley.

Moos, R. (1976) *The human context: Environmental determinants of behavior.* New York: Wiley.

Moos, R. (1979a) *Evaluating educational environments: Methods, procedures, findings and policy implications.* San Francisco, Calif.: Jossey-Bass.

Moos, R. (1979b) Improving social settings by social climate measurement and feedback. In R. Munoz, L. Snowden, & J. Kelly (Eds.), *Social and psychological research in community settings.* San Francisco, Calif.: Jossey-Bass.

Moos, R. (1981) *Work environment scale manual.* Palo Alto, Calif.: Consulting Psychologists Press.

Moos, R., Clayton, J., & Max, W. (1979) *The social climate scales: An annotated bibliography (2d ed.).* Palo Alto, Calif.: Consulting Psychologists Press.

Moos, R., & Moos, B. (1981) *Family environment scale manual.* Palo Alto, Calif.: Consulting Psychologists Press.

Moos, R., & Trickett, E. (1974) *Classroom environment scale manual.* Palo Alto, Calif.: Consulting Psychologists Press.

Waters, G. (1979) The family environment scale as an instructional aid for studying the family. *Teaching in Psychology,* **6,** 162–164.

Wetzel, J. (1978) Depression and dependence upon unsustaining environments. *Clinical Social Work Journal,* **6,** 75–89.

CHAPTER 7

Ecological Approaches to Working with Families of Disturbing Children

SUSAN SWAP

Parents and teachers identify a significant number of young children as having behavior problems. These behavior problems are disturbing to us: They stretch our tolerance, remind us of the frustrating limits of our abilities to control or change others, and often challenge our feelings of competence and self-esteem. Frequently the parents of these children are seen as the source of the problem and are themselves targets for intervention.

The ecological perspective provides a fresh look at the participation of parents in disturbing interactions and offers productive options for understanding and altering them. This chapter identifies the assumptions of the ecological model concerning "disturbing" children and their families and reviews several ecological assessment devices and procedures for evaluating disturbance. After summarizing four major types of programs and services that are currently designed for parents, an ecological model for working with parents is suggested.

ASSUMPTIONS OF THE ECOLOGICAL MODEL ABOUT THE "DISTURBING" CHILD

Assumption 1:   The Child is Not Disturbed

The central assumption of the ecological model is that deviant behavior is the result of complex interactions between the child and the ecosystem in which the disturbance is occurring. The disturbance is not located exclusively in the child: The child is not defined as ill or emotionally disturbed (Rhodes, 1970; Hobbs, 1975; Swap, Prieto, & Harth, 1982). Consider these examples. Children in institutions who engage in high frequencies of head bumping and masturbation may be responding to the lack of adult contact, educational materials, programs of actitivies, and a visually-stimulating environment. Active 5-year old boys with limited attention spans and poor visual-motor coordination may respond with physical aggression in a kindergarten that requires long periods of sitting quietly to complete ditto sheets filled with faded numbers or letters. A brain-damaged infant may be significantly delayed in acquiring language if the caretaker is unable to respond systematically and supportively to the child's limited efforts at speech. In each of these simplified examples, the disturbing behavior of the child needs to be understood as the product of interactions between the child's characteristics, the characteristics of the environment, and the interactions among them.

Proponents of the ecological model agree that in order for a behavior to be considered disturbing, a concerned adult must identify it as such, and that the standards which define what is disturbing are culturally relative. Hallucinations, stingy behavior, or authoritarian child-rearing practices may be highly valued in some cultures and deplored in others (see, for example, Rhodes and Paul, 1978). The range of behaviors that is acceptable may also vary considerably. Rubin and Balow (1978) report, for example, that in a very large sample of schools in Minnesota, over 50% of the boys were considered to have behavior problems by one or more teachers over the 6-year period of the study. This study suggests that the definition of normal behavior is quite narrow, at least within elementary school classrooms in Minnesota.

In summary, the ecological model suggests that we reexamine the common assumption that the child is "the one" who is emotionally disturbed. This reexamination is justified on several counts: decisions about what kind of behavior is disturbing is culturally relative and context specific; disturbing behavior does not occur in isolation but in interaction with others; negative reciprocal interaction patterns can create, maintain, and increase the frequency of disturbing interactions, whereas positive reciprocal interactions can lessen or eliminate disturbance.

It is important to state clearly though, that adherents of the ecological model do not assume that the child is a blank slate. Children are different; some children have characteristics that many people find irritating or unusual. Whether these characteristics develop into frequent episodes of disturbing behavior depends on the interaction of the child with others. Sometimes the child's characteristics are so unusual as to provide a "main effect"; that is, most parents or caretakers would have difficulty creating an environment for the child that would prevent the emergence of disturbance. Nonetheless, the ecological model suggests environmental adaptation may lessen disturbance even in this extreme case. The model is most powerful, however, in helping us to question our assumptions about children whose behavior is not initially so extreme or unusual; in encouraging us to question whether we are creating "disturbed children" by establishing behavior standards that are too rigidly narrow; or creating cultural blueprints for school or home environments that systematically lead to deviant behavior in many children. The optimistic implication is that learning more about ecosystems and how they affect children and families could have tremendous potential for preventing and ameliorating disturbance.

Assumption 2:   Interactions Within an Ecosystem Are Systematic

A second assumption of the ecological model is that the interactions among the variables are systematic. As Salzinger, Antrobus, and Glick (1980) explain:

Not only do the environmental factors influence the child, but the child, in response, influences his or her environment, and the changed environment thereupon exerts a different effect on the child. The child and environment thus constitute a system, an ecosystem of which feedback is a central characteristic. (p. 3)

Bromwich (1980) provides a clear example of systematic interaction cycles in a family with a young child whose social, cognitive, and language behavior deteriorate rapidly between the ages of 10 and 24 months. The professional staff that worked with the family felt that the child's regression was at least partly organic and not "caused" by his environment. Bromwich (1980) observed, however,

So many things seemed to deteriorate at the same time that it was impossible to determine which came first—the infant's change in behavior or the mother's emotional upheaval aggravated by the infant's regression. It is probable that the infant's deteriorating behavior was stressful to the mother, who, in turn, became increasingly disturbed and therefore less able to meet the child's mounting needs. (p. 15)

Assumption 3:   Interventions Must Alter the Ecological System

Because disturbing behavior occurs and is maintained in a particular context, interventions must not ignore that context. Hobbs (1975) insists that "the objective is not merely to change or improve the child but to make the total system work" (p. 114).

Removing the child from the context in which disturbance occurs, treating the child, and then returning the child to an unchanged environment are considered to be both ineffective and unethical. Treatment gains are rarely maintained, and only the child bears the stigma and responsiblity for failure (Hobbs, 1975; Fahl & Morrissey, 1979; Cautley, 1980).

Assumption 4:   Ecological Interventions Are Eclectic

In trying to alter disturbing interactions within an ecosystem, ecologists borrow from many disciplines. For example, a goal may be to improve the skills or knowledge of any member of the system. Behavioral strategies, a course in child development, private tutoring, or art classes offered in a museum might be recommended. Legal, psychiatric, or medical services; respite care; referral to a quality day-care program; or altering the physical environment of an apartment or classroom might be appropriate to a given situation. A child may even be temporarily removed from a discordant situation (e.g., Hobbs, 1966). But in this case, simultaneous interventions would also be directed at parents, teachers, and/or other significant members of the child's community. Goals of these efforts might be to add to parents' or teachers' skills or help them to change their priorities or expectations, revise their perceptions, or acquire new resources.

Assumption 5:   Interventions in a complex ecosystem may have unanticipated consequences

Because of the complex interactions in a given ecosystem, interventions designed to change specific variables may have unanticipated consequences. For example, family counseling may lead a couple to seek a divorce; a home intervention program that emphasizes particular childrearing values and practices may cause a rift in a close extended family where alternative values and practices are common; taking Ritalin for hyperactivity may lead a child to feel that his "good" behaviors are a result of the medication rather than his effort or skill and that "bad" behaviors are a result of failure to take medication (Whalen & Henker, 1980).

Although it is impossible to foresee all the unanticipated consequences of an intervention, Willems (1977) makes a compelling argument that ecologists must carefully research these interdependencies to ascertain what kinds of unintended effects occur most frequently and why. He comments:

Altogether new, system-wide domains of data seem indicated because: 1) successful modifications may produce unintended effects in the repertoire of the target person, 2) failures or marginal successes may be governed by variables that have not even been contemplated as yet, 3) with varying degrees of success on the target person, there may be unintended effects in the larger social or environmental network, 4) success may be temporary for reasons that are little understood, and 5) success may be situation-specific for reasons that lie beyond simple contingency principles. (p. 25)

The number and complexity of direct and unintended effects are multiplied exponentially when one considers the results of interventions on a community or national level, such as the passage of P.L. 94-142, which guarantees free, appropriate education to all handicapped children.

Assumption 6:   Each Ecosystem Is Unique

No two children, families, classrooms, or ecosystems are exactly alike. The networks that define each system also vary over time. Ecologists need to develop a much more complete body of research that will help to sort out important variables, feedback cycles, and changes over long periods of time. This research may lead to common processes that ecologists may follow in studying and intervening in natural settings, despite the fact that the variables themselves and their interactions will differ.

ASSUMPTIONS ABOUT FAMILIES OF DISTURBING CHILDREN

Assumption 1:   The Family Is Not to Blame

Beginning perhaps with Kanner's (1943) hypothesis that autism was caused by "refrigerator parents," it has been commonplace for clinicians to blame the family, particularly the mother, for disturbance in a child. This orientation was supported by observation and work with many families with a disturbed child, where signs of stress, poor communication, and dysfunctional interactions were evident (e.g., Bermann, 1973; Laing & Esterson, 1964). The presumption was that the child's dysfunction was a result of the parents' mismanagement, abuse, or lack of love for the child.

Recent research, however, suggests that the development of a healthy or problematic relationship between mother and child is the result of sequences of mutual reciprocal influence. In studying mother–infant attachment, for example, Bell (1974), Sameroff and Chandler (1975), and Clarke-Stewart (1977) document these conclusions and emphasize the importance of the infants' individual differences in shaping the mothers' caretaking patterns.

Thomas, Chess, and Birch (1968) and Thomas and Chess (1977) in their longitudinal study of the effects of temperament on development, focused specifically on the evolution of behavior disorders in children. They concluded that parents were neither good nor bad, but functioning in an optimal or suboptimal manner with a given child at a given time. They also discovered that in many families where a disturbing interaction pattern had developed, providing information to the parents about their observations and hypotheses and recommending specific alternative management practices helped the parents interrupt these destructive cycles.

The focus on the family as the cause of the child's problems continues to be a dominant approach in clinical practice. Many programs, for example, insist that parents (or at least the mother) receive counseling as a condition for accepting the child. Family therapy may include the child's extended family in the assessment and treatment of the "patient's" disorders. For many parents, involvement in counseling or therapy has been helpful both to them and to their children. But other parents have bitterly resented the implication that they are "at fault" for their child's problems. They have actively sought alternative explanations and immediate, practical solutions to the problems in daily living which the children create. This excerpt from *Parents Speak Out* (1978) represents the feelings of impotence and rage experienced by some parents required to participate in psychoanalytically based treatment:

So much has been written about the abuse of parents of autistic children by traditional psychiatrists that even one more word seems superfluous, yet the abuse continues and thus so must the protests. We worked with two doctors at that school (sequentially—we weren't *that* bad!). Neither ever came right out and said "You caused it," but everything they did say was based on that premise. Our involvement with a parent organization was viewed as a way of avoiding our emotional duty to our child; never mind that he was improving dramatically, in no small part because of what we had learned through that involvement. Our failure to need their kind of help was "blocking"; our by-now angry fighting back, "resistance." The real mind-blower for Doctor Number One was my refusal to admit I hated and resented Eddie because I had to turn down a graduate fellowship when full-time study would have kept me away from him too much. Doctor Number Two picked up the theme and kept "working with me" ("on me" is more like it) to admit my anger. Finally I blew: "You bet I'm angry, Dr. B., and I know what I'm angry at—you!" (Akerley, 1978, p. 42)

In addition to support for the ecological position emerging from the interaction research, several further developments have added strength to the ecological view that disturbance is not the parents' "fault," but a product of the reciprocal interaction between the child and others in a particular environment. One development has been the inability of researchers to find support for the hypothesis that parents' behaviors have caused disturbance in children with certain behavioral disorders. For example, in his review of over 100 studies conducted after 1965, Schopler (1978) found no evidence for a relationship between parental practices and the onset of early infantile autism. He concluded that the research prior to 1965 was time bound and did not control for experimenter bias. Paternite and Loney (1980) sought to identify relationships between childhood hyperkinesis and home environment. They evaluated 57 environmental variables, including multiple measures of SES, family stability and relationships, parental social competence, parental discipline practices and styles, and structure and routine provided in the home. The authors found it particularly noteworthy that there were *no* environmental predictors for the core indicators of hyperkinesis. They did find, however, that poor parent-child relationships and urban residence were associated with high levels of aggression in children. Their deceptively simple conclusion: "that relationships between symptomatology and the environment differ for different types of symptoms" (p. 125) should suggest caution in blaming parents for children's mental illness.

A second development supporting an interactionist approach to childhood disturbance is the growth of child advocacy groups which are organized by parents for certain handicapping conditions (e.g., the National Society for Autistic Citizens; the National Association for Retarded Citizens and their local branches). These groups have been extraordinarily effective in supporting action by the courts and the legislature that have extended services to their children. "Unanticipated effects" of these efforts seem to include feelings of increased self-esteem and internal control among parents who have participated; the creation of new types of services for children and their families; and educational campaigns to inform professionals of parents' rights, needs, and expertise in relation to their children. Parents in these groups generally see themselves as partners with professionals in helping their children (see, e.g., Gorham, 1975). The idea that they are to blame for their children's disorders is not acceptable.

On the other hand, there are currently no national organizations for parents of children whose psychological diagnoses are more ambiguous and less severe, such as for parents of children who are hyperactive, school phobic, acting out, or withdrawn. Professional and conventional wisdom continues to support the notion that parents of these children are "doing something wrong." This "wisdom" often adds to the stress of having a difficult child, exaggerates parents' feelings of incompetence, and prevents their reaching out to other parents and professionals for help.

A third factor which has lent support to an interactionist perspective is the increased recognition that professionals who diagnose and treat disturbing children and their families are strongly influenced by the values and expectations of their own subculture. As we begin to recognize that subcultural expectations and values differ and have integrity within their own context, we may be less likely to define differences as deviant, and parents who cultivate those differences as blameworthy. As Salzinger, Antrobus, and Glick explain:

Take, for example, what sometimes appears to be hallucinatory behavior in Haitian children attending a child psychiatry clinic in New York City. Not only might the hallucinatory behavior prove to be non-psychotic, but actually functional, learned in the context of a cultural tradition that continues to foster the practice of a folk mysticism in place of modern urban medicine. The extent to which some of the behaviors in any subculture resemble symptomatic behaviors in the majority culture is a researchable question and one that has clear implications for diagnosis. (1980, p. 4)

After describing three factors that support a view that "parents are not to blame," it is also important to note a development which tends to reinforce the "pathological parent" orientation. This development is the insight that parents of handicapped children experience stages of mourning as they recognize that the perfect child which they anticipated will never exist. These stages (as summarized in Seligman, 1979, and originally presented by Kübler-Ross, 1969) include denial, bargaining, anger, depression, and acceptance. Progression through these stages is fundamental to the acceptance of the loss and a normal and healthy process for coping with it.

The very useful contribution provided by these insights has sometimes been distorted as professionals apply them to working with parents. In extensive inservice and group work with parents of handicapped children and the professionals who serve them, I have seen three oversimplifications. Professionals assume that parents are "in a stage" when they respond with anger or apathy to a professional intervention. When parents are labeled as "angry" or "denying," the possible legitimacy of their concerns may be avoided. A second problem is that a too-rigid belief in stages may cause us not to recognize variability among and within parents as they try to cope with a handicapped child. For example, a couple may not experience the stages at the same time or even in sequence. Parents do not talk of "achieving" acceptance, but rather describe a series of often painful plateaus as they struggle to accept the reality of their child's handicap at each new developmental phase. A third problem is the tendency to overidentify a parent with a stage label, failing to recognize that there may be many benefits and joys in being the parent of a handicapped child, and that the parenting of that child is only one of many roles that the individual assumes.

The premise that "the family is not to blame" may seem as dogmatic and unrealistic as the contention that it is. The ecological perspective does not suggest that the family's contribution to disturbance should be ignored; on the contrary, it is a primary focus for research. But the ecological perspective *does* suggest that the parents do not "own" or cause the disturbance. The family's behavior is influenced by characteristics of the child and the many ecosystems of which they are a part. "Blaming" the parents ignores the reciprocal nature of disturbance. It also appears to be a counterproductive, even destructive strategy for supporting changes in parents' behaviors and attitudes. Other approaches to intervention are sorely needed.

Assumption 2:   Children, Family and Community Factors Interact to Produce Disturbance

In order to understand disturbance and intervene effectively in a family system, we need to unravel some of the complex variables that interact to produce disturbance. We will consider a small sample of the variables that may contribute to the triggering of disturbing interactions in a given system, including characteristics of the child, the family, and the larger community.

Characteristics of the Child

Some children are more difficult to parent effectively than others. The child's temperament, ability, motivation, health, and responsiveness to adult initiatives influence adults' responses. Thomas and Chess's (1977) longitudinal study cited earlier, has been helpful in elucidating one cluster of temperamental characteristics labeled the "difficult child syndrome" which was common to 10% of their sample. Difficult children exhibited irregularity in biological functions, negative withdrawal responses to new stimuli, nonadaptability or slow adaptability to change, and intense mood expressions that frequently were negative. Although Thomas and Chess found that children with these characteristics were somewhat more likely to develop emotional problems than other children in the sample, they also found that disturbance definitely was not inevitable. In fact, they discovered that several of these difficult infants developed into highly energetic, productive, and well-adjusted children. One important contribution to this outcome appeared to be parents who could maintain their sense of competence despite the child's negative, intense reactions, who could be consistent and firm in setting limits, and continue to encourage their child to adapt to new situations. In short, parental flexibility and skill could prevent the development of behavioral disturbance, even in children who were very difficult to parent.

A child characteristic does not have to be commonly recognized as difficult or unpleasant to be troublesome to a parent. "Goodness of fit" or a match between child characteristics and parental expectations is another useful concept offered by Thomas and Chess (1977). An ambitious, highly energetic father may be continually disappointed in a son with a low activity level who is easily distracted. But a busy homemaker with two other children might find the same child a delight: His low activity level and willingness to be easily distracted when he is "getting into things" could make the difference between a reasonably calm day and chaos. Thomas and Chess found that

...*any* temperamental trait or pattern in any individual child could significantly enter into the development of a behavior disorder, if the environmental demands and expectations were sufficiently dissonant with the child's behavioral style (p. 37, italics mine).

Many other child variables have been implicated in the development of a disorder; for example, lack of responsiveness to the caretaker, including failure to mold to the mother's body and absence of eye contact; low birth weight; and a disfiguring or handicapping condition. These conditions generally require extensive adaptation from parents; and professionals encountering these children often experience the same feelings of rejection and incompetence that parents report in meeting the child's needs. Bromwich (1980) provides an example of her early intervention staff's interaction with an 18-month-old child, born two months premature and suspected of brain damage:

Although the infant was quite responsive to the staff most of the time, he took some time to warm up to them at almost every session. (Sessions were held regularly, every other week.) Moreover, there were times when he was passive and sometimes even rejecting of the staff's attempts to engage him in play. His socially difficult behaviors were discussed with the parents, and the staff's experience of feeling rejected by the infant was also shared with them. The team's acknowledgment of their occasionally unrewarding experiences with the infant was considered important because it had the effect of relieving the parents' feelings of inadequacy. They could see that *the infant* may have contributed to their own unsuccessful attempts to interact with him. (Bromwich, 1980, p. 89)

Family Characteristics

Each of us probably has an image of what the ideal family should be like. It is very difficult to determine how ideal a family must be to contribute to the development of a healthy child; to identify which characteristics, though desirable, are not essential and which characteristics seem to be consistently associated with families of children who are referred for psychological services. Two intensive investigations will be summarized here which have attempted to differentiate the characteristics of families with referred and psychologically healthy children.

Love and Kaswan's (1974) sample included 91 families of children aged 8 through 12 who were perceived by elementary school personnel as needing psychological treatment for serious social and emotional difficulties, and 29 families whose children were described by teachers as functioning adequately. The control children were chosen to match a randomly selected third of the troubled children. All the children were from Los Angeles and represented a wide range of socioeconomic backgrounds. Matching was successful on all characteristics except family composition, with 48% of the referred group coming from homes with a single parent or a stepparent versus only 24% of the nonreferred group. Data included observations of the families in an unstructured situation and during a communication task, verbal ratings by family members on Adjective Rating Scales and by parents on Parent Behavior Inventories, verbal reports from teachers, and observations of the child in school.

Lewis, Beavers, Gossett, and Phillips (1976) explored interactions among families which included an adolescent referred for psychological services. The sample consisted of 12 middle-and upper-middle class families. In identifying a control group, the authors were interested in locating families of healthy adolescents who were functioning either adequately or optimally. Consequently from an original group of 33 "normal" control families, they worked intensively with the six families who ranked highest on their Health-Pathology Scale (the "optimal" group) and six families who scored lowest (the "adequate" group). These three groups of families participated in five videotaped Family Interactional Tasks (e.g., Family Strengths, Family Closeness, Plan Something Together). In addition, the 12 nonreferred families agreed to 3 hours of clinical interviews, to tape-recorded individual interviews of each family member, and psychological tests.

The characteristics of the families with referred children were strikingly similar across the two studies. Both found that the referred families:

1.   did not like their neighbors; anticipated negative interactions from those outside the family; and showed limited initiative in seeking contacts outside the family.

2.   had low levels of respect for family members and low self-esteem;

3.   had communication styles which were confusing and inconsistent. Lewis et al. also mention communication which is distancing and obscuring; Love and Kaswan emphasize the tension, irritation, and ignoring that occur as well as highly evaluative messages.

4.   did not have a strong parent coalition or a stable, effective family structure;

5.   shared ineffective methods of trying to influence one another, including extensive efforts on the part of all family members to exert control over each other.

Lewis et al. (1976) found that "adequate" families shared many of the characteristics of the families with adolescent patients. But they also shared four characteristics that seemed to inoculate them against deterioration. These fascinating results are presented on the following page:

The adequate families resembled patently dysfunctional or midrange families in their oppositional attitudes, only modest respect for subjective world views, use of distancing communication mechanisms, less than firm parental coalitions, reliance upon simple explanations of human behavior, reduced spontaneity, and a tendency toward blandness in individual characteristics. The strengths of these adequate families which have militated against the development of individual symptomatology or family system dissolution included high initiative resulting in multiple family involvements with neighborhood and community, predictability of structure and function, high levels of self-esteem (often based upon favorable contrast of one's family to less fortunate others) and a firm belief in the value of the family. (Lewis, Beavers, Gossett, & Phillips, 1976, pp. 202–203)

It is not possible, of course, to determine what caused the families of referred children to develop dysfunctional patterns based on the information available to the authors of these two studies. In some cases, the referred child's difficult characteristics may have precipitated a crisis by contributing to the parents' feelings of low self-esteem, ineffectiveness, or lack of respect for their spouse. In other cases, existing problems in the marriage and dissatisfaction with life roles may have caused parents to ignore or devalue the child or the marriage. The child's behavior problems may have been precipitated by problems within and between the parents. On the other hand, "adequate" parents may resist disturbance because of the special strengths, resilience, or adaptability of the child. The child's healthy growth may contribute to parents' self-esteem and generate a positive emotional climate. The ecological model suggests that each family pattern is unique, and a healthy or disturbing child is a product of many factors operating over time.

Characteristics of the Community

As Kenniston et al. (1977) have documented, many American families today are under severe stress. One-fourth of our children are raised in poverty, with appropriate levels of nutrition and medical care unavailable to them. Unemployment and inflation are still high. The numbers of children from single-parent families are increasing dramatically but the availability of quality day-care and after-school care is not.

Families of children with special needs may have difficulty obtaining services. Although P.L. 94-142 guarantees a free, appropriate education to all handicapped children between the ages of 3 and 21, there are restrictions. For example, only severely emotionally disturbed children are provided for under the law. Moderately disturbed and socially maladjusted children are excluded (Raiser & Van Nagle, 1980). Even though severely disturbed children are eligible for educational services, a survey by the Bureau for Education of the Handicapped in 1978 indicated that only one-fourth of these children *were* being helped (Kauffman, 1981). Noneducational services may not be accessible, particularly to the poor. For example, respite care is not supported by public funds and is largely unavailable to parents seeking to maintain handicapped children at home. For those populations not covered by P.L. 94-142 (children under 3 and adults over

21), there is duplication, fragmentation, and overlap of services, a backlog of clients in need of services, and lack of universal access to services, particularly for individuals in urban and rural communities (see Meisels, Berkeley, & Godfredsen, 1980, for a review of early intervention policies and programs).

The implications of these facts are profound for families seeking to provide adequate psychological and physical resources for their children. For some families, severe external stress, particularly multiple stresses, may precipitate inadequate responsiveness to children's needs. Bromwich (1981) offers a good illustration of this point. Her staff was successful in meeting their intervention goals in 16 of the 30 families of high-risk infants with whom they worked. Of the remaining 14 families, 6 were low-income and disorganized, and/or with teenaged parents. She explained that effective intervention required that the parents be concerned about the infant's development and that they consider the needs of the infant to be a high priority in their lives. Sometimes these conditions could not be met:

Even from the perspective of outsiders, such as the staff, the six families had burdens to carry and stresses in their lives that outweighed the relatively minor problems that their infants had. The staff was aware of the primary needs of these families and knew that until their immediate life crises could be overcome or at least ameliorated, the parents would not be able to focus adequately on their infants or on the quality of their parenting. The staff spent much time with most of these families...exploring community resources of the kind that they needed the most and that they needed most immediately....Considering their areas of greatest needs, these families might have gained most from broadly conceived social services such as high quality infant and child care facilities, vocational training programs, and personal and marriage counseling. (p. 143)

As an interaction perspective might predict, however, the presence of high levels of external stress does not guarantee crisis in the family nor unresponsiveness to children's needs. Bromwich found, as did Lewis et al., that high self-esteem and initiative to identify and use resources to meet the needs of the family could offset the effects of multiple stresses. These parental strengths will be considered more fully in reviewing the effectiveness of family intervention programs.

A child's school is also a significant aspect of the community of most parents. Whether a child is identified and labeled as emotionally disturbed depends on the relationship between the family and the school. Lack of congruence between the values and expectations of parents and teachers can be troublesome to children. Behaviors that are acceptable or even encouraged at home may be considered inappropriate at school. It is possible for parents and teachers to resolve these value conflicts, and to develop mutual expectations and appropriate interventions. But it does appear that such value conflicts are increasing in our society. According to McAfee and Vergason (1979), increased mobility has fractured the traditional parent-school alliance which was based on shared community values, when teachers' and administrators' values were reflected in the values of the community as a whole. They explain that since World War II:

Schools came to be more frequently administered by professional educators who were not identified with the community. Teachers in inner city schools often commuted from the surrounding suburbs. Now, the educational values of the school may not reflect those of the students, the parents, or the community. Children who are bussed from various locales meet the same clash of values. The difference in values may be real or perceived, but its effect is supported by differences in attire, appearance, recreation habits, and other variables. Communities have been changing rapidly in socioethnic composition—and values and expectations reflect the egress and influx of socioethnic groups. (p. 2)

Of course, value conflicts between home and school do not automatically lead to children behaving inappropriately or becoming identified as disturbed. It is clear, though that children in minority groups are overrepresented in special classes, as are children of low socioeconomic status (Richardson, 1980). The assignment of a child to a special class is a complex process. Mercer (1973) discovered a series of "traps" that propelled a child toward classification as mentally retarded in Riverside, California. She learned that the child had to attend the public schools (because the Catholic school had no special classes). The child had to fail; continue to perform unsatisfactorily; be perceived by the teacher as having low academic competence, poor adjustment, poor work habits, low competence in English, and few friends; be referred to a psychologist and do poorly on an intelligence test; and have parents willing to agree to the label. Richardson (1980) adds that assignment of children to different mental retardation facilities "will vary depending on the kinds of services available, the number of places available in each service, and whether a service has an opening at the time of assignment" (p. 81).

It is difficult for us to recognize the "traps" in our own communities that lead children into and out of particular labels and services. But it is nonetheless useful to look beyond the characteristics of the child in trying to understand the nature and persistence of disturbance.

Summary

The ecological model suggests that disturbance is a product of reciprocal interaction between a child and the ecological systems of which he or she is a part. Disturbing interactions can be precipitated by unusual characteristics in the child, by dysfunctional family patterns, by external stresses imposed on the family such as poverty and unemployment, or any combination of these factors. None of these factors inevitably causes disturbance in the child. Flexible and effective parental management can lessen the distressing quality of a child's unusual behaviors; adaptable, resilient children can resist disturbing family circumstances; parents with high self-esteem and with initiative to identify and use resources can survive multiple external stresses. Whether or not a child becomes labeled as disturbed depends on the contributions of the child, the family, and the larger community as they emerge in patterns of unique, reciprocal interactions over time.

ECOLOGICAL APPROACHES TO FAMILY ASSESSMENT

Assessment Procedures

We have described many variables that may contribute to the growth of disturbing interaction patterns in a family setting. A wealth of scales and naturalistic observation procedures has been developed which helps us to assess various dimensions of family interactions. Making a selection of instruments and/or procedures depends on one's goals. For example, the investigator may be particularly interested in studying the child in a family setting or in contrasting settings (such as home and school); in looking at the family as a system and evaluating the capabilities and interactions of each family member; or in studying the family as part of a community, and exploring the family's social networks or utilization of resources. One's goals may be to conduct research, provide clinical services to families, or to influence legislative policies and programs.

Richardson (1980) summarizes the dilemma and the opportunity confronting the investigator with an ecological perspective:

The profusion of environmental factors that may influence a child's development creates a dilemma for any investigator. To prevent being overwhelmed, it is essential to be able to relate each factor selected to the specific research purpose using theory and previous research findings relevant to the purpose....Existing scales are a useful source of ideas and items, but research instruments generally have to be carefully tailored to meet the specific needs of the particular research project. Only careful pretesting in the field will determine whether parts or the whole of existing instruments are relevant and meaningful to the subjects in the new study. (p. 95)

An ecological assessment of a "disturbing" child must examine those aspects of the ecosystem that are most important in interaction with the characteristics of the child. Examples of assessment procedures that emphasize different aspects of a child's ecosystem are provided below.

The Child at Home or School

Various methods have been used to evaluate how a child functions in a given setting. For example, Thomas, Chess, and Birch's (1968) work on temperament has led to the development of rating scales to be completed by parents or teachers, which assess the temperament of infants (Carey, 1973) and 3 to 7 year olds (Thomas, Chess, & Korn, 1977). In addition, they have proposed guidelines for interviews with parents in clinical practice that would provide information about the child's characteristics and generate insights about current problems. Using a similar conceptual framework, Hall and Keogh (1978) found that collecting data from teachers about a child's temperament was useful in understanding a child's school career. These data proved very useful in distinguishing among children in kindergarten and first grade who developed behavior and/or academic problems and those who did not. The *interaction* of the children's academic ability and temperamental characteristics with the teacher's expectations was useful in predicting school failure among "high risk" children.

Several observation instruments have been specifically developed to study the problem behavior of a target child in specific settings. For example, Wahler, House, and Stambaugh (1976) created a procedure called "The Ecological Assessment of Child Problem Behavior" which can be used at home or school. The first step in the assessment is an interview with significant adults to identify problem behaviors and the specific situations in which these behaviors occur. The interview is used as the basis for data collection by the significant adults about their own behavior as well as the child's. In addition, a clinician or impartial observer collects observational data in 30-minute samples about adult and child behaviors and interactions at home or school: For example, observers evaluate adult and peer initiations (such as nonaversive and aversive instruction and social attention) and five classes of desirable and deviant child behavior (such as compliance-opposition, sustained work, and social approach). The clinician and other participating adults compare their findings, diagnose the problem, and use their data to plan appropriate interventions.

Wahler et al. (1976) found this procedure yields rich, reliable information, uses the clinician's time efficiently, and provides a meaningful or valid index of problem interactions between the target child and other people in that child's environment.

Several observation instruments have been developed to evaluate disturbing teacher–child interactions (e.g., Fink, 1970; Buchan, Swap, & Swap, 1977; Simon & Boyer, 1974). Kounin (1970) studied the contribution of several environmental variables to deviant behavior among disturbed and nondisturbed school children. In observing teacher–child interactions, for example, he learned that teachers who were skillful in managing transitions and in programming to relieve boredom avoided much deviant behavior. Academic subsettings had a significant influence on behavior, with highest rates of school-appropriate behavior for disturbed and nondisturbed children occurring in small group recitation periods, followed by class recitation, seatwork in teacher's sphere, and seatwork not in teacher's sphere. From his results, it appeared that deviant behavior was more clearly related to classroom management and structure than individual differences in children.

The Family as a System

Sometimes an investigator seeks to discover the origin of disturbing behavior by examining interaction patterns within a family system. Bermann (1973), for example, was puzzled by reports of a kindergarten child who often behaved in an aggressive, negative manner in school, but apparently presented no problems at home. He decided to observe Roscoe at home, and found that indeed he was very compliant and eager to please at home. But he also saw that he was consistently rejected and avoided by all family members. Bermann developed a coding scheme that was sensitive to the quantity and quality of family interactions. For example, he supported his conclusions that Roscoe played the role of a scapegoat in the family, in part by presenting the comparative low frequencies with which conversations were initiated with the target child versus other family members. He also displayed the disproportionate amount of antagonistic, disapproving, and accusing initiatives Roscoe received and the absence of any "joyful" initiations. Bermann used the rich observational data generated by many visits as the basis for a complex clinical picture of each family member. His relationship with the family eventually helped him to understand the extreme pressures the family was experiencing from within and without and the reasons for their rejection of Roscoe. Despite this understanding, he lost the parents' trust by confronting them too precipitously in therapy. As he followed the case over a 10-year period, he poignantly catalogs the failure of clinical intervention efforts to respond to the complexity of the family's patterns and needs, and his inability to help Roscoe.

Another method for gaining insights into family interaction patterns is provided by Lewis et al. (1976). They used the Beavers-Timberlawn Family Evaluation Scale to assess various aspects of family interaction, including family structure, mythology, negotiation style, autonomy, and family affect. Ratings were based on videotapes of family interactions during structured tasks. In addition, protocols for individual interviews with adults and children offered a useful tool for comparing individual responses in a one-to-one and family setting. The rich literature on family therapy provides many further examples of approaches and methods for evaluating family dynamics, structure, and health (see, e.g., Chasin & Grunebaum, 1980).

Family Networks

The connections between family members and the outside world often play a crucial role in the rearing of children. Cochran and Brassard (1979) define a social network "as those people outside the household who engage in activities and exchanges of an affective and/or material nature with the members of the immediate family." They discuss several characteristics of networks such as the nature of the relationships, their structural properties (network sizes, interconnectedness, and diversity) and location (geographic proximity, continuity over time). They hypothesize some direct relationships between these network properties and abilities in the developing child (see Figure 7.1).

Hartman (1978) developed a paper-and-pencil simulation called an "ecomap" as an assessment and intervention tool. She explains:

It maps in a dynamic way the ecological system, the boundaries of which encompass the person or family in the life space. Included in the map are the major systems that are a part

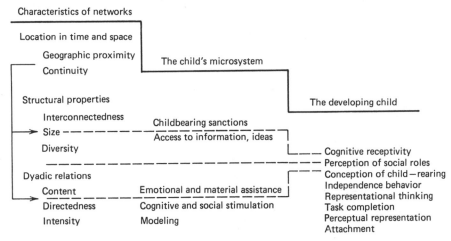

Figure 7.1. Network, microsystem, and child. (From Cochran, M., & Brassard, J. (1979) Child development and personal social networks. *Child Development,* **50,** 601–616.)

of the family's life and the nature of the family's relationship with the various systems. The eco-map portrays an overview of the family in their situation; it pictures the important nurturant or conflict-laden connections between the family and the world. It demonstrates the flow of resources, or the lacks and deprivations. This mapping procedure highlights the nature of the interfaces and points to conflicts to be mediated, bridges to be built, and resources to be sought and mobilized. (p. 467)

An example of a completed eco-map is provided in Figure 7.2. Hartmann gives many examples of the usefulness of the tool to clients and therapists for initial diagnosis, for building relationships, and for evaluation of intervention efforts.

A second example of an assessment procedure that increases our understanding of family networks is the Community Interaction Checklist developed by Wahler (1980). He explains:

This is a parent self-report instrument requiring mother and father recall of their separate extrafamily interactions over a twenty-four hour period. The interactions are coded to reflect: *identity* of the other party (friend, kinfold, helping-agency representative, business person), *valence* of the interactions (aversive to positive on a seven-point scale), *duration* of the interaction, and *distance* of the interaction from home. (p. 190).

Wahler summarizes previous work which indicated that long-term treatment success is threatened by parental insularity. In comparison with treatment-success mothers, insular mothers initiated few contacts and generally rated those contacts they did have as aversive. Wahler adds that insular mothers frequently are subjected to coercive requests for compliance both from their children and the helping professions. These requests are experienced as punishing and as "psychological traps." Moreover, because of their insularity they do not receive

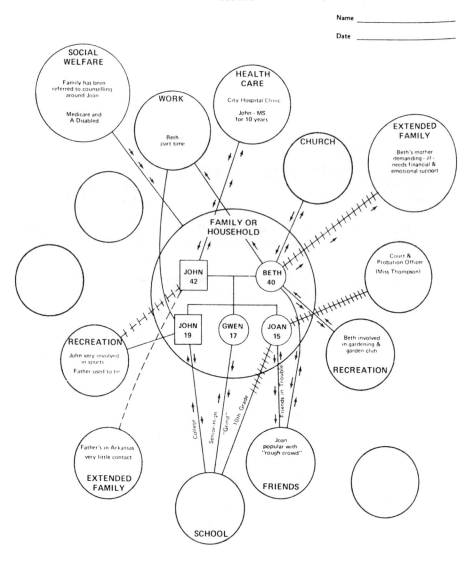

ECO-MAP

Name _____

Date _____

SOCIAL WELFARE

Family has been referred to counselling around Joan

Medicare and A Disabled

WORK

Beth - part time

HEALTH CARE

City Hospital Clinic

John - MS for 10 years

CHURCH

EXTENDED FAMILY

Beth's mother demanding - ill - needs financial & emotional support

FAMILY OR HOUSEHOLD

JOHN 42

BETH 40

JOHN 19

GWEN 17

JOAN 15

Court & Probation Officer (Miss Thompson)

Beth involved in gardening & garden club

RECREATION

RECREATION

John very involved in sports

Father used to be

College

Senior High

"Grind"

10th Grade

Friends in Trouble

Father's in Arkansas very little contact

EXTENDED FAMILY

Joan popular with "rough crowd"

FRIENDS

SCHOOL

Fill in connections where they exist.
Indicate nature of connections with a descriptive word or by drawing different kinds of lines;
———— for strong, – – – – – for tenuous, //////// for stressful.
Draw arrows along lines to signify flow of energy, resources, etc. →·→ →
Identify significant people and fill in empty circles as needed.

Figure 7.2. Diagramatic assessment of family relationships. (From Hartman, A. (1978) Diagrammatic assessment of family relationships. *Social Casework,* **59,** 465–476.)

reinforcement for changes in parenting style that might have resulted from treatment. Wahler hypothesizes that less-directive treatment styles may produce better success. Assessment of parent insularity, therefore, seems crucial in determining the style and nature of the treatment selected for a family as well as a potent variable contributing to the success of treatment.

A new procedure for assessing a child in an ecosystem has been developed by Hobbs (1980). He explains:

To classify a child using the proposed system, the first step is to develop an "ecological assessment and enablement plan." This is a systematic audit of assets and deficits in the child's ecosystem with respect to requirements for service. The assessment involves: (a) identifying sources of discord in the ecosystem as well as sources of strength that can be used to improve the goodness of fit between the individual and important people and places in his life; and (b) specifying what services are required to enable the child to make reasonable progress toward achievable developmental goals. (p. 276)

Table 1 illustrates a summary table of the ecological assessment and enablement plan for a child with multiple problems.

The diagnostic procedure includes an assessment conference attended ideally by "all the people who have something of substance to contribute to the shaping of a service plan" (p. 277). Traditional assessment procedures which are focused on the child are used, if appropriate (such as an intelligence test or an electroencephalogram), but significant effort is also applied to identifying "environmental determinants of effective functioning...such as the removal of access barriers and the provision of prosthetic devices, having a hot meal, or providing a teacher or pediatrician who understands the coping problems of handicapped children." (p. 275). The goal of the conference is to provide a record that functions as a "blueprint for specifying what must be done in order to achieve agreed-on objectives" (p. 277). The significant advantages of this diagnostic approach are that a fixed diagnosis is avoided and diagnosis and treatment are linked.

EVALUATION OF ECOLOGICAL ASSESSMENT PROCEDURES

There is as yet no simple answer to the question, "How do I conduct an ecological assessment of a disturbing child?" The answer depends on the nature of the problem and the context in which it occurs. But the ecological perspective has provided several useful new procedures and instruments, such as those described above, and has allowed us to attempt some generalizations about what an ecological assessment might include.

First, it is essential that information be collected about the child in the environment(s) in which the disturbing interactions are occurring. Ideally, an investigator would enter this environment and collect data about several variables, including information about the frequency and types of disturbing

Table 7.1. Ecological Assessment and Enablement Plan

Client: Robert Washington

Liaison: Margaret Smith

Date of Assessment: May 15, 1978

Date for Review: June 15, 1978

Service required	Who's responsible?	By whom?	By what date?	At what cost?	Source of funds?	Criterion?	Follow-up?
1. Admission to Cumberland House	Margaret Smith	Mother	June 1	$1500 month	Dept. of Mental Health	Return to special education class-room	None
2. Dental work	Nurse-practitioner						
3. Nutrition program	Smith						
4. Assessment for epilepsy	Nurse-practitioner	Dr. Ronald Bates	July 15, 1978	$350	Medicaid	Freedom from seizures	If epileptic, provide medica-tion and periodic checks.
5. Removing from drugs	Smith & Nurse-practitioner						
6. Activity program on weekends	Uncle						
7. Uncle to see Bobby	Uncle						
8. Program at Cumberland House	Smith						
9. Control of temper	Bobby						

From: Hobbs, N. (1980) An ecologically oriented, service-based system for the classification of handicapped children. In S. Salzinger, J. Antrobus, J. Glick. *The ecosystem of the "sick" child.* New York: Academic Press.

interactions and the conditions that precipitated them. As we have seen, several observation instruments that code child-problem behavior in context have been developed which simplify this task. But other more efficient data-gathering procedures also yield valuable information, such as observation of the family in a structured setting or interviews with family members or school personnel about current problems.

A second generalization is that it is important to collect information about situations in which problems do *not* occur and about resources and strengths that exist within the child and the system. Comparison of situations (time, place, physical environment, persons present) which lead to disturbing interactions and those that do not, allows one to identify the critical variables more precisely and thus avoid being overwhelmed by the profusion of choices. Identification of strengths in the system is fundamental to the development of an effective, efficient, and stable intervention plan. All of the instruments or procedures described above reflect this principle.

A third generalization is that the search for causes of disturbing behaviors is a very complex process. We have considered three levels of "search": the child in single settings, the child in contrasting settings, the child and family in a community network. To an ecologist, the inclusion of any one of these levels is preferable to assessing and treating a child in isolation. But the results one obtains depend on the lenses through which one is looking. With greater magnification, one may exclude important elements outside the focal point but gather rich data within it. If one chooses a lens that permits a wide scan of many elements, essential elements may be blurred or overlooked, but the whole is preserved. Another view is provided by the time frame selected for analysis. To continue our analogy, a time exposure has been an invaluable source of information about the behavior of plants and stars. In studying children, a historical view, a developmental view, and a current view have distinct advantages and disadvantages. The ecologist must struggle in making those choices as he/she assesses a "disturbing" child. Having made them, however, the work of other investigators should provide some useful maps, tools, and procedures to guide the search.

PROVIDING SERVICES TO PARENTS OF DISTURBING CHILDREN

Many types of programs are offered to parents of disturbing children by many different groups and agencies. In this section of the chapter, we describe several formats for parent involvement, consider their effectiveness, and present a model for an ideal program of services, based on an ecological perspective.

Current Models for Parent Involvement in the Treatment of Disturbing Children

Four characteristic formats for parent involvement will be presented as a sample of current approaches to working with parents: (1) family counseling and therapy; (2) parent education; (3) parent as co-therapist; (4) parent as decision-maker or trainer.

Family Counseling and Therapy

Therapeutic services are available to individual family members, parents, and entire families through hospitals, clinics, social service agencies, and therapists in private practice. Although the psychodynamic model is the basic guide for intervention, a vast array of techniques and approaches is used. Common goals of the therapist are to help the patient(s) gain insight into the causes for patterns of behavior that are dysfunctional and to provide support and guidance to the patient(s) as they attempt to change these behaviors or to deal with life crises.

The concepts and approaches of family therapy are particularly germane to this chapter on working with families. As a relatively new and developing area, it is not easy to identify and cluster the array of techniques that is currently being used. But Chasin and Grunebaum (1980) have identified three basic approaches to diagnosis and treatment in family therapy. They suggest that efforts to diagnose family predicaments are guided by: (1) a historical approach, in which the history of the family is assessed as it affects current patterns; (2) an interactional approach, which focuses on an assessment of dysfunctional aspects of current family structures and behavioral sequences; or (3) an experiential approach, which assesses the subjective quality of an individual's experience in a family.

They classify treatment approaches as emphasizing *understanding* (the therapist interprets how past influences illuminate current problems and patterns); *transformation* ("The therapist strategically directs the family in order to modify and correct its dysfunctional moves, sequences, and structure" (p. 10); and *identification* (the therapist and older family members promote new identifications to "relax the grip of toxic introjects and destructive loyalties among family members," p. 10). Although practicing therapists inevitably blend these approaches in the diagnosis and treatment of any particular family, Chasin and Grunebaum believe that their schema makes the panoply of current techniques intelligible.

In contrast to some other approaches to working with families (these will be reviewed below), the psychodynamic approach to family therapy considers family members as patients and assumes the existence of deeply rooted and significantly dysfunctional interaction patterns. In the case of therapy with families where one child has been identified as disturbed, the assumption is that the family has played a major role in providing the child with distorted views of self, other people, and relationships (see Eisendrath, 1980). Consequently, pathological characteristics, fixations, and defenses of the parents are diagnosed and treated.

Programs for Parent Education

Tavormina (1974) identifies two major approaches to parent education: those that are "feeling-based" and those based on behavioral principles. He explains that the goals of both parent education approaches are to help parents become more familiar with concepts of child growth and development, to help them clarify their roles and those of their children, and to increase parents' understanding of the complexities of everyday situations to enable them to make better management decisions. In the feeling-based approach, emphasis is placed on parental awareness, understanding, and acceptance of the child's feelings; in the behavioral approach, the emphasis is on teaching parents to manipulate their responses to the child in order to affect the child's subsequent behavior.

Parent education groups may have many different sponsors, such as guidance clinics, schools, continuing education programs, or private organizations. The meetings are of varying duration (often 4–8 weeks) with groups of different sizes and composition. Goals are determined by parents and leaders together: leaders often have specific content to transmit; parents have particular concerns about child rearing that they want resolved. Groups are sometimes designed specifically for parents of disturbed children (e.g., Reed, 1978), but more often children and parents are attempting to cope with the "normal" perplexing stresses of growth (e.g., Gordon, 1970).

Two assumptions that direct parent education programs are that parents sometimes need more information about how to be effective parents, and that parents can learn these skills if they are taught correctly. In addition, a common philosophy is that difficulties in parenting and child behavior problems are normal. In fact, parents often find the discovery that other parents *also* sometimes feel furious, ineffective, depressed, or frustrated one of the most reassuring aspects of their experience.

Often such groups function to prevent more serious problems. Negative cycles may be interrupted; families whose problems seem unresponsive to skill training may be referred to other services; groups may form close connections with one another and continue to meet without a leader, thus preventing insularity.

One of the most thoroughly researched programs of parent education which uses the social learning approach has been developed by Bruce Baker (1980). Baker and his associates developed instructional manuals aimed at parents of retarded children and covering the areas of self-help skills, speech and language, and behavior problem management. "Each manual contains sections on choosing a target skill, teaching, rewarding, and recording progress, as well as fictionalized "minicase" examples, humorous illustrations, and specific program outlines" (p. 206). Baker summarized the results of their study which compared parent education conducted with manuals alone, media-assisted group training, and individual consultation. Baker found that parents trained with manuals alone were as knowledgeable and effective in teaching as parents in the group or consultation conditions, but they reported less confidence in their skills of managing behavior or teaching. Surprisingly, there were no differences in gains between the group condition (nine 2-hour sessions, with videotape demonstrations and role-playing) and the individual consultation condition with the parent and child (nine 1-hour sessions with parent training, videotape replay, and feedback). At a 6-month follow-up, group and individually trained families continued to demonstrate equivalent skills.

Some very interesting variants of these two models have been developed recently. Cautley (1980) and her staff provided home instruction to individual families based on social learning principles. In sessions held three times a week for 3 to 12 weeks, the staff provided guidance and feedback as parents attempted to give clear directions, establish consistent expectations, and give positive feedback. Bolstering parents' self-esteem and confidence, aiding them in solving problems with adult relationships, and helping them find small groups or other community resources became additional goals.

In running a day-treatment program for problem children 2 to 7 years of age, Slaby (1978) discovered that it was possible to add a cognitive dimension to standard behavior management techniques. She was successful in using instruction, demonstration, and role-playing with dolls to explain behavior-change goals and contingencies even to very young children. These procedures improved on standard behavioral approaches by increasing the children's motivation to change their problematic "habits" and by helping them to anticipate the consequences that would occur following different behaviors. Parent training consisted of eight sessions of structured practice of interaction and management techniques between the child and both parents. Behavior management programs were devised by the staff to handle specific behavior problems with input from the child as well as the parents. Her case description of a child using dolls to take the part of the "uncooperative child" or the "parent applying contingencies" is delightful, as is this taped sequence of the conclusion of a final interview between child and therapist:

T: What happens if you have a habit that's *not* good? Does that mean you're bad?

C: No.

T: No? What does it mean?

C: It means you're not being good?

T: Well, you just have a habit.

C: Uh-huh.

T: Can you change habits?

C: (Emphatically) Oh yeah! *Very* easily.

T. Very easily! Have you *learned* how to change habits?

C: Yeah.

T: Did the doll help you to learn how to change habits, do you think?

C: Yeah. And I helped the *doll* learn how to change habits.

Another development is providing educational opportunities to parents and teachers together. For example, a parent involvement program in Ann Arbor, Michigan, used parents and teachers as training teams to present cultural training workshops to teachers and black parents from the community. The goal was to increase communication between home and school in an urban district (Sowers, 1980).

In our own project in a suburban school system (Swap, 1980; Swap, Clark, & Knox, 1980), part of the program consists of providing workshops and courses to parents and teachers together. Workshops on increasing children's self-esteem or identification of learning disabilities in young children build awareness. But courses in which parents and teachers work together on team projects not only build skills in teaching and parenting, but also enhance mutual understanding and frequency of communication. Course topics such as "Fostering Children's Social and Emotional Development," "The Impact of Divorce on Children," or "Fostering a Positive Climate at Home and School" have been popular. Using both parents and teachers as guest lecturers or resource persons highlights the expertise of both groups. Inviting parents and teachers of children with special needs as well as parents and teachers of "normal" children also encourages a rich level of information exchange.

Parents as Co-Therapists

Sometimes it is difficult to distingush between parent education programs that train parents in the rudiments of child development theory and behavior management and parent programs that train parents to become active teachers/ therapists with their children. Both types of programs draw on similar instructional techniques and often offer comparable amounts of direct instruction. There appear to be three major differences. First, the guiding philosophy in co-therapy is that parents are an essential part of the treatment team. They have the most intimate knowledge about the child and long-term responsibility for the child's healthy growth. Bristol and Wiegerink (1979) explain:

It was clear that if gains were to be maintained outside the treatment setting, it would be necessary to have a trained person in the child's natural environment to extend his learning to new situations. The cost of having professionals assume such a role was clearly prohibitive; furthermore, the shortage of such professionals made this plan untenable. A person was needed who had strong reinforcing properties for the child, control over the child's significant reinforcers, and was available for extended contact with the child. The logical person to fill such a role was, of course, the parent. Parent training programs described by Wiegerink and Parrish (1977), Schopler and Reichler (1976), Kozloff (1973), and Bristol (1977) no longer considered parents as patients but rather as partners. (1979, p. 135)

A second difference is that parent education which teaches parents to be co-therapists is a gradual process, where demonstration, feedback, and support (often in the home) are essential. Long-term involvement with a particular school or clinic program is characteristic.

A third major difference is that parents are important not just in maintaining or implementing programs begun at the school or clinic, but in setting priorities, developing curriculum, and identifying new areas for training and ways of teaching them. Parents may decide, for example, that teaching their autistic child to use the toilet is more important than shape identification; that time for a walk or a swing is more important than an extra hour of language tutoring; or that their own involvement as a co-therapist may increase or decrease according to personal needs and the needs of the family as a whole.

Wyatt (1976) describes the development of a co-therapist model in her work with children with language and emotional difficulties. She found that identifying the mother as the primary therapist was consistently useful and successful in treating children with severly defective articulation (in the absence of hearing or neurological impairment), children with defective articulation and secondary stuttering, young stuttering children, and language-delayed children whose mothers were poor communicators. Training generally involved explanation of the mother's own behavior and communication patterns, demonstration of communication patterns appropriate for interaction with young children, helping the mother to understand her feelings toward the child, and follow-up visits once every two or three months.

Involving parents as co-therapists with their child was initiated with Sigmund Freud's work with "Little Hans," a 5-year-old phobic boy. The analysis and treatment of the boy's neurosis was conducted through correspondence with the boy's father. Parent programs using the co-therapy model today are often initiated in educational settings. They are designed primarily to serve children with severe deficits such as retardation and autism, where parent follow-through is sorely needed and parent "complicity" in the genesis of the behavior problems is not suspected. More experimentation with this model in clinical settings with less severely impaired children might be useful.

Parents as Decision-Makers and Trainers

In reviewing the history of parent-involvement programs in the United States, Wiegerink, Hocutt, Posante-Loro, and Bristol (1980) suggest that we are in a phase in which parental responsibility for children's education is growing. This shift has been supported by efforts to establish greater community control over schools, by court battles initiated by parents to guarantee services to their handicapped children, and by a growth in organizations for parents of handicapped children which form strong and organized lobbies. Wiegerink et al. conclude:

During the last decade, the right of parents to be involved has been established in law; the role of parents as advisors and decision makers at both the individual project and state-government levels has been supported; the power of parents to, in fact, attain their rights and to make the educational system more responsive to them has been immensely enhanced. Parent involvement of a substantive nature is now clearly a matter of public policy in the United States. (p. 70).

These words are stirring, but recent research suggests that parent presence or parent signatures in educational decisions for children with special needs may be legally mandated by P.L. 94-142, but trusting relationships, equal partnerships, and actual involvement in making educational decisions cannot be required.

Yoshida, Fenton, Kaufman, and Maxwell (1978), for example, found strong opposition to most types of parent involvement among Connecticut public school planning team members. These planning teams were responsible for designing educational plans and making placement decisions for children with special needs. Although required to invite parents of the child being evaluated to these meetings, the majority of the 1526 educators polled felt that parents should be involved in only 2 of the 24 activities listed: These were gathering information relevant to the case and presenting information to the team. They felt that other areas, such as determining team procedures, developing the instructional program, evaluating the program, interpreting and summarizing information, offering leadership, and finalizing decisions should be the responsibility of the educators.

Some parents wish to be involved in decision-making that relates to program development and policy as well as decisions that concern only their own child. Precedent for this kind of involvement was set in Head Start programs and alternative schools where parent input was fundamental to the operation of the programs. Sowers (1980) reports that more than a million parents and other citizens belong to the more than 60,000 school advisory councils and committees formed in the last 10 years. However, she also emphasizes that "the mechanism alone does not guarantee results in participative decision-making," because administrators do not always welcome these alliances.

Unlike the other formats for parent involvement which we have reviewed, this approach does not involve providing services directly *to* parents. In fact, the assumption that characterizes this approach is that parents should have a role in determining what kinds of services should be offered to children and their families. The parents' perspective as parents and as consumers of existing services should be a fundamental ingredient in making decisions in areas such as community outreach, choice of programs, and styles of implementation. The focus here is not on the parent as patient or learner or even teacher of the child, but as a resource person with valuable information and opinions to share with program administrators on program issues.

A variant of this orientation is to consider parents as valuable resources in working with other parents and professionals (the parent as trainer model). The philosophy is that parents with disturbed or handicapped children have had valuable experience and training that other professionals cannot duplicate (such as in resolving the every day crises of living with the child, in seeking and finding resources, in understanding the feelings and pressures associated with the role of parenting a difficult child), and that other parents will find it easier to learn from people "who have been through it." Professionals may also gain valuable insights and information from parents by working collaboratively with them in providing services to families.

Several programs are experimenting with alternative approaches to working with parents as decision-makers or trainers. For example, Hauser-Cram and O'Leary (1981) report on a parent-teacher partnership model they have developed. The program includes 14 early childhood programs and public school classrooms that serve children with special needs. The three key components of their program are training of parent-teacher-administrator teams in communication skills and strategies, identifying and training parent coordinators for targeted classrooms, and awarding mini-grants. The parent coordinators function as liaisons to other parents, help organize and schedule parent activities and classroom observations, and co-lead parent groups. Mini-grants (up to $400) fund proposals for beginning or further developing parent programs within classroom settings. Thus, parents help formulate and implement programs and policies for the target classrooms.

After two years, the authors have found a number of positive effects: more home tutoring among project parents; significantly more contact between parents and teachers in program classrooms than among parents and teachers in waiting-list classrooms (particularly over instructional issues); the acquisition of career directions and specific new skills among parent coordinators, and increased reports of mutual respect, understanding, and trust among parents and professionals.

In our school-based project to enhance parent-professional collaboration for children with special needs (which has been federally funded since 1978), we have attempted to involve parents as decision-makers and trainers. For example, parents compose one-third of the advisory board which makes final decisions on all project activities. Parents suggest the content for activities offered to parents or parents and professionals together. Parents work collaboratively with professionals in projects such as developing a resource manual for parents or presenting a curriculum fair. Recently, a team composed of administrators and parents introduced the idea of a parent-consultation network, a school-based program for providing consultation from parents to parents. Parents co-lead some parent seminars and provide information to professional staff in workshops and courses.

Bristol and Wiegerink (1979) report on a program developed through a mental health center which uses the parent as trainer model.

Parent education clubs were formed in parent homes, drawing on the parents' natural network of friends or relatives. A parent initiator is trained in group dynamics and is provided with learning packets containing a short introduction to a topic, together with a list of activities for each parent to carry out at home....The center staff act as consultants to the parents, providing materials, films, or speakers during the eight-week sequence or beyond for those "alumni" groups that choose to continue. Different sets of materials are available for normal and handicapped groups. The groups provide not only a learning experience, but the opportunity for mutual sharing and support among parents as well as a chance for some parents to develop leadership skills. (p. 136)

Evaluation of Parent Services

Criteria of Effectiveness

A thorough review of the literature evaluating parent programs is beyond the scope of this chapter. The programs reviewed in the preceding section all offer data to support the effectiveness of their program and/or model. For example, Baker (1980), who used a social learning approach to parent education, provided a summary of their research effort which is partially quoted below:

Parents and children in both training (i.e., group and individual training) conditions demonstrated significant gains on all measures ($p<.001$). Trained parents improved significantly more than controls in programming knowledge ($p<.01$), teaching proficiency with self-help ($p<.001$), and teaching proficiency with play skills ($p<.01$). (p. 209)

Wyatt (1976) using the co-therapy model in working with mothers of children with severely defective articulation reported that her method had been highly successful with children and mothers since they began using it in the 1950s. She claims that 80% of the mothers were cooperative and imaginative in working with their children and that two-thirds of the children learned to speak normally before entering kindergarten.

Even from these limited examples, it is clear that programs collect different information in evaluating the effectiveness of their programs. From my perspective, if one could collect unlimited data, it would be useful to evaluate parent satisfaction and confidence, parent acquisition of new information and/or parents' skills in using this information with their child at home, changes in child behavior or attitudes, and long-term change in child and parent behavior and attitudes. It would also be useful to have objective measures of each of these variables in addition to parent or staff report.

Many programs collect or report on only a few of these variables. As an illustration, in a report of a parent education program based on social learning principles, Dubanoski and Tanabe (1980) presented data suggesting that their trained parents performed better than controls on a paper-and-pencil test requiring answers to four problems related to child behavior and management. Better answers were those that demonstrated appropriate use of any of several behavior techniques. However, only limited data were collected on whether these techniques actually were applied at home and with what results. The authors mention that "a few documented attempts to employ the techniques were reported and discussed in class" and that in a final written evaluation at least half the parents reported changes in their confidence, awareness of factors influencing their child's behavior, use of preventive management, and/or use of reinforcement for desirable child behaviors. In order to evaluate the efficiency of this program, more systematic data on actual parent or child change at home needed to be collected, which ideally would include objective observation reports.

Tavormina (1974) in his critical review of the feeling-based and behavioral approaches to parent education addresses another important issue in establishing criteria for effectiveness. He suggests that these different models utilize different perspectives for defining and assessing outcome:

Although both strategies have been used to deal with similar problems across similar populations, the focus of intervention, the issues addressed in counseling, and the criteria for measuring counseling success differ for each. Consistent with these assumptions, changes in parental cognitions have been the primary success criteria for reflective counseling. Similarly, behavioral counselors key on measuring changes in target behaviors. (p. 827)

Thus, how change is measured and what changes constitute success vary across models. Even within a particular model (such as parent education using social learning principles), there may be different training methods, criteria for success, kinds of data collected, and methods for reporting.

Other Issues in Evaluation

Lebow (1981) does a masterful job of summarizing and discussing issues involved in assessing the outcome of family therapy. He identifies nine significant issues:

the need to consider numerous population and treatment variables, the influence of treatment goals and values upon the research, the difficulties in defining and operationalizing family treatment, the choice between emphasizing integrity of treatment or randomness of sampling, the selection of measurement methods, the controls needed in research design, the extent of generalizability of results, the importance of efficiency of treatment, and the special role of deterioration effects. (p. 167)

All of these issues are relevant to the evaluation of other family-based programs, such as parent education or co-therapy models. This discussion will highlight only one of these issues across program types: population and treatment variables. This issue was selected because it seems particularly crucial from an ecological perspective for evaluating the "goodness of fit" between family and program. Lebow (1981) questions the population uniformity myth that "all families are alike, that they have similar responses to family treatment, that outcome can be summed across diverse kinds of families, and that one need not consider data about the type of families involved in a given study in evaluating research" (p. 168). Clearly, these assumptions are all incorrect if one hopes to gather information about the comparative utility of different treatment types, yet many program descriptions and evaluation reports do not provide sufficient data about their sample to permit an evaluation of the effectiveness of the program for families of diverse types. Recent studies have begun to identify the influence of some family characteristics in predicting the outcome of treatment. Cautley (1980), for example, found that their in-home intervention program was more effective with mothers who were experiencing internal stress as contrasted with external stress or pressure, and who had an adequate social support system.

Bromwich found many variables interacted to produce successful or unsuccessful outcomes in their home-based family intervention program with high-risk infants. These included: the severity of the child's problem, the degree of external stress the family experienced, the family's access to community services or support, the parents' trust of the worker and openness to new information or change, and individual parent characteristics such as self-esteem or resource-fulness. The family's age, developmental stage, ethnicity, structure, and size may also be important to treatment outcome. For example, our own work with parents suggests that several variables may be associated with parents of children with special needs who become involved in co-training or decision-making. Some variables worth exploring would be the parents' age, developmental stage, energy level, articulateness, capacity for abstract thinking, and self-esteem.

Certain kinds of programs may be most useful for certain populations or types of problems. For example, Love and Kaswan (1974) evaluated the comparative effectiveness of three different treatment approaches with disturbing children and their families. After randomly assigning families to treatment conditions, they found that psychotherapy for the child generally was not useful in improving his or her school adjustment as measured by improvement in grades. Treatment approaches that focused on the parents were effective in improving children's school adjustment, but there was a strong interaction effect for socioeconomic level and treatment condition. That is, the most effective treatment for families from higher economic levels was the "Information Feedback" approach, which simply presented parents with the results of the extensive data analysis and gave them opportunities for reflection and discussion. Lower SES families benefited most from 4- to 5-session parent counseling, in which the therapist gave interpretations, suggestions, or advice based on child-rearing principles and clinical experience. The authors conclude:

Our treatment comparisons emphasized the need for a range of interventions for children's developmental difficulties. These apparently will be most effective if they focus on significant adults who deal with the child, and if they permit appropriate matching between the intervention and certain characteristics of these parents and teachers. These involve variation in socioeconomic level and perhaps some psychological characteristics such as predilections for relatively autonomous or dependent relationships. (pp. 230–231)

Thus far we have suggested that it is essential to identify family characteristics in a more systematic and complete way when conducting single program or comparative research on the effectiveness of services to parents. It also seems necessary to collect data on characteristics of families who do *not* receive treatment and why they do not. This information is necessary to evaluate the appropriateness of existing service options for meeting the range of parent needs, and the generalization of program results. Baker (1980) identifies this issue very clearly:

Our experience in recruiting families for training in the Los Angeles area has been consistent with that of other researchers; fewer than 10% of appropriate families who are sent information letters in a targeted mailing join the program. Our successful outcomes, then, might not generalize well to the great majority of families of retarded children, since those in our program are demonstrably different in their motivation for the service and are likely also different in other ways. (p. 213)

He found that joiners differed from nonjoiners in that joiners' children were more retarded and had more behavior problems. Joiners also tended to have been more involved in other school programs, had higher fathers' education, and tended to be from higher socioeconomic levels.

It would be helpful to evaluate joiner and nonjoiner characteristics for several program types, and in cases where parents had a choice of services, to evaluate whether certain types of services were chosen more readily by certain populations. Finally, a community resource analysis would be useful, which identified what services were available to families, the degree to which families were aware of them, and the degree to which families felt such services were designed for "people like them."

Summary

Evaluation of programs of services for families is a complex task. Issues in the assessment of family services have only recently been clearly identified, and new programs for parents are burgeoning. Because programs often use different criteria for evaluations, collect different data, and fail to identify population characteristics in sufficient detail, it has been difficult to compare results within and across program types. Most programs document significant successes with parents. But we know very little about treatment failures, about comparative efficiency and effectiveness of treatments with particular populations, or about why certain parents choose not to participate in existing services.

AN ECOLOGICAL APPROACH TO WORKING WITH PARENTS OF DISTURBING CHILDREN: A SYNTHESIS

In the final section of this chapter, we shall identify the elements of a program of services for parents of disturbing children that is based on the ecological perspective. We will consider the assumptions about parents which will form its philosophical core, and methods for assessing and working with parents in a community setting.

Program Philosophy

As we have seen, within the ecological perspective, disturbance is considered the product of an interaction between the child and his ecosystem. Parents are not to blame for the child's behavior. If the parents are responding to the child's behaviors in a less than optimal fashion, one must dissect the elements of the specific interactions. Characteristics of the child, of other family members, of the physical setting, and of other ecosystems in the community may influence these interactions. Given these assumptions about parents' involvement in disturbing interactions, one might derive some philosophical guidelines for working with them. For example,

1. Parents are responsible for the healthy development of their child and should be active in planning and making decisions related to intervention. Parents should have choices about the role they play in any intervention plan.

2. Parents' knowledge and information about the child and the family should be tapped. Parents and staff should function as partners in problem-solving. The partnership should include sharing information and skills, learning from one another, and respecting the other's expertise.

3. Relevant strengths and resources existing in the child, parents, family, community should be utilized in an intervention plan. The family should be seen as part of a larger network of relationships.

4. The parents' goals, values, and priorities for the child should be respected and acknowledged in a treatment plan. If disturbance is occurring because of a conflict in values between the family and other ecosystems, the conflict should be clarified and alternative solutions generated.

5. The treatment plan should acknowledge parents as persons as well as parents, with several roles and many competing functions to perform. Establishing a climate of trust, providing ongoing support for change efforts, and having realistic expectations about the pace and degree of change in family members would be useful.

Assessment

Ideally, assessment should be a collaborative effort between the professional staff and family members. Data collection should focus on disturbing patterns in the system in which they are occurring. Direct observation is instructive, as well as structured interviews with the child, family members, school personnel, or other relevant ecosystem members. Traditional psychometric and medical evaluations may also be appropriate. Assessment of strengths as well as problem areas is essential to the treatment.

Because disturbance is seen as a result of interactions, identifying any individual as the sole focus for assessment and treatment is counterproductive. Finally, assessment should be directly linked to a treatment plan. Hobb's (1980) service delivery system provides a useful model, because it identifies what is to be done, by whom, at what time; establishes criteria for evaluation; and specifies any follow-up requirements.

Service Programs

Ideally, a continuum of services should be available to parents within the community. Direct service options might include individual and family therapy, parent education programs, and co-therapy models. Inexpensive family recreation opportunities and respite care facilities might also be offered. When possible, these services should be coordinated within a community. Programs offered within a school, religious organization, or community center may seem less stigmatizing to parents than those offered in a hospital or mental health agency, and function to prevent the emergence of more serious or deeply embedded problems.

It seems characteristic for most ecosystems to attempt to function independently from one another. For example, school system staff generally are unaware of educational programs offered to parents through other systems. If a child is referred for medical or psychological treatment outside the school, there is seldom any ongoing exchange of information among school personnel, medical personnel, and parents.

The origins of this kind of isolation are understandable, but its results are wasteful at best: individuals do not take advantage of existing services or their involvement is significantly delayed; staff from different systems engage in treatment of the same child with inconsistent goals and obtain incomplete information on the treatment's effects; existing services are duplicated and necessary services are not initiated.

We need to develop positions within communities for staff who would function in coordinator or liaison roles. In a school, for example, the coordinator could develop and direct inservice activities for parents, teachers, and administrators, work closely with a representative advisory board, establish links with programs in community centers and mental health agencies, and identify and distribute lists of existing community services. In a mental health agency, a coordinator might assess the needs of his or her constituency and identify and develop resources for meeting these needs (e.g., working with parent trainers of parent groups or helping a group of parents and professionals to seek funds for a neighborhood day-care center). Establishing links with hospital personnel and providing inservice education on strategies and skills for collaboration might be another component of the job description. Coordinators from various agencies might develop joint outreach programs that utilize their staff's strengths efficiently and provide more economical services to consumers.

Parent coordinators might be employed by schools or mental health agencies to develop consultation networks, parent groups, school projects such as art fairs or oral history tapes, resource lists and manuals, and/or workshops for staff on parents' perspectives. At the least, school and agency personnel might gain from involving parent consumers directly in decision-making about which needs to meet, in what order, and in what formats. The resources and strengths that parents could offer in program development hardly have been tapped because of their traditional status as patients and/or outsiders. An ecological perspective could alter this orientation and offer parents a choice of roles.

The ecological perspective recognizes the influence of cultural values and norms on the behavior of individuals. Recently, national and state initiatives have sharply reduced available budgets for social services. In many areas, budgets for schools, early intervention programs, mental health agencies, day-care centers, child nutrition programs, and other special programs have been cut significantly. Already it appears that the most frequent response is to maintain direct service to those most in need and to eliminate programs that are more preventive or supportive in function, such as community outreach programs, inservice education for staff, or parent education. There is also a temptation to reduce collaborative efforts with other agencies, because they may interfere with the ability to keep the resources that remain. These solutions have not worked in the past, and there is no reason to suspect that the level of need in families will lessen to parallel our dwindling resources. The challenge to develop creative solutions is compelling.

Ecological solutions are eclectic. They borrow extensively from currently offered programs for parents originating from many disciplines. But the ecological model encourages us to look at systems: the child in several contexts; the parent as a person with many roles in a complex network of relationships. The ecological approach has generated new insights and alternatives in coping with disturbance, and optimistic conclusions about systems' capacity for renewal and significant change. It is an exciting beginning.

REFERENCES

Akerley, M. (1978) False gods and angry prophets. In A. Turnbull, & H.R. Turnbull III (Eds.), *Parents speak out*. Columbus, Ohio: Merrill.

Baker, B. (1980) Training parents as teachers of their developmentally disabled children. In S. Salzinger, J. Antrobus, & J. Glick (Eds.), *The ecosystem of the "sick" child*. New York: Academic Press.

Bell, R.Q. (1974) Contributions of human infants to caregiving and social interaction. In M.L. Lewis, & L.A. Rosenblum (Eds.), *The effect of the infant on its caregiver*. New York: Wiley.

Bermann, E. (1973) *Scapegoat*. Ann Arbor: University of Michigan Press.

Bristol, M., & Wiegerink, R. (1979) In M. Paluszny (Ed.), *Autism: A practical guide for parents and professionals*. Syracuse: Syracuse University Press.

Bromwich, R. (1980) *Working with parents and infants: An interactional approach*. Baltimore: University Park Press.

Buchan, B., Swap, S., & Swap, W. (1977) Teacher identification of hyperactive children in preschool settings. *Exceptional Children, 43*, 314–315.

Carey, W.B. (1973) Measurement of infant temperament in pediatric practice. In J.C. Westman (Ed.), *Individual differences in children*. New York: Wiley.

Cautley, P. (1980) Family stress and the effectiveness of in-home intervention. *Family Relations, 29*, 575–583.

Chasin, R., & Grunebaum, H. (1980) A brief synopsis of current concepts and practices in family therapy. In J.K. Pearce, & L.J. Friedman (Eds.), *Family Therapy: Combining psychodynamic and family systems approaches*. New York: Grune & Stratton.

Clarke, Stewart, K.A. (1977) *Child care in the family*. New York: Academic Press.

Cochran, M., & Brassard, J. (1979) Child development and personal social networks. *Child Development, 50*, 601–616.

Dubanoski, R., & Tanabe, R. (1980) Parent education: A classroom program on social learning principles. *Family Relations,* **29**, 15–20.

Eisendrath, R. (1980) The borderline patient: Individual therapy from a family point of view. In J.K. Pearce, & L.J. Friedman (Eds.), *Family Therapy: Combining psychodynamic and family systems approaches.* New York: Grune & Stratton.

Fahl, M., & Morrissey, D. (1979) The Mendota model: Home-community treatment. In S. Maybanks, & M. Bryce (Eds.), *Home-based services for children and families: Policy, practice, and research.* Springfield, Ill.: Thomas.

Fink, A. (1970) *An analysis of teacher-pupil interaction in classes for the emotionally handicapped.* Unpublished doctoral dissertation, University of Michigan.

Gordon, T. (1970) *Parent effectiveness training.* New York: Wyden.

Gorham, K. (1975) A lost generation of parents. *Exceptional Children,* **41**, 521–525.

Hall, R., & Keogh, B. (1978) Qualitative characteristics of educationally high-risk children. *Learning Disability Quarterly,* **1**, 62–68.

Hartman, A. (1978) Diagrammatic assessment of family relationships. *Social Casework,* **59**, 465–476.

Hauser-Cram, P., & O'Leary, K. (1981) *Parents and schools: A partnership model.* Paper presented at the American Educational Research Association Conference, Los Angeles, California.

Hobbs, N. (1966) Helping disturbed children: Psychological and ecological strategies. *American Psychologist,* **21**, 1105–1115.

Hobbs, N. (1975) *The futures of children.* San Francisco: Jossey-Bass.

Hobbs, N. (1980) An ecologically oriented, service-based system for the classification of handicapped children. In S. Salzinger, J. Antrobus, & J. Glick (Eds.), *The ecosystem of the "sick" child.* New York: Academic Press.

Kanner, L. (1943) Autistic disturbances of affective contact. *Nervous Child,* **2**, 217–250.

Kauffman, J. (1981) *Characteristics of children's behavior disorders* (2d ed.). Columbus, Ohio: Merrill.

Kenniston, K. and the Carnegie Council on Children. (1977) *All our children: The American family under pressure.* New York: Harcourt Brace Jovanovich.

Kounin, J. (1970) *Discipline and group management in classrooms.* New York: Holt, Rinehart and Winston.

Kübler-Ross, E. (1969) *On death and dying.* New York: Macmillan.

Laing, R., & Esterson, A. (1964) Sanity, madness, and the family. Vol. I in *Families of schizophrenics.* New York: Basic Books.

Lebow, J. (1981) Issues in the assessment of outcome in family therapy. *Family Process,* **20**, 167–188.

Lewis, J., Beavers, R., Gossett, J., & Phillips, V. (1976) *No single thread: Psychological health in family systems.* New York: Brunner/Mazel.

Love, L., & Kaswan, J. (1974) *Troubled children: Their families, schools and treatments.* New York: Wiley.

McAfee, J., & Vergason, G. (1979) Parent involvement in the process of special education: Establishing the new partnership. *Focus on Exceptional Children,* **11**, 1–15.

Meisels, S., Berkeley, T., & Godfredsen, M. (1980) *Children in transition: A study of the provision of early intervention services in Massachusetts.* Available from The Cambridge Workshop, 37 Goden St., Belmont, Mass. 02178.

Mercer, J. (1973) *Labeling the mentally retarded.* Berkeley: University of California Press.

Paternite, C., & Loney, J. (1980) Childhood hyperkinesis: Relationships between symptomatology and home environment. In C. Whalen, & B. Henker (Eds.), *Hyperactive children: The social ecology of identification and treatment.* New York: Academic Press.

Raiser, L, & Van Nagle, C. (1980) The loop-hole in Public Law 94-142. *Exceptional Children,* **46,** 516–520.

Reed, J. (1978) Parents/re-ed: Partners in re-education. *Behavioral Disorders,* **3,** 92–94.

Rhodes, W.C. (1970) A community participation analysis of emotional disturbance. *Exceptional Children,* **36,** 309–314.

Rhodes, W.C., & Paul, J. (1978) *Emotionally disturbed and deviant children.* Englewood Cliffs, N.J.: Prentice-Hall.

Richardson, S. (1980) Considerations for undertaking ecological research in mental retardation. In S. Salzinger, J. Antrobus, & J. Glick, (Eds.), *The ecosystem of the "sick" child.* New York: Academic Press.

Rubin R., & Balow, B. (1978) Prevalence of teacher identified behavior problems: A longitudinal study. *Exceptional Children,* **45,** 102–111.

Salzinger, S., Antrobus, J., & Glick, J. (1980) *The ecosystem of the "sick" child.* New York, Academic Press.

Sameroff, A.J., & Chandler, M.J. (1975) Reproductive risk and the continuum of care-taking casualty. In F.D. Horowitz, M. Hetherington, S. Scarr-Salapatek, & G. Siegel (Eds.), *Review of Child Development Research,* vol. 4. Chicago: University of Chicago Press.

Schopler, E. (1978) Limits of methodology: Differences between family studies. In M. Rutter, & E. Schopler (Eds.), *Autism: A review of concepts and treatment.* New York: Plenum.

Seligman, M. (1979) *Strategies for helping parents of exceptional children.* New York: Free Press.

Simon, A., & Boyer, E. (1974) *Mirrors for behavior III: An anthology of observation instruments.* Wyncote, Pa.: Communications Materials Center.

Slaby, D. (1978) *Role-reversal in parent training: A cognitive-behavioral approach.* Paper presented at the Fourth Annual Western Regional Conference: Humanistic Approaches in Behavioral Modification, March 9–11, Las Vegas, Nevada.

Sowers, J. (1980) *Parent involvement in the schools: A state of the art report.* The Parent Involvement Project, Education Development Center, 55 Chapel Street, Newton, Mass.

Swap, S. (1980) *Enhancing parent-professional collaboration on behalf of children with special needs: Year II evaluation report.* Report for the Office of Education, Division of Special Education and Rehabilitative Services, Washington, D.C.

Swap, S., Clark, J., & Knox, L. (1980) Inservice education on parent-professional collaboration: A process of discovery. *The Pointer,* **25,** 53–57.

Swap, S., Prieto, A., & Harth, R. (1982) Ecological perspectives of the emotionally disturbed child. In R. McDowell, G. Adamson, & F. Wood (Eds.), *Teaching emotionally disturbed children.* Boston: Little-Brown.

Tavormina, J. (1974) Basic models of parent counseling: A critical review. *Psychological Bulletin,* **81,** 827–835.

Thomas, A., & Chess, S. (1977) *Temperament and development.* New York: Brunner/ Mazel.

Thomas, A., Chess, S., & Birch, H.G. (1968) *Temperament and behavior disorders in children.* New York: New York University Press.

Thomas, A., Chess, S., & Korn, S. (1977) *Appendix B: Parent and teacher questionnaire.* In A. Thomas, & S. Chess (Eds.), *Temperament and development.* New York: Brunner/Mazel.

Wahler, R. (1980) Parent insularity as a determinant of generalization success in family treatment. In S. Salzinger, J. Antrobus, & J. Glick (Eds.), *The ecosystem of the "sick" child.* New York: Academic Press.

Wahler, R., House, A., & Stambaugh, II (1976) *Ecological assessment of child problem behavior.* New York: Pergamon Press.

Whalen, C., & Henker, B. (1980) The social ecology of psychostimulant treatment: A model for conceptual and empirical analysis. In C. Whalen, & B. Henker (Eds.), *Hyperactive children: The social ecology of identification and treatment.* New York: Academic Press.

Willems, E. (1977) Behavioral technology and behavioral ecology. In A. Rogers-Warren, & S. Warren (Eds.), *Ecological perspectives in behavior analysis.* Baltimore: University Park Press.

Wiegerink, R., Hocutt, A., Posante-Loro, R., & Bristol, M. (1980) Parent involvement in early education programs for handicapped children. *New directions for Exceptional Children: Ecology of Exceptional Children,* **1**, 67–85.

Wyatt, G. (1976) Parents and siblings as co-therapists. In E. Webster (Ed.), *Professional approaches with parents of handicapped children.* Springfield, Ill.: Thomas.

Yoshida, R., Fenton, K., Kaufman, M., & Maxwell, J. (1978) Parental involvement in the special education pupil planning process. *Exceptional Children,* **44**, 531–534.

CHAPTER 8

The Social Network Paradigm
as a Basis for Social Intervention
Strategies

E. MANSELL PATTISON AND GARY S. HURD

The social network paradigm is a powerful conceptual approach to human social relations. Although social network theory has been developed primarily in the domain of social anthropology, we find the implications and applications of social network concepts most relevant to the clinical mental health field. In this chapter we present an overview of the social network paradigm as a theoretical construct, discuss methods and models of social network analysis, and then provide clinical case illustrations of social network intervention strategies.

THE SOCIAL NETWORK PARADIGM

A basic issue in social science theory revolves around how to define operational constructs of human relations, such that we can empirically measure the nature of those relationships. On the one hand we have had *micro-social* studies of family and kinship structure and function. On the other hand are the *macro-social* studies of society and culture. The micro-studies are based on personal relations, whereas macro-studies are impersonal. What has been lacking is an analysis of the *mezzo-social* process that links personal face-to-face process with the impersonal cultural process. This is precisely where social network theory enters (Pattison, 1973 1976, 1977; Pattison et al., 1975).

We can ask a very simple question: What constitutes a person's social universe? Methodologically, we can follow the social links of one person to all his or her face-to-face contacts, then to contacts through others, and finally potential contacts through second-, third-, or fourth-order indirect linkages or connections to persons unknown to our subject (Leinhardt, 1977).

The "small world problem" is an example. You meet a stranger in a strange town and find that you have acquaintances in common. You both comment to each other "it's a small world isn't it?" Or consider the following experiment: You give an envelope to a farmer in Iowa and tell him to give it to a friend to pass along to a friend, and so on, until it reaches an unknown addressee in Boston. We find that the envelope will pass through only four or five intermediaries before reaching the correct person in Boston. These two examples indicate that we do not live in an infinite social universe. Rather we are linked to others in an empirically defineable and finite set of social links or "connections."

What then are the natural limits of the human social universe? Again let us approach the question empirically. Let us start with Mr. Smith, and ask Mr. Smith with whom he interacts directly, those he knows about through others, from there to others who could link Mr. Smith to unknown persons. We can thereby chart his potential social universe. This type of empirical research reveals that the unusual human universe is about 1500 to 2000 persons. This is the size of the original walled cities in Europe, the size of some villages that remain constant for centuries, and the constant size of towns unless urbanization centers arise. These observations suggest that the natural size of a "community" is socio-psychologically about 2000 people. Urbanization is not simply the growth of a community, quantitatively, but rather is a fission and qualitative transformation into a more complex sociocultural organization. A city is comprised of multiple communities, and the gestalt organization of the city is a social construction above and apart from the communities therein (Mitchell, 1969).

The next question is: What are the relationships between the 2000 persons in the community? Social network theory examines the *linkages* or *connections* between persons in this social universe. Let us consider the total community as a Persian rug. The rug exists as a whole. The rug is woven together by many strands of different colored threads. The threads are knotted together as intersections. Now we can analyze the rug in terms of patterns, or colors, or the line one thread follows. Thus depending on our purpose, we analyze the construction of the rug in many ways.

Similarly, a social network analysis of a human community can be conducted in many ways, dependent upon the limiting criterion set. We can look at a community rumor network, political influence network, social service network, money-trading network, and so on. There is no one social network but many social networks of linked social transactions (Boissevain & Mitchell, 1973; Llamas et al., 1981).

LIMITING SETS OF A NETWORK

It is now obvious that one person can participate in many different social network constellations in the community. People of power and influence in the community are people who are multiply linked into many diverse social networks. On the other hand, the person who is linked to few networks or has tenuous linkages has little access to social resources. We can now proceed to define a social network by the limiting criterion of the specific network analysis. As shown in Table 8.1 (Whitten & Wolfe, 1974), we can specify a subjective set or

Table 8.1.   Types of Social Networks

	Limited Network (set) Any extract of the total network based on some criterion applicable throughout the whole network				Unlimited Network
Personal Set	*Categorical Set*	*Action Set*	*Role-System Set*	*Field Set*	
Limited to links of one person	Limited to links involving persons of a certain type or category	Limited to links purposefully used for a specific end	Limited to links involved in an organized role system or group	Limited to links with a certain content (economic, political, etc.)	The social network conceived without application of limiting criteria

From: Whitten, N.E. and Wolfe, A.W. (1974) "Network Analysis." In Honigmann, (Ed.), *Handbook of Social and Cultural Anthropology.* Copyright © 1974 by Houghton Mifflin Company. Used by permission of the publisher and Dorothy M. Kirk.

personal set, which is the view of how a person is connected to all others in his or her social universe. We shall concern ourselves primarily with this set, only because in clinical work we are concerned with the mental health of an identified person.

The other limiting sets are objective and impersonal sets. The *categorical* set would be illustrated by a family network where the category is kinship. An *action* set would be people linked to accomplish a given social purpose. For example, a community mental health team might link school, police, church, and welfare personnel to assist a family. The *role-system* involves people in specific role relationships, such as all personnel in a hospital, office, or clinic. Organizational structure determines the linkages. The *field* set involves linkages of common interest, such as a political network.

The importance of this analysis is to clarify what type of social network one needs to analyze, construct, or intervene in, when we consider some type of social network mental health intervention. Much of the clinical work on "community systems" or "support systems," or "networks" has been ad hoc, without precise definition of the social network toward which the intervention is aimed.

Both objective and subjective network analyses are clinically important. This objective network is arbitrarily defined by the specific criterion that motivates the analysis. For instance, we may wish to examine the objective family network, a work network, a rumor network, a political network, a clinic or day-care treatment network, and so on. In other words, we define the objective frame-reference and then look in the community to see who exists in that objective frame. The community is a tapestry woven of many threads of relationships. In an objective network analysis, we define the specific thread of relationships and follow that thread throughout the community. This is the pattern of analysis used in most community-psychiatry projects of network construction. Clinicians specify the clinical task they wish to accomplish, identify the set of relations they wish to utilize or construct, and then organize or convene that objective network. In sum, *we define the objective network by the social purpose we seek.*

In the subjective network, there is a phenomenological world of relationships as defined and experienced by the individual. The *subjective network can be defined only by the individual.* The subjective network of the individual overlaps many different objective networks, such as family, work, and recreation. The objective network of a person's extended family may include spouse, children, grandparents, in-laws, aunts, uncles, and cousins. Yet the same person's social network—his subjective network—may not include most of these objective kin, but may include his close family, good neighbors, best friends, and work and recreational associates.

NETWORK ZONES

This then leads us to consider how the social universe is constituted from the subjective or egocentric point of view. Obviously we do not relate to a social

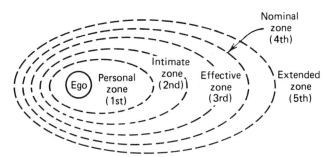

Figure 8.1. Zones of subjective social network. (From Boissevain, J. (1974) *Friends of Friends, Networks, Manipulators and Coalitions.* New York: St. Martin's Press. Reproduced by permission of Basil Blackwell Publisher.)

universe of 2000 persons in an identical fashion. Our network of relationships has psychological and social variations, both structural and functional. Boissevain (1974) suggested that we could arrange our social network relationships into zones, as shown in Figure 8.1.

A *first-order* zone contains the person's nuclear family, with whom there is regular contact, intimate relationships, and high degrees of instrumental and affective exchange. The *second-order* zone comprises close friends, neighbors, co-workers, and relatives who are of high significance to the person and with whom there is a high degree of structured and expectable exchange of affective and instrumental resources. The first and second zones comprise what we call the "intimate psychosocial network."

The *third zone* consists of persons with whom one has less frequent contact, such as distant friends and relatives, or people whom one sees frequently but does not value highly, such as neighbors or co-workers. Here there is a network of *potential relations.* As they make geographic moves, change jobs, or enter different life-stages, people may move between these three zones. The third zone is important as a recruitment area for mobilizing social resources for the person.

The *fourth zone* is the so-called *effective zone.* These include those who are strategically important to a person, and therefore relationships are maintained to some degree, so that use can be made of these resources. This zone might include the family doctor, business acquaintances, neighborhood relations, and so on. The *fifth zone* is the *nominal zone* and consists of people known only casually, by reputation, as representatives of agencies or services. Such persons would relate to the person only if they possessed needed services, resources, or became linked to the individual through intermediaries. Examples might be the minister of a close friend who meets the person through the friend; or a job offer from a manager introduced by a mutual colleague.

We have empirical evidence now to make a rough allocation of people that typically inhabit each of these five zones. In zones one and two, there is a reciprocal function such that these two zones will normally contain 25 to 30 people. Again, this is called the "intimate psychosocial network." Zone three involves 50 to 200 people dependent upon social role; zone four involves 100 to

150 persons; and zone five would include the rest of 1200 to 1500 persons. Thus, there is a rough logarithmic distribution of persons in our social universe.

THE INTIMATE PSYCHOSOCIAL NETWORK

Now we shall return to focus on zones one and two. Over 15 years ago, Pattison began to develop an empirical method to assess the structure and function of ego-centered social networks. We started with a very fundamental criterion set: List all persons who are *important* to you at this time, whether you like them or not. To our surprise, we found that psychologically normal persons consistently listed 25 to 30 persons, who would fall into zones one and two. In some 20 different diagnostic classes of psychopathology we found major attritions in this segment of the social network. This has led us to consider the social network construction of zones one and two as a *basic social unit*.

In order to study the personal psychosocial network, we have devised the Pattison Psychosocial Inventory. This consists of three major elements. First, we ask a subject simply to list all the people who are *important* to him, regardless of whether he likes them or not. These persons are arranged in four subgroups of family, relatives, friends and neighbors, and social or work associates.

Next, the subject specifies which people have ongoing relationships between themselves, apart from their relation to him. These relationships are the links or "connections" within the network.

The subject then rates the nature and quality of interaction between himself and each other person in the network. He does this on the basis of the following five variables that have been shown to be critical elements of significant interpersonal relationships:

1. *Contact.* Is there a high degree of interaction with the other person, whether face-to-face, by telephone, or by letter? A normal person *invests* in those with whom he has frequent contact.

2. *Emotional intensity.* Does the relationship have a strong emotional intensity? The degree of valued investment is reflected in the intensity of feeling toward the other.

3. *Positive vs. negative feelings.* Is the emotion toward the other person positive? Negative important relationships are maintained only in the face of constraint (e.g., a supervisor or spouse).

4. *Instrumental base.* The relationship has an instrumental base if the other person not only is positively valued for himself but also can be counted on to provide concrete assistance when needed.

5. *Reciprocity.* The relationship should be symmetrically reciprocal. If it is, the other person returns a strong positive emotional feeling and may count on the proband, too, to provide instrumental assistance when needed. So there is an affective and instrumental quid pro quo and mutual

exchange of both positive feelings and instrumental assistance between the subject and the others in his personal network.

With this method we have studied a national sample of normal populations and a wide variety of persons with different types of psychopathology. We have discovered three main types of personal social networks. First is a highly replicable social network for normal persons. Second is a "neurotic-type" network common to persons with neurotic disorders, alcoholics, heroin addicts, and other nonpsychotic individuals with long-standing maladaptive behavior patterns. Third is a "psychotic-type" network common to acute and chronic schizophrenics and to persons with major affective disorders.

The network of a normal person has 25 to 30 persons, with 5 or 6 persons in each subgroup (family, relatives, friends–neighbors, social–work associates). Thus, in a normal network the proband relates to about five or six persons in each of these four different subgroups. In a normal network, if the proband is asked to rate these relationships on the basis of each of the five variables listed above, he will rate them highly. That is, he has frequent contacts with most of these people, with positive and intense emotional investment. They provide each other with instrumental assistance, and the relationships are symmetrically reciprocal.

What does this normal social network provide the proband? First, it provides him with a relatively consistent set of norms and social expectations for the management of intercurrent stress. Second, individuals and groups can be readily mobilized in the network to respond to him when he is under stress. Third, there is a rather continuous flow or positive emotional support to the subject. Fourth, the network provides him with ready and available instrumental assistance. Fifth, the network is relatively conflict-free and tends to be stress-reducing, rather than stress-inducing or stress-maintaining. Sixth, the network is semipermeable across many areas of life interaction, so that the subject is consistently reinforced in function throughout his life-space, yet not subject to a single group of people who might impose a closed "group tyranny." Seventh, the network consists of selected persons drawn from a larger pool of other family members, relatives, friends and neighbors, and social and work associates, so that the loss or addition of important persons in the network can be readily accommodated. In sum, the normal social network is a flexible and responsive social resource in which the person is embedded.

The neurotic-type network presents a different picture. There are only about 15 people in the network, with fewer relatives, friends, and co-workers and higher reliance on involuntary ties in the nuclear family. Ratings on the interactional variables are much lower than normals'. There are frequent negative and weak emotional interactions. Many of the 15 persons are seen infrequently or not at all. The connection between persons in the network is half that of normals, each person related to only three others. In metaphoric terms, the neurotic subject is at the hub of a wagon wheel, with individual relationship spokes protruding and with a broken rim that fails to connect the spokes.

This "neurotic-type" network is impoverished and isolating. The subject is neurotically invested in internalized objects that are not present and fails to interact with the real objects in his environment. Real-life interaction is limited by avoidance of contact and by weak or negative emotional valences in the relationships. There is asymmetry in the relationships, so that there are usually expectational debts and obligations felt in the relationships that make the easy give and take of emotional and instrumental assistance difficult. The low degree of connnectedness among network members means that there is no reliable set of social norms and expectations either to guide behavior or to correct distorted behavioral responses. Simply stated, the neurotic interacts with a limited set of sparsely connected individuals and receives little corrective group feedback. There is little opportunity either to observe behavioral modeling of effective coping or to practice effective coping behavior with usual feedback. The social network of persons with neurotic behaviors, consequently, is likely both to induce stress and to maintain or augment stress. Thus, it is more likely to catalyze the transformation of stress into anxiety and then into neurotic-symptom behaviors.

The "psychotic-type" network presents still a different pattern. Here, there are 10 to 12 people in the network, almost all totally interactive with each other. The interpersonal relations are negativistic or ambivalent and highly asymmetric. The subject is caught in and tyrannized by a collusive closed system, with few links to the larger communities of relationships. This social system cannot process high degrees of stress that are readily transformed into anxiety and symptom generation. Further, the system produces conflicting emotional messages and contradictory and confusing instrumental behavior between members of the system. Thus, this system both generates and augments stress and anxiety, while remaining vulnerable to ambient stress.

PSYCHOSOCIAL IMPAIRMENT AND SOCIAL NETWORKS

Our work developed as a result of our increasing interest in the influence social support systems were having on individual coping responses. Cobb (1976), following an extensive review of the literature on family function, concluded that the family plays an important stress-mediating role. Caplan and Lillilea (1976) have extended this notion to include the generic concept of social support systems. There appears to be substantial evidence for the stress-buffering role of social support systems, but until now, as Dean and Lin (1977) have noted, there has been no methodology available to study the exact nature of such "social support."

Increased incidence of stressful life events has been correlated with the onset of psychological disorder in studies of schizophrenics, depressives, and suicide attempters, and in community studies assessing psychiatric impairment. Of particular interest here is the work of Myers et al. (1972). They found that changes in the frequency of stressful life events in a two-year period and changes in psychiatric symptoms were strongly connected: An increase in events was associated with worsening symptoms, whereas a decrease was associated with an improvement or lessening of symptoms. In a follow-up study Myers et al. (1975) investigated persons who did not fit this pattern—that is, those sustaining many stressful events who had lower symptom levels, and those who had fewer stressful events but evidenced higher symptom levels. They found those reporting many events and few symptoms had a higher level of social organization but higher symptom levels than those reporting few events. They concluded that socially integrated persons apparently have lower rates of psychiatric symptoms than those with poorer social integration. They proposed that social supports may act as buffers to moderate the effects of life events and minimize psychiatric symptoms.

The general thrust of these findings has been confirmed by Eaton (1978), who reanalyzed the Myers data using the panel-regression technique. His analysis provided evidence that stressful life events produce mental disorder if the person has not experienced similar stresses before as well as evidence that social supports help mediate or absorb the impact of stress.

Other parallel studies on the relationship between stressful life events and psychological impairment suggest that social supports serve as a modifying variable in the severity of symptom development. Mechanic and Greeley (1976), in a random sample of a student university population, compared the prevalence of treated and untreated psychological disorders. In part, they found that those students reporting more distress had smaller numbers of close friends than those reporting less distress; the friends of the students reporting more distress, in turn, had a higher percentage of emotional problems than the friends of students reporting less distress.

Brown et al. (1975) have shown that, in depressive women, the presence of a close confidant acts as a moderating effect against the onset of depression. Moreover, the presence of other, less intense or more causal relationships appeared not to affect this outcome. They conclude that the presence of an intimate social relationship affords virtually complete protection from a depressive illness following a severe life event or major difficulty.

Two studies by Miller et al. (1976a,b) relate directly to this point. In the first study they examined the association between social supports and selected psychological and physical symptoms in 337 subjects drawn from the list of one general practice. Half had consulted their doctor within the previous seven days and half had not. As in Brown et al. (1975) the results showed that lack of a good confidant was associated with severity of symptoms, whereas having a good confidant was associated with a lack of symptoms. Unlike Brown, however, Miller and his associates found that the absence of casual, less-than-intimate friends was also associated with higher symptom levels in that having at least some acquaintances afforded partial (but only partial) protection against symptom development. In the second study, they sought to examine the relationship between threatening and nonthreatening life events, physical and psychological symptoms, and the degree of social support of the consulters and nonconsulters, using a subsample of the original group for this study. The consulters were shown to have had a greater number of threatening life events, and this appeared as the only dimension discriminating between the two groups. In combined samples, however, threatening life events were strongly related to severity of psychological symptoms and weakly, if at all, to the severity of physical symptoms. Moreover, persons reporting no confidants and few casual friends tended to have higher symptom levels.

These studies indicate that the environmental or social structures surrounding a person (1) significantly influence—or mediate—the impact of stressful events on their lives, (2) affect the severity of both physical and psychological symptoms, and (3) have different structural and interactional characteristics in those with significant depressive illnesses than those with no such illnesses.

Studies utilizing a social network approach consistently demonstrate a correlation between social network structure and psychological function. Blackman and Goldstein (1976), in a study of reciprocity networks and psychiatric symptoms, randomly sampled 20 women (index subjects) and elicited those with whom they "characteristically interacted" (contact subjects). They then succeeded in interviewing 76% of the contact subjects. Their results showed a significant relation between network reciprocity and psychological symptomatology: the less the index subject perceived herself as being tied into a mutual-obligation network, the greater her manifest psychological symptoms as perceived by others.

Three studies have compared the social networks of normals with those of psychiatric patients. Ratcliffe and Azim (1975) compared the social networks of psychiatric patients from two hospitals with controls drawn from households in the same community. Two pairs of samples were drawn from their subject pool to control for marital status, age, and sex. All subjects were required to list significant others who were relied on to meet certain interpersonal needs (those they spent free time with, felt closest to, talked with when troubled, sought advice from, stood by in times of trouble, etc.) and to rate their degree of satisfaction with the relationship. Both married and single psychiatric patients were significantly less satisfied with their personal relationships than were the normal controls. The psychiatric patients reported fewer persons who could be relied on, had fewer voluntary or friendship relations, relied more on their involuntary relationships with relatives, and relied more on professional helpers than those in the control group. In addition, married psychiatric patients differed from their normal counterparts in that they relied less on their spouses.

In a study comparing the social networks of hospitalized medical and psychiatric patients, Tolsdorf (1976) showed that psychiatric subjects reported fewer intimate relations with their network members, listed a greater proportion of these members as family members, and exhibited relatively fewer, but more powerful, persons occupying more controlling and dominant positions. In contrast, the hospitalized medical patients reported more intimate relationships with those in networks less dominated by family members and in which functional persons were their equals.

Consistent findings regarding the networks of outpatients have also been demonstrated. Silberfield (1978) compared two groups of 50 women, one from an outpatient psychiatric practice, the other from a family practice. As a measure of social network, she used a survey method for reconstructing the time that women in each group spent in interpersonal relationships. She found that the social networks of the psychiatric outpatients were impoverished in comparison with those of the family-practice patients, not only in their lack of relationships with many other persons, but also in the amount of time spent with significant others. This held true regardless of whether the relationship was with another family member, a friend, or someone else. The psychiatric patients were less involved with relatives, spouses, or children than the nonpsychiatric patients, having a greater proportion of their relationships with friends than with family members, and they had proportionately fewer close relationships with anyone.

The contacts of psychiatrically impaired persons have also been examined by Post (1962). Using two separate measures, he assessed the prevalence of psychiatric disturbances among the adult "emotionally significant others" of psychiatric patients in treatment. He found, depending on the measure used, that between 42.6 and 44.6% of those adult contacts were rated as psychologically disturbed at some time themselves. "In the author's opinion, 40 percent had shown psychiatric or psychosomatic symptoms concurrently with the patients' illnesses," Post noted. "Over two-thirds of psychologically abnormal adults had exhibited neurotic difficulties; about one-quarter had psychosomatic symptoms, and only one-tenth had, at one time, been suffering from psychoses."

The most direct evidence of the relationship between social network interaction and psychological impairment is found in the work of Kleiner and Parker (1974). They used three measures of psychological impairment: history of nervous or mental disorder, measure of self-esteem, and psychoneurotic-symptom scores. They then measured the degree of importance or salience and the degree of alienation of the individual from his family network, friend network, and co-worker network. They found that alienation from each of the three networks was significantly related to all three measures of psychological impairment. Alienation was cumulatively related to psychosocial impairment, and the degree of alienation and impairment varied directly with the importance of the network.

In summary, these studies indicate a number of things:

1. Personal social networks provide a major source of affective and instrumental relationships for people.
2. Social networks exert both positive and negative sanctions and supports on individuals.
3. Social networks act as adaptive systems by which individual members adjust to complex environments.
4. Social networks provide a basic social unit of analysis by defining a functional social system of relationships.

5. The psychosocial network, these studies suggest, is a fundamental social matrix that can be either health-promoting or pathology-promoting, depending upon its composition and nature.

The studies are also significant in several other respects. First, they provide evidence of the importance of the person's intimate functioning in his social network in relation to his mental health or psychiatric impairment. Second, they have explicitly moved beyond the notion of "psychological impairment" as a process confined solely within the soma and psyche of *individuals,* to an emphasis on *interactional processes,* or relationships between individuals. And third, they point up the etiological importance of the concept of the "fit" or relationship between available social struture and individual coping skills in adapting to stress.

SOCIAL NETWORK AS A MEDIATING PROCESS

This brief discussion illustrates how the normal personal social network may be stress-reducing and anxiety-ameliorating, whereas the neurotic-type and psychotic-type social networks not only fail to help the individual cope with stress, but (because of their very structure) tend to promote and perpetuate maladaptive coping behavior; thus they generate anxiety instead of ameliorating it.

There are a number of mechanisms at work in the normal social network to mediate stress and mediate anxiety. The normal network will usually provide unambiguous emotional and instrumental responses, and it will have a relatively rich repertoire of resources to assist a person in coping with stress so that anxiety does not result. The pathologic network, on the other hand, produces stress through ambiguous and conflicting emotional responses, contradictory instrumental responses, and either social isolation (in the case of the neurotic-type network) or social collusion (in the case of the psychotic-type network).

We recognize that normal networks may also generate stress and conflict. But because the normal network has relatively rich resources in several subgroups, alternative self-regulation mechanisms and self-modification mechanisms arise within the normal interactions of those in the network. The normal network, consquently, tends to be "self-correcting" insofar as network-generated stress is concerned. In the pathologic network this self-correcting interaction is not present, and thus not only is anxiety perpetuated in the proband but the structure of the network itself becomes dysfunctional.

Our final question concerns whether such dysfunctional pathologic networks generate psychopathologic behavior or whether an individual creates his or her own dysfunctional social network. Our current data suggest that the answer is not one alternative or the other but, rather, that both processes reciprocally feed into each other.

We suggest that the process of social development includes critical skills in social network construction. Thus, if a person learns how to create and participate in effective social networks, he will be at less risk of developing psychopathologic symptoms than if he does not participate in such a network. The person who fails to acquire such skills because he has grown up in a dysfunctional social network not only will be adversely affected by the network itself, but also will be unable to build supportive social networks effectively in the future.

In summary, we have shown how a social network analysis of linkages or connections between persons provides a conceptual and empirical approach to social models of mental health intervention. Further, we have indicated the importance of the "intimate psychosocial network" as a primary social unit that mediates one's participation in the larger social universe.

THE DEVELOPMENT OF MODELS FOR SOCIAL NETWORK INTERVENTION

In this section we wish to pursue a more rigorous analysis of social network structure and function (from an egocentric viewpoint), in order to generate a theoretical position for prescribing different clinical social network interventions.

The term *social network* is often used generically, ambiguously, inaccurately, or inappropriately. It is a concept leading to description of the social relations that obtain between people; namely, it is a concept of linkage between people in relation to specific interactional situations. For example, there may be instrumental single links to others: gas station attendant, gas meter reader. Or affective single links to others; a golf partner, bridge partner. Or there may be multiple affective links to other: a golf partner who is also best friend. Or multiple instrumental links to other: a co-worker who also provides car repair service off-the-job. And finally, there are mixed affective-instrumental linkages: a friend and co-worker, a relative who is emotionally close and works with you. Also, interactional links can *change* over time.

We can consider a social network as the entirety of social links between persons in a finite community of relationships. Any given person is therefore part of many *interlocking* social networks. Thus a social network analysis is not ipso facto evident: There is no social network to analyze. Rather, we select an interactional function: a rumor network, an information network, an assistance network, a friendship network, a worship network, a recreational network, and so on. Here social network analysis is a description of the structure and function of the social links of a specific social organization. For most clinical purposes, the a priori defining assumption is the ego-centered social network of the identified patient; and more specifically, the relatively circumscribed "closer" affective and instrumental persons immediately linked through personal contact with the patient, in zones one and two.

In this light, we must stress that a social network is not necessarily a *social support system*. We consider such an assumption to be a major conceptual flaw in most clinical reports about social network intervention. Social networks are just that. They may be supportive, destructive, insignificant, or merely innocuous. Or more precisely, social networks may be comprised of social interactions most of which are supportive, or mostly destructive, or an admixture of a range from beneficient to noxious interactions.

To construct models of different social networks, then, we must address the structural and functional dimensions of specific paradigmatic social networks.

First, let us consider the functional features of a social network, which are as follows:

Instrumental functions: the frequency, amount, and quality of material assistance provided, required, or withheld

Affective functions: the frequency, amount, and quality of emotional exchange (either positive or negative)

Reciprocity: the quality and intensity of obligation incurred or acquired in giving or receiving of instrumental or affective exchange

A closely related function of social networks is "norming": the validation and enforcement of beliefs and behaviors. The frequent interactions of social network members communicate and activate network "norms." Observing the behaviors of one's social alters, the individual network member is provided with good or bad role models, which may influence future behavior. Also there is interactive judgment of actual behavior vis-à-vis norms. Additional aspects of social network involvement are the individual's sense network membership and responsibility toward other members. Thus, not only does the social network provide role models, but it also provides the stage where the roles are enacted and evaluated.

The above-mentioned features of social networks obviously have an older tradition in psychotherapy than that of social network analysis. However, the social network theorists have placed these functions in the definable, and most important here *manipulable,* context of the social network. Social network analysis explicitly recognizes an individual as an interactive element in a set of social actors.

Now let us consider structural features of social network. Structurally, a network is composed of individuals (nodes) who are connected (linked) to one another through socially or behaviorally defined relations. Structural features of social networks include:

Size: the number of nodes in a network

Connectedness: the number of observed links measured relative to the theoretical maximum number of possible links

Flow: the pattern of serial or parallel activations of links

Composition: the number and kinds of relations contained within the network

This last feature might be further elaborated by characterizing each link in the network as either "single-plex," that is, a link defined by only one type of relation, or "multiplex," a link that consists of multiple types of relations.

The investigation of these structural variables, coupled with the ability of social network analysis to examine the behavior of groups and individual members simultaneously, demonstrated the significant influence distant network members may have on each other. Indeed, network members may influence and be influenced by other members in the absence of any direct link (Granovetter, 1973). We must consider an ego-centered social network under two conditions: (1) with presence of ego, and (2) with absence of ego. The latter condition we term "residual network structure and function."

Two idealized networks are represented in Figures 8.2a and 8.3a. It is important to note that each focal ego has similar numbers of links to members and might theoretically share the same composition of social relations. However, the connectedness and the possible activation paths of flows are very different from one another. Figures 8.2b and 8.3b show the residual network configurations when the focal egos are removed from their respective networks. Note that

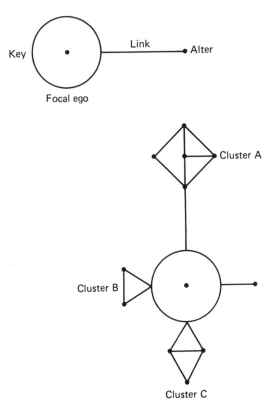

Figure 8.2a.   Weakly interconnected network.

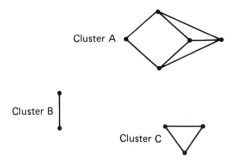

Cluster A

Cluster B

Cluster C

Figure 8.2b.   Residual network (focal ego removed).

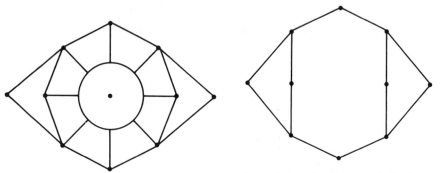

Figure 8.3a.   Strongly interconnected network.

Figure 8.3b.   Residual network (focal ego removed).

the structure of the network in Figure 8.2*a* has almost been destroyed in Figure 8.2*b*, but the second network is largely unaffected in Figure 8.3*b* by the removal of the focal ego. This points out the importance of a network structure on the collective behavior and on the relative significance of members occupying central positions. It is hard to imagine how the network depicted in Figure 8.2*a* could function collectively in the absence of the focal ego. The network of Figure 8.3*a* has no such "critical" member. But a potential liability of this type of network is the relatively greater amount of pressure that might be exerted on each member to conform behviorally to the network norms.

CLINICAL SIGNIFICANCE OF SOCIAL NETWORK FEATURES

Quite clearly, each of the functional components of a social network—locus of support, generation-maintenance, interpretation of social action, norming, provision of role models, and the provision of membership—are of potential interest to the psychotherapist. This is especially true when each of these functions may become noxious through distortion, absence, or withdrawal.

The attention of most network interventions has been to provide identified patients with the presumed benefits of social network participation. In this vein the collective behavior of the social network in response to a crisis is of considerable interest. A social network typically consists of a number of clusters, such as the nuclear or extended family, friends, or co-workers. At the onset of the crisis network, members may attempt to intervene on the precipitating situation or its effect. Often these attempts are successful. Should the clusters fail to achieve a consensus, however, there will be various coalitions in opposition in response to the situation. Then, the principal energies of the network members will be directed to the resolution of this *secondary* conflict. It is also likely that efforts to assist the crisis victim will be inconsistent and contradictory, with a high probability of exacerbating the impact of the crisis. Other network responses of clinical concern are also observed. Quite commonly one encounters collective denial of the situation and this may have a number of motivating factors. The network may be so organized that the affected individuals may be unable to communicate their need to their social network. Or, they may make the situation known to a few network members who may be unable to intervene on the behalf of the patient. It may be that the crisis has been known to the network, but attempts at resolution have failed. In this instance, rather than risk further conflict or failure, the network may extrude the patient or ignore the problems.

We must also consider individual functioning within the context of the network. The resources of the network do not magically appear. Each of the functional components of a social network described above depends on the consensual actions of its members. Should an individual be unable to satisfy the conditions of network membership, then sanctions will be made against him. The sanctions are intended to cause behavioral conformity to the network obligations and not force the individual out of the network. However, the application of sanctions might indeed have the effect of rendering the offending members even less capable of fulfilling their network role. The individuals will in turn suffer more severe sanctions and ultimately be excluded from the network. We note in passing that the "sick role" is a ready alternative to the inability (which can be quite legitimate) to satisfy network obligations.

A particular error in most clinical network reports is to assume that all members of a patient's network are potentially helpful or can be activated. Callan et al. (1975) and Garrison (1977) have observed that not all patient network members are helpful and that some may, in fact, be detrimental to the patient's recovery. Wellman (1979) has placed this in a well thought-out sociological argument. He observes, "(it is)...clear that supportive ties do not come in separate packages but as part of networks which also contain non-supportive ties."

NETWORK PARAMETERS IN CLINICAL INTERVENTION

Greater insight can be gained by noting the various areas of social networks or kinds of network functions that have been the focus of interventions. Two major clinical tasks can be defined: (1) those interventions that attempt to change the functional components of the network, and (2) those that seek to change the structure of the network through strengthening or relaxing various links. We can further divide the clinical task into: (1) change of the patient's (ego's) function or position in the network, or (2) change of the residual network function and structure.

This analysis allows us to organize a matrix composed of four types of "network deficits" juxtaposed against four types of network interventions. This could potentially yield 16 paradigmatic models as shown in Table 8.2. However, we cannot yet assay a completely systematic description, which eventually may be unrealistic from a clinical or theoretical perspective.

Table 8.2.   Comparison of Network Problem Area with Intervention Category

		INTERVENTION CATEGORIES			
		Patient Behavior	*Network Structure*	*Augment Coordinate*	*Replace*
N E T W O R K	Ego Function	A			
	Residual Function			B	C
M O D E L S	Ego Structural	D	E		
	Residual Function		F		G

First, we shall consider four types of network deficits:

EGO FUNCTION.   The function and resources of the network are not an issue but the identified patient is experiencing difficulty in satisfying his network commitments. Examples of this type of problem are role conflict, inability to satisfy role obligations, ineffective communication, poor coping skills, or role difficulty such as unexpectedly becoming the mediator between conflicting network clusters.

RESIDUAL FUNCTION.   The overall network function is impaired. The patient's behavior is a reflection of problems in the network. A general example of this type of problem is the impoverished network. This may range from a lack of social network, lack of resources within a network, or a network experiencing such a variety of problems that all of its resources are committed. Residual function problems can be more subtle than those presented above. One example of this we call the redundant network. This is where most or all of the network relations are of the same type or typically fulfill the same functions. This type of network may be found in isolated nuclear families or where most or all of one's social network is comprised of work associates. Another example of a residual function problem is the inactivated network such as described in the preceding discussion of network responses to a crisis.

EGO STRUCTURAL: Briefly, the focal individuals are restricted in the range of their network activities by the restriction of their social links. An excellent example of this problem is found in the case of divorce. The dissolution of the marital link profoundly alters the structures of the surrounding social network. This can be visualized from the perspective of children who belong to two parental networks that have become separate. The children are the only members in the original network who continue to link what has become two separate network systems.

RESIDUAL STRUCTURAL: This category of problem is illustrated in Figures 8.2a and 8.3a. Should this focal person become incapacitated or removed from the network, the critical functions of the network become impossible. This loss of network structure, due to the inherent liability of this type of structure, may lead to a secondary network deprivation for the remaining members. The problems are twofold: (1) the focal ego may find it difficult to maintain the network, and (2) remaining members may not have the ability to reconstruct a viable network (such as a deserted adolescent).

In the same sense, the network suggested in Figure 8.3a, having no central or critical member, may perceive no threat to its ability to function from the loss or disability of a member. A straightforward criterion for evaluating whether a residual structure problem exists is to appraise the network's ability to function in the absence of the focal member. Should the network either be unable to function or be essentially unchanged, there exists a residual structure problem.

MODELS OF INTERVENTIONS

We can now consider how to fit clinical descriptions of network interventions into Paradigmatic models in the matrix of Table 8.2.

First would be the condition of Ego Function problems. Here the clinical goal is to improve the coping capacity of the patient vis-à-vis the existent social network. Changes in social network are primarily functional, and aimed to improve patient integration into an effective network. Thus, this would be Model A, with a focus on change in patient network function, and the emphasis on altering the patient's routine interaction with his or her social network.

Second, we consider the interventions appropriate in Residual Function problems. In this case the patient has reasonable coping skills but lacks an adequate social network matrix. Model B has the clinical goal of coordinating and augmenting the efforts of existing potential linkages to generate more robust social network actions. Examples would be the screening-planning-linking methodology developed by John Garrison and his colleagues (Garrison, 1974). Additional examples would be extended kin network interventions with drug and alcohol abusers (Kaufman & Kaufman, 1979). Model C, where extant or potential links are lacking, one would "re-imbed" the patient in a new social milieu. Alcoholics Anonymous is an excellent example of "network replacement" of a drinking buddy network by a sober buddy network.

Third, we consider the Ego Structural problems. In Model D the focus is on teaching the patient to recognize the network structure and his or her own position in the network. Model E seeks to restructure the network through changing the interactions of a restricted number of network alters. Examples would be found in the altered structure consequent to conflict resolution. Also the work on marital dysfunction by Boszormenyi-Nagy and Spark (1975) corresponds to this type of intervention.

Residual Structural problems constitute the last network area to be considered. Model F is represented by the large network collations described by Speck and Attneave (1973) and by Rueveni (1979). Here they focus on restructure of the network per se as the primary clinical goal, so that the identified patient has a new and different social network with which to cope, hopefully in a more effective manner. Model G reflects the need to generate a social network for those individuals who have been "lost" to their prior network by geographic or social mobility. Also included are recently deinstitutionalized patients with no effective or surviving social network. Examples of this type of intervention are "halfway houses" or "step-houses." The model also is reflected in memberships in community organizations, even though these may not have been the result of clinical intervention.

A RATIONALE FOR SOCIAL NETWORK CLINICAL INTERVENTION

Although the clinical validity of social network interventions might seem self-evident, many observers tend to evaluate such clinical strategies in terms of individual psychotherapy, from which most clinical treatment theory has been generated. Therefore, we shall briefly discuss clinical theory in terms of social systems interventions.

Our approach is neither psychological nor sociological. Rather, we view human behavior as the *product* of an interaction between individual psychology and the social field. Hence we use the term *psychosocial* to label the *system of behavior.*

We define therapy as a healing intervention on behalf of a *specific individual* who has indefinable dysfunctional behavior. This may be internal behavior (thoughts, feelings) or external behavior (words, actions). There are other healing interventions in the history of medicine that are quite properly conducted on the behalf of people in general, such as water, fluoridation, vitamin enrichment of bread, public sanitation, and so on. Such general system interventions, without a specific individual target, might be termed medical care but not medical therapy.

In terms of mental health, we deem it important to distinguish levels of system intervention, some of which are therapy, others of which are care. Still other levels of system intervention that utilize mental health skills and knowledge are not properly subsumed under a sickness-health paradigm because different social sanctions and norms operate to regulate professional intervention. For example, organizational consultation is often provided by mental health consultants. The social sanction is not based on a "sick" organization that requires "healing." Rather, the mental health professional offers skills and knowledge from one professional arena that may be useful in another arena but under a nonmedical set of role norms.

There is a clear social sanction to define certain individual behavior as "sick" in terms of mental health parameters. There is also social sanction to "treat" the sick individual. In the development of current mental health concepts we have moved toward a more social view of human behavior. In so doing, we seek social sanction to define and treat a social unit comprised of more than one person.

We have gained social sanction to define and treat "sick" families as a social unit. At this point there is much conceptual confusion. On the one hand, critics maintain that only an individual can appropriately be defined as sick, and that a social unit cannot be labeled as sick. On the other hand, some family therapists assert that there are no sick individuals, only sick families; the individual psychopathology is defined as a reflection of the family. Thus if the family were well, the individual would be well.

We take neither position. The social purpose of defining a person of a social unit as sick is integral to the social sanction to treat that person or social unit. Thus we may label any social unit, family, neighborhood community, organization, city, or government as sick. But we do not have the social sanction to do so, nor do we have the social sanction for treatment intervention. We gain social sanction to define and treat to the extent we can demonstrate appropriate skills and knowledge that justify a social mandate to treat.

The professional mandate for treatment is rooted in the individual, for the farther we depart from the individual, the weaker the social mandate to define and intervene. Family therapy did not develop because of the discovery of sick families, but rather from the demonstration that the family was inextricably linked with the defined sick individual. We have demonstrated that intervention with the family produced healing in the individual. We have thus gained sanction to define the family social system as sick and engage in family treatment *as a system.*

Therefore, we can define an individual as sick, and we can define the family as sick. But we do not have a mandate to treat a sick family that has no identifiable sick individual. But let us go a step further. The *degree* of intimate relationship between the individual and a social network is critical to the extension of a treatment mandate. For example, grandparents and cousins of a sick individual may be closely linked to be properly involved in treatment. But if grandparents and cousins are not involved in the family life of the individual, they may properly disclaim involvement. The extreme end of this process is the sick worker in an office staff. Here, it would usually be difficult to link the social unit of office staff behavior to the genesis and maintenance of the individual sick behavior. Similarly, the office staff would probably disclaim involvement in the treatment of the individual. And surely it would be an impossible task to gain social sanction to define the office staff as sick and "treat" the office staff.

In this section, we are concerned with the extension of the social mandate to define and treat *social system units.* However, we wish to differentiate fully the professional mandate for treatment intervention. The inception of psycholotherapy at the turn of the century was based on the germ theory of illness. There was one person who had a germ that produced one syndrome of illness. Treatment was produced by the medical specialist who administered technical procedures on the patient. Thus psychotherapy, based on this model, was a technical procedure that one specialist performed upon one person. Psycho-therapeutic methods have moved from the one-to-one dyad of psychoanalysis to multiperson, multirelationship modes of psychotherapy contingent upon the effective interaction of a social system of people. It is apparent that a social system approach to therapy stands a distance from psychotherapy as defined by the one-to-one situation. More importantly, the attempt to "fit" social system therapy techniques within the conceptual domain of individual psychotherapy is not only unclear but inappropriate. Rather, we suggest that we need to devise a new conceptual model of psychotherapy for social system intervention, appro-priate to these techniques. We propose two models of psychotherapy: a "personal" model and a "system" model. We see these two models of psycho-therapy as complementary rather than competitive, for they have different treatment goals and methods.

Gardner Murphy has observed that from the time of Aristotle until late in the nineteenth century, psychology was the study of individual minds. Group interaction and interpersonal relations were problems for the historian, the moralist, the jurist, and the political economist. Psychotherapy was born in an intellectual era in which perhaps only a one-to-one model of psychotherapy could have been built. A social psychology of human relationships built on the work of William McDougall, Cooley, Durkheim, Giddings, Ross, Tonnies, and especially George Herbert Mead, began to stir an intellectual ferment that was to shake psychological thinking loose from its individualistic moorings.

In the 1920s social scientists began to study "natural groups" in society, based on the conviction that the solution to "social problems" could be facilitated by the study of social interaction and normal social groupings. This empirical research approach was translated into social-work practice with groups. But interestingly, the "social group work" method has remained defined as *not* psychotherapy. The empirical study of natural groups in the community also gave rise to social welfare and social action programs. Yet here also such intervention was not defined as psychotherapeutic. In both instances, because specific people were not identified as "sick," these types of intervention were not considered to have therapeutic potential.

Finally, in the 1930s, Kurt Lewin formulated his now famous "field theory." In brief, field theory posits that each individual exists in an interpersonal field of relationships. Each person exerts an influence on every other person in that field. But in addition, each person exists in a particular place in that field, with a cumulative effect on him from the juxtaposition of all around him. Lewin uses the term *valence* to symbolize the positive and negative tugs and pulls that impinge the magnetic forces upon the individual.

Lewin proposed that the behavior of the individual is the product of two forces. One is the internal psychological structure of the person; the other is field characteristics.

One can change behavior in two ways. First, we can intervene in the internal psychological structure of the individual. This is the traditional model of "personal" psychotherapy. The second method consists of intervention with the social field, such that the individual exists in a different field. This is the model of "system" therapy.

The early development of multiperson therapeutic situations may be seen as an application of general principles of Lewinian field theory. Other extensions of field theory are exemplified in small-group sociology, social psychology, and role theory. Persons operate in a social field, which to a significant extent determines behavior. Thus one can create a social field of therapeutic benefit to the emotionally disturbed person. Cody Marsh, a pioneer in group therapy methods, coined a succinct motto of this theory: "By the crowd they have been broken; by the crowd they shall be healed."

This concept of social field is an impersonal concept, however. The destructive or beneficient effects of the social field are not dependent on the particular personalities or relationships of the individuals who comprise the field; rather, it is the sociological structure of the field that determines its impact. Cody Marsh was thus quite correct when he used the word *crowd* in his aphorism.

When we shift the focus of clinical concern to families and persons linked together by their instrumental and affective relationships to each other, we observe a more complex and different sociodynamic. For here we have not only the effects of impersonal sociological group function, but also the effects of instrumental and affective linkages that exist between members.

Edward Jay (1964), an anthropologist, attempts to differentiate between the *impersonal social field* and the *personal psychosocial network*. He suggests that in a social field: "There is no hierarchy, no nucleated denser focus of relationship or center. The only center would be one unit from which we are looking outward in a given arbitrary distance. Every unit is in this sense a center. The units of the field may be individuals, families, communities, or other social aggregates, but the field as such does not constitute a 'group' with corporate qualities and cohesiveness." In contrast, Jay defines a network as the totality of all the units *connected by a certain type of relationship*. A network has definite boundaries.

The focus of study of such a psychosocial network, then, is on the nature and quality of these specific connecting relationships that set the particular pattern of the network. For example, a family is a social network characterized primarily by specific affective connections, whereas a factory work team is a social network characterized primarily by specific instrumental connections.

What we have observed over the past 30 years is a step-by-step recognition of the psychosocial network in which the patient is embedded; moving from parents and child to nuclear family, to extended family, and finally to a complex social network that may include nuclear family, various kin, friends who have "affective" links, and persons such as ministers and supervisors who have "instrumental" links.

The major conceptual shift relating to therapy, revolves around the focus of therapeutic intervention. In the one-to-one personal model, the assumption is made that psychotherapy will effect change in the individual that will enable him to behave differently in his social fields and social networks. In contrast, in the multiple-person system model, we assume that by tightening and loosening the affective and instrumental linkages which exist in the network, different options for behavior will be presented to the "patient," and consequently the patient will behave differently. Thus, the focus of psychotherapy in the system model is to change the interactional characteristics of the psychosocial network. This model explicitly assumes that human behavior is significantly determined by the characteristics of the social field or social network—hence the therapeutic emphasis lies here, rather than on changing the individual per se.

There are at least two major corollaries to this thesis. First, in the one-to-one, personal model, the definition of normality is essentially an *idealistic* one, that is, the mature genital character, whereas in the system model the definition of normality is an *adaptive* one, that is, capacity to operate effectively in the person's social field and network. Second, the personal model focuses on characterological change, whereas the system model focuses on behavioral change.

THE PERSONAL VERSUS SYSTEM MODEL

We now briefly outline some distinct differences between a personal and system model of psychotherapy. Our aim is to illustrate that the two models do not compete but rather are complementary models, for each is addressed to different psychotherapeutic goals.

The system model of psychotherapy is actually the oldest. It is the model of the shaman, the primitive healer, the folk healer. In primitive society if a member became "sick," it was matter for public concern, for a necessary worker was lost to the small society. Hence, it was in everyone's interest to make sure that the sick person was restored to function. There was little margin for functionless members of the community; everyone was needed to keep the small society functional. When a person became emotionally "ill," there was a generally accepted societal explanation for the cause of the illness. Further, everyone in the small society knew what healing procedures needed to be carried out. And everyone knew what the shaman would do in his healing rituals.

The goal of healing was to restore the ill person to his usual mode of operation and function in the social system. There was no questioning of the values or patterns of function of the social system. In other words, there was a value consensus between healer-patient-society. And there was a healing consensus between healer-patient-society. The healing procedures were a multiperson enterprise that involved healer-patient-society.

In contrast, the personal model of psychotherapy developed with quite a different rationale. The goal was not to help the patient return to function in his social system in the same manner. Rather, it was to help the patient to examine his social system, examine his pattern of function in his social system, and perhaps function in a different social system altogether.

Now the personal model could only come into existence in the face of several other social considerations. First, the person was not immediately required for the society to function, he or she could remain dysfunctional for extended periods of time. Second, the person had available to him a variety of value systems from which he could choose, that is, he did not live in a one-value society. And third, the person had available alternative social systems into which he or she could move.

In the system model, privacy is antitherapeutic, for it is public pressure, public response, and public support that enables the person to move rapidly back into his or her accustomed social function. In the personal model privacy is paramount, for it is privacy that enables a person to achieve distance from and perspective on his behavior within the social system. The privacy of the personal model allows the patient to explore alternatives without public pressure, without public response, and without public support.

Thus we can see that if our psychotherapeutic goal is rapid return of a "sick" person to accustomed social function, then we may choose the system model to capitalize on the "public" that comprises the patient's social system. This is psychosocial system therapy; it is a public therapy. The difference between the primitive shaman and the psychosocial-system-model therapist is that the therapist may aim at changing some characteristics of the social system, not merely use the social system as did the primitive shaman.

If our psychotherapeutic goal is change of personality with the concomitant development of capacity to choose among alternative social systems, then the personal model of psychotherapy in the traditional psychoanalytic sense becomes the model of choice.

The advantage of having two models of psychotherapy is that the psychotherapist may be freed from the attempt to make very different types of therapeutic interventions fit into a model that is inappropriate (hence experiencing conflict over a variety of technical, social, and ethical issues). Further, the psychotherapist clearly can take advantage of the strengths of either model, instead of combining one model to achieve the goals of the other model.

The differences between the two models are charted in Table 8.3 for comparative purposes.

Table 8.3.   Two Models of Psychotherapy

	Personal Model	System-Model
GPA:	To change personality structure	To reinforce adaptive personality structure
Patient relation to social system	May choose to change social systems	Seeks to return to social system
Therapist relation to social system	Is given social sanction to stand apart and question	Is given social sanction to help social system function better
Psychotherapy vis-à-vis the social system	Occurs at a distance	Occurs in an ongoing system
Privacy of psychotherapy	Of paramount importance	Antitherapeutic
Members of psychotherapy	Therapist and patient	Therapist and social system
Focus of psychotherapy	Individual patient (patient directly)	Total social system (patient directly)
Role of psychotherapist	To catalyze capacity of patient to develop self-direction	To catalyze capacity of social system to function more effectively
Definition of patient	Self-defined or deviant as defined by society	Secondary to definition of social system
Definition of therapist	Professionally defined role	Secondary to definition of responsible social system

CLINICAL ILLUSTRATIONS OF
SOCIAL NETWORK INTERVENTION STRATEGIES

In this final section, we provide clinical vignettes to illustrate in practical terms our theoretical and conceptual formulations. Several compilations have described a wide variety of clinical strategies (Erickson, 1975; Gottlieb, 1981; Mitchell & Trickett, 1980; Pattison, 1982; Mueller, 1980). We will not review all the wide variety of clinical innovations that might properly be termed social network interventions, but will give illustrations of the principles enunciated.

*Model A.   Changing the Functions of an Existent Social Network
(The Case of a Schizophrenic Girl)*

Jane, a 22-year-old Oriental single female who was living at home while attending college, was hospitalized with acute symptoms of a florid psychosis. Her symptoms included paranoid ideation, persecutory delusions and hallucinations, marked psychomotor agitation, flat affect, and cognitive and conative disorganization.

Jane was selected for social network intervention because the ward staff noted that whenever members of her family visited, her acute symptoms would dramatically diminish, only to reappear after the visits.

Jane completed the Pattison Psychosocial Inventory and named nine important people: Mother; Father; Sister #5, age 14, Sister #4, age 15; Sister #1, age 26; Brother-in-Law (husband of Sister #1); Favorite female cousin; best girlfriend at college; estranged boyfriend.

We then interviewed the parents to determine whether there were other persons with whom Jane had important relationships (keeping in mind the inclusion and exclusion phenomenon). They reported that the family had few social relations and few relatives in the United States. But they did add six more persons of potential significance: Sister #3, age 21 (a professional student living 300 miles away and omitted by Jane); Jane's former longtime boyfriend, who is a frequent visitor; Mother's older brother, Uncle #1; Mother's younger sister, Aunt #1; Husband of Aunt #1, who is Uncle #2, Neighbor, an older woman who lives next door.

A review of the family history revealed important characteristics of Jane's social network. Her family had immigrated to the United States from the Orient before the children were born. The father was a college graduate with a good civil service job. As an alien, he had remained socially aloof from his co-workers and had no neighborhood friends. The mother had not learned to speak English until the last five years. She therefore remained in the home almost exclusively. She had been taught English by the woman neighbor, who was the only neighborhood contact for the entire family.

In the past five years, the mother's older brother (Uncle #1) and younger sister with husband (Aunt #1 and Uncle #2) had also immigrated to the same city. These relatives afforded some social contact for the family, but lived several hours distant, thus reducing contact.

The mother expressd great reluctance in involving her relatives, because of the family shame of having a psychotic daughter. She actively resisted the relatives' involvement until the father asserted his willingness to comply. Significantly, Aunt #1 and Uncle #2 were the parents of Jane's favorite female cousin.

Both parents were reluctant to involve Sister #3, who had just entered graduate school and lived far away. Nevertheless they reluctantly agreed to fly Sister #3 to the city for a network collation. (We insisted on this because of the psychodynamic significance of absent family members, which is well described in the family therapy literature.) It is noteworthy that Jane, who is Sister #2, had omitted Sister #3 as an important person, which increased our attention to this excluded member.

The former boyfriend was included because he was the only consistent "outsider" who visited the family home, and was in fact a good friend to all of the five sisters and the parents. He had stopped dating Jane over a year ago, but remained a friend of the family.

In summary, we were presented with a psychosocial network that the psychotic patient described as having nine members—note the psychotic network size ranges from 8 to 12. Further examination of spurious membership revealed the *inclusion* of an estranged recent boyfriend, and the *exclusion* of a sister. The relative resources are intrinsically small—with interaction limited by distance. The family as a whole, as well as the patient, has almost no contact with significant others, except for one cousin, one girlfriend, one neighbor, and one former boyfriend. Thus the linkages of the social network are overexclusive. There are almost no linkages to the external world, and the patient lives in a tight interlocked matrix of relationships.

ORGANIZATION OF THE NETWORK COLLATION

The parents were charged with contacting and collating all of the network members for a 3-hour evening session. All the identified members arrived on time. The therapist (EMP) introduced all members to each other, and indeed did not even know who many of the members were. The purpose of the network collation was explained as an effort to assist the patient in her treatment.

Jane was then brought to the room. EMP repeated his previous explanation to Jane and to the network. Next, EMP asked Jane to sit beside him in the center of the room. Jane was asked to place each network member in a specific space around her that best represented the relationship between Jane and that member. This is a direct application of the technique of "family sculpting" (see Figure 8.4). This technique is useful because it symbolically represents each object relationship with ego, it pictorially graphs out the network constellation to all, and it

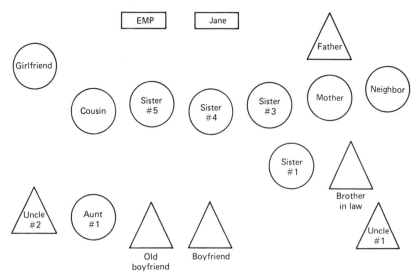

Figure 8.4.   Sculpted network collation.

organizes the network so that the therapist can readily identify each sector of the network.

Several observations can be made of the organization:

Jane places herself in alliance with Father.

Mother and all the female sibs are placed in opposition to Jane.

The excluded Sister #3 is placed in direct opposition to Jane.

The female cousin and female best friend are placed in alliance, alongside Sisters #4 and #5.

Estranged boyfriend and former boyfriend are placed in alliance,

Mother is placed in alliance with woman neighbor.

The three older relatives are placed at a distance from the rest of the network.

A final word must be said about therapeutic concept and method. Our approach is predicated on systems theory. We are operating on the assumption that major and significant dynamics are found in the operation of the system. The therapeutic strategy is aimed at changing the perceptions of roles and role behavior of the members of the system. This is akin to the "structural change" method of family therapy adapted to the larger social network (Pattison et al., 1975).

The role of the therapist in this large complex system may be likened to that of an orchestra conductor. The conductor arranges the players in sections (dynamic alliances revealed in the sculpting arrangement). Then the conductor asks the orchestra to play. When different sections play out of tune or different tunes, the conductor identifies the discrepancy, attempts to resolve it, and attempts to achieve congruent playing of the same tune by all sections.

To continue the analogy, if an individual player (patient) tries to play (behave), while different sections play different tunes (different role definitions and expectations), the player (patient) will be placed in conflict about which tune (behavior) to follow. The result is player (patient) decompensation.

The therapeutic task of the conductor (therapist) is to listen to each section of the orchestra, rather than to individual players. Each section will play a specific tune (dynamic theme). The identification of section tunes (alliance themes) allows for identification of tune (theme) discrepancy. Resolution of discrepancy makes it possible for the entire orchestra (social network) to play the same tune (role behavior). Consequently, the individual player (patient) now hears one tune (role expectation), and may respond by playing the same tune (behavior) that the entire orchestra is playing.

The next technical problem for the conductor (therapist) is to direct the orchestra (social network) to play a healthy tune (healthy role definition) instead of playing an unhealthy tune (psychotic role definition).

In the following transcript, the reader may note both discrepant role definitions, and healthy or unhealthy role definitions. As the network intervention progresses, we can identify the efforts toward discrepancy reduction and healthy role definition.

The Network Intervention

EMP: Come in, Jane

JANE: Oh no! What are you all doing here? (Cries) I love you all. This is too much. I love you. I love you. (Parents rise and run toward Jane.)

JANE: Stop! Go away! I hate you. I don't want you here.

EMP: (Asks parents to return to seats. Approaches Jane, asks her to take his hand and come with him to sit down.)

JANE: I will if they stay where they are. (Jane sits down with EMP.)

EMP: (Asks Jane to place all persons in sculpted arrangements. She does so.)

EMP: (Restates purpose for meeting. Thanks everyone for interest and concern expressed for Jane by coming to meeting.)

EMP: Now, Jane tell us what your problem is.

JANE: (Points to estranged boyfriend): He is the problem!

EMP: Why is he the problem?

JANE: He stopped going steady. He hates me.

EMP: (To estranged boyfriend): Is that so?

ESTRANGED BOYFRIEND: Yes. She became too jealous. She became suspicious of me if I even talked to another girl in class.

JANE: That's not true! You lie. I was not jealous. You just deserted me.

EMP: Can anyone else help us here?

OLD BOYFRIEND: Yes. That's the same reason I stopped dating Jane. She acted the same way with me. She was always jealous of other girls. I couldn't stand it.

JANE: You're both alike. I hate you both. You're bad. You both lie.

EMP: Can anyone else give us some information?

BEST GIRLFRIEND: I think it is terrible, the way both these boys treat her. Jane is sweet and wonderful. She isn't the jealous type. I've known her for 4 years now, and I can tell everybody what a wonderful person she is. She's not the bad one like these boys say.

FAVORITE COUSIN: That's right. I've known Jane for 6 years. We are really close. She is certainly not the jealous type. Why, she is just the opposite. She always says how much she loves her sisters and cares for them.

BROTHER-IN-LAW: Well, I don't know about them. From what I see, the boys are right on target. I think Jane is really competitive with her sisters. She sure acts jealous with her sisters.

JANE: No! No! I love my sisters, they love me! I'm not jealous of the...

SISTERS #4 and #5:   (Crying): That's right. We love you, Jane (They reach out and embrace Jane.)

SISTER #3:   Well, I don't! I hate Jane. I loathe her. I can't stand her. I hate you, Jane!

JANE: I hate you! You never were any good. I'm better than you. I'm prettier than you. I hate you.

EMP: (Constrains Jane and Sister #3 from attempting to hit each other): Wait a minute. Sisters #4 and #5 say they love Jane and are not competitive. But Sister #3 is just the opposite?

SISTER #1:   That's not quite right: Jane is jealous and competitive. She's been that way all the time. But it's been worse with Sister #3. In fact, they haven't talked to each other for 5 years.

EMP: Is that correct?

SISTER #3:   Yes. I hate her. I haven't said a word to her for 5 years.

JANE: Yes. I hate her. She's the cause of all my problems.

EMP: You mean your boyfriends are not the problem?

JANE: No! Sister #3 is my problem. I hate her. She hates me. I want to kill her. Then I'll be okay.

EMP: Well, now, can anyone tell how this problem came about with Jane and Sister #3.

MOTHER: I don't know. But they were born 9 months apart. They were like twins. I dressed them the same and made them twins. They always fought. They always tried to outdo each other. Jane became the pretty one. She got all the boys. Sister #3 was the brainy one. She got the grades. I think Jane is jealous because Jane flunked college, and Sister #3 was admitted to graduate school.

SISTER #1:   Yes, that's true. They were always competitive. I think Jane tried to hold on to her boyfriends to prove that she was better than Sister #3.

BROTHER-IN-LAW: Yes. I sure believe that from what I've seen.

BOYFRIENDS: Us too! Boy oh boy, are we relieved—it's not us!

EMP: Well, let's review here: We all seem to agree that the boyfriends are not the source of the problem. Yes? (All nod.) But there does seem to be disagreement about Jane acting jealous and competitive. Cousin, Best friend, and Sisters #4 and #5 all agree with Jane. Sisters #1 and #3 and Brother-in-Law along with boyfriends, see Jane the opposite. How can we resolve this? Who can give us some more information?

MOTHER: Well, the girls sure fought a lot.

EMP: Explain.

MOTHER: Well, first it was just Jane and Sister #3. Then it got gradually worse. Jane started to fight with all of them.

EMP: Is this true?

SISTERS #4 and #5:   Yes. She fought with us. She hit us. We hate her!

JANE: I hate you. You're all alike. I hate you all.

EMP: Jane, you hate all your sisters?

JANE: Yes.

EMP: Why?

JANE: They hate me first. They don't like me. They avoid me. They don't want to have anything to do with me.

EMP: Is this true?

SISTER #1:   Yes, it's true. I hate to admit it. It's true. Jane was always nosy, so snoopy. So competitive. We couldn't stand her. We wouldn't let her play with us.

EMP: So the truth is that you four sisters did hate Jane, did keep secrets from her, did exclude her? (All four nod guiltily.) How come this kept going on in the family? Why didn't somebody change this bad pattern?

MOTHER: I tried. I tried. But I can't.

EMP: What did you try?

MOTHER: I saw Jane attack her sisters and they'd fight back. I tried to interfere. But Jane would attack me. She'd hit me, and bite me, and scratch me. I was afraid of Jane.

JANE: You better be. I hate you, Momma. You love them. You don't love me.

MOTHER: (Cries): Jane, Jane, how can you hate me? I love you.

JANE: No you don't. And I don't love you. Daddy, Daddy, I love you, you're the only one who loves me. (Jane turns to her father, and they mutually embrace in tears.)

FATHER: There, there. Of course, I love you. Don't cry.

EMP: Let's see what's happening here. Father, do you always comfort Jane?

MOTHER: Sure he does. He's the only one who can handle her. You see, this is what always happens. I just can't handle the girls. It gets so bad when the girls fight that I have to call him to come home from the office to straighten things out.

EMP: Father, do you do that?

FATHER: Yes. Reluctantly. I don't see why she can't handle the girls. I have to make up all sorts of excuses to leave the office in the middle of the day. I think a mother should be able to handle her own daughters.

EMP: Do you all agree that mother should be able to handle her daughters?

UNCLE #1:   Of course. But I think it is a shame that Mother is left alone.

NEIGHBOR WOMAN: She is alone. She had no one to talk to. She couldn't even speak English. I taught her. I'm her only friend. I try to make her feel better. But she's treated so badly.

UNCLE #1:   Well, this is really bad news. I didn't know this was going on. My sister shouldn't be treated like this. Things have got to change. Father, you have to stop this!

AUNT #1:   This is surely shameful. We should have known about this. We wouldn't have let this go on. (To Jane.) You are indeed bad! You have no right to attack your mother. You should not hate your mother. You should love your sisters. You must change!

UNCLE #2:   That's right. Jane, you must respect your mother. You should not run to your father. I expect my daughter (Cousin) to respect her mother. You are my niece. You should act respectfully to your mother. Running to your father is no excuse.

UNCLE #1:   Right. Running to the father is not an excuse in a good Oriental family.

COUSIN: I guess that's right. I never saw this side of Jane. I always saw the sweet, concerned Jane. But, Jane, you must learn to love your mother and sisters.

JANE: No, no. I hate them. They hate me. (Cries—turns to embrace Father again.)

EMP: Well, Father—can you help Jane here? She wants to love Mother, but can't bring her love and hate together.

FATHER: I don't know—what do I do?

EMP: You can't allow Jane to see you as all good and Mother as all bad.

FATHER: Well, that's true. I'm not all good and Mother's not all bad. Jane, that's true. You shouldn't hold onto me.

JANE: I hate you! You don't love me. You're just like Mother. I hate you both. I want to get out of here. (Jane jumps up to run.)

EMP: (Restrains Jane gently by the hand): Wait, Jane. You don't have to run. Everyone is here because they do love you, even if they get very angry with you at times. You, too, can love them and still be angry with them. Is that right? (All members of network nod approval.) (Ensuing are statements by members that you can love someone and also be angry.) (Jane starts to cry in heavy sobs.)

MOTHER: I love you, Jane, and I want you to love me. (They cry and embrace.)

SISTER #5:   I love you, Jane, and I want you to love me. (They cry and embrace.)

SISTER #4:   I love you, Jane, and I want you to love me. (They cry and embrace.)

SISTER #1:   I love you, Jane, and I want you to love me. (They cry and embrace.) (Suddenly there is a tension: Jane and Sister #3 face each other.)

SISTER #3:   It's been 5 years. I want it to stop. I want to start over. Forgive me. It's been half my fault. I do love you, even if we have fought all our lives. (Sister #3 approaches Jane with arms open.)

JANE: I love you. Forgive me. I love you.

(Jane and Sister #3 stand locked in a crying embrace. Everyone in the room cries.) (Jane sits down. Everyone quiets down.)

JANE: I hate you. I hate you all. I don't trust any of you. (She tries to jump up to leave. EMP again gently restrains.)

EMP: It's all right. This is a new experience for you. Everyone is getting the story straight. Everyone has to learn to tell the truth now. You can feel love and hate together, just as they do.

JANE: No, I can't.

EMP: Yes, your family friends here can help you now.

JANE: I hate them. They hate me.

EMP: Well, let's see if that's true. Is that true?

FATHER: Well, I love Jane. But she frightens me when she says that she hates me. I just want her to love me.

EMP: Hate and love go together. You have to learn not to be frightened by Jane's hate. Now don't act frightened. Respond to Jane—now.

FATHER: Okay, Jane, you frighten me. But I can live with that, I guess.

MOTHER: Me, too. If you have to, feel hatred, but don't forget the love.

(Ensuing members reiterate the theme of integrating love and hate.) (Jane listens and then proceeds to tell everyone how hard it is to both love and hate them at the same time.)

EMP: (Concludes session with negotiation with different members for specific tasks including: (1) Relatives to visit mother frequently and decrease isolation; (2) Family members to take turns visiting Jane in hospital; (3) Sister #3 to write regularly to Jane; (4) Girlfriend and Cousin to remind Jane of lessons learned here; (5) Father to stop playing refuge for Jane; (6) Sisters to support mother in her role as maternal authority; (7) Mother to practice her new role of self-responsibility.)

Subsequent follow-up revealed that family members visited regularly with Jane, and adhered to the above negotiations to a substantial degree. The family reported great satisfaction with the network intervention. Some four months later, Jane was asymptomatic.

The apparently positive resolution of symptoms, however, is not the point of this report, because Jane also received medication and individual therapy. The network intervention may have contributed to the therapeutic process, but that can only be an inference. Rather, we wish to use this transcript to highlight the dynamics of the social change network process, both in retrospect and in the process of change.

Analysis of the Network

The initial sculpting arrangement provides clues to the dynamic alliances that unfold in the network operation. However, it does not indicate what the content of the alliance themes will be.

The patient externalizes her network conflict onto a relatively neutral and external member (estranged boyfriend). The network accepts this externalization before the session.

The attempt to maintain the externalization and the image that Jane is good is attacked by the two-boyfriend alliance. They cannot initially overcome the network acceptance of externalization to protect the network status quo. Jane is reinforced in her externalization and good-bad object splitting by the Cousin-Girlfriend alliance in coalition with the Sister #4 and #5 alliance.

The therapist identifies the discrepancy. A marginal network member (Brother-in-Law) serves as a catalyst to "reframe" the issue, not in terms of boyfriend relationships, but in terms of sister relationships. This allows Sister #1 to clarify the conflict, which can then be consensually validated by the sisters and the mother. At the same time, the behavior of the sisters reveals the exclusionary behavior that serves as the reality core for the paranoid elaboration by Jane. Further, the more primitive level of competition for maternal love is revealed in mother's rearing of the "twins." This fundamental competition is acted out ultimately in the mutual five-year estrangement.

Thus, we see that the intimate family dynamics are quickly revealed and explicate the dynamic sources of the paranoid symptomatology. The inability of Jane to resolve good-bad object splitting is related to the network operations. The sisters deny their collusion and reinforce denial. Meanwhile, two different network alliances split in their perception and definition of Jane as either all good or all bad. To the boyfriends, Jane is an all-bad object. To her cousin and girlfriend, Jane is an all-good object. The network alliances perpetuate and reinforce the good-bad splitting with Jane. Jane cannot resolve her denial and splitting processes because, in part, the network is maintaining them.

There is a similar good-bad splitting between mother and father used by Jane. The parents are so socially isolated with few relatives, and no friends or neighbors. Thus, there are no external reality inputs to influence parents' roles, and the parents reciprocally reinforce the good-bad splitting by Jane.

Mother is supported only by the neighbor woman, who does not have enough potency and reinforcement by others to strengthen mother's role function. Both mother and father protect the status quo—avoiding potential familial shame and guilt—by keeping the few relatives at a distance.

In sum, we have a small closed social network, relatively devoid of modifying external connections. The dynamics of network operation provide a pathogenic source of interpersonal relations, and further serve to reinforce pathological dynamics of operation.

The intervention with the network reveals the externalization defense. Clarification of the nidus of conflict makes it impossible for the network to maintain secrets, collusion, denial, or discrepancy. An alternative healthy resolution of basic object splitting and ambivalence is presented, and actually experienced and practiced in reality. Dysfunctional role behavior is identified, and alternative role definitions are offered. The members practice interaction in the new roles. Contracts are explicitly negotiated to reinforce the new role allocations and to "open" the network to broader member interaction. As a result, the patient is now confronted with not only a redefined role for herself, but a set of modified roles for other network members. Further, some steps have been taken to identify common new themes of network response to the patient, which are not only consistent throughout the network, but also consist of a set of more healthy and reparative social responses to the patient.

Model B.   Coordinating and Augmenting Existing Potential Social Network (The Case of a Suicidal Girl)

On December 17, the University Hospital psychiatric consultation service received a consultation request from the orthopedic ward regarding an 18-year-old single white girl who was being treated for multiple injuries sustained in a motorcycle accident. The previous evening the patient was found to be overly drowsy, slow to respond to conversation, with slurred speech. She had taken an overdose of sleeping medications, which she had been accumulating surreptitiously. When questioned, she said, "It didn't matter, I don't want to live. Don't bother me. I want to join my boyfriend, my husband to be."

In the past several years, the patient had been attracted to the hippie movement and had adopted a "drop-out" attitude toward life and her family. She had been dating a 20-year-old man who had similar interests. The girl's parents did not approve of the relationship and openly expressed their dislike of the boyfriend. The couple left for Wyoming against the wishes of both sets of parents. On October 7, while riding a motorcycle together, they were involved in a head-on collision. The boyfriend was killed instantly, whereas the patient sustained serious injuries. A large body-encasing cast was placed on her for orthopedic injuries.

At the University Hospital she was polite but distant to her parents, as well as to the nursing staff. The one relationship that seemed meaningful to her was that with the orthopedic resident in charge of her case. On the evening of December 16, this resident had made arrangements to change the traction on her leg. She stayed away from a ward Christmas party to await him. However, on the way to the hospital the doctor himself had an accident. The patient was informed of this accident in somewhat ambiguous terms, because the extent of his injuries was not known. The patient showed no demonstrable reaction to this event. But one hour later she was found in the depressed suicidal state described. (In retrospect, the accident of the physician reactivated the same reaction as the death of her boyfriend, the physician having been ascribed a transference-determined role; that is, they had a relationship that existed in opposition to the rest of the world.)

The ward staff found the girl increasingly uncooperative the next morning, and during the day the medical staff and nursing staff became increasingly angry with each other for failing to establish rapport with the girl. A psychiatric consult was requested. The psychiatric resident interviewed the girl, but she refused to talk to him and told him to leave her alone. He wrote a dejected consultation note, telling the orthopedic staff that he could be of little use to them because the patient would not talk to a psychiatrist. The girl became more lethargic. The staff thought she was surreptitiously taking more pills, which they assumed were being brought in by her hippie friends. She was placed in an isolation room and forbidden visitors. Her mental condition seemed to deteriorate.

I interviewed the girl late on the second day after her suicide attempt. She was resolutely negativisitic toward anyone she perceived as part of the establishment or who represented any type of authority. I did find out that she liked to talk with the Presbyterian minister from her family's church, and that she was angry at not being able to visit with her hippie friends, several of whom also had a social relationship with the same Presbyterian church.

At this point I elected to explore the characteristics of the social network of this girl both within the hospital and outside it. A plan was worked out with the psychiatric resident to systematically interview all persons we could determine who had some current relationship with the girl.

First, we found that both the medical staff and nursing staff had given up on any attempt to establish a working relationship with the girl. Each staff blamed the girl for creating a problem with the other staff. Thus we found that the girl was being made the scapegoat for interstaff conflict.

Second, we found that her parents and the dead boyfriend's parents were both trying to visit her, but were avoiding each other in the hospital. Each set of parents blamed the other for the fate of their child. However, each set of parents also blamed the girl for her current behavior, which they asserted made it impossible to talk to the other set of parents. Thus the girl was the scapegoat for the interfamily conflict.

Third, we found that the Presbyterian minister was interested in talking with the girl, as were her hippie friends whom he knew. In view of the suicidal attempt, however, neither the minister nor the hippies felt that they should interfere with staff or parents. Further, they were fearful that if they visited the girl, they might somehow precipitate further depression and another suicide attempt.

Fourth, we found that the medical staff and nursing staff had no communication with either set of parents, the minister or the hippies. Both the hospital staff and the kin and friends were reluctant to approach each other. The staff viewed the family and friends with suspicion, as possibly contributing to the girl's depression, whereas the family and friends felt the hospital staff was being hostile to them and did not care about the welfare of the girl.

With the information at hand regarding the scapegoating and blockades in the social network, we decided to inform the girl that we would not conduct any psychiatric treatment with her, but that the psychiatric resident would be visiting with her family, friends, and staff to work out a hospital program for her. Thus the social network of the patient, which consisted of multiple blockades in a dysfunctional network, was defined as the focus of therapeutic intervention.

First, a meeting was arranged with the minister at his church, which included all of the hippie friends that had visited the girl. The girl's problem was thoroughly discussed with this group, and they agreed to a program of daily visitation with the girl. Second, several meetings were arranged with the medical and nursing staff, together and separately, to outline the problems that had been uncovered in her social system. The issues of interstaff conflict were aired and discussed. Concrete plans for specific nursing care were devised and reviewed daily with both the medical and nursing staff. Further, meetings were held between the two sets of parents and the medical and nursing staff to discuss and determine the management of the patient. Specific roles for the behavior of the parents were established.

Subsequent meetings between the parents and hospital staff were held to maintain the agreed-upon role contracts. The hospital staff also met with the minister and the hippie friends, and their roles were defined and agreed upon by both groups. Third, meetings were held with each set of parents and with both sets of parents together. Their mutual hostilities and projections were explored and resolved in several joint sessions. Their mutual roles in visiting with the girl were outlined and agreed upon. Subsequent meetings were held with the parents to reaffirm and sustain their roles with each other and with the girl.

All of these network contacts were made within several days. Within the first week the girl became brighter, more communicative, and less depressed. She became demanding and engaged in very active, albeit hostile, interactions with many people. Her clinical depression cleared rapidly, and she was able to go home on a weekend pass (the weekend was uneventful). A subsequent surgery and hospital stay in February was also uneventful, and the patient was considered by the hospital staff to be a "good" patient during her second hospitalization. Subsequent follow-up revealed a satisfactory convalescence and no recurrence of her clinical depression.

Model C.   Development of New Linkages to Re-Create a Social Network (The Case of the Alcoholic Woman)

A 50-year-old woman called the alcoholism clinic asking for help. She stated that she was so intoxicated from a drinking binge that she could not take care of herself and that she was suicidal. Two clinic staff persons drove out to the woman's house, which was located 20 miles away in an isolated canyon. The woman was found to be living alone. She was both isolated and lonely. Her recurrent depressive moods led to alcoholic binges, which in turn reinforced her guilt and depression. She had no friends or relatives. She was not currently working. There were four neighboring homes; however, the woman stated that although she knew the neighbors casually, she had never wished to impose on them. She felt both guilty and ashamed of her condition and tried to hide from her neighbors.

After this situation was discussed, and permission was granted by the woman, the two staff members went to call on the four different neighbors. In this particular circumstance the women all knew each other and had casual friendly relations. They all expressed concern for the alcoholic woman who was their new neighbor. However, they had not wished to impose themselves because of her apparent desire for isolation and lack of interest in making friends with the neighbors.

The four neighbor women were invited to the home of the alcoholic woman, and a group discussion was held for the rest of the afternoon. The neighbor women were eager to volunteer their help. They each volunteered to provide for cooking and home care until the alcoholic woman was able to care for herself. They arranged a schedule of daily visits in rotation.

The clinic staff returned every week to meet with the entire group, while also maintaining daily telephone contact with both the alcoholic woman and the four neighbors. After several weeks of intimate involvement, the woman was able to resume the management of her own home. She entered therapy in the alcoholism clinic and obtained a job. She has continued to maintain a close relationship with the four neighbor women who assisted her through her crisis.

SUMMARY

In this chapter we have described the social network paradigm as a conceptual and methodological approach to *mezzo* social system analysis. Social network connections link the individual to the larger community social structure and function. The social network can promote mental health or produce mental illness. Our models of social network analysis provide a powerful tool to examine possible social network parameters of psychiatric disorders, and an explicit rationale for the development of clinical interventions.

REFERENCES

Blackman, S., & Goldstein, K. (1976) Reciprocity networks in the community and manifest psychological symptomatology. Paper presented at 39th annual meeting, Eastern Psychological Association.

Boissevain, J. (1974) *Friends of friends, networks, manipulators and coalitions.* New York: St. Martin's Press.

Boissevain, J., & Mitchell, J.C. (1973) *Network analysis: Studies in human interaction.* The Hague: Mouton.

Boszormenyi-Nagy, I., & Spark G. (1975) *Invisible loyalties.* New York: Harper & Row.

Brown, G.W., Bhrolchain, M.W., & Harris, T.O. (1975) Social class and psychiatric disturbance among women in an urban population. *Sociology,* **9**, 51–58.

Callan, D., Garrison, J., & Zerger, F. (1975) Working with the families and social networks of drug abusers. *Journal of Psychedelic Drugs,* **7**, 119–125.

Caplan, G., & Lillilea, M. (1976) *Support systems and mutual help.* New York: Grune & Stratton.

Cobb, S. (1976) Social support as a moderator of life stress. *Psychosomatic Medicine,* **37**, 300–314.

Dean, A., & Lin, N. (1977) The stress-buffering role of social support. *Journal of Nervous Mental Diseases,* **165**, 403–417.

Eaton, W. (1978) Life events, social supports, and psychiatric symptomatology: A reanalysis of the New Haven Data. *Journal of Health and Social Behavior,* **19**, 230–234.

Erickson, G.E. (1975) The concept of personal network in clinical practice. *Family Process,* **14**, 487–498.

Garrison, J.E. (1974) Network techniques: Case studies in the screening-linking-planning conference method. *Family Process,* **13**, 337–351.

Gottlieb, B.H. (Ed.) (1981) *Social networks and social support.* Beverly Hills: Sage Publications.

Granovetter, M. (1973) The strengths of weak ties. *American Journal of Sociology*, **78**, 1360–1380.

Jay, E.J. (1964) The concepts of "field" and "network" in anthropological research. *Man*, **64**, 137–139.

Kaufman, E., & Kaufman, B. (1979) *Family therapy of alcohol and drug abusers*. New York: Gardner Press.

Kleiner, R.J., & Parker, S. (1974) Network participation and psychosocial impairment in an urban environment. Research report, NIMH Grant #19897.

Leinhardt, S. (1977) *Social networks: A developing paradigm*. New York: Academic Press.

Llamas, R., Pattison, E.M., & Hurd, G.S. (1981) Social networks: A link between psychiatric epidemiology and community mental health. *International Journal of Family Therapy*, **3**, 180–193.

Mechanic, D., & Greeley, J.R. (1976) The prevalence of psychological distress and help-seeking in a college student population. *Social Psychiatry*, **11**, 1–14.

Miller, P.M., & Ingham, J.G. (1976a) Friends, confidants, and symptoms. *Social Psychiatry*, **11**, 51–58.

Miller, P.M., Ingham, J.G., & Davidson, S. (1976b) Life events, symptoms, and social support. *Journal of Psychosomatic Research*, **20**, 515–522.

Mitchell, J.C. (Ed.) (1969) *Social networks in urban situations*. Manchester: Manchester University Press.

Mitchell, R.E., & Trickett, E.J. (1980) Task force report: Social networks as mediators of social support. *Community Mental Health Journal*, **15**, 27–44.

Mueller, D.P. (1980) Social networks: A promising direction for research on the relationship of the social environment to psychiatric disorder. *Social Science in Medicine*, **14**, 147–161.

Myers, J.K., Lundenthal, J.J., & Pepper, M.P. (1972) Life events and mental status: A longitudinal study. *Journal of Health and Social Behavior*, **13**, 398–406.

Myers, J.K., Lundenthal, J.J., & Pepper, M.P. (1975) Life events, social integration and psychiatric symptomatology. *Journal of Health and Social Behavior*, **16**, 421–427.

Pattison, E.M. (1973) Social system psychotherapy. *American Journal of Psychotherapy*, **17**, 396–409.

Pattison, E.M. (1976) Psychosocial systems therapy. In R.G. Herschowitz, & B. Levy (Eds.), *The changing mental health scene*. New York: Spectrum.

Pattison, E.M. (1977) A theoretical-empirical base for social systems therapy. In E. Foulks (Ed.), *Current perspectives in cultural psychiatry*. New York: Spectrum.

Pattison, E.M. (Ed.) (1982) *Clinical applications of social network theory*. New York: Human Sciences Press.

Pattison, E.M., DeFrancisco, D., Frazier, H., Wood, P.E., & Crowder, J. (1975) A psychosocial kinship model for family therapy. *American Journal of Psychiatry*, **132**, 1246–1251.

Post, F. (1962) The social orbit of psychiatric patients. *Journal of Mental Science*, **109**, 759–771.

Ratcliffe, W.D., & Azim, H. (1975) Social networks of psychiatric patients and normals. Paper presented at Canadian Psychiatric Conference.

Reuveni, U. (1979) The family therapist as a systems interventionist. *International Journal of Family Therapy*, **1**, 63–75.

Silberfield, M. (1978) Psychological symptoms and social supports. *Social Psychiatry*, **13**, 11–17.

Speck, R.V., & Attneave, C.C. (1973) *Family networks*. New York: Vintage Press.

Tolsdorf, C.C. (1976) Social networks, support, and coping: An exploratory study. *Family Process*, **15**, 407–417.

Wellman, B., & Leighton, B. (1979) Networks, neighborhoods and communities. *Urban Affairs Quarterly*, **15**, 363–390.

Whitten, N.E., & Wolfe, A.W. (1974) Network analysis. In *The handbook of social and cultural anthropology*. Chicago: Rand-McNally.

PART THREE

Ecological Models: Applications at the Community System Level

The delay in implementing and applying ecosystemic concepts in the area of clinical and community practice can be readily understood by considering the problems encountered in selecting and in writing chapters for this part of the volume. Although we are familiar with the presentation of individuals and families in the clinical setting and with preventive efforts aimed at the incidence of individual problems or of family problems, it becomes difficult to rethink these issues from the perspective of larger and more complex systems.

Clinical settings that deal with populations at the lower end of the socioeconomic scale have clearly illustrated the dilemma presented to clinicians. The clinician is trained to treat pathology. But the individual may be discharged "free" of pathology and still return to inflate readmissions rates, simply because there is nowhere else to go. The person who is "cured" but unable to compete in the community confronts the clinician with a simple fact of life: The absence of psychopathology is relevant only to tertiary prevention. Mental health is in the hands of the community, not the therapist.

When extended to more contemporary issues of clinical practice and preventive mental health, the difficulties are equally clear. For the majority of the population, traditional psychopathology is not relevant. We struggle as a contemporary society with powerful influences on the quality of life: with the stress of work settings, of fragmented and reorganized personal and family relationships, with the complexities of urban and technological systems, and with the impact of community environments on the daily life of the individual.

Cronkite, Moos, and Finney have approached the context of adaptation by providing a perspective on community and treatment environments. The chapter illustrates a cutting edge in contemporary behavioral research and professional practice; the vague concept of "milieu" has been slowly and painfully extended and specified so that only recently can we directly confront the evaluation of environments in a way that is relevant to both the delivery of mental health services and the organization of community life.

Bechtel has again confronted the cutting edge by tying the body of ecological research and the theoretical perspectives of ecological psychology to the individual. The interactions or "bond" between individual and community have been known to exist, but the precision and scope of ecological psychology allow that bond to be explored and evaluated in specific ways.

Marsella presents yet a different perspective on the relationship between the individual and community, organizing the known research and theory on stress and coping and utilizing the theoretical perspectives of modern interactionism to approach psychopathology specifically at the population level. Again, although molar community and social process has been known to impact the incidence of specific disturbances of mental health, it is only recently that these data can be used in a systematic fashion and in the context of a model applicable to the practitioner.

The final chapter in this part by Goodhart and Zautra addresses most directly the central issue that emerges from the organization of this section: the quality of life of each individual. The volume of research on quality of life is massive, and thus presents a formidable task to the authors. The application of this substantive area to the level of practice and intervention has implications beyond the specific quality-of-life area; the current state of the art of professional and community practice makes a new set of demands on the professional. Only a decade ago, a few specific theoretical models and a few limited techniques were a sufficient basis for professional practice. But the current state of the art demands a breadth of knowledge and complexity of potential assessment and intervention techniques that may largely redefine professional practice over the next decade. It is rare at this time for the clinician or practitioner in either a private practice or organizational setting to apply directly such substantive bodies of knowledge as quality-of-life research; Goodhart and Zautra illustrate the possibility of such an application, and in the process suggest a new level of responsibility for the practitioner.

CHAPTER 9

The Context of Adaptation:
An Integrative Perspective on Community
and Treatment Environments

RUTH C. CRONKITE, RUDOLF H. MOOS, AND JOHN W. FINNEY

Over the past few years we have conducted an extensive research program to examine the environmental factors that influence health and well-being among patient and community groups. Our studies, and those of other investigators, have shown that the characteristics of the settings in which people function and the personal and coping resources they employ are related to individual and family adaptation. In this chapter, we take stock of some of the conceptual insights and empirical findings that have accrued from this work. More specifically, we present a conceptual framework to integrate the major sets of factors that lead to variations in adaptation, describe underlying patterns of social environments and procedures for assessing them, and examine the influence of the social environments of psychiatric treatment programs and of families and work settings on individual functioning. We then discuss the practical implications of the foregoing material for formulating and evaluating individually and environmentally focused interventions.

AN INTEGRATED CONCEPTUAL FRAMEWORK

The conceptual framework shown in Figure 9.1 provides a synthesis of the major sets of factors that influence stability and change in individual and group functioning. The model illustrates a social-ecological perspective on person-environment transactions and on the consequences of those transactions for adaptation. This type of perspective is becoming prominent in developmental psychology (Bronfenbrenner, 1979), gerontology (Lawton & Nahemow, 1973),

Preparation of the chapter was supported by Veterans Administration Medical Research funds, by NIAAA Grant AA-2863 and by NIMH Grant MH16744. We wish to thank Dani Lawler for her valuable help in preparing the manuscript.

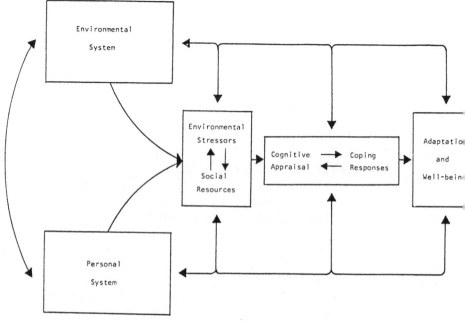

Figure 9.1.   A social-ecological model of human adaptation.

health psychology and behavioral medicine (Moos, 1979a), and clinical and community psychology (Heller & Monahan, 1977). We call this framework social-ecological to emphasize the inclusion of social-environmental (e.g., social climate) and physical-environmental (i.e., ecological) variables (see Moos, 1976; Ch. 1).

In our conceptual framework each set of variables influences every other set. For example, the model specifies the existence of two systems—the personal and environmental—each of which helps to shape the other. That is, some of the characteristics of environments reflect the personal resources of the individual functioning in them, whereas individual qualities (such as personality traits, attitudes and expectations, and personal resources) are affected by the environmental context. The personal and environmental systems combine to influence physical and psychological adaptation both directly and indirectly via mediating factors.

Although research on social resources has proceeded independently of that on stressors, we believe that these two sets of factors need to be considered together. Accordingly, the first set of intervening factors is composed of stressful life circumstances and social resources. Stressful life circumstances have been consistently related to symptoms of physical and psychological disturbance (Rabkin & Streuning, 1976), whereas persons with better social resources have been found to function more adequately, in part because social resources foster "protective" processes that help individuals to resist the effects of potentially harmful environmental conditions (see Cobb, 1976; Moos & Mitchell, 1982). As the model indicates, personal and environmental factors are important determinants both of stressful life circumstances (an impulsive individual has high propensity to experience life stressors; crowded housing conditions can lead to stressful personal relationships) and social resources (a person with low self-esteem may be less able to create a supportive social network; the press of work in a job setting may hamper the development of positive relationships among co-workers).

The next step in the framework involves cognitive appraisal and coping responses. Although the environmental and personal systems, as well as stressful life circumstances and social resources, can affect adaptation directly, cognitive appraisal and coping responses usually are essential mediating factors (Lazarus, 1980). Appraisal processes involve the perception and interpretation of environmental stimuli. These processes must be considered in order to understand the selection of coping responses and the potential impact of environmental circumstances on individual functioning. Not only is the use of coping responses determined in part by personal and environmental factors, but coping efforts may also change the environmental system (increasing the level of order and organization in the family), the personal system (seeking and obtaining information that may change expectations), or stressful circumstances and social resources (switching to a job with less pressure, actively increasing involvement in social groups).

This framework is presented as a heuristic aid to the reader in integrating the material to follow. It should be noted that the fully nonrecursive nature (i.e., bidirectional paths) of the model precludes estimating causal effects with statistical techniques; it does, however, reflect the complexity of the phenomena with which we are dealing. Our own research has explored some of the linkages among stressors, social resources, coping responses, and individual functioning (Moos, in press; Moos & Moos, 1983), and has focused on the relationship between variables in the environmental system (mainly social climate factors) and adaptation. In this chapter, we review some of that work. Given the community-clinical thrust of this volume, we emphasize research on psychiatric treatment programs and on the family and work settings in which people are located during and after treatment. We then describe how one might intervene in these settings to facilitate individual and system adaptation.

THE ENVIRONMENTAL SYSTEM

Environmental variables can be conveniently conceptualized in terms of four major domains (Moos, 1976): (1) social climate factors, (2) physical and architectural factors, (3) organizational factors (policies and procedures), and (4) suprapersonal characteristics (i.e., the aggregate characteristics of the individuals functioning in a setting). Each of these domains can influence health and adaptation directly, as well as indirectly via the other sets of factors specified in the framework. Although all four of the environmental domains can mutually affect one another, we view the social climate as the key mechanism by which the influence of the other domains is transmitted. That is, we believe that the impact of architectural, organizational, and suprapersonal factors is channeled primarily through the type of social climate they help to create.

Accordingly, much of our work has involved the development of a set of Social Climate Scales to assess the social environments of 10 different types of settings (Moos, 1974a; Moos & Lemke, 1982). Three of these are treatment-oriented settings (hospital-based and community-based psychiatric programs and community care facilities for older people), three are primarily settings in which most people function (families, work settings, and social and task-oriented groups), two are educational settings (student living groups and high school classes), and two are total institutions (correctional institutions and military basic training companies).

The dimensions (subscales) of these scales have been derived from a combination of conceptual classification and empirical analysis of data obtained from respondents in the relevant setting. These vastly different settings can be described by three similar sets of dimensions: relationship dimensions, personal growth or goal orientation dimensions, and system maintenance and change dimensions. The specific dimensions included in the relationship and system maintenance and change domains are similar in most settings, although some environments impose unique variations. The goal orientation dimensions measure the underlying aims toward which the environment is directed and consequently vary somewhat more from setting to setting. We provide examples here of the dimensions assessed in hospital-based (Ward Atmosphere Scale; WAS) and community-based (Community-Oriented Programs Environment Scale; COPES) psychiatric treatment programs, and of those measured by family (Family Environment Scale; FES) and work (Work Environment Scale; WES) settings (see Moos, 1974a).

Relationship dimensions assess the extent to which people are involved in the environment, the degree to which they support and help one another, and the extent to which they express themselves freely and openly (see Table 9.1 for examples). Each setting has an involvement or cohesion dimension. Involvement in a treatment setting reflects how active and energetic patients are in the day-to-day functioning of the program, for example, their pride in the program, feelings of group spirit, and general enthusiasm. Cohesion in a family reflects the degree to which family members participate and are emotionally involved with each other. Involvement in a work setting measures employees' concerns about and commitment to their jobs and the enthusiasm and constructiveness they display. The degree of support present in an environment is particularly important. The dimensions of support in treatment programs assess how helpful patients are toward one another and how concerned and helpful staff are toward patients. Peer cohesion and supervisor support in work settings assess friendship and open communication among employees and between supervisors and employees.

Table 9.1. Three Domains of Social Climate Dimensions

Type of Setting	Instrument	Domain		
		Relationship	Personal Growth	System Maintenance and Change
Hospital-based and community-based psychiatric programs	Ward Atmosphere Scale (WAS) / Community-Oriented Programs Environment Scale (COPES)	Involvement Support Spontaneity	Autonomy Practical orientation Personal problem orientation Anger and aggression	Order and organization Clarity Control
Family settings	Family Environment Scale (FES)	Cohesion Expressiveness	Independence Achievement orientation Intellectual-cultural orientation Recreational orientation Moral-religious emphasis	Organization Control
Work settings	Work Environment Scale (WES)	Involvement Peer cohesion	Autonomy Task orientation Work pressure	Clarity Control Innovation Physical comfort

193

Personal growth or goal orientation dimensions measure the basic goals of a setting, that is, the areas in which personal development and self-enhancement are emphasized. As previously noted, the nature of these dimensions varies somewhat among environments as a function of their distinctive purposes and goals. For example, hospital or community psychiatric programs may stress autonomy, practical orientation, and/or personal problem orientation, whereas the primary dimensions along which personal growth occurs in family settings are independence, achievement orientation, intellectual-cultural orientation, active-recreational orientation, and moral-religious emphasis. Work settings tend to vary in their emphasis on autonomy, task orientation, and work pressure.

System maintenance and change dimensions deal with the extent to which an environment is orderly and clear in its expectations, maintains control, and responds to change. The basic dimensions are order and organization, clarity of expectations, control, and innovation. For example, clarity in a treatment program measures the extent to which patients know what to expect in the day-to-day routine of the program and the explicitness of the program's rules and procedures. Clarity in a work milieu assesses the extent to which employees know what to expect in their daily routine and how explicitly rules and policies are communicated.

These three domains of social climate variables—relationship, personal growth or goal orientation, and system maintenance and change—can characterize the social environments of varied settings. The fact that other investigators have used conceptually similar sets of social-environmental variables, indicates that these domains are of general relevance (Fraser, 1981; Stern, 1970; Walberg, 1976). At a minimum, we believe that all three domains must be evaluated to obtain a reasonably complete picture of the social environment of a setting.

Constructing Typologies of Social Environments

The social environments of different settings can be described by their profiles on the dimensions of the appropriate Social Climate Scale in the same way that an individual's personality characteristics can be depicted by an MMPI profile. Moreover, just as some personality theorists and researchers have found it conceptually useful to formulate taxonomies of personality types, the development of environmental typologies can facilitate conceptual and empirical analyses. For example, the potential utility of a taxonomy of treatment programs is apparent when we recognize that interactions between type of patient and type of treatment environment may account for a substantial portion of the variance in patient behavior and treatment outcome. Guided by such considerations, we have developed empirical typologies of the social environments of families (Moos & Moos, 1976), of high school classrooms and university student living groups (Moos, 1979b), and of hospital-based and community-based psychiatric treatment programs (Price & Moos, 1975; Moos, 1975).

We provide an example here by considering four types of treatment settings.

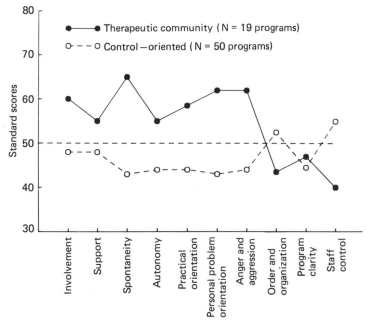

Figure 9.2. Ward atmosphere scale profiles for therapeutic community and control-oriented treatment programs.

Figure 9.2 contrasts therapeutic community and control-oriented treatment programs. The therapeutic community programs emphasize patient involvement in program functioning, open expression of feelings, active preparation for patient release, and concern with personal problems. There is little focus on program planning, neatness, clarity of expectations, or staff enforcement of rules. The basic rationale is that emphasis in the relationship and goal orientation areas helps patients to recover, and that too much focus on system maintenance restricts patients' autonomy and provides them with an overly structured, inhibiting setting. In contrast, the control-oriented programs are oriented primarily toward staff control of patient behavior. Strict rules for patient behavior and staff determination of those rules are the most salient program characteristics. Considerable emphasis is placed on neatness and on carefully planned and structured activities.

Two quite different types of treatment programs are shown in Figure 9.3. The relationship-oriented programs focus on interpersonal relationships, especially on the extent to which patients are encouraged and supported by staff and other patients. These programs also show moderate emphasis on the goal orientation dimensions, and in contrast to therapeutic community programs, there is a focus on order and organization and clarity of expectations. The action-oriented treatment programs display average or below average emphasis on all dimensions

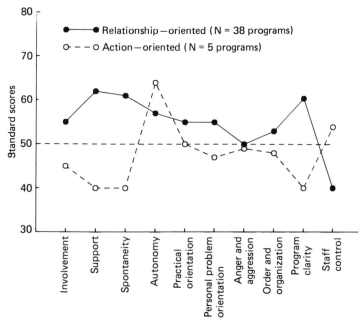

Figure 9.3.   Ward atmosphere scale profiles for relationship-oriented and action-oriented treatment programs.

except autonomy and staff control. This type of program is oriented toward encouraging patients to be independent and self-sufficient. An important focus is to counteract the "secondary gain" (the reinforcement a patient can obtain from being sick, such as being taken care of and not having to work) frequently associated with psychiatric hospitalization by encouraging patients to develop their individual resources in preparation for early release.

We have also identified six distinctive types of families: expression oriented, structure oriented, independence oriented, moral-religious oriented, achievement oriented, and conflict oriented (for methodological details and descriptions of the six empirical subtypes, see Moos & Moos, 1976). In addition to suggesting distinct types of family and treatment orientations, such typologies may be useful in program evaluation studies, because some kinds of family settings can enhance successful treatment outcome. Furthermore, the "match" between the characteristics of treatment and family settings may affect posttreatment functioning. A therapeutic community or relationship-oriented program may have a greater positive impact on patients from families oriented toward expressiveness or independence than on patients who return to families characterized by a high degree of structure or by considerable conflict. Although the empirical work has yet to be conducted, these considerations are also relevant to describing and classifying work settings.

Determinants of Social Climate

The WAS profiles presented in the preceding section illustrate the substantial variations that exist among the social environments of treatment settings. Why do social environments develop in such disparate ways; that is, what factors affect the emergence of an emphasis on support, or on autonomy, or on control? As previously noted, we believe that physical and architectural, policy and program, and suprapersonal factors can influence the type of social environment that emerges in a setting. For example, physical and architectural features can affect social climate directly (more cohesive climates may develop in treatment settings with more social-recreational aids) and indirectly through their impact on program functioning (treatment facilities with more available space may facilitate patient activities and thereby increase patient autonomy). Physical features can also affect social climate indirectly through their influence on the types of patients and staff who decide to enter a setting (facilities characterized by better physical features may attract more socially competent patients, who in turn promote a sense of cohesion and comfort). Policy and suprapersonal factors can influence the social environment of a setting through similar types of processes.

The development of the Multiphasic Environmental Assessment Procedure (MEAP; Moos & Lemke, 1982), which measures physical and architectural, organizational, suprapersonal and social climate variables, afforded the opportunity to examine these hypotheses about the interrelationships among the four domains of environmental factors. The MEAP focuses primarily on community care settings for older people, but the conceptual framework and general approach it embodies are applicable to other types of settings as well (Wandersman & Moos, 1981 a & b).

Analyzing MEAP data from over 90 sheltered care facilities, we found that cohesion among residents was more likely to develop in settings with more physical amenities (such as attractive decorations in the halls), with better social-recreational aids (such as lounges furnished for casual conversation), and with more available personal space and architectural choice (such as individual temperature controls in residents' rooms). Such settings also tended to have more socially competent and functionally able residents, as well as policies that provided these residents with broader personal choice and more opportunity to participate in making decisions about how the setting should be run. As expected, a climate of independence was more likely to develop in facilities that allowed their residents more flexibility in organizing their daily lives and more control over certain aspects of facility policies (Moos & Igra, 1980). These results support the idea that architectural, organizational, and suprapersonal factors can influence the social climate of a setting.

We return to these considerations regarding the characteristics of social climates and their determinants when we discuss environmentally focused intervention strategies in a later section. Now, we turn our attention to the relationship between treatment and extra-treatment settings (specifically, family and work settings) and treatment outcome as observed in studies of psychiatric and alcoholic patients.

EVALUATING THE IMPACT OF TREATMENT AND EXTRA-TREATMENT SETTINGS

Treatment Environment and Treatment Outcome

There is considerable evidence suggesting that the treatment environments of psychiatric programs can influence treatment outcome. Some studies have focused on the relationship between individual patient's perceptions of the treatment milieu and their posttreatment functioning, whereas others have examined program-level relationships between treatment environments and treatment outcome. For example, relative to patient-related variables (demographic and intake symptom factors) and other treatment variables (type of program and treatment experiences), perceptions of the treatment program (COPES) were among the strongest predictors of outcome in a six-month follow-up of alcoholic patients (Cronkite & Moos, 1978). In a study of inpatient (WAS) and outpatient (COPES) alcoholics' perceptions of their treatment environment, Fischer (1979) found that patients who perceived more emphasis on personal problem orientation, the open expression of anger and aggression, and clarity of rules and program procedures reported more positive treatment outcome (as indexed by longer periods of abstinence and less frequent and shorter drinking bouts).

With respect to program-level relationships, programs that are most successful with less seriously disturbed patients emphasize the discussion of personal problems and the open expression of angry feelings, combined with a well-organized and moderately structured context that is also oriented toward patient autonomy, independence, and preparation for release back to the community (Moos, 1974b). Consistent with these results, Bale and his colleagues (in press) found that drug abusers were most likely to have their impulsive behavior challenged in programs oriented toward dealing with personal problems, where expectations and social contacts were clearly defined. Dropout rates were higher and treatment outcome was less positive among patients treated in a program that had strong demands for involvement and participation, but lacked organization and clarity of expectations.

These findings indicate that the preferred treatment environment for less seriously disturbed patients is high on the relationship dimensions (especially involvement and spontaneity), on the treatment program dimensions of autonomy, practical orientation, and personal problem orientation, and on program clarity, but low on staff control (see the WAS profile for the relationship-oriented programs shown in Figure 9.3). Preferred programs for more disturbed chronic patients, on the other hand, are likely to be well-organized and structured and to inhibit the open expression of anger and aggression. For instance, Klass, Growe, and Strizich (1977) studied the relationships between treatment environment and treatment outcome (length of time out of hospital after discharge) among 14 programs composed of chronic patients. The number of violent episodes resulting in injury was higher in programs that emphasized anger and aggression, but lower in programs that emphasized organization. Conversely, patients who were treated in programs characterized by high levels of organization and suppression of anger and aggression spent longer periods of time out of the hospital. We have also found that programs which emphasize structure and staff control are most successful in keeping long-term chronic patients out in the community (Moos & Schwartz, 1972).

Overall, these results are consistent with the view that more disturbed patients who are treated in highly organized programs which emphasize impulse control may internalize some of the social structured norms of the program and therefore stay in the community longer after discharge. Thus, although a therapeutic community- or relationship-oriented program may provide a therapeutic milieu for less disturbed patients, it can be detrimental for more disturbed or chronic patients. Individuals who are functioning marginally (such as chronic schizophrenic patients) need a well-structured setting that insulates them from too much interpersonal stimulation, whereas individuals who are functioning more adequately are more likely to benefit from a milieu that emphasizes autonomy and self-understanding.

The notion of an interaction effect between treatment program structure and level of patient personal resources (particularly cognitive functioning) on adaptation is reinforced by the findings of McLachlan (1972; 1974). He observed that patients with lower conceptual levels (poorly socialized and impulsive, or compliant and dependent on authority) rated themselves as more improved during treatment and indicated reduced alcohol consumption at a 6 to 12 month follow-up when they had been exposed to more structured inpatient treatment (directive group psychotherapy) and aftercare (weekly group meetings). On the other hand, persons with higher level cognitive systems (independent and self-assertive or empathic and cognitively complex) indicated greater self-rated improvement and reduced posttreatment drinking behavior after less-structured (nondirective) treatment and aftercare (occasional written contact or informal meeting with program alumni). "Mismatched" persons (i.e., lower conceptual level patients in less-structured treatment environments, or higher conceptual level individuals in more structured settings) had poorer outcomes than either of the two "matched" groups.

There is additional evidence to indicate that the most beneficial type of substance abuse treatment environment varies depending on patient characteristics. We found, for example, that perceptions of personal problem orientation (COPES) were related to positive treatment outcome among men but not among women alcoholic patients (Cronkite & Moos, in press). Along similar lines, Linn and her colleagues (1979) examined the relationship between ethnicity, COPES perceptions of the treatment environment, and attrition from a drug abuse program. Although the white dropout and completer groups did not differ in how they perceived the program, black patients who perceived the program as more spontaneous, autonomous, practical, and insight-oriented were more likely to remain in treatment.

A related idea is that the effectiveness of program staff may be a function of the match between their orientation toward treatment and the treatment environment of the program in which they are located. Boyle (1979) found evidence of such interaction effects between psychiatric aids' attitudes toward mental illness and the atmosphere of the ward (WAS) on which they were placed. Aids who believed in being kind and benevolent to patients were more effective (as indicated by supervisors' ratings) on wards that were high on relationship and treatment program dimensions, whereas aids who felt that interpersonal factors were relatively unimportant in the etiology of mental illness were more effective on wards that were high on the system maintenance dimensions.

Extra-Treatment Factors and Treatment Outcome

Although characteristics of treatment settings are related to treatment outcome, they "explain" only a limited proportion of the variance in outcome. We believe that information on extra-treatment factors such as family and work environments, stressors and social resources, and appraisal and coping responses can aid in better understanding the recovery-relapse process and, in turn, generate more effective treatment strategies that consider patients' life circumstances and personal resources (Moos, Cronkite, & Finney, 1982).

Along these lines, we have explored the relationship between treatment outcome and the characteristics of the family and work settings to which individuals returned after residential treatment for alcoholism. We studied a group of over 120 such patients and their families and found that an increased frequency of stressful life events was related to more negative family environments, whereas the reliance on problem-focused coping responses to life stressors promoted positive interaction among family members and resulted in more cohesive family milieus. Patients in family environments that were high on conflict and low on cohesion and expressiveness tended to report more anxiety, depression, and physical symptoms. In addition, families in which the alcoholic member showed worse treatment outcome tended to express less concern about one another, to discourage individual thinking, to deemphasize recreational and religious activities, to be disorganized, and to exhibit more conflict and control than families of patients whose treatment outcome was more positive (Finney, Moos, & Mewborn, 1980; Moos, Bromet, Tsu, & Moos, 1979; Moos, Finney, & Chan, 1981). In general, these results emphasize the importance of family cohesiveness in promoting the positive treatment outcome of alcoholism (Orford et al., 1976).

In examining the perceived work environments of alcoholic patients, we found that positive relationships among employees and between employees and their supervisors were related to better functioning only among patients *not* living in family settings. Alcoholic patients not in families, who saw their work environments as emphasizing more task orientation, clarity, and innovation also tended to show better social and psychological functioning (Bromet & Moos, 1977). To explain these findings, we reasoned that the marriage situation acts as a buffer against stress and improves the likelihood that a patient will make a good adjustment (Clum, 1975). Consequently, although dissatisfaction with the job may be viewed with greater detachment by married patients, an unsatisfactory work situation can take on greater significance and have a more adverse effect on the posttreatment functioning of unmarried patients.

Our conceptual framework suggests that personal characteristics have indirect as well as direct effects on adaptation. In an attempt to estimate a model roughly similar to the one shown in Figure 9.1, we found that a substantial portion of the total effect of patient characteristics on adaptation (treatment outcome in this instance) was indirect, or mediated by treatment and post-treatment factors. For example, patients with higher sociodemographic status were more likely to participate actively in treatment and to return to less stressful life situations after treatment. Thus, patients' personal resources may reflect not only what they "bring to treatment," but also what environmental resources or stressors they will return to after treatment (Cronkite & Moos, 1980).

Similarly, the conceptual framework may further our understanding of the way in which treatment effects can be filtered through posttreatment factors. Although we found that the direct effect of treatment on outcome was weak, we also observed that its total effect was more substantial and could be traced to its cumulative indirect effects via posttreatment factors. Specifically, treatment was linked to reduced stressors and more effective coping responses, which in turn were associated with improved posttreatment functioning (Cronkite & Moos, 1980).

These findings suggest that treatment may be more effective when oriented toward patients' posttreatment life circumstances. The benefits to be derived from such an approach are indicated in an evaluation of a "community reinforcement" program that emphasized rearranging marital, occupational, and community resources (Azrin, 1976). This program involved special marital, family, and job counseling, access to job search services, and an active program-related social club. Patients in the program experienced greater success than a matched control group of individuals who received only standard hospital treatment.

Information about extra-treatment factors that are related to treatment outcome can help to identify obstacles to the maintenance of program gains and to suggest strategies for program reformulation. The value of focusing on such factors has been shown in recent investigations of the posttreatment precipitants of relapse episodes (Marlatt, 1977; Marlatt & Gordon, 1979). Many relapses occur as the result of exposure to high risk situations, such as stressful factors in family, work, and other interpersonal settings. Conversely, social network resources and coping processes can facilitate positive treatment outcome and contribute to the recovery process.

In order to incorporate extra-treatment environmental considerations in planning treatment and aftercare programs more effectively, we need to increase our understanding of the ways in which community settings influence adaptation. Accordingly, we turn now to studies that have explored the relationship between family environments and some of the other variables in our conceptual framework, and to research which has focused on the link between family and work settings and the health and adaptation of nonpatient groups.

COMMUNITY SETTINGS AND THE ADAPTATION PROCESS

In the following section, we describe research that has considered the reciprocal effects of family environment and the behavior and adaptation of adults and children, and the relationship between work environment features and job satisfaction and morale.

Coping Strategies and the Family Environment

Several studies have explored the relationship between coping styles and the social environments of families under stress. Maynard and his colleagues (1980) examined the manner in which wives managed the hardships associated with family life in the police profession. By asserting themselves through developing self-reliance and managing the demands and stressors associated with their husbands' occupation (unpredictable work schedules, the stress of life-threatening events, armed conflict, etc.), wives were able to enhance family cohesion, expressiveness, and independence. They also minimized family conflict and control through such coping efforts as building social support, developing and maintaining relationships with other family members and friends, and maintaining family integration (emphasizing role maintenance). In a study of wives of servicemen missing in action, Boss (1980) reported that highly instrumental wives (e.g., independent, competitive, self-confident, etc.) dealt more effectively with the absence of their husbands (i.e., were more able to assume the family roles vacated by the husband). Their instrumental personal guidelines and ability to psychologically close out the father role (lowering psychological father presence) were in turn related to less conflicting family milieus. In another study, the use of avoidance coping strategies by a community sample of married couples was linked to a more negative family environment (Cronkite & Moos, 1983). Together, these studies indicate that the way in which family members cope with stress affects the family milieu (see Figure 9.1).

Family and Work Resources and Adaptation

Coping strategies can affect the family environment, and, in turn, the family (and work) environment can affect subsequent adaptation and well-being. In a study of a representative group of community families, Holahan and Moos (1982) constructed a Family Relationships Index (FRI) composed of the FES cohesion, expressiveness, and conflict subscales and a Work Relationships Index (WRI) composed of the WES involvement, peer cohesion, and supervisor support subscales. These indices were used to examine the connection between the perceived quality of family and work support and complaints of depression and psychosomatic symptoms. In general, employed men and women who perceived more family and work support, and nonemployed women who perceived more family support (as measured by the FRI and WRI) reported less depression and fewer psychosomatic symptoms. When initial levels of maladjustment, stressful life events, and quantitative measures of social resources were controlled, the results showed that decreases in social support in work and family settings were generally related to increases in psychological distress for both men and women over a one-year period.

In a comparison study on roughly the same group of families, Billings and Moos (1982) examined the stressful effects of the work environment on personal functioning and the stress-buffering value of work and family social resources. Work stressors were measured by a composite set of four WES subscales (high work pressure and supervisor control in conjunction with low autonomy and clarity), whereas the WRI and FRI were used to measure work and family resources. Work stressors had a greater impact on men, but supportive social resources provided more attenuation of such effects among men than among women. Although work stressors generally had less effect on men whose wives were employed, high stress in women's work settings was associated with less family cohesion and independence as perceived by their husbands. These findings indicate that the personal relationships developed in family and work settings can buffer the adverse effects of stress and that individuals may be affected indirectly by environmental factors they do not experience personally (such as when the pressure of a husband's or wife's work milieu influences family functioning). Generally, certain aspects of the environmental system can be conceptualized as stressors and social resources and, in turn, related to individual and family adaptation (see Figure 9.1).

Just as in the case of treatment settings, clinicians and researchers have hypothesized that the match between the characteristics of individuals and their family and work settings can affect health and well-being. In this connection, Wetzel (1978) tested the hypothesis that a woman will be vulnerable to depression if her tendency toward independence or dependence is not supported by the environment. She studied groups of depressed and nondepressed women who had families and worked outside their homes. Dependent women who perceived their work environments as low in clarity (i.e., as not giving them needed structure) tended to be depressed, as did independent women who saw their work environments as high in clarity (i.e., as providing too much structure). Similarly, women who were independent but not in an autonomous family environment were more likely to be depressed, as were dependent women in autonomous family environments. In a further study of 150 depressed and 150 nondepressed men and women, Wetzel and Redmond (1980) reported additional support for the hypothesis that when one's predisposition toward dependence or independence (the personal system) is not sustained by work and family environments (the environmental system), one would be vulnerable to depression.

FAMILY ENVIRONMENTS AND CHILDREN'S ADAPTATION

Children's Personal Resources and the Family Milieu

Several additional studies illustrate the link between the environmental and personal system (see Figure 9.1) by focusing on the way in which the family environment can help to shape the development of relatively stable dispositional characteristics (such as internal-external control and impulse control). For example, reasonably cohesive relationships, stable expectancies (order and organization), and an active expressive family life may help build adolescent competence, self-responsibility, and an internal control orientation (Schneewind & Engfer, 1979).

In another study of the relationship between family environment and adolescent personality, Forman and Forman (1981) asked high school students and their parents to complete the FES and the students to complete the High School Personality Questionnaire (HSPQ). Families in which the FES relationship dimensions were emphasized tended to have children who were relatively free of anxiety. Assertiveness and self-sufficiency characterized children in families that supported independence and achievement, whereas children in families that were actively involved in religious and ethical issues tended to be insecure and guilt-prone. Families that emphasized organization and control had children who were seen as relaxed, suggesting that clear rules and well-defined limits can have positive effects. Taken together, these studies indicate that children in cohesive well-organized families tend to be more relaxed and self-confident.

Children's Functioning and the Family Milieu

Aside from shaping relatively stable personal resources, the family environment has also been linked to behavioral and emotional problems among children. For example, Fowler (1980) examined the relationship between the family environment and behavioral problems among prekindergarten children. Manifestations of such problems as developmental delay, speech and language deficits, and behavioral displays of aggression were associated with a less cohesive family environment. Signs of shyness and anxiety were associated with lower family organization and structure. Moos and Billings (1982) studied a group of children of recovered and relapsed alcoholic patients and found that children with more emotional symptoms (such as depression) tended to reside in families that showed more conflict and less cohesion, organization, and congruence of perceptions between parents.

In a study using an Overall Family Attitude Measure (OFAM), Mercer, Hundleby, and Carpenter (1978) reported that the family environment was related to adolescent drug use. For boys, there was less use of alcohol and tobacco in families that were high on warmth and support, whereas for girls, high family warmth and support was related to less use of alcohol, tobacco, and marijuana. In addition, girls who saw their families as less socially oriented were less likely to use alcohol, whereas those who saw their families as disinterested were more likely to use marijuana. These findings suggest that a supportive family may reinforce adolescents against drug use, and/or that children in supportive family environments may spend more time at home and thus spend less time with peers in situations where drugs are easily accessible.

Satisfaction and Morale in the Workplace

As noted earlier, the stressful aspects of work settings may lead to poor employee morale and performance. For instance, the Berkeley Planning Associates (1977) examined employee characteristics and organizational and work environment factors related to "burnout" in 11 Child Abuse and Neglect Demonstration Projects. There was less employee burnout in projects that emphasized job involvement, peer cohesion, and supervisor support, and that had an efficient, autonomous, task-oriented environment with explicit rules and policies. As expected, staff burnout was positively related to perceived work pressure. In addition, such organizational factors as high job formalization, centralization of program decision-making, and large caseload size were related to higher work pressure and to less employee-perceived emphasis on interpersonal relationships, and on autonomy, task-orientation, and clarity. These relationships between burnout and the work environment remained significant even after these organizational factors and demographic variables were controlled.

Characteristics of the work environment that contribute to burnout are likely to affect the quality of employees' performance as well as their openness to innovation. McClure and his colleagues (1980) gave the WES to teachers as part of a larger study of an innovative problem-solving training procedure in a public middle school. The teachers saw their work environments as highly pressured and as lacking in supportiveness, clarity, task-focus, and innovation. This stress-inducing environment led the teachers to experience severe burnout and to perceive the intervention study and associated in-service workshops as a burden rather than an opportunity. Improving the work environments of teachers and other service-oriented professionals may be an effective first step toward improving the quality of the programs they provide for their clients.

The WES has also been used to explore the factors contributing to mass "psychogenic" illness in industrial plants. For instance, some workers in a shoe factory reported experiencing headaches, light-headedness, and dizziness in response to a strange odor in the workplace. Because environmental testing in the plant produced essentially negative results, a behavioral factors evaluation was undertaken. In comparison with nonaffected employees, those affected generally perceived more work pressure, less peer cohesion and supervisor support, and a lack of organizational structure and clarity in the work milieu. The authors concluded that psychogenic illness in the workplace may be precipitated in part by psychological job stress and perceptions of the work environment as lacking in orderly and coherent group functioning (Colligan et al., 1979; Murphy & Colligan, 1979).

SOCIAL-ENVIRONMENTAL INFLUENCES ON ADAPTATION

The overall findings of the studies we have reviewed illustrate the importance of the role of the environmental system in our conceptual model of human adaptation. Supportive interpersonal relationships in family and work settings are generally associated with better individual and family adaptation: less shyness and anxiety, fewer physical and emotional symptoms, and better adaptation to stressful life circumstances and crises. Well-organized settings with clear rules and procedures also tend to be associated with these functioning criteria, as well as with higher morale and less burnout in the workplace. In addition, an emphasis on autonomy and task orientation in work settings and an orientation toward independence, achievement, intellectuality, and recreational pursuits in family settings, are positively related to functioning and adaptation. Conversely, as might be expected, an emphasis on time urgency and pressure in the work milieu is related to dissatisfaction and burnout. Furthermore, overly restrictive structure and control are associated with depressed mood and lack of ability to reorganize family roles realistically under stress.

These findings on the connection between adaptation and stressors and resources in family and work settings are basically similar to those we described earlier in psychiatric treatment programs. They are also consistent with the results of studies in educational and correctional settings (Moos, 1975; 1979b). As such, the findings point to the utility of thinking of "treatment" in broader terms. With respect to alcoholism treatment, for example, Tuchfield (1977) has argued:

By expanding our definition of "treatment" to include informal social processes that facilitate the resolution of alcohol problems, we can increase the likelihood of specifying optimal (and thus economically more efficient) strategies that integrate informal treatment resources with formal modalities. Such a perspective requires that we adopt a comprehensive view of individuals within their specific environments. In doing so, institutions will be more likely to provide services responsive to the individual needs of patients. (p. 1812)

The findings we have reviewed provide some guidelines about the potential "impacts" of specific aspects of social environments, although additional studies are needed to examine the interrelationships among setting characteristics, as well as the variations in their relative influence in different contexts. As we have seen, the match between personal characteristics (sociodemographic factors, dispositional tendencies or attitudes) and the work or program milieu can affect the onset of depression among working women, treatment outcome among subgroups of psychiatric patients, and the effectiveness of staff in a psychiatric program. Moreover, among employed husband-wife pairs, the effects of stress in one partner's work setting may influence the couple's family milieu or the other partner's functioning. There is also some evidence that the characteristics of families under stress or in crises may change in accordance with the spouses' coping styles. Future research in this area should be conducted in light of a general conceptual framework that considers the relationship between personal and environmental factors, as well as the coping and social resources that mediate the effects of these factors on human adaptation.

FORMULATING ECOLOGICALLY ORIENTED APPLICATIONS

Our review has pointed to some of the features of community and treatment settings that are related to individual and system adaptation and to recovery from debilitating psychiatric and addictive conditions. We have also identified some of the environmental features that influence the social climate of settings. The findings regarding the antecedents and consequences of social environments are important not only because they provide us with a better understanding of some of the determinants of human functioning, but also because they can be applied in a number of different ways. We have summarized such practical applications as describing and comparing environments, formulating clinical case descriptions, and enhancing environmental competence elsewhere (Moos, 1979b, 1979c; see also Moos & Fuhr, 1982 included as Chapter 6 in this volume). Here, we describe how social climate assessment can be used to facilitate and monitor change in treatment programs, families, and work settings.

The Process of Environmental Change

The methods we have used to facilitate environmental change involve four steps: (1) systematic assessment of the social environment, (2) feedback of environmental data to participating groups with particular emphasis on real-ideal differences in setting perceptions, (3) planning and instituting changes in the organizational, physical design, and/or suprapersonal features of the setting, and (4) reassessment of the social climate. Because there is no specific "end point" to this process, a continual cycle of assessment, change, reassessment, and so on may occur (for a review of relevant studies, see Moos, 1979c). Indeed, survey-guided feedback using the Social Climate Scales seems most effective when there is an effort to utilize ongoing formative evaluation to help settings remain responsive to the changing needs of their members and to instill problem-solving norms and skills in participants (Finney & Moos, in press; Shinn, 1980).

Changing the Climate of a Psychiatric Treatment Facility

The Community-Oriented Programs Environment Scale (COPES) was used to evaluate and facilitate change in a residential treatment center for disturbed adolescents (Moos, 1974b, Chaps. 4 and 11). In the initial testing, residents and staff showed some fairly large disagreements about the characteristics of the program environment. For example, staff saw more emphasis on both support and autonomy than residents did, whereas the emphasis on involvement and spontaneity was seen as higher by residents than by staff. On the other hand, residents and staff did agree that the program was oriented toward expression of personal problems and of anger and aggression. Data from an administration of the ideal form of the COPES indicated that both staff and residents had fairly similar views as to what would constitute an optimal treatment environment.

The resulting information was collated and fed back to the participants by a "change facilitator." The dimensions from the COPES afforded a comprehensive, systematic structure which allowed staff and residents to conceptualize and discuss the treatment environment in terms of a common set of concepts. Innovations in four organizational system areas were attempted in an effort to produce a more desirable social environment.

1. Some involving activities (e.g., a dance, a picnic) were initiated so that residents would participate in enjoyable endeavors together. This was an effort to increase cohesion and reduce the overly rigid problem-solving focus of many of the activities of the house, which tended to have a dampening effect on both residents and staff, thereby decreasing their involvement.

2. A specific procedure for obtaining peer support when residents were having personal problems was instituted. Any resident could call a "game" when he or she wished. The other residents would then meet to talk about the problem and assist the person in seeking a solution, or at least to feel better about the situation.

3. A resident government system was instituted, but initially it functioned poorly because there was no agreement about the activities for which residents would be responsible. Once specific areas of responsibility were defined by staff and residents, the resident government became a meaningful organizational innovation.

4. Residents were given responsibility for teaching new residents their specific job obligations in the house, and a new system by which each resident rated all other residents on several behavioral scales was developed. In addition, new residents were required to keep a journal of their initial activities in and their reaction to the house. The journal was kept for two weeks and was used to help set specific personal goals on which the adolescent could focus while in residence.

The COPES was readministered approximately six months after the initial testing. On 7 of the 10 dimensions, residents felt their treatment environment was closer to their ideal at the second than at the first testing. The largest changes occurred in the relationship dimensions of involvement and support, and treatment dimensions of autonomy, and the system maintenance dimensions of order and organization and of program clarity. Residents and staff, however, felt that the program was further from their ideal in its emphasis on personal problem orientation and on anger and aggression, indicating the need for further work in the change process (for other studies using the COPES or WAS to monitor and change treatment settings, see Curtiss, 1976; Gripp & Magaro, 1971; Bliss, Moos, & Bromet, 1976; Mosher, Menn, & Matthews, 1975; Ryan, Bell, & Metcalf, 1982; Verinis & Flaherty, 1978).

Changing the Social Climate of a Family

Fuhr, Moos, and Dishotsky (1981) used the Family Environment Scale (FES) to diagnose problems in a couple who had sought therapy, and to monitor the effects of the organizational, physical, and suprapersonal environmental changes which were implemented during the course of therapy.

John and Mary Cartwright* were in their late twenties and had been married for two years. Mrs. Cartwright had a 9-year-old daughter from a brief, previous marriage. Mrs. Cartwright was in close contact with her three older brothers, who were frequent guests and lived in the Cartwright's home for several weeks at a time. Mr. and Mrs. Cartwright entered therapy to discuss her drinking problem and to explore a lack of warmth and cohesion in their relationship. Mrs. Cartwright's drinking was often triggered by her brothers' demeaning and antagonistic remarks. Rather than expressing her anger, she drank heavily until she often blew up in a violent rage. Managing their daughter's behavior was also problematic, because neither parent was effective in setting limits. The Cartwrights also complained of a chaotic and disorganized family life. On a typical day, Mrs. Cartwright would get up late and rush to work. She was often late arriving home to prepare dinner, and her husband refused to help. Mr. Cartwright, who was a law student, would often react to the familial disorder by withdrawing to the library or elsewhere outside the home.

The Cartwrights completed the FES in three ways. They each gave their impressions of the current family environment. Because Mrs. Cartwright's brothers apparently had a significant impact on the family, the Cartwrights also used the FES a second time to describe what the family was like when her brothers were present. The FES was administered a third time to indicate how they saw an ideal family environment.

The FES profiles of their current situation confirmed the therapist's impressions in most areas. A combination of moderate to high expressiveness and independence, and low organization and control was perceived by both partners—similar to the expression-oriented family mentioned earlier in reference to the family typology (Moos & Moos, 1976). The adverse influence of Mrs. Cartwright's brothers was shown by the couple's descriptions of the family milieu when the brothers were present. Both agreed that cohesion and expressiveness were much lower, whereas family conflict was higher during the brothers' visits.

In the feedback process, the therapist's first step was to identify areas of

*The names and details in this case study have been altered to preserve the anonymity of the family.

consensus in the couple's perception of an ideal family environment. Both spouses wanted more cohesion, less conflict, and more cultural and recreational activities. The couple found this feedback encouraging, because they had not been aware of the congruence in their value systems. With feedback on their actual family environment, Mr. Cartwright realized his lack of assistance in housework, compounded by the family's scheduling problems and poor planning activities, significantly contributed to family tension and conflict. This problem was addressed by an organizational/suprapersonal environment change—a person was hired to provide part-time household help. Feedback of the FES scores with and without Mrs. Cartwright's brothers at home strongly underscored their deleterious effect on the couple's relationship. Coincidentally, the Cartwrights had to move to a new home at this time (a physical environment change), and this move allowed them to institute an abrupt change in relating to Mrs. Cartwright's brothers and to develop more control over the friends their daughter brought home (two indirect suprapersonal environment changes).

Three months later, the FES was readministered and the improvements were substantial, as would be expected from the couple's relatively high initial agreement on therapeutic goals. Cohesion and organization were seen as higher, whereas conflict was reduced. In addition, cultural and recreational activities had increased, although both partners felt that more change was needed in these areas.

Changing the Social Climate of a Work Setting

In a recent study, the WES Real and Ideal Forms were used to facilitate change in the work environments of three general medical units (a burn treatment unit, a surgical unit, and a neonatal intensive care unit). The staff in each unit was provided with feedback on the WES results and on the discrepancies between their actual and preferred work milieus. The burn treatment unit staff, for example, showed large discrepancies in that they perceived average or below-average (relative to normative data) emphasis on all WES dimensions except autonomy and wanted to increase emphasis on every dimension except work pressure and supervisor control (Koran, Moos, Moos, & Zasslow, 1983).

Target areas for change were identified in the feedback process and a liaison psychiatrist worked with each unit's staff to formulate and implement environmental innovations. For example, on the burn unit, a number of organizational changes were instituted; individual responsibilities for burn technicians, nurses, and physicians were clarified in group meetings, shifts were changed from 8 to 10 hours, regular times for other staff to meet with physicians were established, and so on.

After the intervention period, staff in each of the three units felt that the actual work setting was closer to their preferred work setting on one or more dimensions as indicated by readministration of the WES three to nine months later. Each unit showed positive changes on two of the three relationship dimensions and two of the three units showed increases in task orientation and staff autonomy and decreases in work pressure. The burn treatment team perceived significantly more emphasis on autonomy, involvement, and peer cohesion six months after as compared with prior to the intervention procedure. These results indicate that the WES can be used to make work environments more satisfactory for the persons working in them—a seemingly necessary condition for the development of an effective treatment environment.

CONCLUSION

Information from environmental assessments need not be limited to its application to environmental *change* efforts. As Price (1979) points out, social climate data can be used to *create* optimal environments or to *select* such settings for individuals. With respect to the former, data on participants' beliefs about an ideal setting can be used to establish the social-environmental specifications for the creation of a new setting—for example, a halfway house. Selection of an optimal setting could also be facilitated by using social climate data. An alcoholic patient, for instance, could use the WES to describe an ideal work situation, and an appropriate milieu could then be selected on the basis of actual WES profiles from several possible contexts; e.g., different departments within the patient's company.

   Although the findings we have reviewed are encouraging, a great deal remains to be learned about the effects of community and treatment environments on individual and group adaptation. The conceptual framework we outlined at the beginning of this chapter charts one promising course for future research. Increasing our understanding of the causal processes that result in the differential effects observed when diverse people function within complex environments, will enable us to specify "optimal," growth-enhancing social contexts for different individuals. Moreover, continuing research on the determinants of varying social climates should eventually enable us to intervene more effectively in treatment and community settings to bring about desired changes. Ultimately, the knowledge acquired from such research may result in individually tailored, ecologically oriented treatment strategies which produce treatment gains that are more resistant to the "decay" so often seen with traditional, client-centered approaches.

REFERENCES

Azrin, N.H. (1976) Improvements in the community-reinforcement approach to alcoholism. *Behaviour Research and Therapy*, **14**, 339–348.

Bale, R., Van Stone, W., Kuldau, J., Engelsing, T., & Zarcone, V. A prospective controlled study of narcotic addiction treatment in three therapeutic communities: Process and two-year follow-up results. *Archives of General Psychiatry*, in press.

Berkeley Planning Associates. (1977) Evaluation of child abuse and neglect demonstration projects. Vol. IX, Project management and worker burnout. Springfield, Va.: National Technical Information Service, (NTIS No. PB-278 446).

Billings, A., & Moos, R. (1982) Work stress and the stress-buffering roles of work and family resources. *Journal of Occupational Behaviour,* **3,** 215–232.

Bliss, R., Moos, R., & Bromet, E. (1976) Monitoring change in community-oriented treatment programs. *Journal of Community Psychology,* **4,** 315–326.

Boss, P. (1980) The relationship of psychological father presence, wife's personal qualities and wife/family dysfunction in families of missing fathers. *Journal of Marriage and the Family,* **42,** 541–549.

Boyle, W. (1979) Predicting and producing effective psychiatric aids. Unpublished doctoral dissertation, Department of Psychology, St. John's University, New York.

Bromet, E., & Moos, R.H. (1977) Environmental resources and the posttreatment functioning of alcoholic patients. *Journal of Health and Social Behavior,* **18,** 326–338.

Bronfenbrenner, U. (1979) *The ecology of human development.* Cambridge, Mass.: Harvard University Press.

Clum, G. (1975) Intrapsychic variables and the patients' environment as factors in prognosis. *Psychological Bulletin,* **82,** 423–431.

Cobb, S. (1976) Social support as a moderator of life stress. *Psychosomatic Medicine,* **38,** 300–314.

Colligan, M., Urtes, M., Wisseman, C., Rosensteel, R., Anania, T., & Hornung, R. (1979) An investigation of apparent mass psychogenic illness in an electronics plant. *Journal of Behavioral Medicine,* **2,** 297–309.

Cronkite, R.C., & Moos, R.H. (1978) Evaluating alcoholism treatment programs: An integrated approach. *Journal of Consulting and Clinical Psychology,* **46,** 1105–1119.

Cronkite, R.C., & Moos, R.H. (1980) Determinants of the posttreatment functioning of alcoholic patients: A conceptual framework. *Journal of Consulting and Clinical Psychology,* **48,** 305–316.

Cronkite, R.C., & Moos, R.H. (1983) The role of predisposing and mediating factors in the stress-illness relationship. Social Ecology Laboratory, Stanford University and Veterans Administration Medical Center, Palo Alto, Calif.

Cronkite, R.C., & Moos, R.H. Sex and marital status in relation to the treatment and outcome of alcoholic patients. *Sex Roles,* in press.

Curtiss, S. (1976) The compatibility of humanistic and behavioristic approaches in a state mental hospital. In A. Wandersman, P. Poppen, & D. Ricks (Eds.), *Humanism and behaviorism: Dialogue and growth.* New York: Pergamon.

Finney, J.W., & Moos, R.H. Environmental assessment and evaluation research: Examples from mental health and substance abuse programs. *Evaluation and program planning,* in press.

Finney, J., Moos, R., & Mewborn, R. (1980) Posttreatment experiences and treatment outcome of alcoholic patients six months and two years after hospitalization. *Journal of Consulting and Clinical Psychology,* **48,** 17–29.

Fischer, J. (1979) The relationship between alcoholic patients' milieu perception and measures of their drinking during a brief follow-up period. *International Journal of the Addictions,* **14,** 1151–1156.

Forman, S., & Forman, B. (1981) Family environment and its relation to adolescent personality factors. *Journal of Personality Assessment,* **45,** 163–167.

Fowler, P. (1980) Family environment and early behavioral development: A structural analysis of dependencies. *Psychological Reports,* **47,** 611–617.

Fraser, B.J. (1981) Learning environment in curriculum evaluation: A review. *Evaluation in Education,* **5,** 1–93.

Fuhr, R., Moos, R., & Dishotsky, N. (1981) The use of family assessment and feedback in ongoing family therapy. *American Journal of Family Therapy,* **9,** 24–36.

Gripp. R., & Magaro, P. (1971) A token economy program evaluation with untreated control ward comparisons. *Behaviour Research and Therapy,* **9,** 137–139.

Heller, K., & Monahan, J. (1977) *Psychology and community change.* Homewood, Ill.: Dorsey Press.

Holahan, C.J., & Moos, R.H. (1982) Social support and adjustment: Predictive benefits of social climate indices. *American Journal of Community Psychology,* **10,** 403–415.

Klass, D., Growe, G., & Strizich, M. (1977) Ward treatment milieu and post-hospital functioning. *Archives of General Psychiatry,* **34,** 1047–1052.

Koran, L.M., Moos, R.H., Moos, B., & Zasslow, M. (1983) Changing hospital work environments: An example of a burn unit. *General Hospital Psychiatry,* **5,** 7–13.

Lawton, P., & Nahemow, L. (1973) Ecology and the aging process. In C. Eisdorfer & P. Lawton (Eds.), *The psychology of adult development and aging.* Washington, D.C.: American Psychological Association.

Lazarus, R.S. (1980) The stress and coping paradigm. In C. Eisdorfer, D. Cohen, A. Kleinman, & P. Maxim (Eds.), *Theoretical bases for psychopathology.* New York: Spectrum.

Linn, M., Shane, R., Webb, N., & Pratt, T. (1979) Cultural factors and attrition in drug abuse treatment. *International Journal of the Addictions,* **14,** 259–280.

McClure, L., Pratola, S., Ellis, F., FitzRitson, S., McCammon, S., & Felder, C. (1980) Enhancing social climate and social competence through social problem solving training in a public middle school. University of South Carolina, Columbia, S.C.

McLachlan, J. (1972) Benefit from group therapy as a function of patient-therapist match on conceptual level. *Psychotherapy: Theory Research and Practice,* **9,** 317–323.

McLachlan, J. (1974) Therapy strategies, personality-orientation, and recovery from alcoholism. *Canadian Psychiatric Association Journal,* **19,** 25–30.

Marlatt, G.A. (1977) Craving for alcohol, loss of control, and relapse: A cognitive behavior analysis. In P.E. Nathan, G.A. Marlatt, & J. Loberg (Eds.), *Alcoholism: New directions in behavioral research and treatment.* New York: Plenum Press.

Marlatt, G.A., & Gordon, J. (1979) Determinants of relapse: Implications for the maintenance of behavior change. In P. Davidson (Ed.), *Behavioral medicine: Changing health life styles.* New York: Brunner/Mazel.

Maynard, P., Maynard, N., McCubbin, H., & Shao, D. (1980) Family life in the police profession: Coping patterns wives employ in managing job stress and the family environment. *Family Relations,* **29,** 495–501.

Mercer, G.W., Hundleby, J., & Carpenter, R. (1978) Adolescent drug use and attitudes toward the family. *Canadian Journal of Behavioral Science,* **10,** 79–90.

Moos, R.H. (1974a) *The social climate scales: An overview.* Palo Alto, Calif.: Consulting Psychologists Press.

Moos, R.H. (1974b) *Evaluating treatment environments: A social ecological approach.* New York: Wiley.

Moos, R.H. (1975) *Evaluating correctional and community settings.* New York: Wiley.

Moos, R.H. (1976) *The human context: Environmental determinants of behavior.* New York: Wiley.

Moos, R.H. (1979a) Social ecological perspectives on health. In G. Stone, F. Cohen, & N. Adler (Eds.), *Health psychology: A handbook.* San Francisco: Jossey-Bass.

Moos, R.H. (1979b) *Evaluating educational environments: Procedures, methods, findings, and policy implications.* San Francisco: Jossey-Bass.

Moos, R.H. (1979c) Improving social settings by social climate measurement and feedback. In R. Munoz, L. Snowden, & J. Kelly (Eds.), *Social and psychological research in community settings.* San Francisco: Jossey-Bass.

Moos, R.H. Creating healthy human contexts: Environmental and individual strategies. In J. Rosen & L. Solomon (Eds.), *Prevention in health psychology,* Hanover, N.H.; University Press of New England, in press.

Moos, R.H., & Billings, A. (1982) Children of alcoholics during the recovery process: Alcoholic and matched control families. *Addictive Behaviors,* **1,** 155–163.

Moos, R.H., Bromet, E., Tsu, V., & Moos, B. (1979) Family characteristics and the outcome of treatment for alcoholism. *Journal of Studies on Alcohol,* **40,** 78–88.

Moos, R.H., Cronkite, R.C., & Finney, J.W. (1982) A conceptual framework for alcoholism treatment evaluation. In E.M. Pattison, & E. Kaufman (Eds.), *The American encyclopedic handbook of alcoholism.* New York: Gardner.

Moos, R.H., Finney, J.W., & Chan, D. (1981) The process of recovery from alcoholism: I. Comparing alcoholic patients and matched community controls. *Journal of Studies on Alcohol,* **42,** 383–402.

Moos, R.H. & Fuhr, R. (1982) The clinical use of social-environmental concepts: The case of an adolescent girl. *American Journal of Orthopsychiatry,* **52,** 111–122.

Moos, R.H., & Igra, A. (1980) Determinants of the social environments of sheltered care settings. *Journal of Health and Social Behavior,* **21,** 88–98.

Moos, R.H., & Lemke, S. (1982) The multiphasic environmental assessment procedure: A method for comprehensively evaluating sheltered care settings. In A. Jeger, & B. Slotnick (Eds.), *Community mental health: A behavioral/ecological perspective.* New York: Plenum.

Moos, R.H., & Mitchell, R.E. (1982) Social network resources and adaptation: A conceptual framework. In T.A. Wills (Ed.), *Basic processes in helping relationships.* New York: Academic Press.

Moos, R.H., & Moos, B. (1976) A typology of family social environments. *Family Process,* **15,** 357–372.

Moos, R.H., & Moos, B. (1983) Adaptation and the quality of life in work and family settings. *Journal of Community Psychology,* **11,** 158–170.

Moos, R.H., & Schwartz, J. (1972) Treatment environment and treatment outcome. *Journal of Nervous and Mental Disease,* **154,** 264–275.

Mosher, L., Menn, A., & Matthews, S. (1975) Soteria: Evaluation of a home-based treatment for schizophrenia. *American Journal of Orthopsychiatry,* **45,** 455–467.

Murphy, L., & Colligan, M. (1979) Mass psychogenic illness in a shoe factory: A care report. *International Archives of Occupational and Environmental Health*, **44**, 133–138.

Orford, J., Oppenheimer, E., Egert, S., Hensmen, C., & Guthrie, S. (1976) The cohesiveness of alcoholism-complicated marriages and its influence on treatment outcome. *British Journal of Psychiatry*, **128**, 318–339.

Price, R. (1979) The social ecology of treatment gain. In A. Goldstein, & F. Kanfer (Eds.), *Maximizing treatment gains: Transfer enhancement in psychotherapy*. New York: Academic Press.

Price, R., & Moos, R.H. (1975) Toward a taxonomy of inpatient treatment environments. *Journal of Abnormal Psychology*, **84**, 181–188.

Rabkin, J., & Streuning, E. (1976) Life events, stress, and illness. *Science*, **194**, 1013–1020.

Ryan, E., Bell, M., & Metcalf, J. (1982) The development of a rehabilitation psychology program for schizophrenics: Changes in the treatment environment. *Journal of Rehabilitation Psychology*, **27**, 67–85.

Schneewind, K., & Engfer, A. (1979) Okologische perspektiven der familiarem sozialisation. (Ecological perspectives on family socialization). In H. Walter & R. Oerter (Eds.), *Okologie und Entwicklung (Ecology and development)*. Federal Republic of Germany: Ludwig Auer Donauworth.

Shinn, M. (1980) Assessing program characteristics and social climate. In A.J. McSweeny, R. Hawkins, & W. Fremouw (Eds.), *Practical program evaluation*. New York: Thomas.

Stern, G. (1970) *People in context*. New York: Wiley.

Tuchfield, B.S. (1977) Comment on "Alcoholism: A controlled trial of 'treatment' and 'advice.'" *Journal of Studies on Alcohol*, **38**, 1808–1813.

Verinis, J., & Flaherty, J. (1978) Using the Ward Atmosphere Scale to help change the treatment environment. *Hospital and Community Psychiatry*, **29**, 238–240.

Walberg H. (1976) Psychology of learning environments: Behavioral, structural or perceptual? In L.S. Shulman (Ed.), *Review of research in education (Vol. 4)*. Itasca, Ill.: Peacock.

Wandersman, A., & Moos, R. (1981a) Assessing and evaluating residential environments: A sheltered living environments example. *Environment and Behavior*, **13**, 481–508.

Wandersman, A., & Moos, R. (1981b) Evaluating sheltered living environments for retarded people. In C. Haywood, & J. Newbrough (Eds.), *Living environments for developmentally retarded persons*. Baltimore, Md.: University Park Press.

Wetzel, J. (1978) The work environment and depression: Implications for intervention. In J. Hanks (Ed.), *Toward human dignity: Social work in practice*. Washington, D.C.: National Association of Social Workers.

Wetzel, J., & Redmond, F. (1980) A person-environment study of depression. *Social Service Review*, **54**, 363–375.

CHAPTER 10

Patient and Community, The Ecological Bond

ROBERT B. BECHTEL

BACKGROUND: THE FOUNDING AND DEVELOPMENT OF ECOLOGICAL PSYCHOLOGY

In 1947, Roger Barker and Herbert Wright, child psychologists, established the Midwest Psychological Field Station in Oskaloosa, Kansas. The purpose of the station was to provide a field location where the total impact of the environment on child development could be studied. The research began with close observations of children's daily behavior. The observation developed into a technique called behavior specimen recording (Barker & Wright, 1958; Wright, 1967). But it soon became apparent that the important units of environmental influence were not individuals but behavior settings. These were supra-individual units into which the community population sorts itself to carry out daily activities. Behavior settings were the observable meetings, classes, businesses, and finite activities of the community. They had a regular time, were tied to a given location, and had a definite population. Furthermore, although psychology in general still finds it extremely difficult to predict an individual's behavior, the climate of a behavior setting was very stable, and the accurate prediction of any individual's behavior in that setting was fairly easy to make.

Barker's text, *Ecological Psychology* (1968), outlined the methods for collecting data on all the behavior settings in a community and described how the various scales he developed would provide both quantitative tests and qualitative descriptions of community life. Later studies (Barker & Schoggin, 1973) showed the stability of behavior settings over a period of 10 years. A behavior setting survey of a community usually shows one to two settings per person. Thus, a community of 500 would have 500 to 1000 settings. A complete list of behavior settings accounts for 95% of the working behavior of all residents. Ecological psychology was then used to study differences between the environmental influences of large and small schools (Barker & Gump, 1964), large and small churches (Wicker, 1969) and large and small communities (Wright, 1969). Bechtel and Ledbetter (1976) shortened the time necessary to do a behavior setting survey and developed a questionnaire format to evaluate remote Alaskan communities. Their data were used for developing guidelines to improve the design of such communities. Srivastava (1979) used the behavior setting survey to evaluate and compare treatment environments of teaching parent homes for delinquents, and O'Reilly (1981) used it to evaluate the treatment environment. LeCompte and Willems (1970) used these methods to evaluate a rehabilitation hospital. Bechtel (1979) introduced the use of behavior settings into therapeutic practice. LeCompte (1981) developed a method for observing stress in behavior settings.

Despite these ever-widening uses, ecological psychology has remained outside the mainstream of community and clinical psychology. One of the reasons is that clinicians and community psychologists are not trained in the methods and concepts and find it difficult to bridge the gap between personality constructs and extra-individual units of behavior. Perhaps more pervasive is the lack of regard for the role of daily behavior in the formation of healthy and pathological behavior patterns. Conventional psychology has too often taken a blame-the-victim stance in its explanatory constructs (Lerner, 1980[1]), whereas ecological psychology assumes the basic explanations of human behavior lie in the organism-environment interaction. From the ecological perspective the most important aspect of human behavior to study is the daily behavior of human beings in the natural environment, uninterrupted by conventional data collection.

RESPONSIBILITY THEORY: THE COMMUNITY SIZE, BEHAVIOR SETTING SIZE INTERACTION

In an attempt to gain a cross-cultural perspective on his methods and data, Barker went to England and studied a small town similar to Oskaloosa. Upon examining the comparative data, he discovered that although the English town had twice as many people as the American town, it had less behavior settings per person. In fact, the American town, although smaller, had 1.2 times as many behavior settings. Furthermore, the people in the American town acted in leadership roles within behavior settings three times as often as the English town.

Barker accounted for these differences by developing the theory of undermanning (Barker, 1960). There seemed to be a relationship between community size and behavior setting size and number such that the larger the community, the larger but relatively fewer the behavior settings. Larger communities had larger behavior settings and fewer settings available to each person.

More important were the psychological differences experienced between large and small behavior settings. People in the smaller behavior settings had to perform differently in their roles. Because a small behavior setting had to do

[1]It is Lerner's thesis that in order to believe in a just world, we *must* blame the victim, otherwise society (and we) must take the blame and change. Thus, psychology tends to support the prevailing common sense view.

much the same work as a larger setting, each person in the smaller setting had to take on a larger and more important work load. As a consequence, the obligations and pressure to perform are proportionately greater on people in smaller settings. Each person has to do a wider variety of activities and produce at a higher level.

As a result of these forces, people in smaller settings acquire a greater sense of importance because they are more necessary to the setting. Their experiences are more intense and varied, and their self-confidence is increased. Because of the pace of smaller settings, feedback on successes and failures is more frequent.

To test out his theory in new situations, Barker studied the student behavior in extracurricular activities of large and small high schools. In the book, *Big School, Small School* (Barker & Gump, 1964) it was shown that students in large and small schools participate in about the same number of settings, but that small-school students hold more positions of leadership and responsibility.

Psychologically, small-school students also experienced more competence satisfactions than large-school students. Small-school students felt more responsibility and obligation toward settings than did large-school students. Barker and Gump (1964) conclude that there is a negative relationship between institutional size and individual participation. Wicker (1971) defines the situation in large organizations as essentially overcrowded. Larger settings seem to have decreased forces toward participation and consequently less satisfaction.

Wicker's (1965) study of larger schools, however, showed that the positive psychological benefits of undermanning, although not enjoyed by most students in a large school, are shared by the few students in positions of responsibility. It would seem then, that the vectors producing the positive psychological benefits are not merely size of organization and size of behavior setting but the *responsibility* of one's role in the behavior setting. The smaller size of the organization and the smaller size of the behavior setting merely create a situation where responsibility is likely to be shared.

That responsibility is not always shared even in the undermanned situation is illustrated by Curran and Stanworth's (1971) study of small businesses in England. According to undermanning theory, the employees of these small businesses should be enjoying the benefits of the undermanned situation. It turns out that the employees are not actually as stimulated as the small-school students of Barker and Gump or the small-church members of Wicker (1969). The reason is that most of these small busiesses are run by persons who are somewhat marginal as are the employees. The economic security of the small firm is less stable also. Therefore, although there are some benefits, these selection factors compromise the theoretical possibilities of small-firm benefits. Thus, there is nothing magical about small size; it merely creates the possibility but does not guarantee the condition.

Because responsibility is the key variable, it would be better to use the term *responsibility theory* rather than the more sexist term.

A further complication ensues when situations are discovered where the

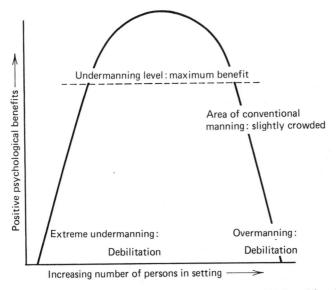

Figure 10.1.   Effects of undermanning and setting size: Inverted U-shaped function.

participants in a behavior setting have too much responsibility. Srivastava (1975) studied a mental health center where the staff was so overworked that they were unable to accomplish their duties. This situation can be labeled extreme undermanning and the undermanning-overmanning relationship can be seen as an inverted U-shaped function in regard to psychological benefits (see Figure 10.1).

Figure 10.1 shows the psychological benefits previously described along the ordinate, whereas numbers of people in the setting/organization are additively represented along the abscissa. Extreme undermanning occurs when there are too few people to perform the behavior-setting roles properly. As greater numbers are experienced the benefits accelerate until an optimum is reached. Note that the optimum is fewer people than are conventionally assigned to most behavior settings. *The number of persons conventionally assigned to roles is considered crowded by this theory.* As one goes down the curve, the benefits quickly decline and the debilitation of overmanning equals that of extreme undermanning.

Of course, the curve represents what usually happens in most organizations, but does not necessarily have to occur. The leaders can simply refuse to share responsibility in an undermanned circumstance. How often this may occur is not known, but some differences may be ascribed to cultural conditions or economic pressures. Nevertheless, on balance, it does seem that smaller organizations in general provide a better climate for giving each individual a greater share of responsibility, and that responsibility seems to be a key factor in the well-being of any member of an organization.

THE HEALTHY COMMUNITY: AN ECOLOGICAL PERSPECTIVE

During my many years as an environmental psychologist, I gave lectures and talks to designers and design students and the question would inevitably arise: How do you design a community? For some time my answer was to design places for all the behavior settings that are found in natural, undesigned communities, but as data accumulated from behavior setting surveys of various kinds of communities, it became apparent that healthy communities could be distinguished from unhealthy community environments by the way the community was designed. The design of some communities seemed to prevent the development of a healthy relationship among residents.

The basic ingredients of a healthy community are found in a particular behavior setting called the *behavioral focal point*. Left to their own devices, the citizens of a community seem to develop their own behavioral focal point. This seems to be the one behavior setting in the community where the greater number of different kinds of people have access. All the men, women, children, including the elderly and minority groups should have equal access to this space. In agricultural villages the behavioral focal point is the weekly market. In small, midwestern towns it is often the drugstore or store/post office combination. One can go to these behavioral focal points and actually come in face-to-face contact with all the inhabitants of a community. It is the place where all the "action" is, where everyone goes to see and be seen, and where one can hear the latest gossip.

Later studies (Bechtel & Ledbetter, 1976) showed that small military bases constructed with a behavioral focal point functioned better because they allowed more business to be transacted informally. In a remote mining community in Australia (Bechtel, Ledbetter & Cummings, 1980), the architect designed a community building that served admirably well as the focal point.

What seems important about this concept is that unless a physical place where people can gather is provided, it becomes difficult to provide face-to-face contact that enables people to know one another.

Behavioral focal points are not bare spots of earth but a place where many community functions converge. It should be a place where residents need not make any social commitment but can go through on the excuse of going to an adjacent function. Thus (as was observed in one study) a teenager can find it absolutely necessary to go to the local store seven times a day without stating baldly that the motive is to "check out the action." A necessity store, a place to sit down and eat and drink with a sprinkling of other complementary services, makes an ideal focal point. The community building of Shay Gap, Australia, is a good illustration.

It should be noted that the actual behavioral focal point, the steps, overlaps with several nearby settings including the post office, the bank, the snack stand, a boutique, and a bulletin board. Waiting in line for the mail is a good place to socialize.

A good behavioral focal point contrasts to one studied in a public housing estate in Cleveland, Ohio. This location was also a stairway but with marked

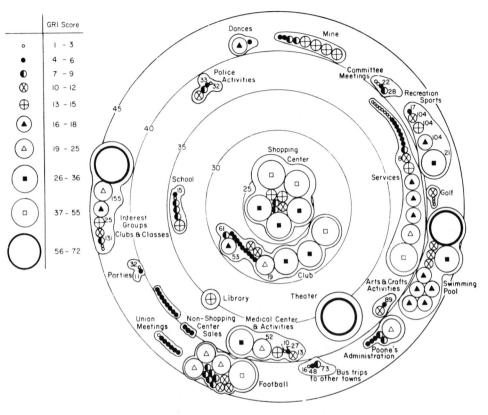

Figure 10.2. Public behavior settings in relation to the behavioral focal point. (From Bechtel, R., Ledbetter, C., & Cummings, N. (1980) *Post Occupancy Evaluation of a Remote Australian Mining Community.* U.S. Army Cold Regions Research and Engineering Laboratory. Courtesy USA CRREL.)

contrast. None of the surrounding activities overlapped, nor were there any reasons to linger. Consequently, the community did not know one another very well and were not able to recognize who was a stranger. The behavior setting survey showed them to be a fragmented community.

Of course, for urban areas, behavioral focal points are much harder to establish. In fact, with the loss of the small "Mom and Pop" stores that once characterized urban neighborhoods, it is increasingly difficult to find a place where residents can gather on an informal basis. Instead, subgroups in each community gravitate to their own focal points such as neighborhood bars, parks, and other "hangouts."

A behavioral focal point does not guarantee healthy relationships in a community, but it does provide a framework in which those relationships can develop. Without it, the community has obstacles to overcome.

As it is with the small towns and military bases, so it is with organizations. Each organization has forces within it to socialize itself into a community. But in most organizations the element of management becomes a critical factor. Thus, when employees ask for a lounge, management that is overcontrolling will refuse out of fear that the employees will become enough of a community to threaten management collectively. It is here that the issues of community and responsibility interface.

The data from ecological psychology suggest that maximizing the amount of responsibility in each peson in a behavior setting tends to produce positive competence experiences. Nowhere has this been shown with more effectiveness than in the job enrichment literature (O'Toole, et al., 1973). Job enrichment is a method of increasing productivity by increasing the amount of responsibility of the front line worker. Instead of tightening the No. 4 bolt on the chassis, the worker becomes part of a team that is responsible for the whole chassis or a major part of it and the team hires its own personnel, repairs its own equipment, and cleans up its own work area. The result is a marked increase in productivity. Yet, job enrichment has been resisted in the United States because it takes too much power away from the manager (Tarrant, 1976).

Clinical Research and Daily Normal Behavior

One of the media sensations in mental health care occurred when Rosenham (1973) introduced "normal" stooges into mental hospitals and discovered that hospital personnel could not differentiate them from other patients. The inability to differentiate normal from abnormal behavior in everyday practice is nothing new. Jackson (1963) discovered that mental health nurses required much more of mental patients to be "normal" than of persons outside the hospital. Recently, Offer et al. (1981) found that therapists tended to see normal adolescents as abnormal.

Such confusions abound in mental health practice. Hornstra et al. (1972) found that patients' view of the therapy process and its goals were far different from staff and their goals for the patient.

One of the reasons for this disparity is the lack of basic knowledge about what constitutes normal behavior and normal expectations of behavior. Common psychological tests of abnormal behavior are standardized by testing mental patients and "non" mental patients on the assumption that something within the patient is different than something within the nonpatient. The problem with this approach is that it does not allow an appraisal of normal behavior in the patient or abnormal behavior in the normal person. The assumption is that virtually all those behaviors that belong to a patient belong to an abnormal sphere.

Behavior settings provide an area of study that is neutral to whether behavior is normal or abnormal. Persons who behave in an unacceptable manner are either changed and accepted into a setting or rejected because of inability to change. Whether an individual is "normal" in the behavior setting framework is judged by his or her behavior across settings.

Patient and Community, The Ecological Bond[2]

The use of ecological psychology in clinical situations is not entirely new. Hanford (1966) describes how ecological principles were applied to change a treatment environment and Gump and James (1970) used behavior setting techniques to study a psychiatric ward. The ecological methods as described by Barker (1968), Barker and Schoggen (1973), and Wicker (1979) have never been adapted for use in a clinical procedure as a part of therapy.

There are four reasons for selecting ecological psychological methods for use in clinical practice. First, these methods involve the daily observable behavior of the client in terms he can understand and deal with. No assumptions are made about inner processes or mysterious forces operating outside his ken. The behavior occurs or it does not. It can be observed by others as easily as the client.

Second, the use of daily behavior records sets up a new relationship between the therapist and client. When the client sees a record of his daily behavior, he becomes his own judge of what needs to be changed and the therapist contracts to help him in this effort. No struggle is needed to uncover hidden motives, which creates an almost adversary relationship between patient and therapist.

There is a third advantage in the use of ecological methods. They allow almost any kind of therapeutic orientation from the simplest kind of behavior modification to more traditional psychoanalytic orientations. Of course, some of the benefits are lost by using certain orientations more than others.

The fourth reason for using ecological methods is that they permit a more objective measure of change in the client's daily behavior. Of course, for therapeutic orientations that are not concerned with daily behavior as a target of change, this is less valuable. But for a quick and reliable measure of the change in a person's daily behavior routine the ecological methods have no equal.

Methods

Barker's studies (Barker, 1968; Barker & Schoggen, 1973) followed by his students (Bechtel, 1977; Wicker, 1979) outline the natural environment of man as a string of behavior settings that can be organized into hierarchies of genotypes and subdivided into 63 separate measures of scales and subscales. The behavior setting survey is the method by which behavior in an entire community is cataloged, encompassing over 95% of the waking hours of every individual.

The behavior setting is a natural occurring unit of human behavior. In a way, behavior settings are the units of behavior into which a community sorts itself to get the business of living done. They are the boy scout meetings, grocery stores, school classes, lawyer's offices, and other natural units of behavior to be seen in everyday life. Each setting is tied to a particular geographic location and has a particular time for occurring. It has a standing pattern of behavior that is understood by all the occupants. The physical surroundings and behavior objects

[2]Portions of this section were presented at the American Psychological Association Annual Convention, New York, 1979.

of the behavior setting are inextricably bound up with the behavior patterns. Each without the other would have different meanings.

Behavior settings are supra-individual units of behavior; that is, they are larger than individual persons. They go on despite changes in personnel. Leaders are replaced, members come and go, but the Lions Club continues to meet regularly.

The individual in any community lives out his life by passing from one behavior setting to another in the daily course of events. His environment consists of the behavior settings he inhabits just as the environment of the mountain lion consists of his hunting territory. In a very real sense, the settings program his daily life for him once he chooses to enter them. The life-style of an individual could be accurately described by listing all the behavior settings he comes in contact with.

Listing the behavior settings that an individual comes in contact with is an ecological psychology technique called the *Behavioral Range.* The technique is administered by having the client list all of his or her activities over a years' time. First, the daily behavior settings are listed such as home, work, travel to work, lunch, evening activities, and weekend activities. Then the full range of a year is covered to include parties, vacations, business trips, dinners, and so on. Then, a final list of behavior settings is made comprising the full behavioral range of the client.

An analysis of each behavior setting is made to determine the role played by the client in each setting. If the client is merely an onlooker and adds nothing to the setting, he or she is given a score of 1. If the person is a member of an audience such as at a play, movie, or sports activity where admission is charged, he is given a score of 2. If the person is a bona fide member of an organization and attends as a member in good standing, he or she is given a score of 3.

If the client is an official of an organization such as a secretary or treasurer, or sergeant at arms, he or she is given a score of 4. If the client is a *leader* in the organization such as a president or vice-president, a score of 5 is given. If the leadership is not shared but of such a character that if the client does not appear the setting cannot take place, then he or she is scored a 6.

Scores of 4, 5, or 6 are grouped together under the label of *performer,* whereas scores of 1, 2, or 3 are called *nonperformers.* The list of settings is then considered in terms of how many settings there are in which the client is a performer versus those in which he or she is a nonperformer.

Also, there are various other measures of the settings that can be made such as *general richness,* but these are fairly esoteric and readers are referred to Barker (1968), Bechtel (1977), or Wicker (1979) if they wish to pursue them further.

Once the behavior setting list is finalized and the performer–nonperformer distinctions made, the client is presented with a behavioral range. The implied or baldly stated question can be: What does he or she want to change? Some clients are appalled by the list itself—some because of its length and others because of its sparseness.

It is hard to avoid the assumptions about leadership implied in the leadership measures. Western culture implies that it is good to be a leader so that behavioral ranges with low scores tend to provoke such responses as "I guess I'm not much of a leader." This is always a good point for discussion with the client to discover how he or she feels about that observation.

Generally, from past research (Barker & Gump, 1964; Wicker, 1968) it has been found that people with leadership roles in settings have healthier attitudes about themselves. It certainly becomes clear from examining the behavioral range whether the client is active in community life, what his interests are, and, more important, where he spends most of his time. For some clients the amount of time spent in certain activities can be a surprise.

Two kinds of responses are solicited from the client. One is how the client feels about the total behavioral range. Such comments as "Gee, I don't do very much," or "God, I'm busy" may reflect the total impact of the pattern.

The second kind of comment is solicited about each behavior setting and how the client feels about his or her role in each setting. Of course, most of these comments are stimulated when the data are being collected by having the client list the settings. It may become apparent which settings are sources of satisfaction, which are merely obligatory, and which are sources of negative feelings. In some cases, it may become necessary to examine typical behavior settings in great detail. This may involve the therapist actually visiting the setting and recording behavior. Some instances of this will be illustrated below.

Another analysis that can be made of the behavior settings is to select a few and visit members of these settings to obtain their description of setting and client behavior. This second description can then be compared with the client's version. This type of analysis is most useful with children because of their greater perceptual selection process. A case history is illustrated below.

Once these discussions reach fruition, the client can be brought to a point of deciding what needs to be changed. For many clients this will seem obvious and no prompting toward a decision is needed. For others, only vague discomforts surface that need to be explored.

Once the changes are decided upon, these can be the essence of the contract between therapist and client. The therapist helps the client toward his own goals of change. The behavioral range list then, can be used as a prechange measure and updated at the end of therapy for a postchange measure.

CASE HISTORIES

Clara (50), an alcoholic, has a rather sparse routine daily behavior pattern. Her daily behavior settings are: Getting up in the morning, breakfast, going to work, coffee-break, lunch, going home, watching television, supper, and going to bed. This weekly routine is varied sometimes by going to the movies with a friend or eating at a cafeteria rather than at home. At different seasons of the year she will also shop in downtown stores or window-shop while walking home from work. On weekends she will usually visit relatives and friends and also watch a *lot* of television. After relating this routine she reflected upon it and remarked: "Gee, I lead a dull life," indicating (at least) she recognized that there was not much potential in the settings she inhabited. When individual settings such as lunch were explored, it was revealed that she usually chose to sit alone. At work she seldom said anything to those around her and had few friends. From looking at the sparseness of her daily behavior Clara was stimulated to try to do something about it and this formed a basis for her therapy contract.

Examining Clara's behavior settings, it is apparent that except for settings where she is the sole participant (such as getting up and breakfast)[3], her participation level hovers between levels two and three, that of an audience. Unless she becomes boss at her job, social lion of the lunchroom, and leader of her family councils, she would not have much chance of level five participation. But even in her sparse environment, there are more chances of level three and even level four participation than she was taking advantage of. One can speculate as to whether this sparse pattern is the typical stripped life pattern of an advanced alcoholic, or whether the sparse pattern itself is partly the cause of drinking to fill the void. Only more historical data can answer the question. In any case, by adding new settings Clara's life can be markedly changed. The behavioral resources as they now exist are only minimally capable of sustaining a healthy life-style. These, of course, are value judgments.

Norma, also 50, and also alcoholic, lives in the same general kind of environment as Clara. She lives in a rooming house, works at the same kind of job, and lives alone. Her daily behavior pattern is far less sparse, however, because as a second job she works at the switchboard in her rooming house, and she has a major interest in dancing which she does at least once a week; she also performs for the crowds at a local dance hall. She has a regular group of friends organized around lunches and shopping visits during the week and weekends. Her participation level in the public settings lies somewhere between the four to five range.

Norma reacted to her behavioral range as a behavioral resource. She became animated when talking about her dancing and her friends. Rather than change her basic pattern, an effort was made to better utilize this resource. Therapy prospects for Norma were especially good, as contrasted to Clara. This also suggests the use of the behavioral range as a selection process for therapy.

Thelma, in her midthirties, is a homemaker with four children. Her presenting complaint was entirely in terms of her husband's treatment of her. The behavioral range did not seem to reveal any stimulus for change of her life-style. With her consent, the therapist visited Thelma in her home about meal time. He merely recorded the family behavior and presented this to Thelma in their next session.

---

[3]These are personal settings as opposed to public settings where anyone is free to enter. Most of ecological psychology concerns itself with public settings, and high participation levels in these settings have been shown to produce feelings of satisfaction, obligation, involvement, and self-esteem.

Two facts became apparent from these data. First, the husband was a past master of handling aggression from his wife. Sample dialogue from the record:

WIFE: "You're a goddamn liar!"
HUSBAND: (Matter-of-factly) "I guess I am."

The second fact, hitherto unsuspected, was that the *main* focus of Thelma's aggression really was her 18-month-old child. Her other children joined in and the little girl took the brunt of everyone's ire. This also was clear in the behavioral record.

After reading the behavioral record, Thelma expressed shock and disbelief at her treatment of the child. Because the treatment of the child was less emotion-laden than the relationship with the husband, this became the target for behavior change and became a model for dealing with the husband at a later date.

It is quite possible that without observation in the home, the behavior toward the youngest child would not have been uncovered. Posttherapy observation of a similar meal time demonstrated more positive interactions between mother and child. During the course of therapy Thelma overcame her repressions and "kicked out" her husband after which she maintained she was much happier. It certainly changed her daily behavior pattern.

Michael, a fourth grader, was admitted to inpatient services. His diagnosis was encopresis (a form of extreme constipation).

A professional social worker took down Michael's Daily Behavior Record as he saw it, then got a second version from his mother, and a third from his teacher's point of view. A number of discrepancies were noted between child and mother and between child and teacher. Michael had the times of his school classes and recesses correct and agreed with mother and teacher about visits and playmates. His disagreements were largely with his mother about getting up time, dressing, breakfast time, school bus time, the amount of time he spends alone after school before his mother arrives, and how much help he gives in doing the dishes. These points were found to be centers of conflict between mother and child. In fact, Michael was quite busy, in his mind, helping with dishes, cleaning house, and being his mother's companion. In public settings Michael was constantly under pressure from his teacher who was constantly reprimanding and punishing.

Because Michael was using inpatient services, his behavioral record was presented to his therapy team. They felt the amount of activity seemed unusual for a person his age.

When confronted with the behavior record and the interpretation of the therapy team, the mother tearfully admitted her overdependence on Michael and the use of him as a husband substitute. Unfortunately it was not possible to use a second behavioral record at the end of therapy to test whether the behavior activity level had changed. Michael was discharged as improved on his symptoms.

CONCLUSIONS

Ecological psychology is not a therapy in itself nor does it necessarily favor any therapeutic method. Its usefulness lies in the relatively complete view that can be provided of a client's behavior outside of the therapy session. The data collected can be used as a pre-post evaluation of progress in therapy, or more directly as a contract for change between therapist and client. The Behavioral Range record can provide insights into client behavior which might take many hours of therapy to reveal, and often the direct observation of behavior is so self-evident that the client can interpret his or her own behavior directly. Behavioral records can also overcome blocks in therapy. The benefit of the use of ecological techniques is to provide a new perspective on client behavior that is currently not found in either collecting case history information or in therapy sessions themselves.

A RESPONSIBLE FUTURE: IMPLICATIONS FOR THE APPLICATION OF ECOLOGICAL PSYCHOLOGY

Because it deals with so many facets of human life, in order to embrace the significance of ecological psychology, a professional must step outside the limits of any one discipline. The community-individual interface is a composite of many elements involving individual makeup, organizational structure, cultural imperatives, and the design of the environment. An understanding of how all of these focus on the individual in behavior settings is necessary to understand how any individual functions. Past therapeutic emphasis has dealt entirely with changing an individual to adapt or strengthen him or her to social and environmental forces. Ecological assumptions are that something in the environment must change along with the individual or any change in the individual will not last. That bitter lesson has been learned by many a therapist who watches painstakingly cultivated changes in a therapeutic course dissolve on contact with the environment.[4] From a more ecological point of view, too many therapies are changes limited only to the therapeutic behavior setting itself and do not generalize to other settings.

From the ecological point of view efforts at change should be focused on the client's behavioral range; in other words, *outside* the therapeutic session itself. Furthermore, improvement, or change, cannot be valid unless there are changes in the behavioral range.

Responsibility theory shows a way of tying the client to his or her own life by dealing with his behavior in the community. The assumptions are not that the client will improve merely by adding behavior settings and leadership roles, but that whatever therapy is applied will result in increased responsibility on the part

[4]Perhaps more harmful to future knowledge about human behavior are the therapists who failed to understand that successful therapy involved behavioral range changes of which they were unaware.

of the client, and that increased responsibility is the element which will carry the client beyond the therapeutic contact.

But the greatest promise of ecological psychology lies more in the area of prevention. With the understanding that a healthy organization of community is one that shares responsibility, a blueprint can be drawn for healthier organizations and communities. The organizations that are too directive need to be changed. The greatest challenge is how we move from being treaters of individual clients to diagnosis and treatment of organizations, communities, and ultimately, societies. The work is just beginning. We understand how to design better communities, we know the principles involved in redesigning failing communities, but too little is known about how community and individuals interact to permit us to heal individuals by direct intervention in community behavior settings.

The future of research in ecological psychology lies in two directions: community and individual experiments. Community experiments will test how far deliberately increasing shared responsibility will go toward increasing health. Experiments with individuals will ultimately test how useful behavioral ranges can be in understanding and changing human behavior.

The facts are that experiments in deliberately undermanning therapeutic communities have already been tried with success. It is a lesson that has been learned and forgotten.

The first example was the Hampstead orphanages under Anna Freud (Freud, 1969). The basic principle used to share responsibility in the environment was to assign the attendants specific children rather than have them treat all of the children as an anonymous group. There was an initial period of turmoil because the children resisted "belonging" to anyone, but then a period of positive change developed.

This lesson was learned again when Colarelli and Siegel (1967) completed the H Ward experiment at Topeka State Hospital. The same principle was used to share responsibility among patients and staff. In this case, however, the medical and psychological staff that were usually in charge were removed and the attendants were assigned specific patients. Thirty-five schizophrenics who had been abandoned as "hopeless" by medical staff were selected to populate the ward. The aides were nine black females who had not been selected but happened to be employed on that ward. After an initial period of turmoil over the radical change in roles, a truly therapeutic community evolved. Within five years, only five of the patients were not functioning in the community outside the hospital. Perhaps more remarkable than the patient change was the change in personality exhibited by the aides. They grew from somewhat passive, noncommitted individuals to people who challenged authority, thought for themselves and exuded a confidence that was in marked contrast to their former behavior.

But why did we not learn these lessons? Probably for the same reason that industry does not embrace job enrichment: The authorities involved—psychiatrists, superintendents, and other officials—have too much of an investment in the way things are now done.

Some readers will recognize that these examples are also good examples of what is now called *deinstitutionalization*. A careful examination of the deinstitutionalization literature shows that the key principle of sharing responsibility is very much the same as with responsibility theory.

It would seem then, that we have the proven technology for changing our organizations and communities into healthier places with great potential for preventive benefits. What are we waiting for?

REFERENCES

Barker, R. (1960) Ecology and motivation. In Marshall Jones (Ed.), *Nebraska Symposium on Motivation.* Lincoln: University of Nebraska Press, 1–49.

Barker, R. (1968) *Ecological psychology.* Stanford: Stanford University Press.

Barker, R., & Gump, P. (1964) *Big school, small school.* Stanford: Stanford University Press.

Barker, R., & Schoggin, P. (1973) *Qualities of community life.* San Francisco: Jossey-Bass.

Barker, R., & Wright, H. (1955) *Midwest and its children.* New York: Harper & Row.

Bechtel, R. (1977) *Enclosing behavior.* Stroudsburg: Dowden, Hutchinson & Ross.

Bechtel, R. (1979) The use of ecological methods in clinical practice. Paper delivered at the American Psychological Association Convention.

Bechtel, R., & Ledbetter, C. (1976) *The temporary environment.* U.S. Army Cold Regions Research and Engineering Laboratory.

Bechtel, R., Ledbetter, C., & Cummings, N. (1980) *Post occupancy evaluation of a remote Australian mining community.* U.S. Army Cold Regions Research and Engineering Laboratory.

Colarelli, N., & Siegel, S. (1966) *Ward H.* New York: Van Nostrand.

Curran, J., & Stanworth, J. (1978) Some reasons why small is not always beautiful, *New Society,* 627–629.

Freud, A. (1969) The Hampstead child-therapy course and clinic. In *The writings of Anna Freud,* **5,** International Universities Press, 3–25.

Gump, P., & James, E. (1970) *Patient behavior in wards of traditional modern design.* Environmental Research & Development Foundation.

Hanford, D. (1966) *Ecological psychology and treatment.* Paper presented at the symposium on community services for the mentally ill, joint meeting of Washington and Oregon State Psychological Associations, Ocean Shores, Washington.

Hornstra, R., Lubin, B., Lewis, R., & Willis, B. (1972) Worlds apart: Patients and professionals. *General Psychiatry,* **27**(4), 553–557.

Jackson, J. (1963) *A conceptual and measurement model for norms and roles.* Comparative Studies of Mental Health Organization, Lawrence: University of Kansas.

LeCompte, W. (1981) The ecology of anxiety: Situational stress and rate of self-stimulation in Turkey. *Journal of Personality and Social Psychology,* **40,** 712–721.

LeCompte, W., & Willems, E. (1970) Ecological analysis of a hospital. In John Archea, &

Charles Eastman (Eds.), *EDRA Two.* Proceedings of the Second Annual Environmental Design Research Association Conference, 236–245.

Lerner, M. (1980) *The belief in a just world,* New York: Plenum.

Offer, D., Ostrov, E., & Howard, K.I. (1981) The mental health professional's concept of the normal adolescent. *Archives of General Psychiatry,* **38**(2), 149–152.

O'Reilly, J. (1981) A comparison of two correctional treatment facilities for juvenile delinquent males. Unpublished master's thesis, Department of Psychology, University of Arizona.

Rosenham, D. (1973) On being sane in insane places. *Science,* **179,** 250–251.

Srivastava, R. (1975) Undermanning theory in the context of mental health and environments. In D.H. Carson (Ed.), *Man-environment interactions, Part II,* Dowden: Hutchinson & Ross, pp. 245–258.

Srivastava, R. (1980) *Ecological approach to environmental evaluation of residential treatment homes for delinquent youths.* Environmental Research and Development Foundation.

Tarrant, J. (1976) *Drucker: The man who invented the corporate society.* Cahners Books.

Wicker, A. (1968) Undermanning performances and students' subjective experiences in behavior settings of large and small high schools. *Journal of Personality and Social Psychology,* **10,** 255–261.

Wicker, A. (1969) Size of church membership and members' support of church behavior settings. *Journal of Personality and Social Psychology,* **13,** 278–288.

Wicker, A. (1979) *Introduction to ecological psychology.* Monterey: Brooks-Cole.

Wright, H. (1967) *Recording and analyzing child behavior.* New York: Harper & Row.

Wright, H. (1969) *Children's behavior in communities differing in size.* Lawrence: University of Kansas.

CHAPTER 11

An Interactional Model
of Psychopathology

ANTHONY J. MARSELLA

INTRODUCTION

Interactional Models of Behavior

The most critical problems facing the field of psychopathology today are
conceptual in nature. The ways we choose to conceptualize a disorder guides our
thinking and sets the limits on possible insights regarding its etiology, classification, and treatment.

In the past, theories of psychopathology have been oriented toward biological,
psychological, and sociological systems of explanation and description. Typically, schools of thought and practice developed around these orientations and
little effort was made to synthesize approaches. In fact, it became rather
fashionable for scientists and professionals to identify with a particular
orientation. Even today, we find the majority of mental health professionals
labeling themselves as "biologically oriented," "behaviorally oriented," or
"psychodynamically oriented."

One of the unfortunate consequences of this tendency has been our reluctance
to view psychopathology as a problem that is related to all of these areas. Clearly,
psychopathology, like normal behavior, is a function of an individual's
biological, psychological, and sociocultural experience. However, its roots reside
not only within the individual but also within the innumerable situations to
which the individual is exposed. This combination comprises the individual's life
experience, which is the ultimate basis of both normal and psychopathological
behavior.

Increasingly, scientists and professionals are becoming aware of the necessity
of accounting for psychopathology in terms of the simultaneous interaction of

Preparation of this paper was partially supported by NIMH Grant No. 5 R12 MH31016-03, awarded
to the author for participation in the NIMH WHO Collaborative Study on *The Psychosocial
Determinants of the Outcome of Severe Mental Disorders.*

both organismic and situation variables. By themselves, each of these variables is insufficient to explain the etiology, manifestation, course, and outcome of psychopathology. But together they offer the possibility of understanding the spectrum of forces involved in human behavior. This new orientation is called interactional theory.

The minimum requirements of an interactional model of human behavior include the following: (1) there must be person, situation, interaction and behavior components, (2) the critical variables in each of these components must be stipulated, (3) the interactional contact variables should yield a new level of variables which accommodates person and situation variables and which provides the context for behavior, (4) the subsequent behavior pattern should be linked with the person-situation components via feedback mechanisms. Within this framework, behavior emerges as the ongoing adaptational changes of the person-situation interactions reflecting forces of both of these fields as well as an emergent quality that is derived from their combination. The occurrence of behavior at both covert and overt levels brings about changes in the subjective and objective aspects of the person and the situation in an ongoing stream of activity that is essentially *life* itself.

A general interactional model of behavior advanced by the author is presented in Figure 11.1. As this figure indicates, the person is a product of both *external* (i.e., environmental and cultural) and *internal* (i.e., biological and psychological) forces. This product is equal to the sum of all of these forces in continual interaction plus an emergent quality which is the result of all the particular forces acting together. Within this context, no force operates independently of other forces but rather must constantly be in interaction with other forces across time.

The second element of this model relates the person to the situation. The person and the situation are in constant interaction with one another and the variance accounting for behavior is a function of the simultaneous interaction of these two force fields. Behavior, whether normal or abnormal, is the ongoing adjustment to the particular product of forces from person and situational sources acting in concert at a given time. Figure 11.1 also points out the obvious feedback implications of behavior for both the organism and the situation.

An Interactional Model of Psychopathology

In many respects, the model detailed in Figure 11.1 can be considered a "master model" for interactional theory. It is general enough to provide a framework for understanding the flow of forces in human behavior but it does not account for specific behavior patterns. As a result, it is necessary to posit other models that specify particular variables and relationships associated with topics like psychopathology. Beginning in 1967, the author initiated a series of studies on an interactional model of psychopathology as a function of the interaction of stresses and resources in combination with certain demographic and personality markers. Through the use of multivariate data analysis procedures it was

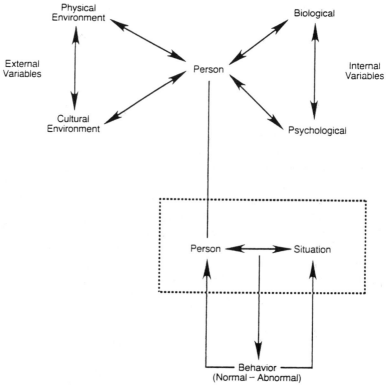

Figure 11.1.   General interactional model of human behavior. (From Marsella, A.J. (1982) Culture and Mental Health: An overview. In A.J. Marsella, & G. White (Eds.), *Cultural conceptions of mental health and therapy.* Hingham, Mass.: G. Reidel Publishing Co.)

possible to relate these different classes of variables to one another. Figure 11.2 provides an overview of this specific interactional model of psychopathology. It will be discussed in greater depth later in the chapter.

Some Issues in Interactional Models

It is critical for readers to recognize that interactional models of behavior represent a major paradigmatic orientation for psychology and the other behavioral sciences. It is an orientation that is quite old but one that has gained broad popularity only in recent years. This is because its conceptualization is so complex that it exceeds the linguistic and methodological tools necessary for its examination.

For example, if we conclude that behavior is a function of the simultaneous interaction of organismic-situational variables, then we need to create a new concept which accounts for these variables in interaction as a new unit of analysis. Andreas Angyal (1941) did this when he coined the term *biosphere* for

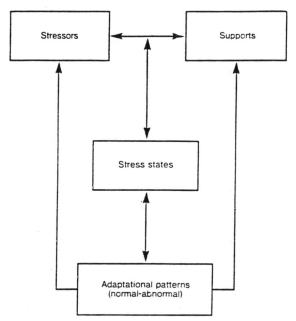

Figure 11.2. Basic components of proposed interactional model of psychopathology. (From Marsella, A.J., & Snyder, K. (1981) Stress, social supports, and schizophrenia disorders: Toward an interactional model. *Schizophrenia bulletin,* 7, 152–163.)

this new unit. But the problem is that both our language and our research methods are insufficient to capture the blend of these two force fields. Clearly, the person and the situation are never separate from one another; however, we separate them in psychology. Indeed, different theories have chosen to emphasize one over the other.

Yet another conceptual and methodological problem encountered in interactional theory involves the problem of subjective versus objective aspects of what is occurring in the organism and in the situation. This is the age-old problem of phenomenology, and our only hope for its resolution may reside in conducting research studies that consider both subjective and objective perspectives.

Purpose of this Chapter

The purpose of this chapter is to discuss an interactional model of psychopathology that can be applied to different patterns of mental disorders. This model was first utilized in 1967 in a series of studies on psychopathology among urban Filipino men (e.g., Marsella, Escudero, & Santiago, 1969; Marsella, Escudero, & Gordon, 1971; Marsella, Escudero, & Brennan, 1973). Modifications in the model were examined in subsequent publications (e.g., Kuo, 1977; Lee, 1979; Marsella and Snyder, 1981). All of these studies were based on a conceptual system that considered patterns of psychopathology to be a function of the interaction of stresses and resources. The stresses assessed included the amount of frustration, conflict, and tension associated with marital, child-rearing, housing, employment, interpersonal relations, and nutritional aspects of life functioning. The resources were associated with the particular philosophies of life, social supports, and crisis behaviors used in coping with stresses. Through the use of multivariate data analysis procedures such as factor analysis, it was possible to relate distinct patterns of psychopathology to the stress and resource interactions. Adaptations of this model of psychopathology have been posited more recently by Andrews et al., (1978), Cobb (1976), Dean and Lin (1977), Johnson and Sarason (1979), and Zubin and Spring (1977). The model has found its components represented in the new *DSM-III* approach to classification (American Psychiatric Association, 1980).

The remainder of this chapter is divided into two major sections. The first section provides a historical analysis of the current interest in interactional theory beginning with conflict between Aristotelean versus Galilean models of causality. The second section discusses the specific components of the proposed interactional model of psychopathology.

HISTORICAL PERSPECTIVES

Aristotelean versus Galilean Causality

Perhaps the earliest roots of interactionism as a general conceptual system can be traced to the conflict between Aristotelean versus Galilean notions of causality. Aristotle (384–322 B.C.) suggested a model of causality based on a simple linear relationship between two or more directly related variables. It was a view that dominated much of Western thinking until the Middle Ages. At this time, Galileo (1564–1642), the Italian astronomer and physicist, argued for a different model of causality. For Galileo, the "cause" of an event resided in the interdependencies among an object ad its surroundings. Relation properties thus became critical in determining causality. Although it is an oversimplification, Galilean thinking was the basis of contemporary "field theory" in physics and it was from this model that subsequent interactional models of human behavior were to emerge in the late nineteenth century.

German Ideological Thought

During the nineteenth century, psychology was in its period of infancy and there was considerable debate among various German scientists and philosophers regarding the determinants of behavior and the appropriate methods for its study. The legacy of Kant, in German ideological thought, had raised a number of perplexing issues about the relationship between object and perceiver. It had shaped a rigid distinction between the outer and the inner with all of its accompanying conceptual difficulties. Many famous figures in the history of psychology became involved in resolving these issues, including Ernst Mach, Wilhelm Wundt, Wilhelm Windleband, Heinrich Rickert, Edmund Husserl, Wilhelm Dilthey, and Edward Spranger. By the onset of the new century, a split had developed between those individuals favoring an experimental and empirical approach to behavior and those favoring a philosophical and experiential approach. At this point, efforts were made to synthesize these differing perspectives. The principal figures in these efforts were William Stern and the Gestalt psychologists.

The psychological perspective advanced by Stern was based on the concept of "wholeness." For Stern the critical feature of any effort to explain behavior resided in the fact that any element was always embedded in a whole. He sought to continually events and concepts in terms of their being a meaningful bounded unity that subsumed the various critical parts into one coherent unified concept. Stern wrote:

The methodological requirement that scientific psychology always preserve the correlation between part and whole, salience and ground, analysis and totality applies without exception. (Stern, 1938, p. 15)

Stern articulated the importance of "wholeness" in human behavior with vigor and persuasiveness, especially in his role as Director of the Hamburg Psychological Institute from 1916 to 1933. One of his disciples was Kurt Lewin (1890–1947). It was Lewin who advanced the first psychological system that can truly be termed "interactional" in nature. His system was called "topological" or "field" theory. Lewin was also influenced by the early Gestaltists: Max Wertheimer, Wolfgang Kohler, and Kurt Koffka. The Gestaltists and William Stern were the psychologists who applied the concepts of "field" theory from physics to psychology. By this time, field theory had emerged as a central concept in the work of Maxwell, Hertz, and Einstein. All of these physicists were committed to the belief that relational properties among various forces were building blocks of causal analysis. Gardner Murphy, in his popular text on the history of psychology, wrote:

The era of atomism began to come to an end and particles began to be understood as aspects of field relationships.... It is within this frame of reference, notably the developments in physics, that one must understand the development of field theory in psychology. The movement began when modern physics invaded the Gestalt psychology. (Murphy, 1949, p. 298)

Interactionism in the 1930s and 1940s

In Lewin's writings, we find the first systematic effort to understand behavior in terms of the simultaneous interaction of organismic and environmental variables. Lewin wrote:

In psychology one can begin to describe the whole situation by roughly distinguishing the person (P) and his environment (E). Every psychological event depends upon the state of the person and at the same time on the environment, although their relative importance is different in different cases. Thus we can state our formula $B = f(S)$ for every psychological event as $B = f(PE)$. The experimental work of recent years shows more and more this twofold relationship in all fields of psychology. Every scientific psychology must take into account whole situations, i.e., the state of both person and environment. (Lewin, 1936, p. 11)

During this same period, a number of other theorists also advanced interactional theories, including Kurt Goldstein and his student Fritz Perls, and Egon Brunswik and Andreas Angyal. Andreas Angyal is particularly important because more than any other theorist, he tried to develop a new conceptual language for psychology, a language that addressed the organism and the environment as a holistic unit for analysis. He called this unit the "biosphere." According to Angyal (1941),

The biosphere includes both the individual and the environment, not as interacting parts, not as constituents which have independent existence, but as aspects of a single reality which can be separated only by abstraction.... Every process which results from the interplay of organismic autonomy or environmental heteronomy is a part of the life process, irrespective of whether it takes place within the body or outside of it. The realm in which the life process takes place has been termed the "biosphere." (Angyal, 1941, pp. 99–101.)

Still others who became supporters of the interactional model in this period included Henry Murray and Jacob R. Kantor, both well-known American personality theorists. Kantor was one of the earliest writers in this area and has not been given the credit he deserves. He was influenced by Adolph Meyer, the famous psychiatrist associated with "psychobiological" approaches to psychopathology. Kantor (1933) believed that the individual interacts as a whole with certain stimuli. He noted the individual does not exist in a vacuum but rather in an environmental setting and the subject matter of psychology is the "interbehavior" of the individual with objects, events, other individuals and groups.

Henry Murray (1938) posited a similar notion. He wrote:

Since at every moment, an organism is within an environment which largely determines its behavior, and since the environment changes...the conduct of the individual cannot be formulated without a characterization of each confronting situation,...The organism and its milieu must be considered together, a single creature-environment interaction being a convenient short unit for psychology. A "long unit"—an individual life—can be most clearly formulated as a succession of related short units of "episodes." (Murray, 1938, p. 39)

Unfortunately, there is a sizable gap between theory and the methodology necessary for the validation of a theory. This is true of the interactional positions suggested by Lewin, Angyal, and others. The concepts they suggested made good intuitive sense but were impossible to study through empirical research. As a result, these theories had less influence on psychology.

By the 1960s, Lewin, Kantor, Angyal, and Goldstein had died, Perls had turned to Gestalt therapy, and Murray and Brunswik's theories had failed to capture the energies of new generations of psychologists. But at the very same time, a number of forces were active that would launch yet another era of concern for interactional perspectives. For example, the work of Brunswik and Lewin was being implemented by Roger Barker, who advanced the concept of "ecological" psychology (Barker, 1968). In addition, many clinicians and clinical scientists were evidencing increased interest in "social ecological" theories as the basis of community psychology (e.g., Mann, 1980; Kelly, 1981). But perhaps more than other events, the emergence of the "consistency versus specificity" issue served to focus interest once again on interactional theories of behavior.

The "consistency versus specificity" issue was stimulated by the publication of Walter Mischel's book, *Personality and Assessment.* In this book, Mischel argued that there was no evidence to support the concept of personality traits as determiners of behavior. He contended that behavior was not consistent across situations but rather, varied as a function of specific situations. As a result of his arguments, the specificity versus consistency issue emerged as a source of extensive debate.

Mischel's conclusions were challenged by numerous researchers, including Block (1962), Alker (1972), Wallach and Leggett (1972), and Marsella and Murray (1973), who argued that Mischel made many errors in his interpretation of trait research. Marsella and Murray (1973) published a study which concluded that consistency in behavior was itself a personality trait, because some individuals were more consistent than others in similar situations. Indeed, they argued that inconsistency (i.e., unpredictability) was one of the primary problems associated with psychopathology. Mischel (1973) and Bem (1972) reaffirmed the specificity position in subsequent publications and the debate has continued under new guises including the "stability versus change" issue in personality development.

Recent writers regarding the "stability versus change" issue include Brim and Kagan (1980) and Rubin (1981). For many years, researchers believed that personality development halted around the teen years or in early adulthood. For example, Freud and Sullivan halted personality development in late adolescence. But others such as Erik Eriksen and Abraham Maslow suggested that personality development occurred throughout the life span. Levinson (1978) and Sheehy (1977) raised appealing arguments regarding the continual growth and development of personality throughout life.

The "stability" position assumes that there is considerable constancy and identity in human personality across time and across situations. In contrast, the "change" position asserts that human beings constantly grow and change and thus do not manifest stability. Similar behavior does not occur across time even with similar situations because of continual personality change. Zick Rubin (1981) pointed out the unreasonableness of the "stability versus change" debate. Rubin stated:

Now that researchers have established beyond a reasonable doubt that there is often considerable stability in adult personality, they may be able to move on to a clearer understanding of how we can grow and change, even as we remain the same people we always were. It may be, for example, that if we are to make significant changes in ourselves, without losing our sense of identity, it is necessary for some aspects of our personality to remain stable. "I'm different now," we can say, "but, it's still me." (Rubin, 1981, p. 27)

At roughly the same time that Mischel was launching his attack on trait psychology and stimulating a return to interactional positions, other researchers were independently rediscovering the virtues of the interactional position. In the first instance, Endler and Hunt (1968, 1969) revived an interest in interactionalism by studying responses to various anxiety-provoking situations. Then, they used analysis of variance to partial out the variance due to person, situation, and interactional variables. In many respects, the basic contribution of Endler and Hunt was to point out the usefulness of statistical methods in identifying the contributions of person versus situation variables in research studies. Endler subsequently joined David Magnusson from Sweden in publishing a series of volumes and papers on the value of the interactional model (e.g., Endler & Magnusson, 1976).

In 1973, Bowers published an important review paper on "situationalism," in which he reported on 11 studies that examined person versus situational contributions to behavior. Bowers grouped the studies into three groups depending on the type of research method used. Among the seven studies using "behavior observation," three favored the *person* and four favored the *situation*. In contrast, among four studies using "self ratings," three favored the *person* and one favored the *situation*. Finally, among eight studies using "stimulus-response questionnaires," five favored the *person* and three favored the *situation*. In brief, although more studies favored the contributions of the person variance over the situation variance, the differences were only slight and no clear conclusion could be reached.

Summary

From the time of the alternative models of causality proposed by Aristotle and Galileo to the present-day conceptualizations of interactional theories of human behavior, there has been continual debate about the determinants of human behavior. The early personality theorists (e.g., Kantor, Lewin, Goldstein, Angyal, etc.) probably came the closest to providing a "true" interactional model of human behavior via their concern for the simultaneous interaction of both person and situation variables. Subsequent efforts to evolve interactional models have fallen short of resolving the issues proposed by these earlier theorists, although they have served to crystallize and to elaborate these issues. It would also be fair to conclude, however, that contemporary researchers have done more to examine the methodological aspects of interactional models in spite of the lack of substantive progress.

The next section of the chapter discusses a model of psychopathology that considers some of the requirements necessary for establishing an interactional theory. The basis of the model is the articulation of person, environment, and interactional components. The person component is represented by the coping or support dimension; the environmental component is represented by the stressor dimension; the interactional component is represented by the stress state dimension. The last component of the model is the psychopathology dimension. This is represented by the specifications for behavior shown in Figure 11.1. Psychopathology, as specified, is considered to be an outcome of stress state parameters. The latter, in turn, is a function of the simultaneous interaction of stressors and supports. Each of these components is divided into a number of categorical members which can be measured for inclusion in a multivariate analysis necessary for linking the components.

AN INTERACTIONAL MODEL OF PSYCHOPATHOLOGY

Stress

the conept of stress subsumes many other concepts and many disciplinary areas of inquiry. Cofer and Appley (1964) recognized this problem years ago when they stated stress

...has all but preempted a field previously shared by a number of other concepts...it is as though, when the word stress came into vogue, each investigator who had been working with a concept he felt was closely related, substituted the word stress for it and continued in his same line of investigation. (Cofer & Appley, 1964, pp. 441, 449)

The term *stress* came into vogue in the early 1950s with the work of Wolff and his colleagues at Cornell University (Wolff, Wolf, & Hare, 1950). The next two decades literally exploded with publications on stress.

As is well known, our current knowledge about stress developed largely from the work of early pioneers in physiology and medicine including Charles Darwin, Claude Bernard, Walter Cannon, Helen Flanders Dunbar, Franz Alexander, and Hans Selye.

Hans Selye's work was of special importance because he posited a universal human response to stressors. This response was termed the "general adaptation syndrome" and was considered to be invariant, regardless of the stressors that evoked it. But, a problem with the universal response description was that it could not account for the specific disorders which individuals developed. As a result, it was necessary to posit two conditions for a given disorder: (1) a generalized response pattern theory, and (2) a specific response pattern theory. Although few researchers have disagreed with Selye's notions about the changes that occur in the "general adaptation syndrome," a number of different theories have been suggested to account for the specific disorders that develop. These theories include those that emphasize (1) genetic weaknesses, (2) acquired vulnerabilities, (3) acquired organ-emotional response patterns, and (4) personality pattern determinants. To these theories, we can now add a fifth theory. The fifth theory suggests the specific type of disorder developed is a function of organismic-situational interactions. The organism can be represented as a coping response system that functions at biological, psychological, and sociological levels. The situation can be represented as a source of stressors. The "simultaneous" interaction of stressors and coping or support systems results in a stress state which conditions particular behavior patterns that may become maladaptive. It is important to recognize these premises assume "stress" is the general foundation of psychopathology, while the specific determinants reside in the interactional patterns of the stressors, coping, and stress state relationships. Thus, both organismic and situational variables determine the particular patterns of psychopathology that an individual develops.

In this chapter, psychopathology may be considered "adaptational" because it represents response patterns to psychological and physiological stress states. These conditions are elicited by external/internal stimulus patterns that are stressors. *Stressors* is the term I will employ for "any event/object/process which elicits a state of change in an organismic system." As was noted, it is my belief that the particular pattern of psychopathology developed is a function of the stressor/stress interactions. This pattern is in a continual state of change, although the variations may be minor. If we are to understand the various clinical parameters associated with psychopathology (i.e., symptom displays, disability profiles, courses, prognoses), it is necessary for us to delineate first those parameters of the stressors, coping, and stress states that are critical in the proposed model. In this section we will deal only with the first two elements of the equation: stressors and stress states.

Stressor Parameters

Although there are numerous stressor dimensions that could be explored, my research has tended to emphasize three parameters: category, content, and descriptors.

Stressor Category

Stressor category refers to the particular life functioning area from which the stressors are emanating. For example, stressors might be associated with such specific areas of functioning as housing, employment, health, marriage, child rearing, recreation, nutrition, interpersonal relations, and so forth. Obviously, these are not discrete categories and it is clear that although one category may emerge as a major source of stressors, eventually it can carry over into other categories of functioning. Nevertheless, these categories do provide a beginning point for referencing the contextual source of various stressors. It is certainly possible that specific categories may be distinctly linked to particular patterns of stressful experience by posing patterns of stressors that are unique.

Stressor Content

Stressor content refers to the particular type of stressor that develops in a given category. Examples include "loss" of job, spouse, status, or wealth; other possibilities include "confusion" over roles, "conflict" in expectations, "frustration" due to blocked goal seeking, "discrepancies" between certain aspiration-achievement patterns in employment, housing, marriage, and so forth. The stressor content essentially focuses on the quality of the "demand" characteristics of the stressor. Within this context, stressor content can be considered to be related to certain response patterns.

At a more general level of analysis, stressor content can be classified according to such categories as the following: (1) acculturation stressors, (2) role conflict stressors, (3) goal-striving discrepancy stressors, (4) value conflict stressors, (5) life-change stressors, (6) role deprivation stressors, (7) noxious stressors (e.g., noise, temperature, toxins), (8) social change stressors, and (9) nutritional deprivation stressors. As these examples indicate, stressors can be related to a spectrum of situations that involves conflict, deprivation, frustration, confusion, and so forth.

Stressor Descriptors

Stressor descriptors refer to various parameters of stressors that are capable of being measured. As noted previously, the stressor descriptors can be applied to biological, psychological, and sociological levels of functioning. Some of the more important parameters include the following:

1. Frequency—How often does the stressor occur?
2. Intensity—How much demand does the stressor impose?
3. Duration—How long does the stressor last?
4. Shape—Is the stressor sporadic, continuous, ascending, descending, linear, curvilinear, etc.?
5. Complexity—Is the stressor complex (i.e., additive, multiplicative)?
6. Discriminability—Is the stressor interpretable and/or identifiable?
7. Controllability—Is the stressor capable of being controlled by either personal or social responses?
8. Familiarity—Is the stressor familiar? Has the organism had previous experience with the stressor?
9. Predictability—Is the stressor predictable or consistent?
10. Conflict—Does the stressor have positive and negative valences?

Stress States

Stress states are the organismic experiential conditions that emerge from the interaction of stressors and supports. Stress states are experienced at biological, psychological, and sociological levels of functioning much as stressors and supports exist at multiple levels. Several stress states dimensions are important in the proposed model.

Stress State Contents

Stress state contents refers to particular patterns of organismic experience characterized by positions on the following three parameters: (1) system overload–system underload, (2) positive–negative, (3) high arousal–low arousal. In the authors' opinion, these three parameters represent basic functional dimensions of human experience that are relatively independent of one another and that capture fundamental poles of human experience. The authors believe these three parameters have particular relevance for psychopathology beause their representational properties may shape maladaptive patterns by conditioning organismic and situational cues. For example, a stress state consisting of *high* overload, *negative* experience, and *high* arousal might condition a confused, delirious, and agitated profile of psychopathology.

In contrast, patterns of underload, negative experience, and low arousal might condition a withdrawn, flat, apathetic, hallucinatory profile. Particular stress states can be differentiated along these parameters and linked with distinct patterns of psychopathology. If particular patterns are experienced over long periods of time, they can shape distinct epistemological orientations (i.e., distinct orientations of causality, time, and space). Implicit within any affective and cognitive state is a sense of causality, time, and space. Thus, if we are highly aroused, we experience the world according to a different causal pattern. We may see causality as a function of contiguity of events (e.g., superstitions) rather than in terms of "logical" relations. Similarly, our concept of time is altered so that events may seem longer or shorter than they may seem under different arousal conditions.

Essentially, the nervous system codes reality according to our experience. If we experience reality at particular levels of arousal, overload–underload, and positive–negative affect with their distinct epistemological implications, then particular patterns of reality will become the normative experience. In a previous paper, the senior author argued these points by discussing the consequences of individuals taking LSD over long periods. Under LSD, reality (i.e., causality, time, space) is altered. The drug experience causes the nervous system to code new reality experiences. Thus, even when the drug is no longer used, the drug reality experience may emerge as a competing reality to that of the "normal state" (Marsella & Price-Williams, 1975).

Stress State Parameters

Stress state parameters refer to descriptors that can define the stress state at either a specific or general level of functioning. The specific stress state parameters suggested are the same as those listed as stressor parameters (i.e., frequency, shape, etc.).

Support (Coping)

A third component of the proposed model is the support or coping dimension. This component includes all of the biological, psychological, or sociological aspects of human functioning that mediate stressors. In this regard, the final stress state experienced by the organism is a function of the stressor-support interaction. Similar stressors can have totally different implications because of individual variations in the supports that mediate them. Stress states are clearly a product of these two components.

Supports can exist at several different levels of human functioning. At a biological level, the organism's state of health is very important in combatting disease and in providing the necessary strength to cope with the demands of life. Excessive fatigue, malnutrition, organ impairment, and so forth can lead to many problems, especally in the face of severe stressors. The energy and endurance needed to cope with stressors are greatly impaired and limited in the face of physiological problems. Thus, it is clear that biological coping is a critical part of dealing with life stressors.

At a psychological level, it is important to understand the role of cognitive mediation of stress. The use of defense mechanisms to deal with anxiety are familiar from psychodynamic psychology. In addition, the stress inoculation techniques of cognitive behavior modification have gained great popularity within the last decade. In previous research on the cognitive mediation of stressors, my colleagues and I (e.g., Marsella, Escusdero, & Gordon, 1972) found that individuals tended to use four different types of life philosophies to cope with stress. These included the following: (1) *Religion* (e.g., "One must pray and trust in God in times of trouble."); (2) *Self-directed behavior* (e.g., "People can solve their problems by planning and thinking through situations."); (3) *Projection* (e.g., "Most peoples' troubles are generally the result of the malice of others."); and (4) *Optimistic fatalism* (e.g., "Things happen according to destiny...what will happen, will happen.").

Our ability to construe the stressors we encounter in particular ways is a critical part of our response to them. Our perceptual processes enable us to defuse potentially pernicious stressors by viewing them in ways that permit us to reduce their severity and negative implications. This can be done by conscious or unconscious thought processes. In this respect, the psychological mediation of stressors is a potent source of coping and support.

Supports also exist at social levels of functioning, especially in terms of family, friendship, and social welfare networks and support systems (see Gottlieb, 1981). Research has indicated that social support systems are critical determinants of the course and outcome of severe psychiatric disorders such as schizophrenia, depression, and neurotic disorders (e.g., Marsella & Snyder, 1981; Henderson, Byrne, & Duncan-Jones, 1981; Hammer, 1981; Beels, 1981). Social support networks can now be readily studied because a considerable number of research instruments have been developed for utilization with both normal and abnormal populations.

In brief, supports or coping resources represent an important dimension of human functioning in the face of stressors. They exist at biological, psychological, and social levels and their indices can be included in any conceptual model of psychopathology.

THE SPECIFICATION OF PSYCHOPATHOLOGY

If we are to make any progress in psychopathology, it is critical to obtain some method for increasing the specificity of our observations. The use of broad clinical labels with minimal attention to specific clinical parameters can only hinder our understanding. A system for classifying behavior is needed which offers a more systematic analysis of those behaviors we associate with psychopathology. I would like to suggest an alternative strategy that could prove useful for relating maladaptive behaviors to the three components of the model: stressors, supports, and stress states (see Figure 11.2).

An Alternative Classification Strategy

Rather than focusing on symptoms in general, it might be useful for researchers and theorists to specify those behaviors associated with psychopathology along two dimensions: (1) Functional systems and (2) Simple and complex response parameters. Although human behavior can be separated across many different categories, potentially valuable implications exist for grouping it according to various functional systems of behavior. These include: somatic, sensory, perceptual, motor, cognition, affective, and interpersonal and self. Each of these functional systems has a number of functions that it performs at varying degrees of involvement with the other systems:

1. Somatic: reproduction, repair, rest, nourishment
2. Sensory: information, acquisition and processing
3. Perceptual: information sorting, interpreting, judging
4. Motor: coordination, movement
5. Affective: arousal, emotion
6. Cognitive: symbolic behavior (verbal, imagistic), language, memory
7. Interpersonal: sociability, appearance
8. Self: purpose, meaning, coherence

These are the systems involved in human behavior—both normal and abnormal. Abnormal behavior differs from normal behavior not in terms of the kinds of responses of the different systems, but rather in terms of the attributes and the situations in which the responses occur.

Some of the more important response attributes for studying abnormal behaviors include the following:

1. Quantitative

    Response Activation: Present or Absent

    Rate: Low–High

    Duration: Brief–Long

    Latency: Slow–Fast

2. Qualitative

    Appropriate: Appropriate or Inappropriate

    Situational Appropriateness: Is the response appropriate to the situation?

    Inconsistency: Is the response inappropriate to the preceding response?

    Interpenetration: Does the response intrude in a sequence but belong to another sequence?

    Perseveration: Does the response occur repeatedly?

    Interruption: Does a response suddenly stop?

    Fragmentation: Are responses random and inefficient?

    Incongruence: Are responses split up?

    Conflict: Are two or more response sequences incompatible?

    Antecedents: Is a response inappropriately related to a stimulus that sets it off?

Within this context, researchers and clinicians are able to specify the "symptoms" in more detail. This permits a greater understanding of their properties.

OVERVIEW OF PROPOSED MODEL

The previous sections discussed the four major components of the model: stressors, social supports, stress states, and psychopathology. Each of the first three components was discussed with regard to the various parameters assumed to be relevant to understanding, describing, and predicting the etiology, onset, expression, course, and prognosis of various forms of psychopathology.

The purpose of the previous sections was to suggest that psychopathology can be conceptualized as adaptive efforts that reflect the complex interaction of various stressor, social support, and stress state parameters. This approach is closely related to newer theoretical and research strategies which emphasize interactional relationships between different variables and variable categories.

This chapter is a step toward the development of an interactional model of psychopathology. It delineates some of the variables that should be considered in conceptualizing psychopathology. Figure 11.1 indicates these variables.

In the future, it will be necessary to develop quantifiable indices of these variables and to specify or to hypothesize relationships among them. Empirical studies will then comprise the final test of the model's utility.

One of the major problems confronting the interactional theories and research strategies is that of data analysis. Clearly, multivariate methods are required because of the many variables involved. In addition to factor analysis and regression analysis, researchers are currently exploring the possibilities of applying topological mathematical concepts to behavioral science topics under the rubric of "catastrophe theory" (Zeeman, 1975).

Each of these methods has its own distinct advantages and disadvantages. All, however, offer researchers opportunities to examine many variables in interaction, and obviously, multivariate methods approximate "true" life conditions more accurately. One of the most unfortunate aspects of much current research is that it often fails to examine variables within a multivariate context.

There are numerous possibilities for increasing our understanding of psychopathology by emphasizing interactional approaches. By themselves, neither stressors, stress states, nor supports can provide a sufficient solution to the puzzles of psychopathology. But together, they offer us the chance to raise new questions about an old problem.

REFERENCES

Alker, H. (1972) Is personality situationally specific or intrapsychically consistent? *Journal of Personality,* **40,** 1–15.

American Psychiatric Association (1980) *Diagnostic and Statistical Manual III.* Washington, D.C.: American Psychiatric Association.

Angyal, A. (1941) *Foundations for a Science of Personality.* Cambridge, Mass.: Harvard University Press.

Andrews, G., Tennant, C., Hewson, D., & Vaillant, G. (1978) Life event stress, social support, coping style, and risk of psychological impairment. *Journal of Nervous and Mental Disease,* **166,** 307–316.

Barker, R. (1968) *Ecological Psychology.* Stanford, Calif.: Stanford University Press.

Beels, C. (1981) Social support and schizophrenia. *Schizophrenia Bulletin,* **7,** 58–72.

Bem, D. (1972) Constructing cross-situation consistencies in behavior: Some thoughts on Alker's critique of Mischel. *Journal of Personality,* **40,** 17–26.

Block, J. (1968) Some reasons for the apparent inconsistency of personality. *Psychological Bulletin,* **70,** 210–222.

Bowers, K. (1973) Situationalism in psychology: An analysis and a critique. *Psychological Review,* **80,** 307–336.

Brim, O. and Kagan, J. (Eds.) (1980) *Constancy and change in human development.* Cambridge, Mass.: Harvard University Press.

Cobb, S. (1976) Social support as a moderator of life stress. *Psychosomatic Medicine,* **38,** 300–314.

Cofer, C., & Appley, M. (1964) *Motivation: Theory and research.* New York: Wiley.

Dean, A., & Lin, N. (1977) The stress-buffering role of social support. *The Journal of Nervous and Mental Disease,* **165,** 403–417.

Endler, D., & Hunt, J. McV. Generalizability of contributions from sources of variance in the S-R inventories of anxiousness. *Journal of Personality,* **37,** 1–24.

Endler, N., & Hunt, J. McV. (1968) S-R inventories of hostility and comparisons of the proportion of variance from persons, responses, and situations for hostility and anxiousness. *Journal of Personality and Social Psychology,* **9,** 309–315.

Endler, N. & Magnusson, D. (1976) *Interactional psychology and personality.* Washington, D.C.: Hemisphere Publishing.

Gottlieb, B. (Ed.) (1981) *Social networks and social supports.* Beverly Hills, Calif.: Sage Publications.

Hammer, M. (1981) Social supports, social networks, and schizophrenia. *Schizophrenia Bulletin,* **7,** 45–57.

Hwang, K.K. (1976) Social stress and psychological adaptation in Taiwan. Unpublished doctoral dissertation. University of Hawaii, Honolulu, Hawaii.

Henderson, S., Byrne, D., & Duncan-Jones, P. (1981) *Neurosis and the social environment.* New York: Academic Press.

Johnson, J., & Sarason, I. (1979) Moderator variables in life stress research. In Sarason, I., & Spielberger, C. (Eds.), *Stress and anxiety.* Washington, D.C.: Hemisphere Publishing.

Kantor, J. (1933) *A survey of the science of psychology.* New York: Principia Press.

Kantor, J. (1955) Interbehavioral psychology. In M. Marx (Ed.), *Psychological theory.* New York: Macmillan.

Levinson, S. (1978) *The stages of a man's life.* New York.

Lewin, K. (1936) *Principles of topological psychology.* New York: McGraw-Hill.

Mann, L. (1979) *Community psychology.* Glencoe, Ill.: Free Press.

Marsella, A.J. (1982) Culture and mental health: An overview. In A.J. Marsella, & G. White (Eds.), *Cultural conceptions of mental health and therapy.* Hingham, Mass.: Reidel.

Marsella, A.J., Escudero, M., & Brennan, J. (1975) Goal-striving discrepancy stress in urban Filipino men: II. *International Journal of Social Psychiatry,* **21,** 282–291.

Marsella, A.J., Escudero, M., & Gordon, P. (1971) Stresses, resources, and symptom patterns in urban Filipino men. In W. Lebra (Ed.), *Transcultural mental health research in Asia and the Pacific.* Honolulu, Hawaii: East-West Center Press.

Marsella, A.J., Escudero, M., & Santiago, C. (1969) Stresses, resources, and symptom patterns in urban Filipino men. Paper presented at Second Conference on Transcultural Mental Health Research in Asia and the Pacific. University of Hawaii, Honolulu.

Marsella, A.J., & Murray, M. (1973) Diagnostic type, gender, and consistency versus specificity in behavior. *Journal of Clinical Psychology,* **30,** 484–488.

Marsella, A.J., & Price-Williams, D. (1974) Hallucinogens and epistemic organization. *Bulletin of the Menninger Clinic,* **38,** 70–72.

Marsella, A.J., & Snyder, K. (1981) Stress, social supports, and schizophrenia disorders: Toward an interactional model. *Schizophrenia Bulletin,* **7,** 152–163.

Mischel, W. (1968) *Personality and assessment.* New York: Wiley.

Mischel, W. (1973). Toward a cognitive social learning reconceptualization of personality. *Psychological Review,* **80,** 252–283.

Murphy, G. (1949) *Historical introduction to modern psychology.* New York: Harcourt Brace Jovanovich.

Murray, H. (1938) *Explorations in personality.* New York: Oxford Press.

Rubin, Z. (1981) Does personality really change after 20? *Psychology Today,* **15,**(5), 18–27.

Sheehy, G. (1977) *Passages.* New York: Ballantine.

Stern, W. *General psychology from the personalistic standpoint.* New York: Macmillan.

Wallach, M., & Leggett, M. (1972) Testing the hypothesis that a person will be consistent: Stylistic consistency versus situational specificity in size of children's drawings. *Journal of Personality,* **40,** 309–322.

Wolff, H., Wolf, S., & Hare, L. (Eds.) (1950) *Life stress and bodily disease.* Baltimore, Md.: Williams & Wilkens.

Zeeman, E. (1976) Catastrophe theory. *Scientific American,* **234,** 65–83.

Zubin, J., & Spring, B. (1977) Vulnerability—a new view of schizophrenia *Journal of Abnormal Psychology,* **86,** 103–126.

CHAPTER 12

Assessing Quality of Life
in the Community:
An Ecological Approach

DARLENE E. GOODHART AND ALEX ZAUTRA

INTRODUCTION

How a problem is defined greatly determines what is done to solve it. The definition of a social problem, in the words of Caplan and Nelson (1973),

...determines the attempts at remediation—or even whether such attempts will be made—by suggesting both the *foci* and the *techniques* of intervention and by ruling out alternative possibilities. More specifically, problem definition determines the change strategy, the selection of a social action delivery system, and the criteria for evaluation. (p. 200).

For most of its history, the "problem" for community mental health and community psychology has been to reduce rates of mental disorder in society (Heller & Monahan, 1977). Dominated by the traditions of clinical psychology and psychiatry, the causes of mental disorder were seen to reside within the individual, taking such forms as intrapsychic conflict, faulty learning history, and inability to delay gratification. To reduce psychopathology in society, therefore, meant extending treatment to as many troubled individuals as possible, particularly to previously excluded groups such as minorities and the poor.

In recent years, there has been growing dissatisfaction with this definition of the problem (Heller & Monahan, 1977). Primarily, it ignores the contribution of such environmental stressors as poverty, pollution, and discrimination to human suffering, and turns attention away from systems-level interventions that could reduce distress more effectively (e.g., Price, 1974). However, shifting blame for psychopathology away from persons and onto environments is not a satisfactory solution either (Rappaport, 1977). It implies that persons are passive victims of outside forces, and disregards the fact that, to a degree, persons shape their own environments, as well as being shaped by them. Thus a more accurate and complete definition of the problem of psychopathology would view it as the result of troubled relations between person and environment, rather than as the result of deficiencies within either one alone (Caplan & Nelson, 1973).

There are even further questions as to whether psychopathology should be the *only* problem for community work. Instead, helping the community to develop its strengths and resources should also be a problem needing attention (Sanford, 1972). An orientation is called for that adopts the quality of life (QOL) in the community as the dominant concern. A QOL orientation includes the alleviation of distress, but does not stop there. It also considers how positive mental health (Jahoda, 1958) can be promoted by fostering opportunities in communities for members to find satisfactions and develop competencies.

The emergent ideology in community mental health and community psychology, then highlights the importance of both person and environment, and how person-environment relations affect QOL, with QOL encompassing not only adjustment to difficulties, but positive mental health as well (e.g., Heller & Monahan, 1977). Interventions following from this ideology would include both person and environment in efforts to prevent psychological maladjustment, but perhaps more importantly, would seek to enhance positive mental health in its own right. To guide these interventions, research is clearly needed. However, this research must generate understanding of problems and progress in communities in ways other than those derived from the study of individuals. An ecological perspective can be particularly promising in this regard (Rappaport, 1977). Its defining feature is to consider persons in the context of environments, and how transactions between person and environment affect QOL.

The purpose of our chapter is to discuss the utility and application of an ecological perspective for the assessment of the QOL of individuals in communities. QOL assessment is defined as a research activity designed to generate information about the QOL of individuals, and about how QOL is maintained and modified by person and environment. In keeping with the discussion above, QOL is seen as encompassing both psychological adjustment and positive mental health (see Zautra & Goodhart, 1979). Psychological adjustment reflects the level of adaptation to environmental demands, and the degree to which person-environment relations enable basic tension-reduction needs (e.g., safety, security, affiliation) to be met. Positive mental health reflects the degree to which person-environment relations foster the development of competencies, achievements, life satisfactions, and opportunities for environmental mastery.

The power of an ecological approach to QOL assessment is that it provides a framework for both person and environment to be considered simultaneously when planning and evaluating strategies for intervention in the community. Strategies responsive to person-environment interrelationships can remedy social problems and foster QOL more effectively than strategies that consider person or environment alone. In addition, an ecological approach can contribute to the development of theory regarding forces within persons and environments that promote and hinder QOL in communities.

To give a brief overview of the chapter, we first present a preliminary conceptual framework for understanding and assessing QOL in the community from an ecological perspective. The framework takes as its point of departure the significant events in the lives of community members, such as marriage, job loss, and retirement. Methods for measuring QOL and life events are considered next. To illustrate our ideas, we present an example of an ecological assessment of QOL from our own research in a tri-city community. Following this, we offer a sampling of primary prevention strategies to improve QOL that could follow from assessment of QOL from an ecological perspective. Possible directions for future research are then considered, and the chapter is concluded with an overall summary of the major points.

AN ECOLOGICAL FRAMEWORK OF QOL IN THE COMMUNITY

Lewin's (1951) renowned equation, $B = f(P, E)$, signifies that behavior is a function of person and environment. In this section, we present a preliminary ecological framework that considers QOL as a function of person-environment relations. The primary settings for these relations are the significant life events of community residents (Lazarus & Cohen, 1977), such as marriage, job promotion, retirement, and physical illness. Life events make the limits and opportunities of environments known to persons. Life events also enable persons to gain awareness of their strengths and deficits, develop coping skills, and alter their environments. To understand QOL in the community thus requires a thorough understanding of life events. Although several comprehensive descriptions of events have been offered (e.g., Dohrenwend & Dohrenwend, 1974), more attention must be given to the context of personal and social forces in which an event occurs (Hultsch & Plemons, 1979). The same event in a different context has very different psychological meanings and effects (Neugarten & Datan, 1973). The significance of an ecological perspective of QOL is the fact that the psychological and social "environments" of events are highlighted as key determinants of their outcomes.

Our ecological framework is intended as a conceptual tool for understanding QOL, and also as a tool for integrating data from applied community research into useful form for program planning, intervention, and evaluation. We emphasize that this framework is offered only as a guideline for these efforts, not as an empirically validated model. Future research is needed to test the adequacy and accuracy of our thinking, and to add substance to these beginning formulations.

The section presents major considerations regarding life events and their contexts that need to be included in an ecological perspective of QOL. It also integrates these considerations into an overall framework to describe how the event context can shape the nature and course of reaction to an event and its ultimate outcome for QOL. Because of the length and number of ideas presented, the reader may wish to refer to the summary at the end of the section before proceeding.

Preliminary Assumptions

Conceptual frameworks typically make preliminary assumptions. As a prelude to the remainder of the chapter, we present three assumptions that underlie our ecological framework of QOL. The first assumptions hold that both person and environment must be considered together as a unit of analysis. Interactions between person and environment are reciprocal processes (Lazarus & Cohen, 1977). Persons shape and, in turn, are shaped by their environments, and similarly, environments affect and, in turn, are affected by the persons embedded within them. QOL arises out of these mutual interactions and interdependencies between person and environment, and cannot be adequately understood outside this framework (Lazarus & Cohen, 1977).

The second assumption proposes that QOL is a product of the *fit* between person and environment (Pervin, 1968). Fit refers to the degree of congruence between opportunities and demands from the environment and the individual's needs, abilities, and expectations (French, Rodgers, & Cobb, 1974).

The third assumption regards the implications of person-environment fit for human service planning and community development. It pertains to the notion of multiple environments, or "niche breadth"(Mills & Kelly, 1972) in communities. Person-environment fit does not connote fitting everyone to one "best" environment (e.g., Rappaport, 1977). Adaptive behavior varies depending on behavioral styles of the individual and normative requirements of the setting. To enhance QOL in communities, then, the interventionist and social planner must increase the diversity of settings (or niches) to which persons with different behavioral styles can adapt (Rappaport, 1977).

Person and Environment Inputs

Persons and environments each make inputs into the person-environment equation. From persons come a variety of characteristics, such as beliefs, choices and values, strengths and vulnerabilities, and goals and motivations. Personality theory is replete with examples of dimensions on which person can be described. Studies of person-environment fit have focused primarily on three of these dimensions, demographic characteristics (Weschler & Pugh, 1967), capacities for life maintenance and environmental mastery (e.g., Lawton & Nahemow, 1973), and motivational factors such as needs, wants, and preferences (e.g., Kahana, 1975; Stern, 1970).

Descriptions of environments as inputs into the person-environment equation have been offered by Barker (1964) in his theory of behavior settings, and by Moos (1973) in his conceptualization of social climates. Environments also have been construed in terms of systems theory (e.g., Bronfenbrenner, 1977). Furthermore, environments have been differentiated into living and nonliving components, into social units (e.g., family, peer groups, co-workers), and into community organizations and institutions (e.g., family, peer groups, co-workers), and into community organizations and institutions (e.g., church, business, social service agency) (Holahan & Spearly; 1980; Lazarus & Cohen, 1977).

To have an impact on individuals, however, environments must be translated into forces that influence behavior directly (Lewin, 1951), say by affecting resources and obstacles for meeting needs and goals, or by affecting the behavior of others in the social field. Environmental forces that act directly on persons can be described as demands and supplies (French et al., 1974). Demands are external requirements that call for a response from the person. A job or family, for example, demands the performance of certain role requirements and activities. Supplies are external resources that help persons meet demands, as for example, financial assets, care-giving social networks and institutions, and community and cultural values. (Note that demands and supplies can emanate from persons as well.)

Life Events as Person-Environment Transactions

Persons and environments represent the raw inputs into the person-environment equation. The primary units of transaction between person and environment are the major events in the experience of life in the community (Lazarus & Cohen, 1977). Events have been typically viewed as environmental in origin, with unidirectional effects on persons. As Lazarus and Cohen (1977) point out, however, there are difficulties in "speaking as if...events necessarily originate independently of the person's contributory activity, that is, as solely environmental events rather than as transactions between persons and environment" (pp. 89–99). For example, events such as divorce, job promotion or job loss, and vacation are at least partly the product of the person's coping activity, performance virtues and inadequacies, decisions, and resources. Persons also modify the physical and social environment through life events (Altman & Lett, 1970).

Functions of Life Events

Events serve two main functions in the life of the individual: as markers and as processes (Danish, Smyer, & Nowak, 1980). When viewed as markers, events signify milestones or transitions. For example, pregnancy is a transition point in the life experience. To the person and to others, it signifies the beginning of a family, and initiates an entire sequence of new events, such as childbirth, child starting school, and child graduating and leaving home. The life experience is given shape, direction, and meaning by periods of major change, rather than by periods of stability (Lowenthal & Chiriboga, 1973).

Events also function as processes in the life course. The actual experience of the event as an unfolding series of daily changes assumes an importance of its own. Thus for the individual woman, pregnancy may be as much the morning sickness and the swelling stomach as the signal of life's progression. When viewed as processes, events have a beginning, a middle period of coping and adaptation, and usually come to some sort of resolution in time (Caplan, 1964).

Cognitive Appraisal Processes and Life Events

Life events can have no impact on QOL, however, unless perceived and comprehended. These functions are accomplished through cognitive appraisal processes (Lazarus, Averill, & Opton, 1974). Cognitive appraisal is an invariant part of the response to events for all persons. It represents the means by which the signficance of the event for well-being is judged and evaluated (Lazarus et al., 1974). Appraisals mediate the entire sequence of reaction to events, beginning with the initial perception of an occurrence, following through to its resolution. The same life event will not have uniform meaning and impact on all persons. Depending on the cognitive appraisal, an event stressful for one person can be neutral or positive for another, or to the first person at a different time.

Several aspects of life events can be particularly important in cognitive appraisals. These relate to the amount of change (Holmes & Rahe, 1967) and to the desirability of change (Vinokur & Selzer, 1975) brought about by an event (see also Redfield & Stone, 1979). The significance of amount of change as a salient dimension in event appraisals derives from a homeostasis model of behavior (Selye, 1956). Under ordinary conditions, person and environment are in a state of homeostasis or dynamic equilibrium maintained by the person's habitual regulatory mechanisms, and by customary environmental demands. When a particular person-environment transaction departs from the norm, stress is precipitated, and the transaction may become a significant life event. The amount of stress precipitated by an event is directly related to the magnitude of the deviation from the typical life course, and hence, the amount of readjustment effort required to restore equilibrium to person-environment relations (Holmes & Masuda, 1974). Note that the absence of life events, or underload, may also be stressful (Levi, 1974). Viewed from the perspective of change being the dominant concern, an absence of events may represent a change from an ongoing steady state to a new level in which significantly fewer adjustive demands are made on the person.

Once a change in ongoing person-environment transactions is perceived, its meaning and significance for well-being are evaluated (Lazarus et al., 1974). A major distinction among events in this regard pertains to desirability (Vinokur & Selzer, 1975). Some events may represent positive changes in the previous state (e.g., marriage, purchasing a house, school graduation), whereas others may represent negative changes (e.g., illness, divorce, job loss) (Dohrenwend, 1973; Parkes, 1971). Negative events rather consistently have been found to predict psychological distress and maladjustment (e.g., Vinokur & Selzer, 1975), perhaps by signifying personal failures or losses of valued attributes and objects. Positive events may augment well-being and life satisfaction, possibly by signifying important achievements, personal competencies, or gains of desired attributes and assets (Zautra & Reich, 1980). Paradoxically, however, positive events may also raise levels of distress under some conditions (Block & Zautra, 1981).

Psychological and Social Contexts of Life Events

As stated above, events and their effects are mediated by cognitive appraisal processes, one important appraisal being the perception of change in ongoing life patterns, and another the evaluation of the desirability of the change. However, change and desirability have no meaning in the absolute. Instead, a standard or reference point is required against which to compare the focal situation. As Lewin (1935), states, "judgment, understanding, perception are impossible without a related background, and the meaning of every event depends directly on the nature of its background" (p. 175). Thus the perception of change can occur only against a background of no change, or change at a different rate. Similarly, the assessment of desirability can be made only with reference to some prior or desired condition. On closer inspection then, cognitive appraisals of life events involve processes of comparative judgment in which an event is compared and contrasted with normative standards.

The next concern is to identify sources from which these standards may be derived. One primary source can be found in the person's own perceptions of his or her self in relation to the psychological world (Sherif, 1967). These perceptions include such aspects of the self-concept as goals and values, needs and motivations, knowledge, strengths and vulnerabilities, as well as other cognitive, affective, and conative dimensions. These self-appraisals form a *psychological context* for experiencing and responding to life events.

Another source of standards of comparison for appraising events can be found in the person's perception of his or her self in relation to the social environment (Sherif, 1967). Much of the experience of life in the community centers around self-perceptions of how and where one fits into the immediate social environment and the larger social structure (Suls & Miller, 1977). These self-appraisals form a *social context* for experiencing and responding to life events.

Not everyone in the social environment is equally salient as a source of normative standards, however. Instead, only certain individuals, those serving as reference groups, are used for social comparison (Festinger, 1954). Perceptions and evaluations of one's situation depend largely on which reference group is employed for comparison purposes (Merton & Kitt, 1950). A key factor in selecting reference groups is the perceived similarity between oneself and potential social comparison persons (Gruder, 1977). Similarity may be along social and demographic dimensions (Merton & Kitt, 1950), as well as along dimensions representing less tangible attributes such as beliefs, attitudes, and abilities (Festinger, 1954). Comparison persons may also be found in groups to which the individual aspires to belong but is not a member (Sherif, 1967). Note that individuals may not be totally free to choose their reference groups. Communities may actively enforce normative standards sanctioning appropriate goals and behavior for its different members.

Of all possible areas of perceived similarity among individuals, age, or life stage which combines age, marital status, and the presence of children, is particularly salient (Baltes & Willis, 1977). There is a growing body of literature in adult development that describes the significance of age peers and age norms for governing reactions to major life experiences (e.g., Birren & Schaie, 1977). In addition, there are other areas of perceived similarity among community members. Although less studied than age, economic status (cf. Catalano & Dooley, 1977) and ethnicity (Zautra & Barrera, Note 1) may be important bases of social comparison.

Normative Life Events

Normative standards for events may be communicated to individuals in many ways, and have many forms of representation within the cognitive structure. However, a major mode of communication and cognitive representation may be in the "language" of life events themselves. That is, normative standards may be embodied by normative life events. Normative events may be thought of in adaptation level (AL) theory (Helson, 1959) terms as representing AL or the point at which no change would be perceived in ongoing person-environment relations. These are events for which the individual has readily available, reflexive coping and adaptation mechanisms, or the "range of stimulation within which adaptive responding is not required" (Cofer & Appley, 1964, p. 336).

As noted above, the psychological and social contexts in which events occur are important sources of normative standards. These standards, then, can be conveyed and cognitively represented by events regarded as normative by psychological or social criteria. From a psychological context, the person's own history of life experiences can serve as important standards of comparison for new events (Lawton & Nahemow, 1973). Past events influence expectancies about likely future occurrences. Also, the repetoire of coping skills, as well as one's psychological vulnerabilities, are much the product of previous person-environment encounters (Lazarus & Launier, 1978). Similarly, appraisals of an event's desirability are influenced by whether a deviation is in a positive or negative direction from expectancies based on past occurrences (Beck, 1971). That individuals do, in fact, use psychological contextual norms for evaluating major life experiences is a central, although usually implicit, notion in life events theory (e.g., Dohrenwend & Dohrenwend, 1974).

With respect to the social context, norms can be represented by high-probability events for the reference groups of which one is (or wishes to be) a member (e.g., Neugarten, Moore, & Lowe, 1965). Age or life-stage peers are especially important, for they set standards governing the time in the life course when certain events are (or are not) supposed to occur (Neugarten, 1976). Certain life experiences occur with greater regularity at particular life stages, as for example marriage, family development, and career advancement in early and middle adulthood, and retirement, illness, and death later in life. Moreover, expectations regarding major life events can be charted (Neugarten & Datan, 1973). As Neugarten (1976) states:

There exists a socially prescribed timetable for the ordering of major life events: a time in the lifespan when men and women are expected to marry, a time to raise children, a time to retire. The normative pattern is adhered to, more or less consistently, by most persons within a social group. (p. 16)

In addition, certain life events cluster for community groups depending on socioeconomic status (Catalano & Dooley, 1977) and ethnicity (Zautra & Barrera, Note 1). Specifically, social losses may be more prevalent for low social status groups and ethnic minorities, whereas social gains may characterize the life experience of higher status, nonminority community members (Dohrenwend, 1973). These experiences form a normative background against which new life events can be appraised.

It is important to recognize that the use of normative standards in cognitive appraisals of events is a highly complex process that must be considered from multiple perspectives. To illustrate, normative events shape not only expectancies, but affect vulnerabilities and coping resources as well. In the case of lower status community groups, undesirable experiences may be congruent with expectations, and less cognitively disruptive. However, their cumulation can reduce well-being by depleting psychological and social resources for coping (Dohrenwend & Dohrenwend, 1981). Moreover, disadvantaged persons may not use each other as reference groups, but instead may compare their situations with middle- or upper-class norms.

Event-Context Congruence

We stated that standards of reference provided by psychological and social contexts are highly important for cognitive appraisals of life events. At this point, we emphasize that it is the degree of *fit* or *congruence* between an event and its context that is of key concern. We thus propose that the concept of person-environment fit, of central importance in ecological models of behavior, be extended to life events as well. It is our major premise that the perception of, course of reaction to, and ultimately, the impact of a life event on QOL depends on the fit of the event with its psychological and social contexts. Because these contexts can be represented by normative events, we can be even more specific: *Responses to and outcomes of life events depend on the congruence of the event with events normative by psychological and social contextual standards.* The amount of fit perceived to exist between an event and normative events we refer to as *event-context congruence*. Event-context congruence signifies whether the present progression of the life experience is synchronous with the prior course, and with the life courses of salient others in the social environment.

Note that psychological and social contexts are intimately interrelated, and standards of comparison from both combine to shape the background against which a given life event is cognitively appraised. However, progressions of events along an inner psychological dimension are not always coordinated with progressions along an outer social course (Riegel, 1975). That is, an event which conforms to psychological norms may be off-time or out of step with the social environment, and conversely, timely, congruent social events may be highly distressing by psychological contextual standards. The manner in which these asynchronies are resolved has important consequences for the individual's continuing growth and development (Riegel, 1975).

Some empirical support has been found for the notion that congruence between an event and its normative contexts may be an important predictor of the event's impact on the QOL. The significance of a psychological context for shaping the outcomes of events was illustrated in a quasi-experimental study by Reich and Zautra (1981) in a college student sample. Groups of subjects were asked to perform varying numbers of activities they found pleasurable, and returned one month later to fill out questionnaires assessing their QOL. Although positive well-being was found to be somewhat higher when more pleasurable activities were undertaken, overall there were no differences among the groups on mental distress. When the frequency of prior negative events reported was statistically controlled, however, interesting group differences emerged. Subjects who both reported more negative events and were asked to perform more pleasurable activities manifested a significant drop in mental distress, as well as an increase in positive well-being, compared with the other groups. The previous negative events may have shaped a psychological context in which stressors were the norm, thus making subsequent pleasurable experiences more cognitively and affectively salient by comparison. But subjects for whom stressors were not the norm (who reported fewer prior negative events) were relatively unaffected by the later positive engagements.

Other research suggests, additionally, that event-context congruence may be an important determinant of event outcome when the subsequent events are negative rather than positive. In a reanalysis of data from an epidemiological survey of psychological disorder, Eaton (1978) found that stressful life events seemed more likely to produce mental disorder if similar events had not been experienced before.

Regarding the social context, there is a growing body of research to suggest that congruence of events with age-group norms is a key predictor of the event's impact on QOL (e.g., Datan & Ginsberg, 1975). Persons frequently compare their own events with high-probability experiences for age peers to determine whether their events are early, late, or on-time in the life cycle (Neugarten, 1976). On-time events, even if "objectively" negative, may be regarded as part of the ongoing life experience, and thus be less distressing than events that occur off-time, or at unexpected intervals. For instance, undesirable events such as illness and death of loved ones may be less upsetting when they occur at normative periods, namely, later in life, than if they occur off-time, earlier in the life course. To illustrate, in a study of psychological adaptation to physical illness, Zarit and Kahn (1975) found that, compared with older persons, younger minimally disabled victims of cerebrovascular accidents (i.e., "stroke") tended to deny their impairments to a significantly greater extent. Younger persons also were less depressed than older ones, suggesting that, affectively as well as cognitively, the former group acknowledged illness-related losses less than the latter. For older victims, the illness may have been developmentally "due," and therefore more psychologically acceptable. For younger persons, however, illness may have represented a greater departure from the norm, and thus have been more unacceptable.

Concern with event timing also suggests that QOL may be adversely affected when anticipated events do *not* occur. For instance, Lowenthal, Thurnher, and Chiriboga (1975) reported that the loss of expected salary increases and promotions was a major source of dissatisfaction for middle-aged men, perhaps because these events were timely, given the man's current position in the life cycle.

Nonnormative social events may not only be distressing to individuals, but they may upset the social environment as well (cf. Jahoda, 1961; Rappaport, 1977). Socially incongruent events may precipitate a host of other occurrences, perhaps the environment's own response to disruption in the steady state. For instance, Block (1980) found that for some life-cycle groups, negative events such as work and family troubles were associated with other stressors, whereas the same events for different life-cycle groups appeared not to have had these "ripple effects."

Event-Context Combination Rules

We have suggested that the degree of event-context congruence determines the impact of events on QOL. However, this regards only the *quantity* of fit between person and environment. We have yet to address questions regarding *quality;* namely, how much congruence (or incongruence) is "good" for QOL? In mathematics, combination rules refer to the means by which independent variables are put together in an equation to produce a particular outcome. In our event-context congruence framework, combination rules refer to alternate predictions regarding the outcomes for QOL resulting from differing amounts of event-context congruence. Three combination rules are discussed: cumulative congruence, critical-level congruence, and optimal congruence (see also Kahana, 1975).

A cumulative congruence combination rule proposes that there is a direct, linear, monotonic function relating event-context congruence and QOL. That is, persons strive to maintain maximum similarity between their own life experiences and psychological or social contextual norms. QOL is enhanced to the degree that perfect congruence can be maintained or reestablished following an event. This combination rule is most consistent with a homeostasis model of life events proposed by Holmes and Rahe (1967; Holmes & Masuda, 1974).

Like the cumulative model, a critical-level combination rule presupposes that QOL is maximized by perfect congruence between an event and normative standards. Some amount of discrepancy can be tolerated without undue effects, however. When a certain point of discrepancy (the critical level) is reached, QOL becomes threatened, with increasingly undesirable outcomes the greater the incongruence (see also Cofer & Appley, 1964, pp. 451–452).

Both the cumulative and critical-level viewpoints assume that upsets in the balance of person-environment relations are inherently undesirable. An optimal congruence combination rule does not make this assumption. Perfect congruence is not thought to maximize QOL, but instead, is as undesirable as extreme deviation from the norm. An optimal congruence rule posits that QOL can be favorably affected by event-context incongruencies, as long as the incongruencies remain within a range of tolerable affect and marginally adaptive behavior (Lawton & Nahemow, 1973; Levi, 1974). In the process of reestablishing balance, new competencies can be developed that enable future demands of greater magnitude and complexity to be handled (Wohlwill, 1966).

This conceptualization is consistent with a growth or development model of human behavior (e.g., Riegel, 1975). Life events that upset preexisting relations between person and environment may serve as precursors to growth. As expressed by Danish et al. (1980), "growth is preceded by a state of imbalance or crisis which serves as the basis for future development. In fact, without crises, development is not possible" (p. 6). Indeed, there is some tentative evidence to suggest that adjustment to major life changes may be hindered if opportunities to adopt new roles and values are impeded. In a small sample of mature women, Hirsch (1980) found that adjustment following recent widowhood and college reentry was lower for women whose social networks may have constrained opportunities to develop new patterns of behavior, thereby pressing for person-environment fit to be reestablished at a pre-event level.

An Ecological Framework of QOL: Event-Context Intersections

We considered some major characteristics of events and their contexts, and proposed that the degree of event-context congruence may be of central importance for predicting the outcomes of events on QOL. We now put these considerations together into a preliminary ecological framework of QOL. Figure 12.1 provides an overview of the framework. The framework is described in terms of major points of intersection between an event and its psychological and social contexts. Through these junctures, the context instrumentally shapes the course of reaction to an event and determines its eventual outcome for QOL. Five points of intersection are delineated, beginning with an event's occurrence and proceeding through to its resolution and future consequences for QOL. The first four points of intersection pertain to the event as a process in the experience of life, one of the functions of events described earlier. The last intersection regards the event as a marker of transition in the life course.

We adopt an optimal congruence combination rule regarding potential outcomes of life events. Incongruencies between event and context can create opportunities for the enhancement of QOL, as well as pose dangers for its reduction (Caplan, 1964). The outcomes that result will depend largely on the degree of event-context discrepancy, with incongruence (or congruence) in the extreme likely to be detrimental, and moderate levels having the greatest potential for desirable effects.

Event Occurrence

The first point of intersection between an event and its context is at the time of event occurrence. Contextual variables influence whether a given person-environment transaction becomes a significant life event. For instance, self-perceived vulnerabilities and strengths determine the changes that can be handled by automatic regulatory mechanisms, and those that require more active efforts at readjustment. Event context also influences the kinds of life events that are likely to occur. The psychological context, representing the person's own needs, goals, and motivations, shapes the nature of behavioral strivings, and thereby creates disruptions of certain kinds in person-environment relations. For instance, advancement in one's career may require major geographic relocations, thus creating change of a certain type in ongoing life patterns. In addition, the kinds of events that occur will be greatly influenced by social norms and involvements. These present certain opportunities and make certain demands that give rise to particular kinds of life events.

Events create asynchrony between the person and his or her psychological state, and/or between the person and his or her social environment (Riegel,

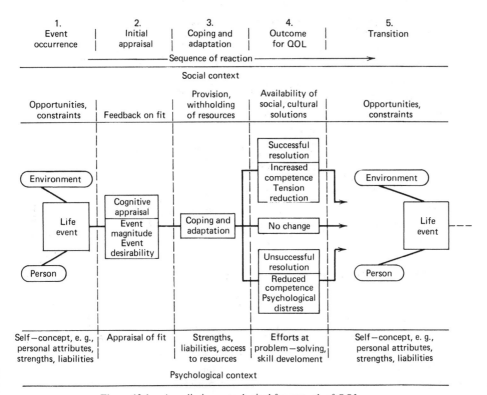

Figure 12.1.   A preliminary ecological framework of QOL.

1975). In essence, events signify that the person is moving at a different rate or in a different direction from psychological or social norms. If the discrepancy reaches a threshold level of perception, an initial cognitive appraisal of the event is made.

Initial Cognitive Appraisal

At the initial perception of change in ongoing person-environment relations, the change is cognitively appraised in terms of its magnitude and desirability. This represents a second point of intersection between an event and its context. Neither change nor desirability can be assessed without standards of comparison. As stated earlier, these standards of comparison are provided by the psychological and social contexts in which the event occurs. Cognitive appraisals involve comparative judgments to evaluate the extent of fit or congruence between the event and its context. To the degree that the event is congruent with the individual's values, goals, self-concept, and coping repertoire (psychological context), and the values, expectancies, or norms of reference groups (social context), it may not be perceived as a significant change, nor necessarily be evaluated as threatening (Neugarten & Datan, 1973). The social environment also may provide feedback (Cassel, 1975) confirming the fit, and to help the individual interpret the meaning and significance of the experience.

In contrast, to the degree that the event represents a departure from normative standards, it will be regarded as a major change or crisis in the life experience (Caplan, 1964). Note that positive as well as negative changes create incongruencies, and therefore, can precipitate crises. The individual is presented with information and demands not encountered before, or which conflict with existing information, behavior, goals, and values (Hultsch & Plemons, 1979), thereby arousing a state of cognitive dissonance (Festinger, 1957). Efforts at dissonance reduction may be hindered by the unavailability of familiar reference points against which to compare one's cognitive and affective state. Comparisons with familiar standards are primary means of reducing arousal and uncertainty in novel situations (Cottrell & Epley, 1977).

In addition, to the extent that the event is incongruent with social norms, the social environment may give negative feedback. For instance, a 55-year-old woman who returns to graduate school for a PhD may engender negative sanctions from others for violating life-cycle norms. This also raises the point that incongruent events can elicit a host of negative events (Jahoda, 1961) due to adverse reactions from the social environment, or the individual's inability to process information effectively and meet behavioral demands of the novel situation. Thus for the 55-year-old woman, entering graduate school may be associated with other stressors, such as conflicts with family and friends and difficulties with course work.

To the degree that the event is highly congruent with psychological and social norms, it will likely result in only momentary disruption, a quick return to equilibrium, and essentially have little impact on the person. Greater event-context discrepancies, however, whether positive or negative, require more extensive coping and adaptation efforts to reestablish fit.

Coping and Adaptation

The perception of change elicits coping and adaptation to restore person-environment equilibrium. Coping and adaptation proceed through a succession of trials until the event-context discrepancy is sufficiently reduced (Lazarus & Launier, 1978). This marks a third point of intersection between event and context, for the context will largely determine the resources available and the obstacles encountered throughout the readjustment process.

The initial response to the perception of change is to engage habitual problem-solving and adaptive strategies (Caplan, 1964), in essence, to call upon customary psychological and social resources for resolving incongruencies. If the event-context discrepancy is not too great, these initial efforts may successfully reestablish balance. That is, congruence may quickly ensue if the demands of the event can be met by skills developed through successful mastery of previous event sequences (psychological context) (Hultsch & Plemons, 1979), or by assistance readily available from others (social context) (Caplan, 1964).

If, however, the event-context incongruency proves too great, coping and adaptation resources may be unavailable or inadequate to restore balance. Individuals may not have had opportunities to develop problem-solving strategies for events that deviate markedly from previous experiences, or through anticipatory coping, to develop strategies for events that deviate from social contextual norms. In addition, should incongruent events precipitate a host of other events that demand energy and attention, few reserves may remain for dealing with the focal situation. Also, the less normative the event, the less likelihood that formal and informal networks will exist to aid in the coping and adaptation process (Danish et al., 1980).

The event context can influence coping and adaptation in other ways as well. The social context provides norms and sanctions governing appropriate coping behavior for different individuals (Lazarus & Launier, 1978). For example, although it may be somewhat permissible for a child to hit another child in anger, the same behavior from an adult would seldom be tolerated. Furthermore, by influencing the likelihood of occurrence of certain events, the context may promote or constrain certain coping and adaptation strategies (Lazarus & Launier, 1978; see also Hultsch & Plemons, 1979). For example, coping by direct action may be less effective under some circumstances than others. One circumstance would be when action had little instrumental value in resolving a difficulty (Lazarus et al., 1974), as for events such as illness and death of a loved one. These events tend to occur more frequently at advanced stages in the life cycle. Older individuals, in addition, tend to function more generally in environments with limited coping resources, such as could be obtained from economic assets and social involvements. As a result, direct action coping strategies may decrease and intrapsychic coping modes increase over the life span (Gutmann, 1969).

If customary coping and adaptation strategies are inadequate to restore congruence, the individual may search for new solutions. Concurrently, defensive and avoidance maneuvers may be engaged to prevent further internal and external disruptions (Lazarus & Launier, 1978). At some point, however, the situation comes to be resolved with a resultant impact on QOL.

Outcomes for QOL

The process of resolving the event involves reestablishing congruence between the person and the psychological or social environment. The resolution may be in the direction of improved mental health or mental illness (Caplan, 1964). The resolution process and its outcome represent a fourth point of intersection between an event and its context.

To the extent that the event-context discrepancy is within a range of tolerable affect and minimally adaptive behavior (Lawton & Nahemow, 1973), the individual's background of skills and competencies may provide a sufficient base for building new adaptive behaviors and successfully resolving the situation. Also, the person may be more open to external assistance that would permit energy to be mobilized for learning new behaviors and making necessary reorganizations in psychological and social structures. Furthermore, to the degree that events fit within the social context, there may exist social or cultural solutions to the problem. In addition, individuals may have opportunities to observe peers model successful and unsuccessful problem-solving strategies.

Successful resolution enhances QOL by leading to increased self-esteem and assurance, to a greater sense of strength, resourcefulness, and environmental mastery, and to a more highly integrated personality (Caplan, 1964). Essentially, congruence is reestablished at a higher level of satisfaction and competency. The psychological adjustment dimension of QOL also may be improved through the development of more effective means of tension reduction, or through the resolution of old conflicts (Rapoport, 1962).

To the degree that event and context are highly incongruent, the outcome may be in the direction of psychological dysfunction and poorer QOL. Significant event-context discrepancies may represent a form of "culture shock," in which the demands of the event are too novel or too complex, given obtained levels of mastery, for skills to be learned for successful resolution. Moreover, the social environment may prove to be ineffective, unresponsive to requests for assistance, or possibly openly antagonistic, should the event deviate too greatly from social norms. As a result of these consequences of poor fit, the individual may become so preoccupied with defense against threat and further disruption, and thereby closed to new information and resources, that the likelihood of finding a satisfactory solution to the problems grows less and less likely (Hultsch & Plemons, 1979). The fit thus reestablished between person and environment is one of defensiveness, reduced self-confidence and esteem, social isolation, and perhaps some personality disintegration.

Events as Transitions

The preceding four points of intersection between event and context consider the event in terms of a progressively unfolding situation, or as a process in the life experience. We noted earlier that events also represent markers of transition in the life course. The outcomes of a life event for QOL affect future person-environment relations and thus become inputs into subsequent events. This represents a fifth point of event-context intersection. The fit reestablished between person and environment from event resolution shapes the course of reaction to future events, as the cycle of response repeats itself from the initial occurrence of a new change through to its resolution.

Poor resolution of an event may lead the person to resist future disruptions in the steady state. Change and exposure to the unfamiliar are avoided. Behavior comes to be dominated by needs for tension-reduction and defense, so as to maintain the tenuous balance of person-environment relations reinstated as an outcome to the previous event. The person may perceive her or himself as more vulnerable (Lowenthal et al., 1975), and consequently, may have more negative experiences symbolizing dissatisfactions, personal failures, or losses, thereby resulting in further declines of QOL.

In contrast, successful resolution of person-environment encounters may encourage future exploratory and competency-building behavior, even though such behavior creates internal tension and results in temporary incongruencies. The person may view him or herself as more challenged (Lowenthal et al., 1975). Correspondingly, she or he may have greater numbers of positive experiences signifying gains, satisfactions, and environmental mastery, with perhaps some negative events caused by disturbing the steady state (Lowenthal & Chiriboga, 1973). In general, QOL becomes increasingly enhanced as successively better fits are established with the psychological and social environment (Riegel, 1975).

In concluding this section, we wish to emphasize that life events and the responses of individuals to them are highly complex and multidimensional. The framework described above offers only an overview of some of the aspects we view as potentially significant. We discussed the psychological and social contexts of events as two possible determinants of reactions to and outcomes of events on QOL. There are other critical contexts of events not covered in our framework, however; for example, cultural and historical contexts (Riegel, 1975; Hultsch & Plemons, 1979), and the physical environment (Altman & Lett, 1970). Also, individual differences in perceptions and reactions must be a key consideration (see Lawton, 1975). Time is a critical factor as well. The same event may be resolved and re-resolved on many occasions, as the individual comes to different perceptions and understandings throughout the life course with each new person-environment encounter.

SUMMARY

Person and environment each make unique inputs into the person-environment equation. The significant events of community life, such as marriage, illness, and retirement, represent primary units of transaction between person and environment. Life events function both as markers of progress in the life course, and as unfolding processes with a beginning, middle, and resolution. For events to have an impact on QOL, they must be perceived and comprehended. This is accomplished through cognitive appraisal processes that mediate the reaction to and outcomes of events. Several aspects of events can be highly important in cognitive appraisals, namely, the amount of change in ongoing life patterns precipitated by the event, and the desirability of these changes.

However, change and desirability can only be appraised in reference to standards of comparison. Standards of comparison for evaluating events are provided by the psychological and social contexts in which the events occur. The psychological context represents the individual's self-perceptions of personal attributes, coping liabilities and assets, needs, values, goals, and other aspects of the self-concept. The social context represents perceptions of oneself in relation to the social environment. Social standards for comparison are provided by reference groups in which the person is or wishes to become a member. Reference groups are selected based on the degree of similarity between the individual and potential social comparison persons. A critical dimension of similarity between oneself and others is age, or life cycle. Social comparison persons also can be found in others of similar socioeconomic status or ethnicity.

Standards of comparison provided by psychological and social contexts can be communicated and cognitively represented in the form of normative life events. Psychologically normative events can be found in the individual's own previous life experiences. These shape future expectancies and the repetoire of skills for coping and adaptation. Socially normative events are high-probability occurrences for reference groups. Normative events for age or life-cycle peers are particularly significant for setting guidelines against which persons evaluate the timeliness of their own experiences.

The degree of fit between an event and normative standards, as represented by normative life events, is of central importance for predicting event outcomes on QOL. There is some empirical support for this notion, with respect to fit within both psychological and social domains. The fit of event to context is defined as event-context congruence. Different predictions can be made as to qualitative outcomes for QOL resulting from greater and lesser degrees of event-context congruence. Cumulative and critical-level viewpoints propose that QOL is maximized to the extent that perfect event-context congruence is maintained. In contrast, an optimal congruence viewpoint suggests that discrepancies within a range of tolerable affect and minimally adaptive behavior can potentially enhance QOL by providing opportunities for the development of new satisfactions and competencies.

Having discussed some major considerations regarding events, contexts, and their interrelationships, we integrate these components into a preliminary ecological framework of QOL. The framework adopts an optimal congruence view that QOL can be augmented by events that are moderately incongruent with psychological and social norms. The framework describes critical points of intersection between event and context during the sequence of response to the event and its resolution. Intersections are found at event occurrence, initial appraisal, coping and adaptation, resolution and outcome, and the transition into future person-environment encounters. At these junctures, the event's context shapes the reaction to and the eventual outcomes of the event on QOL.

MEASUREMENT ISSUES AND STRATEGIES

Like any research endeavor, QOL assessment requires its dependent criteria to be operationalized, and the indicators or predictors of these criteria to be specified as well. In this section, we present an overview of strategies for measuring dependent and independent variables to assess QOL in communities from an ecological perspective. A detailed review of measurement issues in community research is beyond the scope of the chapter. For those wishing to pursue the topic further, the work of Attkisson, Hargreaves, Horowitz, and Sorensen (1978) can be particularly helpful as a starting point.

We begin the section by discussing general objective and subjective approaches to QOL assessment. Objective and subjective criteria of QOL are described next. Following this, we consider objective and subjective strategies for the measurement of life events, event contexts, and finally event-context congruence as the principal indicator of QOL in communities.

Objective and Subjective Approaches

Two approaches to measurement have been taken to assess QOL in communities: These are objective and subjective strategies (Zautra & Goodhart, 1979). Comprehensive descriptions of specific strategies are available elsewhere, and thus will not be considered here (see Attkisson et al., 1978; Hagerdorn, Beck, Neubert, & Werlin, 1976). The defining feature of an objective approach is its reliance on external, publicly verifiable information. Data on external community features (e.g., age, sex compositions, employment rates) are collected by objective means (e.g., census counts, public records) to predict QOL, which is operationalized by objective criteria (e.g., service utilization rates). Social indicator methods (e.g., Bloom, 1975), and social area analysis (Struening, 1975) are two examples of this strategy.

A major criticism of objective methodologies is the uncertainty that they, in fact, do represent community members' own perceptions and evaluations of QOL (e.g., Schneider, 1975). To overcome this difficulty, subjective approaces for assessing QOL have been advocated (Campbell, 1976). The major feature of a subjective strategy is the use of direct reports by community residents on their experience of community life. Data are collected mainly through surveys. Subjective methods, too, have met with criticism (e.g., Bunge, 1975). Potential difficulties include vulnerability to social desirability response bias, idiosyncracy in reports of subjective states, and inability to assess reliably differences in well-being among community groups.

We would, however, argue for a unified approach in which both objective and subjective methods are used to assess QOL. This takes advantage of the strengths of each method and minimizes some of the weaknesses of either when used alone. Objective assessments can provide valuable information on the external community environment, whereas subjective reports can describe the community environment as perceived and evaluated by residents (Zautra & Simons, 1978).

QOL Criteria

We noted at the beginning of the chapter that QOL encompasses two independent dimensions of the life experience: psychological adjustment and positive mental health. Psychological adjustment reflects the degree to which person-environment relations enable individuals to meet basic tension reduction needs, such as safety and security. Positive mental health reflects the degree to which person-environment relations permit strengths, achievements, and satisfactions to be developed and maintained. Dependent criteria of QOL need to represent both aspects of well-being. We briefly discuss objective and subjective criteria of these dimensions, considering first psychological adjustment, then positive mental health.

Objective measures of psychological adjustment have been used fairly commonly in applied community research (see Goodstein, Zautra, & Goodhart, 1980). Most often, utilization rates of human services are the criteria employed. Utilization rates have face validity, are readily available, can be easily quantified, and have some empirical support as to their utility as measures of distress in communities. This criterion has some obvious deficiencies, however, such as its dependence on the availability, cost, publicity, and community acceptability of services.

A number of subjective measures of psychological adjustment are available (see Zautra & Goodhart, 1979). Checklists of psychiatric symptomatology are frequently used in community surveys to assess psychological adjustment. Examples of instruments include the 22-item *Psychiatric Screening Inventory* (Langner, 1962) developed in the midtown Manhattan study and the *Health Opinion Survey* (Leighton, Harding, Macklin, Hughes, & Leighton, 1963) developed in the Stirling County study. Psychological adjustment can also be assessed with measures of negative affects. These may tap the shorter-term emotional response to stressful conditions (Campbell, Converse, & Rodgers, 1976). The Bradburn (1969) *Affect Balance Scale* is a commonly used survey instrument of this type.

Compared with psychological adjustment, there have been fewer strategies developed to measure positive mental health in communities. Maladjustment and distress have commanded the greater share of interest and attention in community work. Also, there is little common understanding regarding the meaning of positive mental health (Danish et al., 1980), a necessary prerequisite for its measurement. Six approaches to understanding the concept are presented by Jahoda (1958). These include attitudes toward the self; growth, development, and self-actualization; personality integration; autonomy; perception of reality;

and environmental mastery. Moos (1974) offers a comprehensive review of specific objective and subjective techniques to measure some to these positive mental health components.

In community surveys, subjective reports of happiness, life satisfaction, and self-esteem are frequently used to assess positive mental health. The Bradburn (1969) *Affect Balance Scale* is a typical measure of happiness (and unhappiness as well). Two of the most comprehensive life-satisfaction inventories were developed in nationwide surveys by Andrews and Withey (1976) and Campbell et al. (1976) to determine level of satisfaction and dissatisfaction in various life domains, such as family, work, leisure, income, social relations, and health. There are a variety of self-esteem measures that can be used in community surveys see (Robinson & Shaver, 1973).

Indicators of QOL: Event-Context Congruence

In addition to selecting outcome criteria, QOL assessments must determine the measures to be used as independent variables, or indicators, of QOL. A variety of community characteristics have served as objective indicators in community research (see Zautra & Goodhart, 1979; Goodstein et al., 1980). Examples include median family income, rates of unemployment and divorce, crime statistics, and demographic variables such as age, sex, and ethnicity. In addition, reports of happiness, life satisfaction, and psychological distress have served as subjective predictors (as well as criteria) of QOL.

The major life events of community residents have been used successfully to predict QOL in communities (Zautra & Simons, 1979; Goodstein et al., 1980), and we would argue for their use as indicators in ecological strategies of QOL assessment. A key requirement for the utility of an indicator is that it be maximally relevant to the variables the researcher wants to measure (cf. French et al., 1974). Life events serve this function, in that they tap directly the psychological meaning and experience of life in the community. Moreover, our ecological framework proposed that QOL is a product of person-environment fit. To evaluate fit, person and environment must be assessed along commensurate dimensions (French et al., 1974), meaning with equivalent scales of measurement. Life events are amenable to this requirement. The state of the person can be assessed using his or her current life experiences. The state of the environment, represented by the psychological and social contexts in which events occur, can be measured using life events as well. As noted earlier, contextual life events can include the person's past experiences and life experiences regarded as normative for similar others in the social environment.

An ecological approach to QOL assessment using life events as indicators calls for three measurement tasks: The first is to assess the events of the person, the second to assess events representing psychological and social contexts, and the third is to compute the amount of fit between events and contexts, defined earlier as event-context congruence. Measures of event-context congruence represent the indicators of QOL. Some objective and subjective approaches that could be taken to accomplish each measurement task will be described briefly.

Measuring Life Events of the Person

Extensive reviews of the measurement of life events are available (e.g., Dohrenwend & Dohrenwend, 1974), and we present only some of the highlights here. Paper-and-pencil checklists on which residents directly report their life experiences are the most common subjective measures of life events in community surveys. Of these instruments, the most widely used seems to be the *Social Readjustment Rating Schedule (SRRS)* developed by Holmes and Rahe (1967). Other life events checklists also have been developed, essentially revisions of the *SRRS*, to include events of relevance for specific populations (e.g., Cochrane & Robertson, 1973), permit evaluations of event characteristics, such as desirability (Johnson & Sarason, 1979) and controllability (Dohrenwend, Krasnoff, Askenasy, & Dohrenwend, 1978), and to equalize the balance of positive and negative items (Block & Zautra, 1981).

Another type of subjective assessment of life events is a critical-incidents technique that identifies important events associated with significant changes in well-being. One early example of this strategy is the "life chart" of psychiatrist Adolf Meyers (Holmes & Masuda, 1974), which asked persons to recall events that clustered around the time of onset of physical illness. Lowenthal et al. (1975) utilize a similar procedure by having respondents retrospectively identify experiences associated with major life satisfactions and dissatisfactions.

Objective methods to measure life events can include having persons in the immediate social environment report on the focal individual's life experiences. A study by Gersten, Langner, Eisenberg, and Orzeck (1974), in which mothers described events that happened to their children, is one example of this procedure.

Measuring Event Contexts

Assessing the psychological and social contexts of life events is a relatively new area, and therefore greatly in need of further development. For the traveler wishing to explore this terrain, we have no maps or charts, but we do offer suggestions for some alternative strategies. To measure the psychological context of events, subjective reports could be obtained directly from residents, or objective reports obtained from others regarding the resident's previous life experiences. Also, prior expectancies and the adequacy of coping skills could be assessed indirectly by asking respondents to rate the desirability of the *outcomes* of their life events (cf. Parkes, 1971). Positive outcomes may signify gains or favorable deviations from prior norms, whereas negative outcomes could signify losses, or unfavorable discrepancies from the pre-event life situation.

Subjective methods to assess the social context of events could include having community members identify normative events for their reference groups, perhaps by asking of events on a checklist, "How normal or typical is this experience for people who are like yourself?" Another subjective method could involve asking about the feedback received from others regarding one's life events. Presumably, if the event fits within the social environment, there should be little negative feedback and perhaps some positive conveyances (cf. Jahoda, 1961).

Objective methods could be used to derive socially normative life events empirically. This requires identifying homogeneous groups of community members and measuring their experiences. For example, theory, judgment, and previous research could be used as guidelines to determine salient characteristics that differentiate subgroups in the community. Such characteristics may include income, ethnicity, occupation, and age or life cycle (i.e., age, marital status, and the presence of children; cf. Campbell, 1976). To identify normative life events for each subgroup, subjective reports of life experiences could simply be aggregated within the subgroup. Another techique that could prove highly interesting involves content analysis of mass media to determine normative events for different community populations. There are a few examples in the literature, using content analysis of magazine fiction to assess normative social roles for subgroups according to age and sex (e.g., Wilson, 1981).

An alternative objective strategy works in reverse of the methods described above. Namely, the researcher first identifies homogeneous clusters of life events, and then uses the event clusters to identify salient characteristics of community subgroups that report similar patterns of life experiences. There are several multivariate techniques that could be employed, such as Q-type factor analysis (Bennett & Bowers, 1976), multiple classification analysis (Bishop, Fienberg, & Holland, 1975), and discriminant function analysis and canonical correlation (Tatsuoka, 1971).

Measuring Event-Context Congruence

Having identified the person's life events and events that represent psychological and social contexts, the next task becomes to evaluate the degree of fit between the two sets of events. Most commonly, fit has been operationalized by simple difference scores obtained by subtracting ratings of persons and ratings of environments, person and environment having been measured on commensurate scales (e.g., French et al., 1974). Similarly, it would be possible to compute discrepancy scores between events and their normative contexts. Another strategy could employ weighting the person's life events according to the amount of congruence with normative events (as will be described in the next section). In addition, a few multivariate techniques could be applicable, as for example, profile classification procedures (Tatsuoka, 1974) to assess similarities between individual and social group patterns of events.

In general, the measurement of person-environment fit is an area much in need of further work, because concern with the issue, and hence its assessment, is a relatively new development in community research. Some alternative approaches assessing fit are reviewed by Pervin (1968). Examples of specific strategies are offered by French et al. (1974) regarding person-environment fit in work settings, and by Stern (1970) regarding fit in the college environment.

QOL IN A TRI-CITY COMMUNITY: AN ILLUSTRATION OF ECOLOGICAL ASSESSMENT

In this section, we present an illustration from our own research of an ecological approach to QOL assessment conducted in a metropolitan tri-city community of the southwestern United States (see Goodhart & Zautra, Note 2 for a comprehensive description of measurement, data analyses, and results of this study). The example is intended to illustrate some possible strategies for the measurement of event-context congruence and its impact on QOL. We would encourage others to explore alternate strategies as well, perhaps by making use of some of the suggestions described in the preceding measurement section.

Data for the tri-city QOL assessment were collected by surveying a probability sample of 537 individuals selected to represent the approximately 250,000 residents of the community. The surveyed group paralleled the highly diverse population of the area, and contained college students at a local university, suburban residents, members of a Mexican-American subcommunity, and a large retirement population. Interviews were conducted in the respondent's home, and averaged 1 hour and 15 minutes in length. Interviews were completed by 85% of the originally selected sample. Four brief measures of psychological well-being administered to each respondent represented the criteria of QOL. These consisted of the *Psychiatric Screening Inventory* (Langner, 1962) to assess psychological symptomatology, the *Positive* and *Negative Affect Scales* (Bradburn, 1969), and a perceived life-satisfaction scale (Andrews & Withey, 1976) to assess satisfaction with different life domains. Information on life events was collected using a 64-item life-events measure (Block & Zautra, 1981) derived from the *SRRS* (Holmes & Rahe, 1967). Revisions of the original *SRRS* had been made to clarify ambiguous items, and to add more positive events. Residents reported whether any of the events on the list had taken place in their lives during the last year.

Two series of analyses were conducted. The first series evaluated the significance for QOL of event congruence with psychological-contextual norms. The second series of analyses examined the impact of congruence between events and norms for the social context.

Event Congruence with a Psychological Context

Perceptions and evaluations of the pre-event life situation can represent normative psychological standards against which new events are appraised. We assessed deviations from these standards by asking whether each event reported by residents on the modified life-events measure had "turned out" positive, negative, both positive and negative, or had no effect. Only events whose outcomes were rated as positive or negative were used in the analyses. Positive outcomes could represent gains over the pre-event situation, whereas negative outcomes could represent losses (cf. Parkes, 1971). Appraisals of events as gains or losses may reflect normative expectancies about the life experience, as well as the adequacy of coping resources for restoring equilibrium following events. Frequencies of gains and losses reported by residents were summed, and the two totals used as measures of event congruence with psychological contextual norms.

It was hypothesized that, by deviating from pre-event norms, both gains and losses would elevate psychological tension. This would be evidenced by more symptoms and negative affects on our measure with more frequent occurrences of events. However, by signifying improvements over the pre-event state, gains could have the added effect of enhancing positive mental health, as would be indicated by greater numbers of positive affects and life satisfactions.

To test these hypotheses, correlational analyses were performed to examine associations of gains and losses with the QOL criteria. Our propositions, in general, were supported by the results. Higher frequencies of losses seemed to reduce positive mental health and increase maladjustment. In contrast, greater numbers of desirable deviations from pre-event norms seemed to enhance positive mental health somewhat, at least with regard to positive affects. As predicted, more frequent gains also appeared to create some difficulties for psychological adjustment, as reflected by increases in negative affects and symptoms. When frequencies of losses were statistically controlled, however, associations between gains and psychological distress were reduced to nonsignificance. Relations between gains and adjustment difficulties may thus be mediated by co-occurring negative experiences, as has been suggested (Block & Zautra, 1981).

Overall, the findings supported the notion that psychological standards of reference can be important in perceptions and evaluations of life events. Deviations of events from these standards, as reflected in appraisals of events as gains or losses over the previous situation, significantly predicted the event's outcome on QOL in our study. Attention to the psychological context of events thus can be highly useful for understanding and assessing the QOL of community residents.

Event Congruence with a Social Context

The significance of event congruence with social-contextual standards was examined using a subsample residents 55 years and older (n = 129) from the surveyed tri-city population. Our concern was with congruence between events and standards for the respondent's age group. To increase homogeneity within the subsample, respondents were divided into two age groups, one of younger persons 55 to 64 years (n = 54), and the other of older persons aged 65 years and above (n = 75). It was believed that the younger and older respondents represented two distinct developmental periods (cf. Erickson, 1953), and thus could have somewhat different age-group norms. Each group was treated separately in all analyses.

The modified life-events inventory was used to construct a 60-item measure of event-context congruence. Potential age group norms for events were derived empirically by calculating the percentage of respondents who reported the occurrence of each event on the measure. Higher-frequency events were considered to be more normative for the age group (see also Neugarten et al., 1968). Each event was weighted based on the percentage of respondents who endorsed it, with incrementally higher weights assigned to events reported by proportionately fewer persons. Weights were integers ranging from 1 to 5, with 1 assigned to events reported by 41% or more of the respondents, up to 5 for each decrease of 10% in event frequency. We were also concerned with the desirability of deviations from age group norms, and so we assigned each event to a positive or negative category a priori. Weighted events reported in the positive and negative categories were summed. The two totals represented the degree to which the resident's own life experiences deviated from age norms, and whether these deviations were in a positive or negative direction. Data analyses were conducted using a multiple regression design for analysis of covariance (see Cohen & Cohen, 1975, Ch. 9) to control for the simple frequency of events.

Positive and negative events that differed from those of the majority of the respondent's peers seemed to affect QOL independently, and sometimes to a greater extent than life events in general. For both age groups, positive events were unrelated to the criteria, unless they represented discrepancies from age-group norms, in which case they seemed to enhance QOL by increasing levels of positive affect. Moreover, nonnormative positive events appeared to serve a preventative function for the younger residents, who reported fewer psychological symptoms with more frequent occurrences of these events.

Negative incongruent events seemed to diminish the QOL of both age groups. For younger respondents, however, it was only nonnormative stressors that reduced well-being, and negative events in general were unrelated to the criteria. For older residents, both normative and nonnormative negative events were detrimental to QOL. Older persons may be more psychologically vulnerable than younger persons to undesirable changes of any kind in their experience of community life.

In sum, the results of the two series of analyses highlighted the need to consider both psychological and social norms governing events. The fit between life events and these normative standards can be an important predictor of an event's outcome on QOL. Community members may evaluate their experiences both by observing movement in their own lives, as well as by observing whether their social environments are moving along with them. Thus an ecological perspective that incorporates both the event and its normative context could prove to be highly useful in assessments of QOL in the community.

IMPLICATIONS FOR PRIMARY PREVENTION

Information about the community ultimately belongs to the community. In addition to taking knowledge for theory development, QOL assessment must give some knowledge back to the community in terms of guidelines for intervention to promote 'QOL. The information from ecological QOL assessments could provide a highly useful data-base on which to design and evaluate primary prevention programs (cf. Heller & Monahan, 1977). Ecological QOL assessment and primary prevention are a particularly good "fit" in terms of philosophies and goals. Both view QOL as arising out of person-environment interdependencies, and the optimization of QOL, therefore, as requiring interventions to maximize person-environment fit. Moreover, ecological QOL assessment and primary prevention view QOL as a function not only of adjustment to difficulties, but of opportunities to enhance positive growth and development.

Primary prevention to improve QOL could use as the point of departure the significant life events of community members (Danish et al., 1980). Prevention strategies could be directed toward reducing or eliminating distress-producing fits between person and environment, and also toward increasing opportunities for more challenging, competency-building fits through significant life events. In Table 12.1 we offer an overview of some directions these prevention efforts could take. We do not claim to be all-inclusive nor completely systematic, but merely give the reader a sampling of some of the possibilities. The entries are cross-classified by target and goal of intervention. Intervention targets can be individuals, communities, or individuals and communities simultaneously. Prevention goals can be to improve person-context fit, meaning fit with respect to life events in general. Prevention goals can also be to improve community-context fit, or fit with respect to normative events for community subgroups, such as minorities, the elderly, or the poor. We will briefly discuss each category, and where possible, cite examples of interventions that have been done in a particular area. Interventions to improve person-context fit will be considered first.

Interventions to Improve Person-Context Fit

At the individual level, efforts can be directed at increasing the adaptability of community members to nonspecific life events. For instance, there may be general problem-solving and coping skills applicable across a range of situations in which individuals can be trained (Danish et al., 1980). One example is a program developed by Spivak and Shure (1974) to teach young children basic skills for thinking through and solving typical interpersonal problems.

At the community level, interventions could focus on reducing environmental stressors such as noise, pollution, and crowding. Catalano and Monahan (1975) describe possibilities that include participation in social planning, urban design,

Table 12.1. A Sampling of Life Event Preventive Interventions

Prevention Goal	Level of Intervention		
	Individual	Community	Person X Community
Person-context fit (to increase fit through events in general)	Training, education, skill building in general problem-solving, coping strategies	Reduce environmental stressors (e.g., noise, pollution, crowding)	Organization development
		Strengthen informal supports	Community organization-social advocacy
	Esteem building	Provide opportunities for challenges	Community development
		Mass media education on general problem-solving, coping skills	
Community-context fit (to increase fit through normative events)	Enhancing life event processes, developmental transitions	Mass media campaigns to reduce negative stereotypes of community groups (e.g., elderly, handicapped)	Community development
	Anticipatory coping strategies	Design environments to meet special physical needs of community groups (e.g., elderly)	Community organization-social advocacy
	Behavior change to reduce likelihood of preventable negative events	Education, intervention with organizations, socialization institutions (e.g., schools) to facilitate developmental transitions, normative crises	Parallel institutions, alternative environments for disenfranchized groups

and consultation on the construction of residential environments to minimize crowding and exposure to excessive noise.

Interventions to increase person-context fit can be directed simultaneously at individuals and communities. One example is a youth advocacy program by Seidman, Rappaport, and Davidson (1980) aimed toward diverting predelinquent adolescents from more serious involvement in the juvenile justice system. Interventions were conducted by college student volunteers who worked in an advocacy fashion with both the youth to build strengths, assets, and self-sufficiency, and with the community to provide educational, vocational, and recreational resources to the youth. Holahan and Spearly (1980) describe other examples of interventions to improve person-context fit by working to increase the adaptability of persons as well as the responsiveness of environments to individual needs.

Interventions to Improve Community-Context Fit

These strategies are targeted specifically around normative events for community subgroups. At the individual level, interventions can be directed toward helping persons deal with normative events more effectively, perhaps by providing opportunities for anticipatory coping, changing behavior to reduce the likelihood of preventable stressors, or teaching persons how to use transitional events (e.g., retirement, menopause) to promote positive mental health. Danish et al. (1980) present a conceptual framework and intervention strategies for "enhancing life-event processes," that is, for using high probability life events as vehicles to augment individual strengths and resources. Maccoby and Alexander (1979) present an interesting approach using the mass media and face-to-face instruction to modify individual health habits that could lead to coronary problems, a high-probability stressor in later life.

At the community level, strategies can be directed toward modifying environmental conditions that create stress for certain community subgroups, such as the poor, the elderly, and the disabled. For instance, the mass media can be used to change social norms and reduce negative stereotypes of these subgroups. Interventions also can be conducted with architects and city planners to design physical environments that enable individuals with special needs (e.g., elderly, handicapped) to function effectively and independently in the community (e.g., Windley & Scheidt, 1980). Furthermore, prevention efforts can environmentally foster competence and satisfaction as outcomes to normative events. For example, Bloom (1971) describes a project designed to smooth the transition of first-year students into college life. Through periodic feedback from questionnaires on their college experience, students were afforded membership in a group having psychological reality, which provided information to promote self-understanding of normative stressors.

Interventions to promote community-context fit can involve individual and communities simultaneously. These interventions both increase individual adaptability and change environmental norms operating on persons with special characteristics. One example is social advocacy for disenfranchised groups (see Rappaport, 1977, Ch. 6). Group skills for negotiating with community power structures are developed, whereas at the same time, interventions are conducted with the community to increase its responsiveness to the group's needs. Creating parallel institutions and alternative environments are other possible interventions in this category. For instance, the needs of the elderly may be served better in age-segregated housing (Rosow, 1968) and retirement communities in which older persons do not have to compete with younger ones for community resources.

SOME DIRECTIONS FOR FUTURE RESEARCH

With roots in clinical psychology and psychiatry, community mental health has inherited a sizable body of knowledge about the inner workings of the person. Only recently have inroads of practical utility for community work been made toward increasing understanding of persons in the context of environments. Much work still needs to be done to develop ecological models of QOL in communities, particularly if these models are to serve as useful bases for intervention and prevention. Life events are highly important in this regard. Whether viewed as processes or markers, understanding events is central to understanding the experience of community life, and how individuals and communities change over time. Although a great deal of progress has been made in recent years, more needs to be known about how persons, and especially environments, shape the course, reactions, and outcomes of life events for QOL. We offer a few possible, and by no means exhaustive, directions for the development of ecological models of events. Three issues are considered. These involve attention to the longitudinal, multidimensional, and systems-level aspects of life events.

Longitudinal Aspects

Life events can have impacts on person and environment that last well beyond the immediate point of resolution (Caplan, 1964). Longitudinal aspects of events pertain to these longer-term effects. One concern for future investigation relates essentially to how, what, and whether persons learn from their past experiences. Of central importance in this regard are the means by which the repetoire of coping skills is expanded or reduced by events. Also of importance are the conditions governing the likelihood that new coping skills will actually be used in subsequent person-environment encounters (Danish et al., 1980). Furthermore, there may be instances when such applications of past coping skills to future problems may not be desirable. For example, different events may present sufficiently diverse adaptive demands so that different strategies for coping would, in fact, be required. To illustrate, persons who prefer active coping styles such as vigilance and information-seeking may deal effectively with most of life's demands. However, active coping may be particularly detrimental for adjustment to certain events such as physical illness (Cohen, 1980). Also, shifts from active to more passive coping over the life course may be necessary for adjustment in the later years (Gutmann, 1969). Research to understand the contingencies governing the long-term development, use, and modification of coping resources could have much utility, particularly for planning prevention programs that maximize gains for QOL from major life events and minimize potential losses.

Multidimensional Aspects

A major issue in this area pertains to the need to incorporate the multiple contexts of a given event into models of person-environment fit. There are many contexts in which an event occurs and must be responded to. We considered two—a personal context and a social context. Yet within each of these contexts there are multiple facets that make up the whole, as represented by the diversity of needs, goals, and personal attributes that comprise a psychological context, and by the multiple social groups in which the individual has or desires membership that make up a social context. Moreover, there are still other contexts, such as the biological state, cultural environment, and place in historical time (Hultsch & Plemons, 1979; Riegel, 1975). Any or all of these contexts can provide standards of reference for evaluating the congruence of a given event. These standards need not be consistent or compatible. In fact, it is very likely that discrepancies will arise between or within contexts, such that an event congruent with one set of norms will be incongruent with another. For instance, persons may be physically or psychologically ill-prepared to make certain normative social or cultural transitions. Greater attention to and understanding of these multidimensional concerns will likely increase the accuracy with which the outcomes of life events can be predicted.

Systems-Level Aspects

We considered how the context of events can influence their effects on individuals. However, an ecological perspective reminds us that relations between person and environment are transactional. Environments affect persons, but persons also affect their environments. Thus arises a systems-level question of how the person's life experiences can affect the context in which the experiences occur. For instance, it has been suggested that positive events may promote a more benevolent social context in communities, perhaps by increasing social interaction and helping behavior (Zautra & Reich, Note 3). Possibly communities function more supportively when their members experience positive emotions from life experiences. There is some evidence for the notion that communities may benefit from their members' positive events. Zautra and Simons (1979) used residents' reports of positive and negative events, aggregated within census tracts, as area indicators of utilization rates of mental health services. Census tract utilization rates were obtained from independent sources (agency records). Findings indicated that neighborhoods characterized by more positive events had lower service use, and moreover, positive events actually discriminated neighborhood utilization rates better than negative events. The same findings were replicated in a separate community study (Goodstein et al., 1980). Essentially, very little is known about the impact of community members' life experiences on the community context. This area of inquiry is likely to be highly promising in the study of community mental health and the maintenance of positive QOL.

Epilogue

Models of person-environment fit are not without their potential pitfalls in QOL assessment and human service planning. For instance, there is the danger that these models could be used (inadvertently or otherwise) to reinforce the status quo for disenfranchised groups in the community. It could be argued, however benignly, that the poor person is "better off" in a poor neighborhood, the mental patient in a mental hospital, or the elderly in a nursing home, because these arrangements do, after all, represent the closest match of person to environment. Although possible misinterpretations and misuses cannot be avoided totally, they may be lessened to some degree should the community researcher and planner keep three questions in mind: "Fit *to* what?" "Fit *for* what?" and "Fit for *whom*?"

The first question, "Fit to what?" pertains to whether person or environment should serve as the referent to which the other is fit. It is certainly possible, and perhaps not too uncommon, for assessments and interventions to be carried out with the notion that individuals should be fit to environments, however stressful or maladaptive the environment. It would alternately be possible to use individual needs, goals, and capacities as the guiding standard, or ideally, to use both as standards whereby person and environment are optimally fit to each other.

Whether environments should, in fact, be matched to the needs of some community members, if such matches promote maladjustment in persons, or deterioration in communities, is another issue. This raises a second question, "Fit for what?" In other words, what outcomes should result if person-environment fit is optimal? Lawton and Nahemow (1973) discuss this issue with regard to old people. The authors suggest that hedging environmental demands downward to meet declining levels of ability, or providing a "too comfortable" fit, may only lead to further deterioration, whereas increasing environmental demands in tolerable units may preserve or augment existing capacities. This proposition has been supported empirically (e.g., Baltes & Zerbe, 1976). Even more seriously disabled elderly can regain some functional abilities with appropriate environmental stimulation and reinforcement (Katz, 1976). Thus efforts to promote fit for the purpose of reducing distress must consider possible consequences for the maintenance of life satisfactions and skills for environmental mastery.

The third question, "Fit for whom?" concerns whether the QOL needs of some community groups are being served by existing patterns of fit at the expense of other groups' needs. By patterns of fit, we refer to the distribution of power and resources in the community. These may be thought of in terms of environmental "supplies" (Caplan, 1964) required by individuals for tension-reduction and positive well-being. The fit between individuals and environments in this regard is obviously better for some community groups than for others (Rappaport, 1977). In our ecological framework of QOL, we considered only the person and his or her immediate environment. Yet, this is only one setting, and it is embedded within multiple interacting and interdependent settings in the larger community (Bronfenbrenner, 1977). Changing a given element in the overall structure will have repercussions at other levels. As Hardin (1969) asserts, we can never do merely one thing. Thus, improving fit for some groups will likely meet with resistance from other groups, who perceive their own access to needed resources being threatened.

Although there are no easy solutions to social problems, QOL assessment can help by identifying how existing distributions of power and resources are maintained, or in Lewin's (1951) terms, the "driving" and "restraining" forces that preserve equilibrium in communities. QOL assessment can also help by focusing on the strengths of individuals and communities, rather than on their deficits, to identify untapped resources that could be brought to bear on remedying undesirable community conditions. Understanding of and sensitivity to the community as an ecosystem (Bronfenbrenner, 1977), in which there are multiple linkages and interdependencies, is a necessary prerequisite to maximizing QOL for all community members.

SUMMARY

The chapter was concerned with the assessment of QOL in communities. QOL encompasses both psychological adjustment to life's difficulties, as well as positive mental health, or the development of competencies and satisfactions. The central purpose of the chapter has been to propose that QOL is best understood and assessed from an ecological perspective as a function of person-environment relations. In particular, QOL depends on the fit between person and environment, or the matching of individual needs and behavioral styles with environmental demands and opportunities. This perspective is highly consistent with the emergent ideology of prevention in community psychology and community mental health.

We developed a preliminary conceptual framework to understand and assess QOL from an ecological perspective. The framework took as its point of departure the significant life events of community members, such as marriage, death of significant others, and job promotion. The framework highlighted the importance of the event's context as a key determinant of the event's impact on QOL. Two such contexts were considered, a psychological context and a social context, with age peers being a particularly important component of the social context. Event contexts provide normative standards against which new events are perceived and evaluated through cognitive appraisal processes. Normative standards can be represented by normative life events, with the previous history of life events and high-probability events for reference groups comprising normative psychological and social occurrences, respectively. We proposed that the degree of fit between an event and contextual standards, defined as event-context congruence, determine the event's outcome for QOL. Alternate predictions were made regarding the effects of differing degrees of event-context congruence: Cumulative and critical level viewpoints would see QOL as maximized by perfect congruence, whereas an optimal congruence approach would predict QOL to be maximized by moderate discrepancies between events and normative standards. We combined the above considerations regarding events, contexts, and event-context congruence into a preliminary ecological framework of QOL. The framework delineated five key points of intersection between event and context at which the context instrumentally shaped the course of reaction and ultimate outcome of the event on QOL.

Objective and subjective strategies to measure QOL in the community from an ecological perspective were reviewed. These included the identification of dependent criteria of QOL and methods to assess life events, event contexts, and event-context congruence, with event-context congruence representing the principal indicator, or predictor of QOL. To illustrate an application of an ecological approach to QOL assessment, we presented an example from our own research on QOL in a metropolitan tri-city community.

Data from ecological assessments of QOL can provide highly useful information for planning, conducting, and evaluating primary prevention efforts in communities. We offered a sampling of prevention strategies to maximize person-environment fit in communities through interventions designed around life events in general, and around normative life events for community subgroups.

Future research is clearly needed regarding the means by which event-context interactions affect and modify QOL over time. Attention must be given to longitudinal and multidimensional aspects of these interactions, and to how they influence and, in turn, are influenced by larger community systems. The chapter concluded with three "dicta" for the community researcher and interventionist regarding the implications of person-environment fit for the assessment and enhancement of QOL.

REFERENCE NOTES

1. Zautra, A., & Barrera, M. *A consideration of the community context in needs assessments of Mexican-Americans.* Paper presented at the Proceedings of the Third National Conference on Need Assessment in Health and Human Service Systems. University of Louisville, March 17–20, 1981.

2. Goodhart, D., & Zautra, A. *An ecological perspective in needs assessment.* Paper presented at the meeting of the American Psychological Association, Montreal, 1980.

3. Zautra, A., & Reich, J. *Positive events and quality of life.* Paper presented at the Proceedings of the Third National Conference on Needs Assessment in Health and Human Service Systems. University of Louisville, March 17–20, 1981.

REFERENCES

Altman, I., & Lett, E.E. (1970) The ecology of interpersonal relationships: A classification system and conceptual model. In J.E. McGrath (Ed.), *Social and psychological factors in stress.* New York: Holt, Rinehart, & Winston.

Andrews, F.M., & Withey, S.B. (1976) *Social indicators of well being: Americans' perceptions of life quality,* New York: Plenum.

Attkisson, C.C., Hargreaves, W.A., Horowitz, M.J., & Sorensen, J.E. (Eds.) (1978) *Evaluation of human service programs.* New York: Academic Press.

Baltes, B.P., & Willis, S.L. (1977) Toward psychological theories of aging and development. In J.E. Birren & K.W. Schaie (Eds.), *Handbook of the psychology of aging.* New York: Van Nostrand Reinhold.

Baltes, M.M., & Zerbe, M.B. (1976) Independence training in nursing-home residents. *The Gerontologist,* **16,** 428–432.

Barker, R.G. (1964) *Ecological psychology: concepts and methods for studying the environment of human behavior.* Stanford: Calif.: Stanford University Press.

Beck, A.T. (1971) Cognition, affect, and psychopathology. *Archives of General Psychiatry,* **24,** 495–500.

Bennett, S., & Bowers, D. (1976) *An introduction to multivariate techniques for social and behavioral sciences.* New York: Wiley.

Birren, J.E., & Schaie, K.W. (Eds.). (1977) *Handbook of the psychology of aging.* New York: Van Nostrand Reinhold.

Bishop, Y.M.M., Fienberg, S.E., & Holland, P.W. (1975) *Discrete multivariate analysis: Theory and practice.* Cambridge, Mass.: MIT Press.

Block, M.A. (1980) A test of three models of positive life events. Doctoral dissertation, Arizona State University.

Block, M., & Zautra, A. (1981) Satisfaction and distress in a community: A test of the effects of life events. *American Journal of Community Psychology,* **9,** 165–180.

Bloom, B.L. (1971) A university freshman preventive intervention program: Report of a pilot project. *Journal of Consulting and Clinical Psychology,* **37,** 235–242.

Bloom, B.L. (1975) *Changing patterns of psychiatric care.* New York: Human Sciences Press.

Bradburn, N. (1969) *The structure of psychological well being.* Chicago: Aldine.

Bronfenbrenner, U. (1977) Toward an experimental ecology of human development. *American Psychologist,* **32,** 513–531.

Bunge, M. (1975) What is a quality of life indicator? *Social Indicator Research,* **2,** 65–79.

Campbell, A. (1976) Subjective measures of well being. *American Psychologist,* **31,** 117–124.

Campbell, A., Converse, P.E., & Rodgers, W.L. (1976) *The quality of American life.* New York: Russell Sage.

Caplan, G. (1964) *Principles of preventative psychiatry.* New York: Basic Books.

Caplan, N., & Nelson, S.D. (1973) On being useful: The nature and consequences of psychological research on social problems. *American Psychologist,* **28,** 199–211.

Cassel, J. (1975) Social science in epidemiology: Psychosocial processes and "stress" theoretical formulation. In E.L. Struening, & M. Guttentag (Eds.), *Handbook of evaluation research.* Beverly Hills, Calif.: Sage.

Catalano, R., & Dooley, C.D. (1977) Economic predictors of depressed mood and stressful life events in a metropolitan community. *Journal of Health and Social Behavior,* **18,** 292–307.

Catalano, R., & Monahan, J. (1975) The community psychologist as social planner: Designing optimal environments. *American Journal of Community Psychology,* **3,** 327–334.

Cochrane, R., & Robertson, A. (1973) The life events inventory: A measure of the relative severity of psycho-social stressors. *Journal of Psychosomatic Research,* **17,** 135–139.

Cofer, C.N., & Appley, M.H. (1964) *Motivation: Theory and research.* New York: Wiley.

Cohen, F. (1980) Coping with surgery: Information, psychological preparation, and recovery. In L.W. Poon (Ed.), *Aging in the 1980's: Psychological issues.* Washington, D.C.: American Psychological Association.

Cohen, J., & Cohen, P. (1975) *Applied multiple regression/correlation analysis for the behavioral sciences.* Hillsdale, N.J.: Erlbaum.

Cottrell, N.B., & Epley, S.W. (1977) Affiliation, social comparison, and socially mediated stress reduction. In J.M. Suls, & R.L. Miller (Eds.), *Social comparison processes: Theoretical and empirical perspectives.* New York: Wiley.

Danish, S.J., Smyer, M.A., & Nowak, C.A. (1980) Developmental intervention: Enhancing life event processes. In P.B. Baltes, & O.J. Brim, Jr., (Eds.), *Life-span development and behavior* (Vol 3). New York: Academic Press.

Datan, N., & Ginsberg, L.G. (1975) *Life-span developmental psychology: Normative life crises.* New York: Academic Press.

Dohrenwend, B.S. (1973) Social status and stressful life events. *Journal of Personality and Social Psychology,* **28,** 225–235.

Dohrenwend, B.S., & Dohrenwend, B.P. (Eds.) (1974) *Stressful life events: Their nature and effects.* New York: Wiley.

Dohrenwend, B.S., & Dohrenwend, B.P. (1981) Socioenvironmental factors, stress, and psychopathology. *American Journal of Community Psychology,* **9,** 128–159.

Dohrenwend, B.S., Krasnoff, L., Askenasy, A.R., & Dohrenwend, B.P. (1978) Exemplification of a method for scaling life events: The PERI Life Events Scale. *Journal of Health and Social Behavior.* **19,** 205–229.

Eaton, W.W. (1978) Life events, social supports, and psychiatric symptoms: A reanalysis of the New Haven data. *Journal of Health and Social Behavior,* **19,** 230–234.

Erickson, E.H. (1953) Growth and crises of the healthy personality. In C. Kluckholn, & H. Murray (Eds.), *Personality in nature, society, and cuture.* New York: Knopf.

Festinger, L.A. (1954) A theory of social comparison processes. *Human Relations,* **7,** 117–140.

Festinger, L.A. (1957) *A theory of cognitive dissonance.* Stanford, Calif.: Stanford University Press.

French, J.R.P., Rodgers, W., & Cobb, S. (1974) Adjustment as person-environment fit. In G.V. Coehlo, D.A. Hamburg, & J.E. Adams (Eds.), *Coping and adaptation.* New York: Basic Books.

Gersten, J.C., Langner, T.S., Eisenberg, J.G., & Orzeck, L. (1974) Child behavior and life events: Undesirable change or change per se? In B.S. Dohrenwend, & B.P. Dohrenwend (Eds.), *Stressful life events: Their nature and effects.* New York: Wiley.

Goodstein, J., Zautra, A., & Goodhart, D. (1980) A test of the utility of social indicators for behavioral health service planning. *Social Indicators Research.*

Gruder, C.L. (1977) Choice of comparison persons in evaluating oneself. In J.M. Suls, & R.L. Miller (Eds.), *Social comparison processes: Theoretical and empirical perspectives.* New York: Wiley.

Gutmann, D.L. (1969) The country of old men: Cultural studies in the psychology of later life. Occasional Papers in Gerontology, No. 5. Ann Arbor, Mich.: Institute of Gerontology University of Michigan-Wayne State University.

Hagedorn, H.J., Beck, K.J., Neubert, S.F., & Werlin, S.J. (1976) *A working manual of simple program evaluation techniques for community mental centers.* Rockville, Md.: National Institute of Mental Health.

Hardin, G. (1969) The cybernetics of competition: A biologist's view of society. In P. Shepard, & D. McKinley (Eds.), *The subversive science: Essays toward an ecology of man.* Boston: Houghton Mifflin.

Heller, K., & Monahan, J. (1977) *Psychology and community change.* Homewood, Ill.: Dorsey Press.

Helson, H. (1959) Adaptation level theory. In S. Koch (Ed.), *Psychology: A study of a science* (Vol. 1). New York: McGraw-Hill.

Hirsch, B.J. (1980) Natural support systems and coping with major life changes. *American Journal of Community Psychology,* **8,** 159–172.

Holahan, C.J., & Spearly, J.L. (1980) Coping and ecology: an integrative model for community psychology. *American Journal of Community Psychology,* **8,** 671–685.

Holmes, T.H., & Masuda, M. (1974) Life change and illness susceptibility. In B.S. Dohrenwend, & B.P. Dohrenwend (Eds.), *Stressful life events: Their nature and effects.* New York: Wiley.

Holmes, T.H., & Rahe, R.H. (1967) The social readjustment rating scale. *Journal of Psychosomatic Research,* **11,** 213–218.

Hultsch, D.F., & Plemons, J.K. (1979) Life events and life-span development. In P.B. Baltes, & O.G. Brim, Jr. (Eds.), *Life-span development and behavior.* (Vol. 2). New York: Academic Press.

Jahoda, M. (1958) *Current concepts of positive mental health.* New York: Basic Books.

Jahoda, M.A. (1961) A social-psychological approach to the study of culture. *Human Relations,* **14,** 23–30.

Johnson, J.H., & Sarason, I.G. (1979) Recent developments in research on life stress. In V. Hamilton, & D.M. Warburton (Eds.), *Human stress and cognition.* New York: Wiley.

Kahana, E.A. (1975) A congruence model of person-environment interaction. In P.G. Windley, T.O. Byerts, & F.G. Ernst (Eds.), *Theory development in environment and aging.* Washington, D.C.: Gerontological Society.

Katz, M.M. (1976) Behavioral change in the chronicity pattern of dementia in the institutional geriatric resident. *Journal of the American Geriatrics Society,* **24,** 522–528.

Langner, T.S. (1962) Twenty-two item screening scale of psychiatric symptoms indicating impairment. *Journal of Health and Human Behavior,* **3,** 269–276.

Lawton, M.P. (1975) Competence, environmental press and the adaptation of older people. In P.G. Windley, T.O. Byerts, & F.G. Ernst (Eds.), *Theory development in environment and aging,* Washington, D.C.: Gerontological Society.

Lawton, M.P., & Nahemow, L. (1973) Ecology and the aging process. In C. Eisdorfer, & M.P. Lawton (Eds.). *The psychology of adult development and aging.* Washington, D.C.: American Psychological Association.

Lazarus, R.S., & Cohen, J.G. (1977) Environmental stress. In I. Altman, & J.F. Wohlwill (Eds.), *Human behavior and environment: Advances in theory and research* (Vol. 2). New York: Plenum.

Lazarus, R.S., & Launier, R. (1978) Stress-related transactions between person and environment. In L.A. Pervin, & M. Lewis (Eds.), *Perspectives in interactional psychology.* New York: Plenum.

Lazarus, R.S., & Cohen, J.G. (1977) Environmental stress. In I. Altman, & J.F. Wohlwill (Eds.), *Human behavior and environment: Advances in theory and research* (Vol. 2). New York: Plenum.

Leighton, D.C., Harding, J.S., Macklin, D., Hughes, C., & Leighton, A.H. (1963) Psychiatric findings of the Sterling County study. *American Journal of Psychiatry,* **119,** 1021–1026.

Levi, L. (1974) Psychosocial stress and disease: A conceptual model. In E.K.E. Gunderson & R.H. Rahe (Eds.), *Life stress and illness.* Springfield, Ill.: Thomas.

Lewin, K. (1935) Psycho-social problems of a minority group. *Character and Personality,* **3,** 175–187.

Lewin, K. (1951) *Field theory in social science.* New York: Harper & Row.

Lowenthal, M.F., & Chiriboga, D. (1973) Social stress and adaptation: Toward the life course perspective. In C. Eisdorfer, & M.P. Lawton (Eds.), *The psychology of adult development and aging.* Washington: American Psychological Association.

Lowenthal, M.F., Thurnher, M., & Chiriboga, D. (1975) *Four stages of life.* San Francisco: Jossey-Bass.

Maccoby, N., & Alexander, J. (1979) Reducing heart disease risk using the mass media: Comparing the effects on three communities. In R.F. Munoz, L.R. Snowden, & J.G. Kelly (Eds.), *Social and psychological research in community settings.* San Francisco: Jossey-Bass.

Merton, R.K., & Kitt, A.S. (1950) Contributions to the theory of reference group behavior. In R.K. Merton, & P.F. Lazarsfeld (Eds.), *Continuities in social research: Studies in the scope and method of the American soldier.* Glencoe, Ill.: Free Press.

Mills, R.C., & Kelly, J.G. (1972) Cultural adaptation and ecological analogies: Analysis of three Mexican villages. In S.E. Golann, & C. Eisdorfer (Eds.), *Handbook of community mental health.* New York: Appleton-Century-Crofts.

Moos, R.H. (1973) Conceptualizations of human environments. *American Psychologist,* **28,** 652–665.

Moos, R.H. (1974) Psychological techniques in the assessment of adaptive behavior. In G.V. Coelho, D.A. Hamburg, & J.E. Adams (Eds.). *Coping and adaptation.* New York: Basic Books.

Neugarten, B.L. (1976) Adaptation and the life cycle. *The Counseling Psychologist,* **6,** 16–20.

Neugarten, B.L., & Datan, N. (1973) Sociological perspectives on the life cycle. In P.B.

Baltes & K.W. Schaie (Eds.), *Life-span developmental psychology: Personality and socialization*. New York: Academic Press.

Neugarten, B.L., Moore, J.W., & Lowe, J.C. (1968) Age norms, age constraints, and adult socialization. In B.L. Neugarten (Ed.), *Middle age and aging*. Chicago: University of Chicago Press.

Parkes, C.M. (1971) Psycho-social transitions: A field for study. *Social Science and Medicine*, **5**, 101–115.

Pervin, L.A. (1968) Performance and satisfaction as a function of individual-environment fit. *Psychological Bulletin*, **69**, 56–68.

Price, R.H. (1974) Etiology, the social environment, and the prevention of psychological dysfunction. In P.M. Insel & R.H. Moos (Eds.). *Health and the social environment*. Lexington, Mass.: Heath.

Rapoport, L. (1962) The state of crisis: Some theoretical considerations. *Social Science Review*, **36**, 211–217.

Rappaport, J. (1977) *Community psychology: Values, research, and action*. New York: Holt, Rinehart & Winston.

Redfield, J., & Stone, A. (1979) Individual viewpoints of stressful life events. *Journal of Consulting and Clinical Psychology*, **47**, 147–154.

Reich, J., & Zautra, A. (1981) Life events and personal causation: Some relationships with distress and satisfaction. *Journal of Personality and Social Psychology*.

Riegel, K.F. (1975) From traits and equilibrium toward developmental dialectics. In W.J. Arnold (Ed.), *Nebraska Symposium on Motivation*. Lincoln: University of Nebraska Press.

Robinson, J.P., & Shaver, P.R. (1973) *Measure of social psychological attitudes*. (Rev. Ed.). Ann Arbor, Mich.: Institute for Social Research.

Rosow, I. (1968) Housing and local ties of the aged. In B.L. Neugarten (Ed.), *Middle age and aging*. Chicago: University of Chicago Press.

Sanford, N. (1972) Is the concept of prevention necessary or useful? In S.E. Golann & C. Eisdorfer (Eds.), *Handbook of community mental health*. New York: Appleton-Century-Crofts.

Schneider, M. (1975) The quality of life in large American cities: Objective and subjective social indicators. *Social Indicators Research*, **1**, 495–509.

Seidman, E., Rappaport, J., & Davidson, W.S. (1980) Adolescents in legal jeopardy: Initial success and replication of an alternative to the criminal justice system. In R. Ross, & P. Gendreau (Eds.), *Effective correctional treatment*. Toronto: Butterworths.

Selye, H. (1956) *The stress of life*. New York: McGraw-Hill.

Sherif, M. (1967) *Social interaction: Process and products*. Chicago: Aldine.

Spivak, G., & Shure, M.B. (1974) *Social adjustment of young children*. San Francisco: Jossey-Bass.

Stern, G.G. (1970) *People in context*. New York: Wiley.

Struening, E.L. (1975) Social area analysis as a method of evaluation. In E.L. Struening, & M. Guttentag (Eds.), *Handbook of evaluation research*. (Vol. 1), Beverly Hills, Calif.: Sage.

Suls, J.M., & Miller, R.L. (Eds.) (1977) *Social comparison processes: Theoretical and empirical perspectives*. New York: Wiley.

Tatsuoka, M.M. (1971) *Multivariate analysis.* New York: Wiley.

Tatsuoka, M.M. (1974) Classification procedures: Profile similarity. *Selected topics in advanced statistics: An elementary approach* (Vol. 3), Champaign, Ill.: Institute for Personality and Ability Testing.

Vinokur, A., & Selzer, M.L. (1975) Desirable versus undesirable life events: Their relationship to stress and mental illness. *Journal of Personality and Social Psychology,* **32,** 329–337.

Wechsler, H., & Pugh, T. (1967) Fit of individual and community characteristcs and rates of psychiatric hospitalization. *American Journal of Sociology,* **73,** 331–338.

Wilson, S.J. (1981) The image of women in Canadian magazines. In E. Katz, & T. Szecsko (Eds.), *Mass media and social change.* Beverly Hills, Calif.: Sage.

Windley, P.G., & Scheidt, R.J. (1980) Person-environment dialectics: Implications for competent functioning in old age. In L.W. Poon (Ed.), *Aging in the 1980's: Psychological issues.* Washington, D.C.: American Psychological Association.

Wohlwill, J.F. (1966) The physical environment: A problem for a psychology of stimulation. *Journal of Social Issues,* **22,** 29–38.

Zautra, A., & Goodhart, D. (1979) Quality of life: A review of the literature. *Community Mental Health Review,* **4**(1), 1–10.

Zautra, A., & Reich, J. (1980) Positive life events and reports of well-being: Some useful distinctions. *American Journal of Community Psychology,* **8,** 657–670.

Zautra, A., & Simons, L.S. (1978) Assessment of a community's mental health needs. *American Journal of Community Psychology,* **6,** 351–362.

Zautra, A., & Simons, L.S. (1979) Some effects of positive life events on community mental health. *American Journal of Community Psychology,* **4,** 441–451.

Zarit, S.H., & Kahn, R.L. (1975) Aging and adaptation to illness. *Journal of Gerontology,* **30,** 67–72.

PART FOUR

Ecological Models: Applications at the Sociocultural Level

When the diversity of human culture is considered, the inclusion of a section on sociocultural process in a volume designed to illustrate an ecosystemic perspective and applications for the practitioner becomes a formidable undertaking. But it is a reality that, even within the limits of conventional professional practice in the United States, the practitioner must deal increasingly with cultural and subcultural differences. Not only the black, Hispanic, and Native American populations present a significant challenge; in the working setting, we are also confronted with the effects of global political process. Within many communities, substantial refugee populations from a dozen countries across the globe are struggling to integrate both personal functioning and community involvement. The events of Vietnam, of Poland, and of the Middle East are not ultimately insulated from professional practice and mental health.

More significantly, as we deal with the impact of specific subcultures on service delivery and professional models of practice, we confront the reality that social and cultural processes are relevant for every client presented to the practitioner and for the majority culture of the community in relation to preventive mental health efforts. The basic norms and values of the community have changed in a striking fashion decade by decade; the mental health issues of the 1950s, 1960s, and the 1970s are sufficiently distinct to direct our attention to the significance of broad social process.

If we have largely ignored these aspects of human behavior in conventional practice, there exists no better illustration of our ignorance than with respect to Native American populations. Not for decades but for centuries the native population of the United States has been largely decimated by an inability or unwillingness to consider the integrity of American Indian cultures. Trimble and Hayes clearly illustrate the specific and practical relevance of subcultural differences in the delivery of mental health services. But the issues presented obviously extend beyond the Native American population.

The chapter by Daniels, Wilkinson, and O'Connor also illustrates the ease with which both researchers and practitioners can fail to perceive critical mental health needs at both the individual and population level. Much of the research and clinical practice relating to black American populations proceeded from assumptions, and confirmed such assumptions in the absence of data and in the absence of effective intervention. Daniels, Wilkinson, and O'Connor approached the issues from an ecosystemic perspective, which allows the accurate development of specific models and intervention strategies for an urban black population.

The integration of sensitivity to subcultural issues, systems models, and the substantial practical dilemmas presented in mental health practice are demonstrated by Szapocznik et al. The subcultural populations presented to mental health jurisdictions in areas of Florida have made evident the realities of such a broad ecosystemic perspective on subcultural differences.

In the final chapter, Hurd and Pattison present what appears to be an issue rarely of practical significance to the working clinician: spirit possession. But a careful reading of the chapter reveals surprises in terms of relevance; what the client often presents to the clinician are not those problems or issues well understood on a rational basis, but those inexplicable and powerful events that seem to come from nowhere and to produce effects beyond the understanding and awareness of the client. Similarly, on a community level, what most fuels our feelings of hopelessness and powerlessness are those events that seem beyond understanding and control.

CHAPTER 13

Mental Health Intervention in the Psychosocial Contexts of American Indian Communities[1]

JOSEPH E. TRIMBLE AND SUSANNA A. HAYES

Act I

Scene I. A small office located in a wing of the village center complex somewhere in western Alaska. (A soft knock at the door. A nonnative counselor swivels in his chair, reaches over, and opens the door. An Eskimo adolescent female is standing there, hands clasped, waiting the polite permission to enter.)

COUNSELOR: "I've been waiting about an hour for you Maryann." (pause) "Please come in and take this chair over here." (Points to a small overstuffed chair located in the corner of the office and then swivels around in his chair, his eyes following the client to her seat. He waits until she sits down and appears settled in.)
"Well, Maryann, I understand you've been having some problems at home and in school. Do you wanta talk about them?"

MARYANN: (Hands clasped and resting on her lap, eyes cast down seemingly fixed on a spot on the floor in front of her.) She responds softly, "I don't know." (a long pause interspersed with a sigh) "Well, maybe."

COUNSELOR: "It seems you're having some heavy arguments with your dad and I understand you ran off for a couple of days. Can you give me some idea of what's bothering you?"

MARYANN: (long pause) "Uhm...I don't know if I can."

COUNSELOR: "Well, could you tell me something about your problems at school? Are you bothered by them?"

MARYANN: (softly) "No...not really bothered."

COUNSELOR: "Are you interested in completing school?"

MARYANN: "I don't know...I think so."

[1]Correspondence concerning this chapter should be sent to the senior author, Department of Psychology, Western Washington University, Bellingham, WA 98225.

COUNSELOR: What about your future...do you have any future plans?"

MARYANN: (long pause) "I don't know...maybe I do."

The session continues in this manner, the counselor struggling to initiate discussion and the client, in a culturally appropriate way, quietly avoids any confrontation or involvement with the counselor. We can assume that the session ends on a frustrating note for both with the counselor puzzled over his ineffectiveness and the client annoyed because the counselor failed to work within a framework sensitive to her cultural orientation.

The scene is not fictitious. It happened much the way it was described. More significantly though is the very real possibility that this scene has been occurring in Indian and native communities for decades. Typically, a non-Indian counselor is employed by some institution to provide and deliver mental health services to the indigenous population. In time the counselor or therapist becomes frustrated with the apparent lack of success with the clients. And, furthermore, he or she begins to have less and less appointments despite overwhelming evidence that the community and individuals are experiencing a multitude of problems.

The frustrating Indian client–non-Indian mental health worker experiences can be avoided. Those intending to deliver mental health programs can be effective provided they operate within a framework sensitive to the cultural milieu in which the intervention effort is to occur. This chapter identifies some of the major characteristics of the cultural milieu—the ecosystem of the American Indian or Alaska Native community.[2] Following this, background information is provided concerning contemporary attempts to understanding tribal-specific concepts of mental health and a review of the literature dealing with counseling and psychotherapy in Indian communities. These sections are followed with material that concentrates on the delivery of services and implications for the future of delivering clinical services to the communities in question. The chapter concludes with some pointed recommendations.

THE CULTURAL MILIEU OF INDIAN COMMUNITIES

As the central theme of this text suggests communities, whatever form they take, constitute an ecosystem; as such, it is imperative that one be familiar with the elements that comprise that system if they hope to operate within it successfully. Indeed, delivering effective mental health services to Indian communities requires knowledge of the community's character (Trimble & Medicine, 1976), the nature of the services available (Manson & Trimble, 1981) and the community's orientation to mental health (cf. Dinges et al., 1981; Trimble et al., 1982). This section discusses the nature of the existing support networks and the major structural and functional elements comprising a "typical" Indian community.

[2]For the sake of convenience the term *Indian* will hereafter be used in lieu of American Indian and Alaska Native. Such a practice is fairly well accepted.

Existing Support Networks

Indeed it would be presumptuous for anyone to assume that mental health-related support systems are nonexistent or loosely pulled together in Indian communities. If this appears to be a bit preposterous, consider the presumptive attitude of early missionaries and certain agencies of the U.S. Public Health Service, namely, that Indian religion and medical capabilities were nonexistent or woefully inadequate and therefore should be changed or developed.

Within most Indian communities, especially those in rural areas and on reservations, one can find at least three human support type systems: (1) an informal yet highly structured helping network; (2) a culture-specific traditional healing system most likely linked to a traditional religious orientation; and (3) a conventional public health service unit supported in whole or part by state and federal funds. Indians living on, near, and at remote distances from the home community are acutely aware of the existence of the three systems. Some avail themselves of the services provided by all three, still others reject one for another using various reasons as a basis for the preferences.

Informal Helping Network

The informal helping network typically consists of a core group of community members. The individuals are not organized nor do they meet specifically to discuss community matters. Rather they are seen as individuals who have the reputation of being able to help in crisis situations, provide assistance in times of dire need, or simply be an ear for someone distressed over a personal or family problem. Many are reluctant to be publicly identified as persons capable of providing counseling assistance—they are usually quite modest, unimposing, and seemingly always available. One Coast Salish informant who serves in this community capacity remarked to one of the authors after an apparent deluge of crisis phone calls and personal visits, "I always seem to make people feel better about themselves—but after they're gone, there doesn't seem to be anyone around to help me deal with the problems I've inherited from those I helped."

Traditional Healers

Most people know of the existence of some sort of folk medicine and healing in Indian communities. Stories about the wisdom, skills, and practices of shaman and medicine men seem to abound in and around Indian communities. Knowledge of the presence of the shaman is widespread, but knowledge about their actual activities is quite restricted and limited to a privileged few.

Access to the services provided by traditional shamen such as the spirit healers among the Coast Salish in the Pacific Northwest are limited mainly to Indians. For the Coast Salish healers there are exceptions and they are usually reserved for non-Indians with Indian spouses. Among other tribal groups access is restricted exclusively to Indians; in some areas, particularly among certain Pueblo groups, the shaman will only see village members and their extended kin.

Most shamen limit their services to functional and psychosomatic based disorders. Few challenge organic based diseases such as cancer, coronary problems, and diseases of the nervous system. Some shamen will refer people with acute illnesses, wounds, and so on, to a community-person skilled in the use of herbal medicine; others may serve in a dual role of herbalist and spiritual healer.

In a number of Indian communities physicians, psychiatrists, and mental health workers are collaborating with the local shaman to improve the delivery of services. Such collaboration is relatively new despite the persistent suggestions of a number of advocates (Bergman, 1974; Attneave, 1974). In a way there may be some wisdom tied in with the reluctance as many collaborative efforts have ended in a tragic failure—for the client and the healer in particular each loses something in situations where the healer is unable to effect a change (Attneave, 1974; Dinges et al., 1981).

A traditional healing system in Indian communities does not mean that all of the local residents subscribe to the orientation. Devout Indian followers of Christian religions, for example, often scoff at the "primitive" ways of the traditionalists and nativists. In addition, many service delivery personnel staunchly refuse to acknowledge the credibility of healers. Carolyn Attneave's (1974) description of a typical view held by a number of professionals is illustrative. One of her informants was quoted as saying:

I'm a careful, hard-working scientific physician. I don't prescribe medications. I don't know about or use therapies that haven't evidence that they do some good. Besides, I'm willing to explain what's what to qualified colleagues—even to patients when they can comprehend. These medicine men aren't about to tell me what they do or how they do it. No! I can't refer my patients to them. That would be unethical. (p. 53)

In some Indian communities, especially among the Coast Salish, it appears that more and more Indians are seeking the services of "Indian doctors" and spiritual healers than a few decades ago. Perhaps this can be attributed in part to the growing interest in Indian pride and identity, coupled with the growing acceptability of seeking the services of a shaman rather than that of other available helping services.

Federal, State, and Local Service Units

The number of federal and state supported mental health service programs located in and around Indian communities is increasing. This growth can be attributed to changes in federal policies toward Indians, increases in the demands for more comprehensive health care, and the recognition that mental health conditions in Indian communities are quite high, especially in the substance abuse areas (Manson & Trimble, 1982).

The federal and state supported services typically are provided through the Bureau of Indian Affairs, the Indian Health Service, and community mental health centers. The type of services offered by these agencies varies and depends on the nature of the problems and availability of staff. Similarly, the degree to which community members respond to the services is a function of the degree to which the services are perceived as culturally sensitive to the life-style orientations of tribal members. A discussion of the nature of these services and community perceptions follows.

The mental health services provided by the Bureau of Indian Affairs (colloquially often referred to as the "BIA" or "the Bureau") are restrictive and most likely more incidental than planned, especially forms of diagnostic counseling and psychotherapy. Services are provided in child welfare cases, family problems, and in educational and vocational guidance programs. The services usually are carried out by mental health professionals, occasionally in collaboration with indigenous paraprofessionals. Clients with acutely severe problems are usually referred to staff at the Indian Health Service.

Most of the public forms of mental health services for Indians are carried out by the Indian Health Service (colloquially "IHS"). Operating on both an inpatient and outpatient basis, psychiatrists (often contracted for one or two days per week) provide services targeted to deal with major emotional and behavioral disorders. Neuroses and alcoholism seem to dominate the list of disorders (Rhoades et al., 1980).

Since the early 1970s numerous urban Indian mental health programs and tribal-based programs have been initiated. Both of these kinds of programs emerged as a result of the Indian Health Care Improvement Act and the Indian Self-Determination Act. Many of the services available from the programs resemble those offered by the IHS; setting them apart though is the proximity of the programs to the community. In many communities Indians must travel great distances to receive the services provided by IHS. The addition of urban and tribal-based programs has lessened the travel burden for many and thus relieved the heavy burden placed upon IHS facilities.

Those intending to work in the area of Indian mental health must be acutely aware of the three helping service systems. They vary in complexity and intensity from community to community and from one geocultural region to another in the United States. Moreover, the clientele likely to obtain a particular service is variable—so much so that on occasion a person may visit both the shaman and an IHS mental health worker to double the chances of recovering.

Ecosystemic Characteristics of the Indian Community

The human support systems described in the previous section exist within a larger fabric encompassing the intimately woven structural and functional components of a native community. Viewed from an ecosystemic perspective these components include the unique characteristics of the physical and environmental setting, the sociocultural characteristics, and the individual Indian people themselves. Each component shares a common core of similarity across almost all Indian communities, especially those in rural areas. But just as there exists some element of similarity, there is abounding variation within and between communities. Knowledge of the intimate character of these components is an absolute necessity for all to work effectively in Indian communities. A brief overview of these components can be instructive.

The Physical and Environmental Setting

The location of housing in Indian communities may appear random, but in fact it is tied quite closely to a land tenure system. The nature of the system typically is reflected in political orientations, participation in Indian ceremonials, degree of Indian blood, and subsistence patterns. Yet in other communities, the distribution of housing and residential patterns may be tied directly to land ownership and not necessarily reflect a social orientation. In still other communities, location of settlements may be distinguished by the continued maintenance of a clan system—the clan indeed is viewed as a viable sociopolitical entity that can be clearly distinguished from others in other sections of the community.

There are some rural Indian communities where small Indian housing settlements are separated from one another by non-Indian land plots. Such settlements, though, tend to be relatively cohesive reflecting a similar sociopolitical orientation among other things. Moreover, although not clearly documented, there is some evidence to suggest that many urban Indian settlements such as those in Denver, Albuquerque, Los Angeles, and Seattle resemble those of certain rural areas. In these instances, though, people from similar tribal backgrounds will comprise the residents of a particular neighborhood; in Seattle, for example, Alaska natives tend to live in one neighborhood, whereas plateau groups tend to reside in another.

The distribution of residential patterns in Indian communities follows definite patterns. The patterns vary but nonetheless represent an element that reflects yet another orientation represented by identifiable sociocultural factors.

Sociocultural Characteristics

Another vitally significant component of the Indian community consists of those elements that comprise the social fabric. These elements include the nature of family and kin relations, age group distinctions, leadership and political patterns, and religious preferences. Although these elements are not necessarily inclusive, they represent those that are most influential in the day-to-day activities of the community.

Most Indian scholars would agree that the most significant element in an Indian community involves familial patterns and relations. In rural communities the patterns are heavily influenced by the extended nature of the family. The extended family pattern similarly can be found in urban areas, but distances there may contribute more to the strength of the cohesive bond than in rural areas.

In small Indian communities there may be a mere two or three families that dominate the total population. And, in these instances, one may find that members of these family groups may hold significant positions in the many tribally owned and federally supported programs. Further, as one might suspect, certain families may not necessarily think too positively about another—the members involved quite often are in the low hundreds. A newcomer to a community may find that identifying members of families typically is a frustrating experience, because there seems to be no end to the extent of the kin relations. As one informant from a small community in Washington's Olympic peninsula put it, "Well, when you get right down to it, we're probably all related to one another around here—but some are just more so than others."

Another element in that social fabric involves affiliations with religious institutions, from the traditional Indian church to orthodox versions of Christianity. Religious affiliations are potent and strongly influence life-style orientations of many community members. Moreover, those who follow traditional Indian practices may also be devout followers of a Christian sect— allegiance to one religious practice does not preclude an involvement in another. The affiliations also may reflect the leanings of certain families within the broad extended family network, obviously affecting preferred belief system and behavioral orientations.

Knowledge of the elements of a community's social system, together with information about physical characteristics of the environment, will immensely improve a would-be mental health worker's effectiveness. Knowledge of these two elements is not sufficient, however, to comprehend the makeup of the community's ecosystem effectively. One must have some understanding of the characteristics of the residents to bring their potential effectiveness level to a reasonable level.

Individual Characteristics

Recently a federal auditor evaluated the operations and participants of a federally supported education program. As part of his duties he was obligated to interview several of the Indian students to get a sense for their perceptions of the program's effectiveness. They came in individually to see him at the appointed times to offer their impressions. At one point, into the office walked a high school sophomore with curly red hair, freckles, light skin, and blue eyes. "And who might you be?" queried the auditor. "Well, I'm Johnny J. and I've an appointment to see you." "Are you Indian?" snapped the auditor. "Of course," answered Johnny, adding, "Would you care to see my tribal identification card?"

The vignette typifies the misconceptions many well-intended non-Indians have about Indians. A large part of the misconceptions is attributed to stereotypy and a distinct lack of familiarity with rural, reservation, and urban Indian features. Reservation communities, for example, typically consist of Indians of various blood quantum mixtures ranging from the "full blood" to those who are one-eighth to even less than that. Occasionally one finds non-Indians living and working in the community who "look more Indian" than many who are enrolled or registered members of the resident tribe.

The variations in physical characteristics are often used as criteria to determine the degree to which one subscribes to traditional or nativist orientations. Quite mistakenly non-Indians often consider so-called "full-bloods" to be more traditional (colloquially, "more Indian") than mixed-bloods. In point of fact, using blood quantum as criteria to determine traditional leanings in some communities would be quite helpful; in other communities it would be disastrous.

Again, knowledge of these characteristics is critical for one to comprehend the ecological nature of Indian communities. The settings, the psychosocial components, and individual Indian characteristics all combine to form a subtle, complex system that requires careful ongoing assessment. Add to the system the types of helping agencies available together with their subtle complexities, and one obtains a profile of a dynamic process demanding constant attention and contemplation. It is against this framework that one must reflect to effect successful mental health intervention efforts.

LITERATURE ON COUNSELING AND PSYCHOTHERAPY WITH AMERICAN INDIANS

Most students and followers of the cross-cultural counseling field are familiar with the underutilization hypothesis, namely, that ethnic minorities tend to underutilize existing community mental health centers even though mental health indicators reveal an enormous need for service (cf. Padilla & Ruiz, 1973; Torrey, 1970, 1972; Sue, 1977; Sue et al., 1978). Further, many followers of the field also recognize the significant problems associated with counseling the culturally different (cf. Marsella & Pedersen, 1981; Pedersen et al., 1981). In fact, within the past decade increased effort and attention have been given to the subject of counseling across cultures. Problems, issues, and recommendations have been presented on topics ranging from use of innovative therapies to training. Articles focusing on the mental health intervention problems and issues of Indians appear in most of the works—the themes are quite consistent, specifically: (1) Indians tend to underutilize existing public services, and (2) efforts must be directed to seek alternative strategies for improving the quality and effectiveness of delivery strategies.

The literature on counseling, psychotherapy, and related mental health intervention approaches as it relates to American Indians is rather limited in number when compared with the body of mental health information in general. A bibliography on Indian mental health compiled by Kelso and Attneave (1981) shows a definite growth in the number of citations, beginning in the 1930s and extending to the present. Altogether they identified some 1400 articles dealing in some manner with Indian mental health—about 75 articles have been identified that in some way focus on conventional forms of psychotherapy and counseling. A review of some of the findings can shed some light on the issues central to the subject of Indian mental health.

Tribal-Specific Concepts of Mental Health Literature

Social anthropologists, psychiatrists, psychologists, and other interested people have long expressed interest in tribal-specific concepts of mental disorders. Late nineteenth-century anthropological descriptions depict an assortment of behaviors from numerous tribes, which depart in some fashion from apparent normative tribal patterns. More detailed accounts began to appear in the literature in the first two decades of the twentieth century, and included descriptions of the classic *windigo* psychosis among the Algonkin speaking people and *pibloktoq* among Polar Eskimos.

From all ethnographic accounts of North American Indian life-styles each tribe had some version of what one might consider to be some behavioral and emotional disorder. Although the variations in labels used to describe them are as diverse as Indian linguistic groups, there is communality in the expressed behaviors themselves. Clement's (1932) classification scheme is useful in pointing out the similarities. Clement found that there are four broad explanations for the causes of disorders throughout the world; specifically, loss of an important substance from the body, introduction of a harmful substance into the body, violation of taboos, and use of black magic and witchcraft. These explanations can be further subsumed soul-loss, spirit intrusion, taboo breaking, and disease sorcery, respectively. Elements of Clement's categories can be found in *all* North American Indian folk belief systems; variations of these categories persist today. Some Coast Salish and Lakota informants claim that beliefs in the traditional explanations are increasing among many community members.

Spirit intrusion is one category that has received considerable attention from behavioral and social scientists. According to Clement (1932) the category "includes all etiologies which hold that disease is due to the presence of evil spirits, ghosts or demons"(p. 190). Belief in spirit intrusion and possession is very common among the Pacific Northwest tribal groups, especially Coast Salish ones (Amoss, 1978). Among these groups those who are thought to be "possessed" display behavior similar to agitated depression. According to Canadian psychiatrists Jilek and Jilek-Aall (1971), the behavior is "often associated with considerable somatization, hallucinatory or illusional experiences. In particular, these symptoms are: anorexia; insomnia; apathy alternating with restlessness; dysphoric crying spells and nostalgic despondency; dyspnoea, precordial sensations and vague spastic pains" (p. 1183).

Accordingly, victims "made sick by spirit powers" *(sye'wen)* are those experiencing anomic depression, probably the result of frustration, discouragement, defeat, and lowered self-esteem (Jilek, 1974). Hallowell (1963) describes a similar pattern of behavior among the Ojibwa *(äkwaziwin)* where attainment of life goals is jeopardized by the intrusion of the spirit of the diseased. Similarly, among eastern subarctic Eskimos an equivalent form of spirit intrusion *(quissaatug)* is found which is characterized by "compulsive passivity, withdrawal and depression...(often) accompanied by brief flurries of manic activity" (Vallee, 1966, p. 64).

Examples of other forms of tribal-specific behavior disorders abound. A generalized review describing mental health concepts of American Indians was developed by Trimble, Manson, Dinges, and Medicine (1983). The review provides a perspective incorporating other related aspects of mental health including prevention, and native-specific concepts of human competence. Other more lengthy detailed descriptions can be found in Boyer's (1964) ethnopsychiatric account of folk psychiatry among the Mescalero Apache, Kaplan and Johnson's (1964) and Dinges' et al. (1982) account of behavioral disorders among the Navajo, and Murphy's (1964) detailed description of shamanism among the St. Lawrence Island Eskimo.

One important aspect of the literature on tribal-specific concepts of behavior disorders is the finding that the beliefs and practices coincide with the values of the group in question. Certainly not all Coast Salish Indians believe in the notion of spirit intrusion. Most, nonetheless, know of it and are aware that many strongly subscribe to it. Another characteristic of the folk psychiatry literature is the linkage with descriptions of shamanism, traditional healing and the role of contemporary psychotherapy and counseling. The next section examines a summary of literature on this aspect.

Counseling and Psychotherapy Literature[3]

As noted earlier there is an obvious increase in the studies of counseling and psychotherapy with Indians. Presently four major reviews of the topic exist that emphasize the role of values in counseling Indians (Trimble, 1976, 1981), use of a social ecological orientation in working with Indian clients (Dinges et al., 1981), delivering mental health services to Indian communities (Manson & Trimble, 1982), and conducting cross-counseling research among Indians (Trimble & Lee, 1981). Other short review articles exist emphasizing the literature on the relationship between the traditional healer and psychiatrists and psychologists (Attneave, 1974), self-perception and perceived alienation (Trimble, in press), and mental health prevention (Manson, 1982).

A common theme appears to exist in most of the Indian counseling and psychotherapy literature. Most writers concur that many Indians seem to experience interpersonal and interethnic problems when they seek professional mental health assistance. This probably occurs because a sizable number of counselors and therapists lack experience and knowledge of the Indian client. Other core themes also run through the literature.

One theme emphasizes that conventional counseling techniques can be inappropriately adapted for use with certain American Indian groups (Spang, 1965; Red Horse et al., 1978). Like many first-time clients, some Indian clients simply may not know what to expect—a client's silence and apparent nonattentiveness could be construed as hostility (Jilek-Aall, 1976). This lack of familiarity contrasts with certain experienced Indian clients—client behavior conforms to the counselor's ethnocentric expectations of "good client behaviors" (cf. Goldstein, 1981). In the latter instance, little if any conflict-reduction or problem solving occurs as the client is merely role playing and probably is not helped by the relationship. In either instance, an internalization of appropriate clientlike behavior fails to occur, presumably deriving from the incompatibility between the counselor's technique and the client's cultural orientation.

---

[3]Assistance in developing this section was provided by our former graduate student, D. John Lee, currently at Tabor College.

Another topic emphasizes providing alternatives for use in counseling American Indians as one solution to preventing intercultural conflict. In the Southwest, Youngman and Sadongei (1974) recommend that counselors focus on traditional mannerisms to guide their interactions with Indian youth. Jilek-Aall (1976) and Attneave (1969) urge clinicians to focus on family dynamics when working with Indian clients. Attneave points out that family network counseling actually mobilizes relatives and friends into a social force that serves to counteract client depersonalization and isolation. Jilek-Aall suggests that a use of mythological themes through storytelling can provide a medium where a client can identify symptoms by expressing personal customs toward story themes.

The delivery of mental health services to Indian communities has attracted some attention. Themes include basic issues emphasizing program inadequacies and needs and descriptions of unique programs (Manson & Trimble, 1982). Certainly one finds the few articles discussing the underutilization of available services mentioned earlier (Torrey, 1970, 1972; Sue, Allen & Conaway, 1978) unique to all ethnic-minority groups (Sue, 1977).

Underutilization describes the circumstances; the causes underlying these patterns, however, are varied. Hippler (1975) argues that some Eskimos, for example, fail to respond to mental health care systems because of their intrinsic belief in magic. He further argues that Eskimos will continue to be nonresponsive to care as long as magic-thinking and beliefs in traditional healers persist.

Beliefs about the effectiveness of mental health care staff are viewed as a major stumbling block in use patterns among a sample of Navajo (Schoenfeld, Lyerly, & Miller, 1971). Patient referrals seemed to be related directly to the attitudes program staff held toward the care-providing agencies. For example, few, if any, clients were referred to the BIA program as attitudes toward staff were largely negative. Further, although the Mental Health Staff was viewed positively, a great deal of mistrust existed between them and other agencies. Interagency suspicions hampered effective delivery of services in the communities.

Urban Indian leaders and community members also share a mutual concern about mental health conditions and availability of services (Borunda & Shore, 1978). According to Barter and Barter (1974), urban Indians believe that their mental health needs are not being adequately met, and the federal government shares the responsibility for providing facilities. Those services that are available are viewed with suspicion and hence are underutilized.

Nonurban and off-reservation Indians apparently experience problems similar to their urban counterparts. Thomas Bittker (1973), following a survey of Phoenix area service delivery facilities, reported that off-reservation Indians have ambiguous status; governments typically considered them to be outside the realm of responsibility. Nonetheless, their needs for services are as great as those Indians from other settings; and they may be even greater considering the limited services available to them.

Many recommendations concerning the operation and programming of Indian service delivery units have been introduced. The two that receive the most support call for more local Indian control (Ostendorf & Hammerslag, 1977) and establishing and directing centers from a cross-cultural perspective (Westernmeyer & Hausman, 1974). Both indeed are simplistic in concept, but are complicated to implement efficiently and effectively. Indian control implies, for example, that there are a number of trained Indian mental health administratots and clinicians.

Two promising options have been proposed and, in some catchment areas, developed and implemented. Bergman (1974) advocated the use of Indian paraprofessionals working in collaboration with non-Indian professionals. Such an effort promotes a number of culturally appropriate ventures, not the least of which is making professionals ever conscious of the bicultural demands of their clients and staff. In a similar vein, Attneave (1974) strongly urged mutual collaboration between traditional healers and non-Indian professionals.

Despite the many criticisms about the collaborative efforts, a few similar programs have been initiated and are operating successfully. In 1969, at the Boarding School in Toyei, Arizona, under the collaborative guidance of Indians and non-Indians, a parenting project was initiated. Navajo houseparents were employed to work closely with students, especially in teaching them traditional skills. The program has been quite successful in keeping emotional problems at a minimum and in improving certain academic skills (Goldstein, 1974). A similar concept was initiated in Portland (Shore & Nicholls, 1977). Essentially, Indian juvenile offenders were assigned to a group home where treatment and support were provided, in many instances involving the parents and relatives.

A number of articles exist describing unique program concepts involving collaborative efforts and use of specialized techniques. Attneave (1969) advocates the use of network therapeutic techniques in clinical settings. Involvement of family members, conceivably even clan members, can assist the troubled family in making transitions, provide positive and healthy role models, and promote family cohesion. Murdock and Schwartz (1978) substantiate Carolyn Attneave's arguments and propose more family involvement in providing care, especially for Indian elderly (cf. Cooley et al., 1979).

Bloom and Richards (1974) and Kinzie, Shore, and Pattison (1972) describe mental health delivery efforts in Alaska and among Pacific Northwest coastal tribes, respectively. In both articles, emphasis is placed on developing programs responsive to the culturally unique needs of community members, promoting close interaction with local staff, and fostering Indian control and management of services.

The literature on culturally-specific mental health disorders and problems, and delivering intervention schemes to Indian communities is likely to follow contemporary trends. Future literature will probably include more empirically based studies evaluating the effectiveness of innovative efforts, detailed analytic case studies describing successful and unsuccessful treatment rehabilitation, and prevention efforts. This increase is likely to be attributed to the growing interests in the subject attested to by the recent formation of National Indian Counselors Association, increased numbers of professionally trained American Indian and Alaska Natives moving into the field, and continuing demands to meet the mental health needs of the first American.

In the meantime, emphasis must be given to the value of exploring procedures that fit with the ethos and life-style existing in Indian communities. Information provided thus far in this chapter described the basic helping systems in Indian communities, the ecosystemic components of the community, and a distillation of literature findings. In the final section of the chapter emphasis is placed on delivering services to the community. Through the use of case study material, examples of successful and unsuccessful attempts at delivering services are offered. Guidelines are provided for effective positive relationships with community members and developing an understanding of the role of a mental health worker in the ecosystemic context of the Indian community. Recommendations for improving future intervention efforts are also provided.

DELIVERING SERVICES TO THE COMMUNITY

The mental health specialist who is assigned to work with reservation-based American Indians or among the 300,000 American Indians living in urban centers usually is not an Indian. In most instances the level and degree of direct, personal, and/or professional experiences with Indians is very limited. Obviously, the challenges to identify, understand, and work with individuals in need of mental health assistance are intensely demanding. Adding personal-cultural differences between therapist and clients to the service delivery process can lead to confusion and frustration for all concerned.

Variations in Cultural Orientations

Currently, the range of cultural orientations that may be observed within the diverse spectrum of native populations covers infinite variations between the extremes of strict traditionalist and strict assimilationist. Adding to this complexity are the specific cultural practices derived explicitly from one's affiliation with a tribe or tribes. There are over 300 tribes in the United States with most tribal groups consisting of units or bands that have their origin in extended family systems. It is important to recognize that no one model of service delivery or one theory of cross-cultural intervention can be effectively employed by mental health specialists who work with persons referred to as American Indians. There are vast differences among individual members of a tribe as well as between members of different tribes. Together with the levels and forms of differences are the individual and group similarities that exist. Following are some examples to clarify these points.

Two sisters, both over 50 have lived all of their lives in a remote village on a large reservation in the Northwest. One sister is very active in the social and political life of her community. She is a strong advocate for educational and economic development of the tribe. Her beliefs on issues of tribal self-determination have been clearly and eloquently annunciated at regional and national conferences. She travels extensively and is a ready and willing communicator among friends or strangers. Her personal manner is that of an open, warm, and gregarious woman.

Many friends and extended family members have harshly criticized her for the positions she has taken on a number of tribal issues. She is sensitive to these objections and is trying to decide if her life would be better in an off-reservation community, where the objections and criticisms would be less intense. An important issue for her is whether or not the separation from her home community would become more difficult than tolerating the negative aspects of her current situation.

The other sister is a very private person. She has been known to keep her children and grandchildren away from school because it interferes with food-gathering seasons or her need for their help with household chores. She strongly objects to the presence of non-Indians on the reservation and regards her sister's activities with disdain. She seldom speaks to anyone other than her family members. When cultural gatherings are held in the village, however, she and her sister partake actively in the preparation and celebrating. Both women speak their tribal band's language as well as English. Both were raised by the same parents and attended the same Indian boarding schools.

Another example reflects the lives of two brothers. One brother is in his early thirties and has a college degree, which has allowed him to take a job as a BIA employee on his home reservation. He has been married, divorced, and remarried. His domestic life is hectic with frequent separations usually occurring after weekends of drinking and partying. There are times when the pressures of his job as an accountant and the conflicts of his family life have placed him in a state of severe depression. He has talked with the pastor of a Christian Church on the reservation because he regards the man as a friend. There is no one else in whom he has confidence or trusts to keep his situation private. He has indicated verbally that he has felt desperate enough to consider suicide as an alternative to living his life as it is.

His brother is in his late twenties. He quit school after completing the tenth grade, is single, and lives in a small house on his parents' ranch. Until his recent employment in the tribe's logging operations, he has done part-time farm labor. He enjoys hunting, fishing, and ranching. His personal goals are defined by his life at present. He has close personal communications with his family and some close friends. He is distant toward strangers and finds social communication with women other than family members very strained. He is satisfied with his life as it is and feels no need to change. He is concerned about his older brother. He thinks his drinking and marriage problems reflect a deep unrest that is related to the confusion of an Indian trying to live in non-Indian ways. He has not tried to talk with his brother about these problems because he thinks there is nothing that he can do to help him.

These examples represent four distinct persons who live on a reservation within a close proximity to each other. Each person has an individual and independent life pattern. Yet, each shares much in common with the other. All of the persons could be considered as prospective clients for a mental health specialist. The likelihood of such services being sought by any one of the four is probably remote. Their problems are complex. A psychologist in an office, bringing formal training in clinical intervention to the reservation, would be ignored by most native people in need of assistance. The professionals have been in and out of reservation communities for years. Few have reached the people.

There could be thousands of examples presented, each being person specific, reflecting complex and problematic personal-cultural situations of the individuals. If a mental health specialist was assigned to work on the reservation of the persons described, how would they be regarded by the native people? What would the specialist need to know about the people? From whom and where could this be learned? How would that information lead to or affect encounters between persons and worker? How helpful would the worker be? These questions are fundamental and reflect some of the most essential concerns of the cross-cultural interventionist.

Assessment Strategies in Reservation Situations

Just as every person's life history provides important information for a mental health worker, the history of a reservation community provides valuable insights into past and existing physical and psychosocial conditions. Historical study will reveal the initial reactions to cultural conflicts between Indian and non-Indian groups. This information can be obtained from the primary sources of government reports of Indian agents and employees assigned to work on the reservations in the years of initial contact. Accounts of military personnel give their perspectives on the way tribes managed to survive or not survive in times of war. The records of missionaries, early teachers, and medical personnel focused on some of the systems that were being introduced. They documented how difficult it was for the native people to accept the sudden presence of so many strange and conflicting practices. They also established a basis for understanding why mental health professionals are regarded with distrust.

Anthropologists and artists often give a perspective that comes at a later time historically. Their comments reflect the cultural-personal confusion and suffering that native people endured (or could not endure) when non-Indian interventions were established on the reservations. These insights clarify and contrast in detail the order and predictability of the precontact communities with the elements observed postcontact. In addition to the written history, some of it blatantly revealing the negative attitudes government, military, religious, educational, and medical personnel were willing to document, there is a wealth of knowledge offered through oral history. With few exceptions, persons who recall the initial contact years are deceased. Their history has been passed on to successive generations. The gathering of this history through personal interviews would provide a psychologist with an expanded and more accurate historical perspective, as well as many introductions to the tribal members. This history is not easily shared. One may hope to be given opportunities to gather this material, but it will be given only if people are confident that it is respectfully and purposefully received.

The "newcomer," "outsider," "stranger," "white" who attempted to ask questions without preliminary contacts, agreements, and approvals would find closed doors and, most likely, uncooperative and suspicious persons. One of the most obvious reasons for this reticence to respond to these forms of inquiries is the volume of curious inquirers that has intruded on Indian towns and communities. Some native people have referred to such visitors as victim-centered researchers. They have "picked the bones and brains" of the people and left with no indication as to the use or interpretation of the information gained. After the fact, the native people have sometimes discovered themselves as "informants" in someone's publication. The survival instinct prevails: Don't talk to strangers. You never know what they might try to do to you.

How does an outsider gain entry and begin to receive recognition and acceptance? One practical guide is to fit yourself into a context familiar to the people so they may readily associate your presence with a role of service or helping. For example, a counselor or psychologist employed by the Indian Health Service could be introduced to some of the native people by the IHS physician. It might take many weeks to become even a physically recognizable person. To get outside of a clinical setting, the mental health specialist may visit community centers, schools, and senior citizen programs with the Community Health Representatives (CHR's) who are often native community members. These types of visits allow the natives to make their assessments of the "newcomer" and formulate some impressions of his/her manner, sense of humor, respect, and rapport with the community and its people. The first step toward developing an adequate assessment strategy among the native people is to give them opportunities to assess you. The observers are far from passive in this process, even though they may give little indication that they are actually watching with intense interest. It may take months, even years, for a mental health worker to develop a sense of how he/she is regarded by the particular individuals with whom they are working and serving. The acceptance of this condition is most difficult for the professional who anticipates working with many clients on a daily basis, much like one would experience in clinics or agencies in the general population centers. The person who cannot or will not accept these conditions of mutual assessment is advised to stay away from the reservation settings. It would not benefit anyone to try and work within a context that one finds objectionable or frustrating.

In addition to these general guidelines, there are many sensitive issues related to the manner or way in which a mental health worker interacts with the people. They want and need to be respected as they are. Their life-space is their own domain. One does not enter that domain in its physical or psychological character unless given permission. As an example, the way in which the handshake is offered to an Indian is an issue of delicate sensitivity. For most Indians the hands are pressed together gently for a few seconds. The firm grasping and shaking of hands that is common among non-Indians is regarded as disrespectful and rude among many native people, especially those living according to the traditional ways. For the "outsider" it is far better to use a form of traditional respect than it is to experiment with more contemporary or progressive manners.

The timing and pacing of verbal exchanges during a conversation are another sensitive point. Initially, most verbal exchanges are very slow paced when compared with the manner of verbal exchange outside of Indian communities. Two persons talking together may stand side by side rather than face to face. Looking downward or away from each other is preferred over looking directly at the person. Words may be few. Pauses between the speakers' comments are frequent and much longer than is common in non-Indian conversations. These differences all relate to customs and values of respect for the individual. A gentle touch is more rsepectful than a firm grasp. A time for quiet reflection on what has been said is more respectful than a fast-paced exchange of words. Giving a person his or her own physical space is more respectful than standing directly in front of them. Keeping one's eyes downward or directed away from another is more respectful than intense or close observation of facial or other characteristics. Taking the process of mutual assessment past the introduction stage, the mental health worker then starts to enter into the daily life patterns of the people. The basic efforts to provide food, clothing, shelter, transportation, and recreation are major concerns, even matters of crisis in many native persons' lives.

A consistent economic reality that most native communities live by is survival. This reality implies that when life's basic needs are met, extensive planning, management, community support, and hard work have been required. When needs are not met, people are engaged in a desperate struggle. This may require that families move into the homes of their relatives, or it may necessitate the sharing of limited food supplies. In substance, the physical and psychosocial constraints of poverty challenge the coping and tolerance levels of many native individuals and families on a regular basis.

The mental health worker who maintains a personal-social distance from the native community in its multifaceted life systems can never access the range and depth of impact that poverty inflicts. Furthermore, the people are unwilling to explain or relate their feelings or the complications of their life circumstances to a person removed from them. The mental health worker who must assess the behavior of the people as they live, needs to become a part of the community life.

Most communities have a range of gatherings that brings members together in open and rather free-flowing events. New community members and visitors are usually welcomed on these occasions. Athletic competitions and exhibitions of the school-age tribal members are usually followed with keen interest. Athletic ability is highly respected, and the people enjoy seeing their youths in sports events. Most Indian communities have also adapted to the celebration of Thanksgiving, Christmas, Memorial Day, Independence Day, and other events including Easter, Halloween, and Valentine's Day. In addition, they have celebrations and memorials reflective of their own traditions. Many of these are open to non-Indians. Being a participant in these events communicates the wish to be with the people. As community members develop a sense of trust and liking for the *person* who is the mental health worker, they will tend to respect the professional work of that *person*.

The forms of assessment that have been described are reflective of a person-place interaction model: the gathering of background (historical) information;

the nonparticipant observer; or the participant observer. The data gathered through these methods would be massive in scope and volume. One might ask if it would be more effective and reliable to use only structured or objective assessment instruments. Based on 14 years of experience with tribal members from a number of reservation communities, we believe this approach to be very unwise for the following reasons:

1. The norms of the norm-referenced tests have been developed with populations that are different from and usually exclusive of native people.
2. Most native people think of and respond to matters of behavior differences, mental or emotional experiences as person specific and unique. Comparing or contrasting an Indian person with other persons or groups could be very offensive if not totally unacceptable. The interjection of a formal test into psychological services could seriously limit and possibly destroy the present or future client/worker rapport.
3. Most native people would find it difficult to relate formal testing situations with mental health services. Mental health is reflective of one's spiritual life. An assessment that represented the dominant society's way of identifying psychoemotional conditions would not be acceptable on the basis of traditional beliefs and practices. The testing situation could easily be regarded as another offensive imposition.

Intervention: Approaches and Techniques

Being aware of the sensitivities of Indians to the assessment process, it logically follows that intervention approaches and techniques would have to be adapted to meet the needs of the particular individuals being served. One must keep in mind that many Indians, both reservation and urban-based, find it difficult to go to medical and dental offices even when there is abundant evidence that assistance is needed. It can safely be said that a small percentage of any native community in need of mental health services would go to a clinic or office, ask for an appointment, and keep it. The following case is cited as an example of the need for alternative intervention strategies when working in a native community.

THE CASE OF ANDY

Andy was a kindergarten student in a predominantly Indian grade school in his home community. Andy's teacher immediately identified him as a severe behavior problem in the classroom. He shouted rather than talked, ran up and down the halls making as much noise as he could while other children walked quietly, fought with his peers, and generally defied most of the teacher's requests. Andy was big for his age and used his physical size as a means of dominating his peers. He would not wait his turn in a lunch line or for a toy that someone else was using at recess or play time.

Andy's teacher, teacher aides, and counselor met to decide what could be done to improve his behavior and help him adjust to school. A basic behavior modification approach was tried. It was found that praise or tangible rewards for positive behavior were as likely to set off a chain reaction of negative behavioral outbursts as they were able to act as a reinforcement for cooperation. When Andy started acting out, his energy would build and he had to be physically removed from the classroom—kicking, screaming, and biting all the way. He was taken to the counselor's office where he was restrained by being held. His crying and rebelling could last for 30 minutes or longer, a draining session for Andy, the counselor, and anyone who had to listen to him. This removal and holding strategy was gradually beginning to show some positive results in that the struggling time was shortening, and a warning of removal sometimes resulted in conformity to the teacher's request.

The counselor scheduled a parent conference with Andy's mother. This took place at her home. The mother indicated that there were many problems in Andy's behavior at home that were similar to his school situation. She felt certain that she could not control her son. She admitted to using a broom handle to strike him when he turned his anger against her. Her fear was that Andy could harm her and the unborn child she was carrying. Andy's mother was frustrated by her own failure to manage her son. She mentioned that Andy's father could manage him very well because Andy knew how strong his dad was and that he did not tolerate disobedience. Due to marital problems, however, the father was not living in the home. When it was suggested that Andy undergo a psychiatric examination to try and determine what he needed and how he could be helped, the mother agreed. She was willing to try anything that would control his violence, especially in her present situation.

A consulting psychiatrist was given a full report on Andy's behavior patterns and also had access to medical records going back to his birth. On the day of Andy's appointment, he was taken from his school to the clinic by his counselor. Andy had expressed concern about going to talk with a stranger, but getting out of school for a while seemed worth the risk involved. When Andy was introduced to the psychiatrist as "someone who wanted to talk with him for a little while," he seemed rather passive. The interviewing room was arranged with office furniture. Andy looked around as if he needed to find something to occupy his attention.

The psychiatrist asked a few simple questions, "How old are you; How do you like school," which Andy did not acknowledge. The counselor was given the nod to leave the room and did so quietly. It was less than 5 minutes before Andy bolted out of the office with a look of desperation on his face, ran down the hallway, and went out the back door. The counselor was told that Andy would not cooperate in the attempts to check his eye-hand coordination. This was hardly surprising information to the counselor.

Andy was found outside running around the trees and shrubs in the clinic yard as fast as he could. He tried to act like he was hiding or indicating that he was not going to be caught. The counselor joined in his game, without saying anything. After a few minutes, Andy couldn't resist the urge to become the game winner and charged at the counselor with a triumphant "gotcha." He was not willing to go back into the clinic. The psychiatrist came outside to talk with the counselor about his brief encounter. Andy happily clowned, rolling on the ground playing "dog."

Obviously, Andy would present any professional with many forms of challenge. However, the psychiatrist invited the problems of this session. The following approach would be recommended in order to engage all persons concerned in a more productive level of communication and involvement.

1. The psychiatrist should have gone to the school to observe Andy in several situations: classroom activities; recess; mealtime; free play. Andy was not given the opportunity to put his "helping" person in any meaningful context. The boy was deprived of an important right.
2. A consultation with Andy's mother should have been scheduled, preferably at home and with the counselor present in order to provide the woman with a familiar person she could relate to and rely on for support if she felt uncomfortable.
3. A consultation with Andy's father should have been requested. This would require meeting him where and when he would select. Many native men regard contact with someone from a mental health program as emasculating. Every effort would be made to provide the man with a positive experience.
4. The initial attempt to engage Andy in a one-to-one exchange could best be arranged during school activities or perhaps during a second home visit. The office setting cannot work in most cases.
5. A detailed record of Andy's usual weekday and weekend schedules should have been noted. This would include wake-up times and related routine, breakfast habits, preparing for school, and getting to school.
6. Based on the results of the preceding sessions, a plan for a home-school cooperation program could have been developed with input and approval from Andy's parents, teacher, counselor, and school staff members who work with him.
7. Periodic observations would have to be made to determine Andy's progress and work out the needed adjustments to his home-school program.
8. It is obvious that Andy's mother needs help in dealing with her son. It is likely that she also needs help with her marital problems and in planning for the birth of her second child. Andy's behavior patterns were brought to school from home. The family as a unit and the individual members need support in resolving the problems they encounter in living with each other.

THE CASE OF PETE AND ALICE

The following case study is presented as a direct contrast to the Andy case. It demonstrates how effectively an ecological intervention can place a mental health worker into the action field of native people. The case is particularly important because it involves a cross-cultural relationship between the counselor and the persons who are clients.

Alice and Pete are husband and wife, married for over 25 years and in their forties. Both were born and raised in reservation communities and experienced a boarding school education, a traditional extended family home life, and the trauma of the federal policy of relocation. However, for most of Alice and Pete's married life, they have lived on their home reservation. Both persons could be described as hard workers, and responsible and reliable community members. They are socially active in the community and their home is a frequent gathering place for parties and dinners with many family members and friends.

Because of Pete's regular employment and Alice's part-time work, the couple is able to meet their economic needs and live comfortably. They have often taken in family members who were without finances or in need of both personal and economic support. It was not regarded as a favor to the families helped, but was treated as a visit. The four children the couple raised are grown and living on their own.

When a new mental health worker came into the community and rented a home in the village near Pete and Alice, it was noted by the couple as an unusual event. Typically, teachers, doctors, lawyers, and other professionals hired to serve the community had lived off the reservation. When the new neighbor was seen walking to the post office or the local store, many of the reservation residents took note. The new worker spoke with people along the way, had friendly and informative conversations with the native woman who was the postmistress, and always made a point of talking with children as they rode their bikes or went through town on errands or visits. This behavior, the visits with the clerks at the grocery store, and the apparent ease with which the person interacted with the community members, was discussed in local circles. Pete and Alice shared in these conversations and decided they wanted to meet this new person.

They made a point of stopping by the counselor's house one day while yard work and gardening was going on. The conversation was very concrete and light: the good weather, the yard work, the condition of the house, the immediate neighborhood. Pete and Alice felt comfortable with the counselor and extended an invitation to dinner that evening. The counselor gladly accepted and thanked Alice for saving the day. Around 5:00 the counselor put some fresh fruit in a sack and walked up to the couple's house for dinner.

It was a long and talkative session. Pete and Alice were curious about the counselor's background and wondered how someone could find their way to such a little town. They shared stories about their background, including growing up when the reservation was still without electricity and water systems. The whole exchange was in a spirit of good humor. It was late at night before the counselor left the couple's home and walked through town reflecting on the evening.

Gradually, the relationship between the Indian couple and the counselor developed into a close friendship. Through this relationship, the counselor also met all of Pete and Alice's family and many of their friends. There were celebrations of traditional and other festive events; namings, memorials, birthdays, holidays. There were also working times spent together including gathering firewood, planting gardens, repairing vehicles, cooking and serving at large community dinners.

In the course of these activities, there was always time for personal conversations. Ideas were exchanged and shared about problems that were mutually recognized. Issues about reservation government, economics, and social problems were discussed. The counselor followed a policy of listening carefully, making observations about the points that seemed unusual or difficult to understand, and generally being careful to keep personal opinions out of the discussions.

When the topics discussed were personal to Pete and Alice, the counselor was aware of the exchanges as a form of counseling. Things that were bothering either person were spoken of in very clear and specific language. The counselor listened carefully and shared observations relating to the concerns expressed. The situations that were problematic centered on interpersonal relationships. An issue that was a regular concern related to the frequency and amount of alcohol that was used at home and in local taverns and meeting places. Pete and Alice both knew that drinking to excess led to fights and separations. They saw this in their own relationship and in that of most of their friends and family. They wanted to change their drinking practices but didn't know how that could be done. They wanted some workable alternatives for their lives.

In times of stress or crisis in the families that the counselor knew, there were requests for help. Often these contacts were made at home or in a variety of settings around the community. Seldom did the community people find it appropriate or necessary to make a call at the counselor's office. That time was usually taken with persons referred for counseling or evaluation by the local alcohol or drug treatment program. Offices were not regarded as places of personal contacts. Most of the Indian people seeking help from the counselor wanted a personal meeting, the privacy of a personal setting, and the freedom to choose their own time for talking. For Pete and Alice, the talk often took place after dinner or on weekends when they went out into the hills and the country to hunt or fish or gather natural foods, worked around their home, or helped in community activities.

As Pete and Alice grew accustomed to including the counselor in many of their social activities, they found support for limiting and sometimes eliminating their use of alcohol. It was possible for them to have an enjoyable weekend with family and friends without drinking.

After several years of consistent counseling in the way that was appropriate to Pete and Alice, they realized they had made some of the changes they had wanted both as individuals and as a married couple. When the counselor moved to a new assignment, Pete and Alice were able to maintain their adjusted living patterns. Without going into any formalized treatment program, they changed some of the interpersonal and social behaviors, which improved their lives and the lives of other community members.

There are several points that may be underlined with regard to this case study.

1. The counselor who moved into the village made a major change in that community. This is further emphasized by the fact that village life was shared by a small, closely-knit group. The counselor's presence created a new realm of social dynamics among the people.

2. The community members had many opportunities to observe the counselor on a daily basis and decide how and when they would initiate a relationship. They were free to ignore or engage the counselor as they wished.

3. The counselor had to be personally adaptive, able to accept the many aspects of the community that were very different from non-Indian communities: being the minority rather than majority member; being somewhat suspect as less than sincere or helpful in purpose or intent; living within a framework of economic poverty, with consistent examples; living in an area that was geographically remote; being on call 24 hours of any day; being relatively isolated from peer support; being expected to live and work as an unusually self-sufficient person.

4. There was never any certainty that the counselor was "on target." Much of the interaction was based on being personally open to the people and accepting of their criteria for professional involvement. Being accepting of the basic life goals and guidelines of the people had to be an integral part of the communications that were shared.

5. In time, this initial testing period of the counselor's acceptability ended. Once the people felt they could rely on the counselor, there was a steady request for services from the community.

6. If the same counselor had lived off the reservation and driven to and from an office as a base for working with the people, there would be a low probability that Pete and Alice could have made the helpful contacts with a neighbor.

Critical Implications

Surveys of Indian communities have consistently revealed that alcohol abuse presents a major threat to the physical and mental health of up to 90% of the adult population. Regular weekend or more extended drinking practices are very common. Community members who do not become involved in such behavior are subjected to teasing or questioning as to their isolation. This is especially true among native men who choose not to join their peers at the taverns or the drinking sessions that take place around the reservations. Teenagers are also affected by similar modeling and peer influences.

A major factor in the perpetuation of substance abuse within native communities is the lack of consistent internal controls. Drinking to get drunk is a commonly accepted practice. In fact, children who see an adult drinking presume that "they are getting drunk." The children themselves often begin drinking as early as six or seven years of age. As they grow older and become more involved in adult activity, the tendency is to adapt to the drinking patterns that surround them. In effect, in many Indian communities the current population has never experienced community life without excessive use of alcohol.

The personal and societal tragedies that have sprung from alcohol abuse in Indian communities are appalling. One can become so accustomed to the consistency of alcohol abuse with life tragedies that the two become synonymous. There is abundant evidence that alcohol abuse has become a subcultural "coping mechanism," a way of "getting into a good mood" or a means of "feeling good." Viewing these circumstances from an historical perspective, alcohol was introduced to most native communities at the same time that economic, social, and cultural traditions were being eroded by the influences and power struggles resulting from contact and confrontation with the non-Indian world. Cultural fragmentation, deprivation of religious freedom and freedom of speech and assembly, war and disease, threatened or eliminated the life coping skills of many native people. As long as the deeper more complex personal and group mental health problems of native people are masked as problems of alcohol abuse, little progress toward improved mental health will be made.

The cultural and personal adjustments required of many American Indians in the contemporary world still exceed the tolerance levels of many individuals. References have been made to the schizoid qualities required of the person who must integrate traditional beliefs and practices with the systems and demands of the dominant society. For many people this duality of life systems is both intolerable and unavoidable. An Indian man or woman taking part in a traditional religious ceremony is able to experience the regeneration of thousands of years of their cultural heritage. That same person drives to the site of that event in a car or on a highway patrolled and maintained by a state or federal government. The religious ceremony that requires several days of uninterrupted participation also requires that the person be excused from their job and other outside commitments. Maintaining psychoemotional equilibrium under the pressure of daily cultural conflicts is the point of origin for many mental health problems.

Within the internal support systems of the native community are the persons who have managed to develop and maintain the psychoemotional strength to live with the conflicts of their duality as native persons and as related and involved participants in the dominant society. Among these community members are those who have managed to raise large families and continue to care for children and grandchildren. They have remained personally strong and given their lives in dedication to their people. Their personal-cultural identity is deeply established within themselves and through their role as vital members of their extended families. They are the lifeblood of the native communities.

Leadership and support for these family-centered and dedicated community members comes, in large part, from the spiritual men and women, the traditional healers of the people. These leaders live with and among the people, yet are distinguished by their knowledge and spiritual powers. Their roots are in the traditions of the native religious practices, yet they are not religious separatists. They may practice a religious faith of the Christian groups and intersperse these teachings and practices with their native religion. Their perspective of the spirit world does not place limits on who and what can be acceptable because of ethnic or cultural origins. These leaders are unifiers of believing persons in a deep and sacred realization of human family bonding.

The practices of healing are tribally and personally specific. A healer may be recognized by some members of a community and discredited by others. The work of some healers is known and credited by many different tribal communities. The work of the healer is one of drawing out and channeling the spiritual reality of the human and natural world around them. It requires physical demonstration and exercising of prayer, singing, chanting, fasting, and sacrificing as in most of the rituals of major religious groups. The role of the healers may vary, but they could be compared with a priest, rabbi, or minister in terms of the sacredness of their position and function among the people.

Personal problems or concerns that an Indian may identify as spiritual in nature are often similar to the problems a non-Indian may consider psychological or emotional. The differences in the way personal problems are assessed are deeply intertwined with cultural values and religious beliefs. Because native religions encompass the total life (inclusive of emotional and psychological activity) are dealt with as religious. Such practices as bathing, sweating, fasting, and meditation are often part of a spiritual purging. These things are done in the company of or under the direction of the spiritual healer. Native medicines, often produced from herbs, roots, leaves, or bark, are also used in the healing process. Such practices are centuries old in the native traditions. Certainly for the native person, these practices are far more meaningful and creditable than a counseling session with a non-Indian stranger.

It would obviously be to the advantage of the psychologist to develop a working relationship with the Indian healers. The psychologist would initially be a learner, seeking to gain some basic knowledge about the religious beliefs and practices of the native people. This sharing would have to take place in the context of a personal relationship between the native person and psychologist. There would be no information shared or exchanged if the traditional healer lacked confidence in the sincerity of the learner. Most healers can readily distinguish the genuinely concerned and caring helper from those who are motivated for other purposes. However, once a psychologist was accepted by the healer, their creditability would be greatly enhanced in the views of at least some native community members. If the healer is not generally respected and accepted, the association could be a less than positive influence in community relations.

The collaborative efforts of the healer and the psychologist would effectively result in a mutual sharing of the mental health services provided to the community. The counselor, using an ecological model of assessment and intervention, would in time establish a living-working rapport with the community. Through this process-intervention, persons demonstrating a level of need appropriate to the work of a healer would be encouraged to seek that help.

Those persons whom the psychologist could help through counseling would remain as clients of the psychologist. It would also be likely that the traditional healer would encourage community members to use the counseling services as a means of sustaining the progress that had been made through his/her intervention.

An alternative to the cooperative relationship of healer and psychologist would be that they work as separate and distinct helping persons. There are many disadvantages to this approach; some of them are as follows.

1. In a close-knit community that has experienced many factionalized services (i.e., BIA, IHS, NIMH, and other grants) the separation of mental health services represents more factionalism.
2. Historically, traditional healers who have worked with and for their community occupy a position of respect and positive regard that a newly arrived psychologist does not and cannot have. The psychologist who works outside of the existing helping system is limited in access to the people by maintaining a separate position.
3. Every Indian community has its unique characteristics including those of its mental health needs. Few if any persons would be more aware of these characteristics than a native healer; the alternative being to expend a great deal of time and effort trying to learn on one's own.

SUMMARY

The field of cross-cultural counseling is expanding rapidly. And, too, interest in providing efficient and effective mental health services for American Indians is rising along with the general interests. What makes this exciting is that finally counselors and clinicians take a serious view of culture and ethnicity. Recent apparent emphasis on ethnicity, however, raises the profound notion that cultural orientations are important aspects in providing for and delivering effective mental health services. Indeed, the constructs of "healthy" and "normal," traditional guiding factors in providing mental health services, are not commonly shared among many clients. Ethnocentric notions of adjustment, adaptation, and coping tend to ignore diverse cultural orientations. And, to some extent, many of the theoretical orientations governing treatment approaches are presumptuous—they preclude the possibility that cultural groups do not have the traditional resources for dealing with human difficulties.

What are the different ways that cultural backgrounds of many American Indians shape interpersonal relationships? How does ethnicity and cultural diversity influence counseling transactions? How can counselors evaluate their own cultural bias? Is counseling itself, as a way of helping others, culturally encapsulated? If so, should it retain primarily a unicultural focus? A string of related questions can be asked. Whatever form they take, however, they are not new to the field of mental health in general. On the other hand, the questions and concerns *are* new to the field of psychological counseling. Far too many counselors have ignored or avoided cultural differences. Some prefer to deal with cross-cultural issues at the academic level, whereas very few attempt to sensitize students, trainees, and other counselors to those cultural concerns. Whatever the case, we must begin to generate supportive data with which we can compare the use of counseling styles and strategies in culturally unique settings. The contents of this text reflect that effort. It is important to remember that simply asserting that culture makes the difference is no longer *solely* acceptable.

REFERENCES

Amoss, P. (1978) *Coast Salish spirit dancing.* Seattle: University of Washington Press.

Attneave, C.L. (1969) Therapy in tribal settings and urban network intervention. *Family Process,* **8,** 192–210.

Attneave, C. (1972) Mental health of American Indians: Problems, prospects and challenges for the decade ahead. Paper presented at the meeting of the American Psychological Association, Honolulu.

Attneave, C. (1974) Medicine men and psychiatrists in the Indian health service. *Psychiatric Annals,* **4,** 1, 49–55.

Barter, E.R., & Barter, J.T. (1974) Urban Indians and mental health problems. *Psychiatric Annals,* **4**(9), 37–43.

Bergman, R. (1974) Paraprofessionals in Indian mental health programs. *Psychiatric Annals,* **4,** 76–84.

Bittker, T.E. (1973) Dilemmas of mental health service delivery to off-reservation Indians. *Anthropological Quarterly,* **46,** 172–182.

Bloom, J.D., & Richards, W.W. (1974) Alaska Native regional corporations and community mental health. *Psychiatric Annals,* **4**(9), 67–75.

Borunda, P., & Shore, J.H. (1978) Neglected minority: Urban Indians and mental health. *International Journal of Social Psychiatry,* **24**(3), 220–224.

Boyer, L.B. Folk psychiatry of the Apaches of the Mescalero Indian reservation. In A. Kiev (Ed.), *Magic, faith, and healing.* New York: Free Press.

Clement, F.E. (1932) Primitive concepts of disease. *University of California Archaeology and Ethnology,* **32,** 185–222.

Cooley, R.C., Ostendorf, D., & Bickerton, D. (1979) Outreach services for elderly Native Americans. *Social Work,* **29,** 151–153.

Dinges, N., Trimble, J., Manson, S., & Pasquale, F. (1981) The social ecology of psychotherapy and counseling with American Indians. In A. Marsella, & P. Pedersen (Eds.), *Cross-cultural perspectives on psychotherapy and counseling.* New York: Pergamon.

Goldstein, G.S. (1974) The model dormitory. *Psychiatric Annals,* **4**(11), 85–92.

Goldstein, A.P. (1981) Evaluating expectancy effects in cross-cultural counseling and psychotherapy. In A.J. Marsella, & P.B. Pedersen (Eds.), *Cross-cultural counseling and psychotherapy.* New York: Pergamon.

Hallowell, A. (1967) The self and its behavioral environment. In A. Hallowell (Ed.), *Culture and experience.* New York: Shocken.

Hippler, A.E. (1975) Thawing out some magic. *Mental Hygiene,* **59,** 20–24.

Jilek, W.G. (1974) Indian healing power: Indigenous therapeutic practices in the Pacific Northwest. *Psychiatric Annals,* **4**(9), 13–21.

Jilek-Aall, L. (1976) The western psychiatrist and his non-western clientele. *Canadian Psychiatric Association Journal,* **21,** 353–359.

Jilek, W.G., & Jilek-Aall, L. (1971) A transcultural approach to psychotherapy with Canadian Indians: Experiences from the Fraser Valley of British Columbia. In *Psychiatry (II) Proceedings of the Fifth World Congress of Psychiatry,* Excerpta Medica International congress series, No. 274. Mexico City, D.F.

Kaplan, B., & Johnson, D. (1964) The social meaning of Navajo psychopathology and psychotherapy. In A. Kiev (Ed.), *Magic, faith, and healing.* New York: Free Press.

Kelso, D.R., & Attneave, C.L. (1981) *Bibliography of North American Indian mental health.* Westport, Ct.: Greenwood Press.

Kinzie, J.D., Shore, J.H., & Pattison, E.M. (1972) Anatomy of psychiatric consultation to rural Indians. *Community Mental Health Journal* **8**(3), 196–207.

Manson, S.M. (Ed.) (1982) *New directions in prevention among American Indian and Alaska Native Communities.* Portland, Or.: Oregon Health Sciences University Press.

Manson, S., & Trimble, J.E. (1982) Mental health services to American Indian and Alaska Native communities: Past efforts, future inquiry. In L.R. Snowden (Ed.), *Services to the underserved: Historical and current issues.* Beverly Hills, Calif.: Sage.

Marsella, A., & Pederson, P. (Eds.) (1981) *Cross-cultural counseling and psychotherapy.* New York: Pergamon.

Murdock, S.H., & Schwartz, D.F. (1978) Family structure and the use of agency services: An examination of patterns among elderly Native Americans. *The Gerontologist,* **18**(5), 475–481.

Murphy, J.M. (1964) Psychotherapeutic aspects of shamanism on St. Lawrence, Alaska. In A. Kiev (Ed.), *Magic, faith, and healing.* New York: Free Press.

Ostendorf, D., & Hammerschlag, C.A. (1977) An Indian-controlled mental health program. *Hospital and Community Psychiatry,* **28**(9), 682–685.

Padilla, A.M., & Ruiz, R.A. (1973) *Latino mental health: A review of the literature.* Washington, D.C.: Government Printing Office, DHEW No. (ADM) 74–113.

Pedersen, P., Draguns, J.G., Lonner, W.J., & Trimble, J.E. (Eds.) (1981) *Counseling Across Cultures.* (2nd ed.) Honolulu: University Press of Hawaii.

Red Horse, J.G., Lewis, R.L., Feit, M., & Decker, J. (1978) Family behavior of urban American Indians. *Social Casework,* **59,** 67–72.

Rhoades, E.R., Marshal, M., Attneave, C., Echohawk, M., Bjork, J., & Beiser, M. (1980) Impact of mental disorders upon elderly American Indians as reflected in visits to ambulatory care facilities. *Journal of the American Geriatrics Society,* **28**(1), 33–39.

Schoenfeld, L.S., Lyerly, R.J., & Miller, S.I. (1971) We like us. *Mental Hygiene,* **55**(2), 171–173.

Shore, J.H., & Nicholls, W.W. (1977) Indian children and tribal group homes: New interpretations of the whipper man. In S. Unger (Ed.), *The destruction of American Indian families.* New York: Association on American Indian Affairs.

Spang, A. (1965) Counseling the Indian. *Journal of American Indian Education.*

Sue, S. (1977) Community mental health services to minority groups: Some optimism, some pessimism. *American Psychologist,* **32,** 616–624.

Sue, S., Allen, D.G., & Conaway, L. (1978) The responsiveness and equality of mental health care to Chicanos and Native Americans. *American Journal of Community Psychology,* **6,** 137–146.

Torrey, E.F. (1970) Mental health services for American Indians and Eskimos. *Community Mental Health Journal,* **6**(6), 455–463.

Torrey, E.F. (1972) *The mind game: Witchdoctors and psychiatrists.* New York: Emmerson Hall.

Trimble, J.E. (1976) Value differences of the American Indian: Concerns for the concerned counselor. In P. Pederson, W.J. Lonner, & J.G. Draguns, *Counseling across cultures,* Honolulu: University Press of Hawaii.

Trimble, J.E., & Medicine, B. (1976) Development of theoretical models and levels of interpretation in mental health. In J. Westermeyer (Ed.), *Anthropology and mental health.* The Hague: Mouton.

Trimble, J.E. (1981) Value differentials and their importance in counseling American Indians. In P. Pedersen, J.G. Draguns, W.J. Lonner, & J.E. Trimble. *Counseling across cultures.* (2nd ed.) Honolulu: University Press of Hawaii.

Trimble, J.E., & Lee, D.J. (1981) Research perspectives on counseling the American Indian. Paper presented at the American Education Research Association meeting, Los Angeles.

Trimble, J.E., Manson, S.M., Dinges, N.G, & Medicine, B. (1983) American Indian concepts of mental health: Reflections and directions. In P. Pedersen, N. Sartorius & A. Marsella (Eds.), Mental health services: The cultural context. Beverly Hills, Calif.: Sage.

Trimble, J.E. (In press) Knowledge of self-understanding and perceived alienation among American Indians. *Journal of Community Psychology.*

Vallee, F.G. (1966) Eskimo theories of mental illness in the Hudson Bay region. *Anthropologica,* **8,** 53–83.

Westernmeyer, J., & Hausman, W. (1974) Cross-cultural consultation for mental health planning. *International Journal of Social Psychiatry,* **20**(1–2), 34–38.

Youngman, G., & Sadongei, M. (1974) Counseling the American Indian child. *Elementary School Guidance and Counseling,* **8,** 273–277.

CHAPTER 14

The Psychosocial Ecology of Urban Black Youth

STACEY DANIELS, CHARLES B. WILKINSON, AND WILLIAM A. O'CONNOR

Socialization theory has in recent years been expanded beyond traditional sex-role training for children to include differences due to social class. Now, the surrounding ecosystem of the child is being regarded as impacting the socialization process. The ecosystem model allows the community to be viewed as composed of subsystems that interact in somewhat predictable ways. The total system can be divided either according to populations or elements of the environment. What must be remembered is that the process is a continuous one of person interacting with environment according to the specific setting.

The socialization process of blacks has perhaps seemed abnormal to social scientists because it does not adhere to the white middle-class norm. The distinctive Afro-American cultural heritage in conjunction with historically low societal status has necessitated that blacks receive different training than their white counterparts in order to prepare for adult roles.

This chapter is based on data drawn from a series of ongoing studies of black urban adolescents and the childrearing strategies utilized by their mothers, but the theory applies to all families. The studies illustrate how the immediate ecosystem impinges on mental health and social functioning in the black family.

THE BLACK FAMILY

Black families have been stereotyped as controlling and authoritarian but preparing for self-responsibility at an early age (Bartz & Levine, 1978; Baumrind, 1972). According to Lewis (1975), Afro-American culture, in contrast to Euro-American, stresses independence, assertiveness, and nurturing for both sexes. Personal uniqueness is highly valued. Although many black families do subsist below the poverty level, much of the research on black families has been criticized

This chapter was supported by grants from the Center for Minority Group Mental Health Programs, National Institutes of Mental Health (MH 24858, MH 33679).

for its presumption of an isomorphic relationship between disadvantaged social and economic position and psychosocial functioning (Kuhn, 1972). Studies have been questioned which impute to ethnic status or personality what may be a function of environmental demands (Baughman, 1971). Families that are headed by females have suffered the additional onus of being stereotyped as inevitably leading to dysfunctional youth, again based to a large degree on methodologically flawed research (Blechman, 1980).

THE ECOSYSTEM

To fully appreciate the dilemma of black families, particularly those headed by a single female occupying a relatively impoverished urban environment, eco-systems theory considers the concepts of the ecological niche and manning. An *ecological niche* refers to a specific subpart of the total ecological system which can be identified by the consistency of interaction between its occupants and the physical surroundings; the concept is similar to that of Barker's (1968) behavior setting, but is an observable unit of persons and physical objects. The niche is a structural reflection of the concept of input site. It is a location in ecological space through which the energy is transferred. The second concept, *manning,* refers to population, the number of occupants that can be supported within a given niche. These two concepts, like all others in ecological thinking, have a dynamic relationship.

It is assumed that any living system is open, that is, sustained by constant interaction with the surrounding environment. It is also assumed that the system is organized and distributes energy in an orderly fashion. The action of the ecosystem can be described in terms of levels of organization and feedback loops (O'Connor, 1977). *Levels* refers to the increasingly complex components in the system, beginning with the smallest molecule of an organism and extending to its societal and cultural networks. *Feedback loops* refer to the cybernetic concept of action processes or paths; actions that produce change are conventionally termed *positive loops*, whereas processes that maintain and stabilize the system are termed *negative loops*.

The concept of a system both open (an input dimension) and organized (an internal process dimension) implies a dynamic equilibrium model. The input dimension extends across levels of organization to sustain cohesion of the total system and differentiation of the subsystems. The internal process dimension at any level of organization maintains both stability and change. The level of input may be considered high or low for a given niche depending on the resources distributed to its occupants; conversely, population may be considered high or low in relation to a niche depending upon the resources available. The concept is analogous to Barker's concept of undermanned and overmanned behavior settings. Undermanning is common when there is relatively low population, and individuals of necessity occupy several settings in more than a spectator or consumer role.

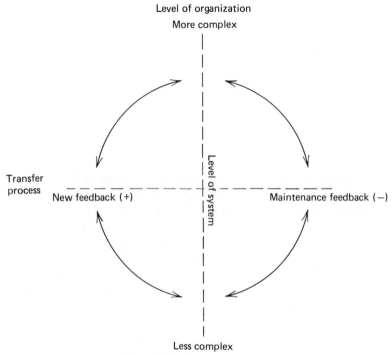

Figure 14.1.   Basic system components.

The black, single-parent female-headed family often occupies a niche or complex of specific settings in the urban environment in which population is relatively high in relation to the resources distributed. Few opportunities exist for roles above that of spectator or consumer. An adjustment in the system is required for the survival of the occupants. Adjustments also occur in the surrounding systems to minimize the energy loss which could be created by a high population niche where resources to provide input are limited.

In human populations, we see this process in its most extreme and unbalancing form in such open "inhuman" activities as war or gross exploitation of the natural resources of one group by another. At a more subtle level, it is an adjustment mechanism that may be delicately implemented through the mechanism of the complementary niche. A complementary niche is one that may be occupied by two groups in a manner which distributes the resources of the niche efficiently by allowing both groups to exchange resources with each other. For example, a population that is viewed as chronically disabled may be institutionalized in this manner. The identified patient does not earn a salary or participate in the economic exchange of the community as a whole but receives only those resources necessary for minimal subsistence. The professional caretakers, on the other hand, receive wages and in return occupy the institutional environment in a "helping" role. The economics of traditional state hospital systems reflect this process: The amount of money necessary to pay staff

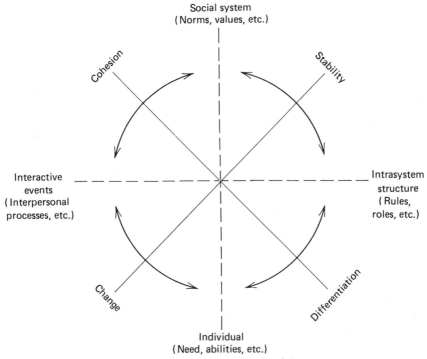

Figure 14.2.   Interactional components of social econosystems.

and maintain the facility is approximately equal to the median income of the communities in the catchment area multiplied by the patient population (O'Connor, 1977).

The mechanism of the complementary niche has been central to adaptation for the black population. Slavery is an example of complementary niche mechanisms in their most extreme form. The contemporary black population must contend with the same process, intensified in the case of the impoverished single-parent family. The community at large is likely to provide services to such disadvantaged populations based on disability: health and mental health services, welfare, unemployment, prison, and the like. The critical adaptation which the family must provide requires that it distribute limited resources and access the community environment in a manner that allows the individual to occupy a noncomplementary niche.

THE ECOSYSTEM'S INFLUENCE ON CHILDREARING

Childrearing strategy involves three levels of the system—the surrounding community, the family system, and the individual. Because the community has limited resources, it provides a distribution or feedback loop that is largely organized to maintain the stability of the total system, a negative loop from community to child. This is not entirely to the disadvantage of the individual child, for the essential mechanisms involve transmission of basic information through educational and other facilities which communicates the norm, expectations, and requirements that the society places upon the behavior of the individual. It is an efficient transfer because it moves down through the system and involves the negative loop. The child, however, must ultimately participate in a positive feedback loop which moves up through the system to the community; that is, must learn to impact, change, and actively cope with the community rather than being the passive recipient of minimal resources through the labeling process, which may propel the individual into a complementary niche or disabled role. As we have noted from basic ecosystems theory, there is an energy loss in this process. Additional input will be required for the child to transfer the negative loop information into positive loop feedback to the system. It is in this way that the family becomes the critical mediating system.

There is a suggestion that specific (if perhaps unintentional) childrearing strategies are adopted on the part of single-parent mothers; these strategies focus largely on the management of the relationship between the family, mother's own pattern of participation, and the available settings that provide resources within the community (O'Connor & Daniels, 1979). It further appears that particular outcomes, which are assumed to be related to the pattern of familial and community processes, are not necessarily related to a single type of system or single level within the total system; some dimensions of behavior may be impacted by one type of setting, whereas other patterns are impacted by both a different level and activity area. Perhaps for a given individual, different patterns of behavior in that individual's life space have been influenced by his/her interaction with different aspects of the total system process.

The essential strategy of successful black single-parent mothers has been this: They provide the child with additional negative loop energy, that is, they provide basic socialization experiences and coping skills to the child. At the same time, however, each mother engages indirectly in a positive loop relationship to the community: She impacts the community directly accessing those most available high resource subsystems in her immediately accessible environment. Through the use of local community organizations, churches, networks of families and friends, and similar subgroups, the black single-parent mother focuses her energy on impacting these systems so that they begin to include and further socialize the child. Her own employment and activities in the community also serve as an example for the child on how best to manage the system. The amount of energy or resources which then returns to the child is sufficiently enhanced to allow the individual child increasing access to and penetration of the community system. In the process, the child derives critical coping skills and community access experiences.

In terms of the family system, of course, a parent may engage in the traditional behavior of providing positive feedback loops; praise, nurturing, support, encouragement, and so on, may otherwise allow the child a sense of personal freedom and worth. It is clear from the research data, however, that the single

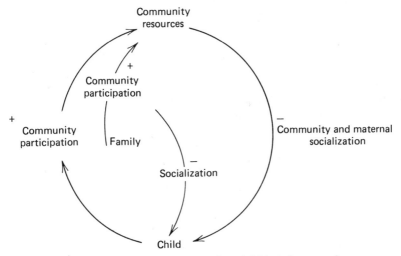

Figure 14.3. Schematic representation of child-rearing strategies.

mother is engaged in a risky and highly consequential ecological maneuver with respect to the surrounding environment, even in terms of those settings and activities she stresses over others. She is confronted with a potentially excluding world, and must manage the system in a fashion that allows the survival of her offspring as independent coping individuals. She is likely, therefore, to be anything but a laissez-faire parent; on the contrary, she will tend to be demanding in her socialization practices. She may require skill conformity to social norms, and will not tolerate disruptive or potentially deviant behavior in her offspring.

With male children, this means stressing concrete areas such as school and work. Her energy is channeled into those areas that may help her son "make something of himself." This emphasis begins at an early age, in many cases during the preschool years. Perhaps there is a tendency to overstress to compensate for the inherent problems for a boy growing up without father presence in the home. Whatever the underlying reason, the object of the process is survival, and it is an accommodation familiar to the black community extending through many generations.

Although there is some belief that sons are preferred, mothers in black families have been said to expect more of daughters, perhaps because of their greater present utility in the family (Graudenz et al., 1976; Davis & Havighurst, 1946; Hoffman, 1977; Schulz, 1969). The very real dilemma for the adolescent black girl has been career versus motherhood; in contrast to her white counterpart, some sort of future employment has usually been necessary. (The black woman might be considered as having had a head start in dual socialization which the feminist movement recently has emphasized for the majority culture.) Increased employment of women, fewer children, and longer lives have resulted in more varied and extended careers for women in general (Hoffman, 1977). Even if the choice is career, whereas men are expected to be continuous breadwinners until retirement, women are expected, at least intermittently, to take breaks for a family. Therefore, the socialization process appears somewhat more difficult and complex for the female child. Much of the socialization and modeling within the family must provide support not only for a developmentally increasing involvement in the external community, but for the potential of forming a new family unit and becoming an adult female with offspring. Ambiguity to these roles may exist within the family unit, and clearly exists within the society. Because roles are more ambiguous and choices less concrete, socialization appears not to be as stringently goal oriented, which influences what skills develop and what choices are made. For example, in our research adolescent girls seeking a job learned to settle for lower pay, whereas boys seemed more inclined to wait for higher wages, perhaps because employment as a goal was not stressed as much for daughters as for sons. Female children, on the other hand, learned to manipulate public agencies much better and at an earlier age than did their brothers, which was a useful skill if the girl later found herself a teen parent (O'Connor, Daniels, & Johnson, 1981).

Further, where a number of offspring are included in the nuclear family unit, the female child may assume parental responsibilities with respect to her siblings. By the age of 16 or 17, two elements must be considered for female children. First, the society clearly provides a variety of active socializing experiences for the male, but may not provide the same resources with the same emphasis for females. Second, the choices facing a female on high school graduation may be more complex, because continuing education or employment must be balanced against the possibility of marriage, pregnancy, and the consequences of these choices. For the male, success is clearly targeted in the education and employment areas; for the female, substantial improvement in her situation and substantial success may also be obtained or impaired through the choice of a marriage partner.

At an anecdotal level, a number of the mothers in the studies appeared to struggle with the difficult role and socialization choices with respect to females. Clearly, they could identify the potential success and survival skills necessary for males. For females, however, the uncertainty of life roles was clear. Some mothers may be unwilling to invest as strongly in the educational and economic attainments of female children given a dangerous role and fragile access to resources. The hopes, dreams, and opportunities may be focused on one child who is usually male, especially if family resources are limited. In some cases, we might speculate that mothers also wish to prepare their daughters for the possibility of lives not dissimilar to their own; lives in which personal success is limited but where the possibility of the success of offspring remains a viable alternative.

Contrary to traditional expectations, the female-headed single-parent black family may not have destructive consequence for male offsprings; the possibility of adequate male identification is clearly available (Wilkinson & Daniels, 1982). For females, on the other hand, the lack of resources and ambiguity of the female role, coupled with poverty and racism, may produce a consequence in the single-parent family which is more difficult to predict. The catalytic interaction of sex roles and racial stereotypes may impact female offspring in particular.

IMPLICATIONS FOR SERVICE DELIVERY

If we wish to consider the implications of these data for preventive mental health efforts, several interesting patterns can be noted. First, one of the most powerful and consistent supports available to a mother may be employment and educational opportunities, potentially impacting specific patterns of psychosocial functioning in adolescent offspring. Second, the consistency of informal social networks within the community and the use of agencies that are not traditionally involved in mental health (i.e., churches) emerge as a second critical area to be considered. As noted in earlier research (Wilkinson & O'Connor, 1977), there is an inverse relationship between the use of formal mental health resources and the use of churches and informal networks; the use of formal mental health resources appears more likely in those families for whom other resource networks are extremely impoverished, and is associated with less favorable outcome.

It has long been recognized within the black community that the provision of services only for the most dysfunctional or deviant members of the community is ultimately a poor investment in the health of the community. Typically, resources may be provided based on disruption to the external society in which a particular disadvantaged or minority group is embedded. Thus the identification of and provision of services for those with mental health, delinquency, employment, and similar difficulties may be to the benefit of society but not of particular benefit to the target group. Such services are simply the most obvious, and in times of economic distress they appear to be the most necessary or prioritized services. In point of fact, support for maternal employment and education have appeared to be more potent constructive influences than any other provided. Further, the fragmentation and labeling involved in service delivery can have negative effects. From an ecological perspective, it is support of the resource availability within the community and access to community resources which become the critical determinants of positive functioning. The ecological model provides a basis for integrating prevention and service delivery; if the mechanisms by which successful functioning may be obtained or clearly identified, then support with resources for those mechanisms and processes can be effectively provided.

Our inferences gain some modest credibility in the context of other ecological research. If the surroundings do impact behavior in a forceful manner, the optimal environment would provide a wide range of resources and relatively small settings which are easily accessible in an optimal manning level. Considering that most mental health centers contacts involve a small proportion of the individual's total time, tend to be intermittent or temporary, do not involve a high performer role, and are most often implemented in large and impersonal treatment settings, then it is likely that much of the influence on life-style and mental health status over extended periods may derive from the multiplex of settings in which the individual is embedded (O'Connor, 1977). Hume's (1975) data with respect to intact white surburban families would support such a view. By contrast, if preventive mental health efforts and services are based largely on data with a preselected dysfunctional population and measures of relatively molecular psychological or interpersonal process, then the only possible models that emerge will focus on such areas as early detection and screening, parent effectiveness in a dyadic communication context, and the like. More molar processes, such as the effects of school size, may not be included in such a perspective.

If the data suggest assumptions on which further study may be based, a second area of application might well involve the relationship between mental health organizations and the surrounding community. The first issue which arises in this context is that of service delivery, the structure and organization of mental health efforts. Traditionally, mental health institutions operate on an essentially pyramidal structure; the size of the organizational unit can be extended, embedding the client in an organization that minimizes the range of activities and level of functioning of the identified patient. It is interesting to note the structural differences between private practice psychotherapeutic service delivery and public institution delivery models. In the private practice setting, accessible only to those with substantial resources, the most highly trained professional engages almost exclusively in a dyadic or small-group relationship with a service recipient; administrative functions, paperwork, scheduling, telephoning, and similar functions are generally relegated to adjunctive or nonprofessional personnel. By contrast, in the large organizational structure of most community mental health centers, it is adjunctive personnel who have a substantial share of patient contact (in the extreme of an inpatient service) and the more highly trained professional personnel who tend to fulfill administrative, legal paperwork, and supervisory functions. Although data exist in abundance on the optimal psychosocial environment for maximizing satisfaction and competence (e.g., in the numerous studies of business organizations), such data have infrequently been applied to the delivery of mental health services. Team treatment systems, continuity of care, tracking and transfer systems, standardized treatment assignment, and routing procedures may all operate to make the client as less an individual as possible, whereas client and therapist struggle to achieve the most personal and individual human relationship possible in that context. If the single-parent data have more general application, such large system processing may be undesirable.

A second perspective on the service delivery problem emerges when the relationship of the organization of community resources is considered. If the community itself is a massive pyramidal structure in which competence and power concentrate at the top and conformity is progressively demanded at the geometrically expanding base, then the system can be viewed as containing a finite amount of resources that is not distributed equally, but which individuals may obtain only by appropriate performance in a given ecological niche. If this is the case, then the mental health system struggles with the revolving door largely at the mercy of the larger surrounding system; for that portion of the client population who lack competencies and resources, an effective psychotherapeutic intervention within the context of the institution may return the individual to a community in which adequate functioning and the maintenance of mental health are not possible; if the individual is sufficiently credentialed and obtains the necessary competencies to occupy a more desirable and less stressful niche, then the potential effect may be to create a new mental health casualty. In this sense, the mental health institution may unwittingly be cast in the role of social scavenger, participating in a triage system in which some individuals may be placed in niches designed to absorb excess population and maintain less functional individuals without loss of overall social control. The single-parent data suggest an alternative role, with a subsystem serving as mediator and access point to the community.

This in turn raises questions about the focus of treatment outcome research: What is considered an outcome and how it is assessed may have a major impact on the development and delivery of services. If, for example, the variables that were seen to have significant impact in the single-parent studies were applied to treatment outcome, then we might well consider the effectiveness of mental health efforts in such terms as the individual's capacity to gain and hold employment, function in social networks, uitilize formal community resources, and the like. Such an approach, illustrated in the state hospital (O'Connor & O'Connor, 1977) and drug treatment (O'Connor & Klassen, 1978) studies provided a view at variance with traditional outcome findings. Although it is unfair in the extreme to burden mental health facilities with the responsibility for an individual's total functioning, it may not be inappropriate to recognize the limited role and the appropriate limits of mental health organization. Serious questions arise as to the ability of mental health interventions to deal with such contemporary social problems as epidemic substance abuse, child abuse, the maintenance of successful marital relationships, the prevention of adolescent pregnancies, and a host of other problems which have been welcomed into the mental health arena with an evident lack of discretion.

Finally, the studies reviewed in aggregate raise interesting questions about the definition of health and illness. On an intrapsychic basis, the concept of the mental illness and treatment techniques which are based on that assumptive view may be appropriate. When the range of potential influences on behavior is considered more broadly, the distinction between health and normalcy becomes an issue. When we consider an individual who is mentally healthy, well-adjusted, or normal, are we in fact assessing positive individual functioning or conventional behavior? Are definitions of mental health (and to a considerable degree the goals of a large-system mental health services) more in support of social control than individual differentiation, and more designed for social cloning than personal growth? It is tempting, for example, to interpret the single-parent findings as reflecting positive mental and effective functioning on the part of the subject children; but the reality, which extends to a variety of other studies, is that we cannot distinguish between positive and effective personal functioning and ordinary middle-class conformity. Klassen's (1977) treatment outcome data, for example, suggest that individuals who were seen as most improved by the treatment facility were often those who changed least but were most typically middle class in patterns of behavior and demographic characteristics on treatment entry.

Treatment and Context

Although it is evident that an ecosystem perspective has some reasonable if speculative applications to the more molar aspects of clinical and community mental health issues, the application of this viewpoint to the therapeutic process itself has been minimal. Although data are lacking, the assumptions might still be applied. The community assigns functions to the therapeutic process which are recognized by the community at large, the client, and the therapist. Thus, clinical process, even on a molecular level, occurs in a context; the therapist, client, and the psychosocial setting form a single and complementary unit. The therapist and client play complementary roles as do psychopathology and treatment within the context of the total ecosystem. Psychotherapy exists for psychopathology, which is ultimately defined by the community; cultures that do not recognize a particular behavior as pathological do not recognize a related form of health (O'Connor, 1977).

The clinical process may be viewed as a function of energy input and distribution in the total ecosystem, as a particular pattern of activity which is impacted both by therapeutic process and by the person's interaction with the total ecosystem. From this perspective, the overall effectiveness of mental health efforts on a community level is related to the capacity of the community's substructures to distribute sufficient resources to meet the needs of community inhabitants. In this sense, psychopathology is a function of normalcy; when normal roles do not allow effective and conventional behavior, deviant roles and behaviors emerge. Psychotherapy then becomes a mechanism for the ecosystem as a whole to correct the imbalance between system demands and occupant needs. The function of the clinician may be as much to support the functioning of the system as to enhance the functioning of the individual.

In this sense, there are three contracts involved in the therapeutic process. The first is an overt contract between the therapist and client: The client presents problems both verbally and by demonstrated behavior, which it is assumed the therapist can help to change. At the same time, however, a more subtle contract exists between the therapist and significant others in the individual client's life space: To the extent that others view certain behaviors as problems and are aware that the client is engaged in a therapeutic process, expectations for change surround the client in his or her significant life relationships. The strategy and the intervention techniques of the therapist interact with the network of anticipated change that surrounds the client outside of the therapeutic context itself. Finally, a clear contract exists between the therapist and the community at large. The therapist is empowered, so to speak, to redefine the status of an individual so that the client may begin to behave differently, present himself or herself differently, become involved in different networks and habits of behavior, join different organizations, and the like. At the same time, limits are set on the power of the therapist; diagnosis and prognosis often reflect the extent to which a community will recognize changes in a person of a particular age, sex, socioeconomic level, symptom complex, and set of life circumstances.

The relationship between therapist and client is interestingly analogous to the processes inferred from the single-parent studies. Mother has a relationship with her child within the family context, but also serves as a mediator with the community as a whole and as a facilitator of access to particular systems and resources. To the extent that the analogy applies to therapeutic process, the effectiveness of the therapist may be reflected not only in the molecular techniques and interactional processes that occur within the therapeutic dyad, but also in the therapist's capacity to interact directly and indirectly with the community at large.

REFERENCES

Barker, R.G. (1968) *Ecological psychology.* Stanford, Calif.: Stanford University Press.

Bartz, K.W., & Levine, E.S. (1978) Childrearing by black parents: a description and comparison to Anglo and Chicago parents. *Journal of Marriage and the Family,* **40,** 709–719.

Baughman, E. (1971) *Black Americans.* New York: Academic Press.

Baumrind, D. (1972) An exploratory study of socialization effects on black children: Some black-white comparisons. *Child Development,* **43,** 261–267.

Blechman, E.A. (1980) *Are children with one parent at psychological risk? A methodological review.* Paper presented at the meeting of the American Psychological Association, Montreal, Canada.

Davis, A., & Havighurst, R.J. (1946) Social class and color differences in childrearing. *American Sociological Review,* **11,** 698–710.

Graudens, I., Kraak, B., & Hauer, D. (1976) Scale to measure childrearing practices and attitudes of mothers of five to six-year old preschool children. *Psychologie in Erziehung and Unterricht,* **23,** 70–79.

Hoffman, L.W. (1977) Changes in family roles, socialization and sex differences. *American Psychologist,* **32,** 644–657.

Hume, N. (1975) *Family adjustment and the psychosocial ecosystem.* Unpublished doctoral dissertation, University of Kansas.

Klassen, D. (1977) Person, setting, and outcome in a drug abuse treatment program. *Psychiatric Annals,* **7**(8), 80–104.

Kuhn, M. (1972) Major trends in symbolic interaction theory in the past twenty-five years. In, J. Manis, & B. Meltzer (Eds.), *Symbolic interaction.* Boston: Allyn & Bacon.

Lewis, D.K. (1975) The black family: socialization and sex roles. *Phylon,* **36,** 221.

O'Connor, W.A. (1977) Ecosystems theory and clinical mental health. *Psychiatric Annals,* **7**(7), 63–77.

O'Connor, W.A., & Daniels, S. (1979) *Psychosocial ecosystems: a multilevel model.*

Paper presented at the meeting of the American Psychological Association, New York.

O'Connor, W.A., Daniels, S., & Johnson, D.H. (1981) Teenage pregnancy among blacks. In P. Aahmed (Ed.), *Pregnancy, childbirth and parenting.* New York: Elsevier-North Holland.

O'Connor, W.A., & Klassen, D. (1978) Person, setting and outcome in drug abuse treatment. *Journal of Consulting Clinical Psychology.*

O'Connor, W.A., & O'Connor, K.S. (1977) An ecological approach to treatment. In Berger, D., & Greenberg, P. *Planning for change in state hospitals.* New York: Springer.

Schultz, D. (1969) *Coming up black.* Englewood Cliffs, N.J.: Prentice-Hall.

Wilkinson, C.B., & Daniels, S. (1982) Black female headed single parent families: parameters for prevention. Unpublished manuscript.

Wilkinson, C.B., & O'Connor, W.A. (1977) Growing up male in a black single parent family. *Psychiatric Annals,* 7, 356–362.

CHAPTER 15

One Person Family Therapy

JOSE SZAPOCZNIK, WILLIAM KURTINES, OLGA HERVIS, AND FRANK SPENCER

The field of psychotherapy had its beginnings with individual-oriented foci for pathology and psychotherapy. In time, efforts to conceptualize problems in terms of dyads emerged in the field, such as the seminal work of Bowen et al. (1958) regarding the schizophrenic mother. The family unit next became the focus of study. In the early 1960s, with the onset of the community mental health movement, the philosophical thrust in mental health continued to expand to encompass extrafamilial systems such as the community, the school, and the workplace. As systems theory developed, scientists increasingly identified symptoms as reflective of dysfunctions or pathologies in large systems. Thus, the symptoms in the individual have been seen as reflective of family pathology, and family pathology has been seen as a symptom of the larger systems within which the family was lodged. The pendulum has begun to swing back. In recent years we have started to acknowledge that systemwide interventions are at best difficult given the difficulty inherent in entering and changing large systems.

In a study conducted at the Spanish Family Guidance Center in 1975–1977, we investigated the added effectiveness that intervention directly in the ecosystem might have over family therapy alone. This study is discussed briefly below. In it, we learned that it was possible to help families effectively without necessarily intervening directly in the ecology. The significance of these findings is that it was possible to affect the family's interactions with its environment by working with the family alone, as long as the conceptualization of the problem remained in broad systems terms.

In a more recent study with elderly Hispanics, we conceptualized the roots of depression in these elders as resulting partially from the interaction between the elders and their ecological conditions. Interestingly, we chose not to affect the ecological conditions per se (which would have required massive community interventions), nor did we choose to treat the elder in a vacuum. Rather, we chose

This work was supported by NIDA Grant No. R18 DA 03224. Elsa Alvarez, Angel Perez-Vidal and Marta Fuentes, therapists in the One Person Family Therapy work reported here provided invaluable input to the conceptual development of One Person Family Therapy. The case reported in this chapter was provided by Elsa Alvarez.

to modify through therapy the interface, that is, the transactions between these elders and their environment.

In these studies, we have learned that dysfunctions in smaller systems or organisms can be conceptualized as caused by the larger systems in which they are embedded. Interventions have not been needed to change the entire suprasystem, however, but only those aspects of the suprasystems that produce a dysfunctionality in the smaller system (i.e., family), or in the individual (i.e., elder or adolescent). In particular, we have learned that in this more limited effort, we can help the smaller system by impacting on the interactions between the smaller and larger system, working at the interface (defined interactionally) between systems.

Most recently, we have investigated the possibility of treating a family problem by working with only one person. We have attempted to assist an adolescent by changing those family system interactions that affect and/or involve the adolescent. In this instance, the family system will of necessity be affected, but typically in those areas that most closely involve the adolescents' dysfunctions. The roots of the One Person Family Therapy are found in the work of Bowen (cf. Carter & Orfanidis, 1976), although we have been guided by structural systems theories such as those of Minuchin (1974, 1976), Haley (1976), and Madanes (1981) on how to intervene in families. The initial work that led to the development of One Person Family Therapy was conducted under the auspices and guidance of Dr. Mercedes Scopetta, Director of the Spanish Family Guidance Center from 1972 to 1977.

The Spanish Family Guidance Center has developed, implemented, and evaluated a number of therapeutic modalities designed to fit the specific needs of populations served. OPFT, as discussed in this chapter, is an example of an intervention modality designed to meet specific population needs. It is designed to offer the advantages of systemwide impact in families that may present themselves initially as unable or unwilling to take part in family therapy. OPFT is conceptualized as a modality that can be used alone or in conjunction with other modalities such as conjoint family therapy (CFT). Immediately following is the historical or systematic research effort from which OPFT has developed. Subsequent sections present the theory and practice of OPFT.

HISTORICAL CONTEXT

The 1975–1977 study (Scopetta, King, Szapocznik, & Tillman, 1977), mentioned earlier, investigated whether both conceptualization and therapeutic interventions needed to be of an ecological variety, or alternatively, whether it was sufficient to conceptualize in ecological structural systems terms (e.g., Aponte, 1974), but intervene structurally only within the conjoint family context (cf. Minuchin, 1974). The study was conducted to investigate within an experimental design the relative effectiveness of two treatment conditions. These conditions were labeled intramural and ecological. In both conditions, presenting problems, supporting dynamics, and treatment plan were conceptualized in ecological structural family therapy terms (cf. Szapocznik, Scopetta, Aranalde, & Kurtines, 1978). However, the nature of the actual therapeutic interventions differed so that in the intramural condition, only those interventions occurring in the therapists' offices and within the conjoint mode were allowed, whereas in the ecological condition, at least two direct interventions were required on aspects of the ecology of the families.

The intramural condition represented a conjoint treatment approach in which the assessment of the family's needs, as well as therapy, took place strictly within the therapist-family relationship. In this condition, interventions that took place outside of the therapist's office and/or outside of the therapist-family relationship were restricted to a minimum. If it became necessary to manipulate an environmental variable, this was done by mobilizing the family members so that they manipulated the environmental variable themselves. With the exception of interventions within the family system, therapists did not intervene in other ecosystems. For example, in a family in which the IP presented problems related to his educational ecosystem, and the parents felt powerless to help their child improve in school, the therapist might encourage the parents to take more interest in the problem and increase their authority. Behavioral options including a meeting at the school for the parents and certain teachers might be discussed, but the therapist would not intervene directly in the educational ecosystem.

In the ecological condition, therapists were required to make a minimum of two direct interventions in at least two ecosystems of the family that were clinically judged to be dysfunctional. These interventions were direct in the sense that the therapist initiated actions aimed at improving the family members' relationships with particular ecosystems outside of the family. Therapists treating families in the ecological condition were also permitted to utilize the techniques of the intramural condition. However, a distinguishing feature of the ecological condition was that the therapeutic system included not only the therapist and the family members, but also representatives of ecosystems with whom the family had dysfunctional relationships.

In the ecological condition, for example, the therapist would make direct contact with the schoolteachers and counselors of the Identified Patient (IP) in the family mentioned above, which had a dysfunctional relationship with the educational ecosystem. The therapist might arrange a psychological evaluation aimed at clarifying educational needs and vocational aptitudes so that the IP's relationship with the educational system could become more meaningful. The therapist might also intervene directly to help the parents become more involved in the educational system of the IP, perhaps by acting as an advocate of the family at meetings with school authorities.

The results of the study indicated that both ecological treatment and intramural treatment were highly effective forms of therapy for these families. In both conditions, the identified patients exhibited highly significant reductions in various areas reflective of psychopathology such as drug abuse, impulse control disturbance, subjective distress, behavioral disturbance, role dysfunctioning, and total psychopathology. In both conditions, families had significantly improved their functioning in relationship to the following ecosystems: educational, occupational, peer, judicial, social services, and recreational. It appeared that when both therapy conditions were conceptualized in ecological structural terms, they were both highly effective and not significantly different from each other. Thus, it was not necessary to intervene directly in the suprasystems. Intervention in the conjoint family alone was as effective as intervention in the conjoint family plus direct intervention in the suprasystems.

BRIEF STRATEGIC FAMILY THERAPY

A large body of literature has evolved that substantiates the effectiveness of family therapy with drug-abusing families. A review of the family therapy field as practiced in the 1970s (Olson, Russell, & Sprenkle, 1980), includes a table listing ten separate treatment strategies within family therapy, such as Structural Family Therapy, Behavioral Family Therapy, and Family Crisis Intervention, cross-tabulated with the presenting problem(s) with which they have been most effective. This article, as well as publications by Coleman and Davis (1978), Stanton (1979), and Kaufman and Kaufman (1979), indicate that family therapy has been found effective and is also widely accepted as a treatment for families with drug-abusing members.

Taking the literature and our past experience into account we have, in own work, conceptualized family problems and interventions through the conceptual lens of Brief Strategic Family Therapy (BSFT). BSFT is a family systems approach which views dysfunctions as a result of maladaptive, repetitive sequences of interactions within a family system and between the system and its ecology. Consequently, it is fundamentally concerned with changing dysfunctional interactions to create a more adequate family organization, one that is conducive to individual and system growth. BSFT is based largely on the structural work of Salvador Minuchin (1974), and the strategic concepts of Jay Haley (1976).

As a natural social system, a family develops ways of organizing itself and transacting business among its members and with its environment. When the system is overloaded with stress, or experiencing situations for which it has not developed coping mechanisms, the family perceives the problem and enters therapy. The most common recognition of the problem is labeled by the family as existing in one of its members, the Identified Patient (IP). Consequently, the family's expectation of therapy is that of IP needs to be changed. The family therapist, however, focuses on the whole group, that is, one of the members may be acting out the dysfunction, but it is in fact the whole family that is under stress, and it is the interactional patterns within the family that are dysfunctional. Thus, the behavior of the IP is perceived in relationship to the concurrent interactions he or she has with the other family members.

Brief Strategic Family Therapy is present and future oriented. Its goal is not the exploration of the past, but rather the manipulation of the present (Minuchin, 1974) as a tool of change. In order to work toward this goal, the therapist looks at sets of interactions, diagnoses those that are pathological, and plans strategies to restructure these interactional patterns in order to implement change.

Brief refers to the fact that therapeutic goals are achieved within a range of 8 to 16 sessions; strategic refers to the notion that sessions are focused and specifically directed toward the remediation of previously identified problems and the achievement of planned goals. *Strategic* also refers to the fact that, prior to each session, a therapeutic plan is devised which identifies the still-existing dysfunctional interactions and develops an intervention strategy to create a situation which promotes new and more functional ways of interacting.

As in Minuchin's Structural Therapy, BSFT techniques fall into two categories: joining techniques and restructuring techniques, *Joining* refers to the therapist's movements to enter the family system for the purpose of creating a new therapeutic system within which she/he can diagnose and effect change. *Restructuring* refers to the actual change-producing tactics.

The creation of a new therapeutic system is an essential preamble to creating change within a family. It is through joining that the therapist can experience and thus diagnose the family's interactions. It is also through joining that the family makes a commitment to the new system, thus minimizing the chances of dropping-out or resisting change. Finally, it is in the process of joining that the therapist establishes her/himself as a leader, a position which facilitates restructuring intervention by making the family ameanable to the therapist's manipulations.

In joining, it is essential that the therapist accept the family organization as is, thus eliminating the possibility of perceiving an artificial system or of alienating the family. The therapist joins by initially *supporting the family structure,* or, *tracking* its patterns of communication (i.e., initially following the content and patterns of communication set up by the family), and by *mimesis* of the family's style, affect, activity, and mood. The above techniques help the family to be at ease and provide the context within which the family can enact the dysfunctional behavior patterns that bring them to therapy. *Enactment* refers to encouraging or facilitating the family to behave/interact in its characteristic fashion. In order to encourage enactment, the therapist systematically redirects communication to encourage interaction between family members rather than family–therapist interaction.

Once a therapeutic system is established, and once the family has been permitted to function in its usual fashion, the therapist is now ready to promote, facilitate, suggest, and actually direct alternate organizations, structural arrangements, and interactional patterns. It is here that the therapist challenges the familial status quo, tests its flexibility for change, and creates situations that permit more functional alternatives to emerge. There are a variety of ways in which change-producing interventions can be made. For example, dysfunctional communication patterns can be blocked by the therapist while new interactions are prescribed. Also, restructuring need not necessarily be aimed at the whole system; it often involves only subsystems within the family.

A number of techniques can be used to restructure and shift family interactional patterns. Some examples are:

1.   *Reframing.* The therapist relabels a process, a person, or an event. An alternative organization, label, or even essence is offered for the entity. This new conceptualization implies a new way of behaving toward that entity.

2.   *Reversals.* The therapist changes a habitual pattern of interacting by coaching one member of the family to say or do the opposite of her/his usual response. A reversal of the established sequence breaks up previously rigid patterns that are pathological, and allows new alternatives to emerge.

3.   *De-Triangulation.* Here the goal is to shift the motion of a triangle because triangulation prevents dyadic relationships from processing and growth. Detriangulation permits the dyad in conflict to transact "business" or feelings directly, and thus more effectively. De-triangulation also frees the third party from being used as the repository of the system's dysfunctions. For example, in the case of a couple in which there is a close alliance between mother and son as well as a strong marital conflict, the father frequently gets back at mother through the son by denegrating and belittling him, as in the case of David below. The son and mother may actually pair up to keep the father distant from the family. When father wants to get to mother, he can do so by placing his son in an IP role. De-triangulation of the son may be achieved by breaking up the alliance between mother and son. This may be done by having the son participate with the father in activities such as sports. Actual de-triangulation can now be accomplished by coaching the son to set boundaries between himself and the parental couple, particularly when conflict emerges between the parents. This can be accomplished by having son leave the scene of argument. Thus, now, when father wants to get to mother, he will have to do so more directly.

4.   *Opening-up Closed Systems.* Closed, or dormant systems give appearances of calm so that the tension can be felt somewhere else in the family. One way to open such a system and thus realistically confront the problem-genesis is to activate it by creating crises (such as magnifying small emotional issues). This in turn activates dormant interactions so they can be dealt with openly and in a new manner.

The new interactions fostered by these techniques in therapy sessions are strengthened by the assignment of tasks. An essential aspect of BSFT is that in order to promote generalization of the new patterns emerging during therapy, the family is given a task (homework) at each session which repeats in the natural context, the in-therapy experience. Thus, various family members are directed to carry out certain interactions at home, after the interactions have been successfully carried out in a therapy session. The task must consist of interactions between persons rather than something that one person can do on his/her own.

ONE PERSON FAMILY THERAPY (OPFT)

The goal of treatment in One Person Family Therapy (OPFT), as in the conjoint model of structural family therapy, is to bring about changes in repetitive and sequential dysfunctional patterns of interactions. Structural family therapy as described by Minuchin, however, lends itself for use principally in the conjoint family mode. OPFT, on the other hand, was developed to bring about structural changes while working primarily with one family member. Because currently used structural techniques generally are designed for direct intervention in the family, several new techniques had to be developed to permit indirect interventions in the family through the One Person (OP).

OPFT was initially developed using a population of drug-abusing adolescents. In a major national survey of 2012 agencies offering services to drug abusers, 93% of those who responded indicated family therapy to be the treatment of choice with drug abusers (Coleman, 1978). This survey, as well as the findings of other researchers (e.g., Van Deusen, Stanton, Scott, & Todd, 1980), however, further suggests that although family therapy is the preferred treatment for this population, including families of drug abusers into treatment is extremely difficult. For these reasons, it seemed desirable to bridge the "wisdom of the field" in terms of the benefits of family treatment with the reality of the unaccessability to treatment of the families of drug abusers. The purpose of the research project in which OPFT was first systematically applied was to demonstrate the feasibility of accomplishing the goals of structural family therapy while working primarily with one person. Another major purpose was to demonstrate the effectiveness of OPFT when compared with the conjoint mode. As noted above, the techniques of OPFT are intended to meet the needs for treatment in cases where families are not available. For the purpose of the initial research project which compared Conjoint Family Therapy (CFT) and OPFT, however, cases admitted to the study were restricted to instances for which the family was available for preassessment and possible random assignment to either a conjoint or a one-person mode. This chapter describes OPFT's therapeutic procedures as applied within the constraints of the research project.

Therapeutic Procedures

The OPFT therapeutic procedures described in this section are intended to illustrate one possible application of OPFT. The steps described here are representative of those used in the research project. For the project, as a first step, the entire family was always seen at the time of admission for a preliminary diagnosis of family structure, administration of pretests, and choosing of the OP. The second step in OPFT is choosing the One Person (OP) who, by virtue of his/her centrality and power, has access to the greatest number of repetitive and complementary dysfunctional behaviors. The third step is to "join" the family (i.e., follow and move through the family's interactional structure through the

OP) in order to be in the position to direct changes within the family. Joining incorporates both establishing a therapeutic alliance and tracking the family through an enactment analogue. The fourth step is the actual restructuring, which is accomplished through a variety of techniques that change the OP's complementary participation and thereby interrupt the flow of dysfunctional interactions. Restructuring in OPFT, unlike the conjoint mode, incorporates both intrapersonal and interpersonal restructuring.

WALKING THROUGH A CASE: DAVID S.

David was 16 years old when he was arrested for dealing in drugs. He had run away from home 4 months earlier. Because of his age, the Juvenile Court judge brought in his parents and placed David in their custody, under the condition that they seek family counseling at our Center.

Diagnostic Interview

As with all of the cases in our project, the first step was the initial interview and diagnostic session with the entire family. During the initial interview, the structural systems diagnosis of the family revealed that David was identified by the family as the principal repository of blame for the family's unhappiness, that is, as the IP. The assessment of family interactions indicated that, on the one hand, mother overprotected David with the support of grandma and grandpa. Mr. S., on the other hand, labeled his son hopeless, denigrating him for his failures, with the support of David's older, "streetwise" brother. Mother and father continually bickered throughout the assessment sessions, and consistently diffused the conflict between them by focusing on David's "problems." At those points father typically turned to David to accuse and denigrate him, while David weakly accepted the onslaught.

How to Choose the OP

The second step in the OPFT procedure is choosing the OP. In order to choose the One Person (OP) who can most effectively function as a therapeutic ally, a number of factors need to be taken into consideration. These factors include: (1) centrality in family interactions; (2) power in the family; (3) availability in both a psychological and practical way. Centrality refers to an individual's position in family interaction and the extent to which interactions are routed through that individual. The most extreme example is an individual who functions as a switchboard for the family in the sense that all communications tend to be routed through that individual. The rationale for making centrality a criterion for choosing a person as the OP is that the greater the number of interactions in which a person is involved, the greater the number of interactions that can be changed by adjusting that person's complementary participation in those interactions.

There are two concepts of centrality. One is the centrality of a person in family interactions. The second is the centrality of a person in the content of the interactions. For example, if mother is a family switchboard and son is the IP, mother is central from a process perspective, but most interactions use the IP's dysfunctions in their content.

Power is closely related to centrality in that centrality, in and of itself, gives a family member a great deal of control over family interactions. However, power in the family is determined not only by an individual's centrality in interactions but also by the extent to which an individual's leadership is successful, or by the extent to which an individual becomes the content of the family's interaction. In choosing an OP, power is important because of the control that the powerful individual exercises over the family's interactions, and thus, the influence that the individual may have in changing these interactions.

There are two cases in which a person's power in the family is derived by virtue of being the content of most family interactions, making that person the appropriate choice as the OP. The first is when the person is exhibiting life-threatening symptomatology, such as suicide attempts or severe drug abuse. These individuals should be worked with directly, so that increased monitoring of their life-threatening symptoms can be conducted. Second, there are some families in which the IP-hood is so rigid that these families cannot accept any other solution to their problems other than for something to be done about the IP. Selection of another family member would seem inappropriate to them, so they would not continue with therapy. In addition, such families are unlikely to continue with treatment when the therapist insists on treating the entire family.

Whereas from a structural perspective, availability might appear to be a more pedestrian notion than power and centrality, it is nevertheless important in choosing the OP. Availability refers to the ease with which a therapist can establish an effective alliance with a family member. An effective alliance requires that the family member be: (1) physically available to the therapist on a regular and mutually agreed-upon schedule, and (2) directly affected by the problem.

In David's case, as in most cases in our research project, the identified patient—David—was selected as the OP. There are several reasons why David was chosen. The first was the rigidity of IPhood, that is, the family's unwillingness to accept the possibility that anything could be wrong with the family other than David. A second reason for choosing David was his centrality. By virtue of his IPhood, in most arguments within the family he was the central content. Finally, David was eminently available because of the Court mandate.

In many respects the example of David is representative of the choice of OP in our study in that in most families the IP was chosen for the OP. This is so because IPhood by its very nature vests the IP as the repository of family conflict, thereby casting the IP in a central role. The centrality of the IP, however, is characteristically built upon dysfunctional interactions between the IP and her/his parents.

Although in most of the families treated as part of the project the IP was selected for the OP, in a few instances other family members were chosen as OPs. In our study this occurred in families where mothers were strongly committed to treatment and were powerfully central by virtue of their switchboardlike function within the family.

Joining

ESTABLISHING A THERAPEUTIC ALLIANCE.   After having diagnosed the family in terms of its characteristic patterns of interactions, the OP alone is brought in for famly therapy. In family therapy, the initial task of the therapeutic relationship is to join the family. In conjoint family therapy, joining is accomplished by accepting the family's interactional patterns and in turn being accepted by the family. The purpose of joining is to place the therapist in a position that will allow her/him to direct changes in the family. In OPFT, because the entire family is not available throughout the treatment sessions, the therapist enters the family, as well as directs change, through the OP. To accomplish this, a therapeutic alliance is established with the OP. The OPFT therapist, in the context of the therapeutic alliance, will continue to track the family's characteristic patterns of interaction through the OP's perception, and will direct changes in dysfunctional interactions by encouraging or directing the OP to change her/his complementary behaviors in these interactions.

In the case of David, the therapist began the joining process on the first session by establishing a therapeutic alliance. David presented himself for the first session dressed in a black jacket and gave the impression of a tough, "streetwise" adolescent. He was initially cautious and cool to the therapist, but later in the session began an enthusiastic recounting of his experiences while he had run away from home. This situation provided the opportunity for the therapist to begin the joining process. The therapist, sensing David's great pride in his adventure and his success in the adult world, listened intently and allowed him to savor his bold adventure. David was allowed to experience the opposite of his initial self-blame and negativism about what he had done. By listening attentively, the therapist and patient shared a critical experience and established a therapeutic alliance that provided a foundation from which to begin to track the family structure and the position of David, the IP, within it.

ENACTMENT.   In CFT, joining is accomplished through techniques such as supporting the family structure, tracking its communication patterns, and by mimesis of the family's style. These techniques help to place the family at ease and encourage the enactment of dysfunctional family interactional patterns. In OPFT, because the family is not present for most sessions, the emphasis necessarily shifts to enactment as the principal technique for "joining the family" including tracking its dysfunctional interactional patterns. Enactment, however, is considerably different in OPFT than in CFT. Whereas in CFT actual enactment of characteristic family interaction takes place, in OPFT, because just one person is present, only an enactment analogue is possible. The *enactment analogue,* as used in OPFT, refers to constructing a representation of the family's characteristic interactional patterns in lieu of actual enactment, which allows direct observation.

What makes an enactment analogue possible and how is it brought about? The most important theoretical and clinical contribution of OPFT as described in this chapter is found in the systematic integration of intrapersonal and interpersonal concepts and clinical interventions within a single approach. The concept of the enactment analogue is built upon the more basic psychological process of introjection. *Introjection* as used in OPFT refers to the process whereby the individual internalizes her/his complementary role in the family's characteristic pattern of interactions.

The relationship between family patterns and introjection can be illustrated by an analogy of a tree and the medium in which it grows. The tree springs out of a genetic background that defines the parameters and limits of what it can be. The tree in its embryonic stage (e.g., the seed) is planted in a growing medium with which it establishes a symbiotic relationship. As the roots grow, they allow the tree to feed itself from what the medium can offer and conversely, the roots provide a function for the medium in protecting it against erosion, and the leaves protect the ground from the harshness of the sun, thus establishing a homeostatic balance. It is interesting to note that complementarity between the tree and its growing medium takes place not only in the process of living but also in the complementary physical form of the roots and their growing medium—with each becoming complementary in form to the other. In other words, the configuration of the soil around the tree exactly complements the form of the tree.

The complementarity of the tree and its growing medium is analagous to the relationship between a child and the family context within which s/he grows. The child comes into the family with her/his genetic background that defines the parameters and limits of what s/he can be. The child and the family quickly establish a symbiotic relationship in the sense that the child's behavior becomes an integral part of family interactions and these interactions in turn, are encouraged and maintained by the child's behavior. The young child learns basic behavioral patterns from her/his early experiences with the family's interactional patterns. As a result, the child learns to behave in such a way that s/he complements the family's interactional patterns. In time, the child becomes a "cog in the wheel" of these interactions in the sense that s/he can respond to, initiate or maintain certain family patterns by her/his behavior. As the child grows up, these basic behavioral patterns become more automatic or introjected. That is, the child has now internalized her/his particular complementary roles in the family dynamics, and has thus successfully internalized the "family structure." It should be noted, however, that the same complementarity that develops between a young tree and its growing medium can also develop between a mature tree transplanted with a new growing medium. Similarly, adults that join a family, such as through marriage, also develop and internalize complementary ways of interacting.

How is this relationship between introjection and family patterns useful in OPFT? In OPFT when the OP is asked to represent her/his family, what the OP usually represents is the behavior of others rather than the self. The therapist assumes from systems theory that for the system to maintain itself, the OP must behave in a fashion that complements the reported behavior of others, that is, the OP has introjected the kinds of behaviors that complement the behavior of others in the family. When these two complements (OP's and others' behaviors) are brought together, the system has been represented symbolically and can be understood from a systemic point of view. How does the therapist use this representation to understand the relationship between what the OP sees in the family, that is, the behavior of others, on the one hand, and the OP's introjected complementary behaviors and the overall system, on the other hand?

In the conjoint mode, when the family comes to the family therapist, typically the parents present their complaints about one family member, known as the IP. The family therapist through her/his understanding of family systems immediately assumes that if an IP exists, then its complement—a family dynamic dysfunction—must also exist. In the case of OPFT, the process is identical but the direction may be reversed. An IP/OP tells the therapist about the *other family members'* behaviors. The family therapist through his/her understanding of the family systems immediately assumes that a complement to the represented behavior must also exist in the IP/OP that supports the maintenance of the reported behavior of others.

Figure 15.1 depicts, using Venn Diagrams, the relationship between reported behaviors of others, the OP's introjected behavior, and family interactional patterns.

The underlying assumption that allows enactment through the processes outlined above is that the OP's complementary role in the family's interactional patterns are introjected. The family interactional patterns are defined as comprising two complementary parts: (1) the OP's own (introjected) behavior in the family context, and (2) the rest of the family's behavior. Because the OP tends to perceive the other family member's behaviors but not her/his own, in the enactment analogue, the OP is requested to represent the other family members' behaviors. Bringing together the family's represented behaviors and the assumed OP's introjected behaviors provides a full picture of the family's systemic, self-reinforcing, and repetitive pattern of interactions.

The process of creating an enactment analogue has limitations beyond those encountered with actual enactments. In particular, the OP's report of the family's behaviors may be distorted. This distortion may introduce some inaccuracies into the structural (interactional) analysis that is used to construct a symbolic representation of the family's interactional patterns. Thus, the therapist may have to resort to a variety of techniques in bringing to life family patterns in order to compare various enactments as expressed or projected through the several techniques. It is suggested that the congruence between enactment and family patterns can be established from the reliability among the enactments (a notion similar to coefficient Alpha in establishing the reliability of items in measuring a single construct).

Several techniques have been used to elicit enactment analogues. Techniques that have been found useful are (1) role playing by OP of several roles, (2) role playing by OP and therapist of complementary roles, (3) empty chair technique—

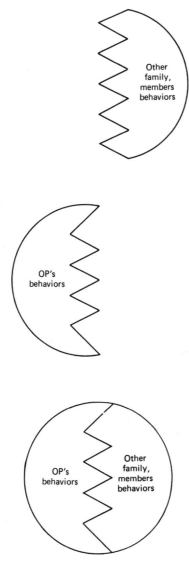

Figure 15.1. Venn diagrams of family interactions.

    1. OP represents other family's behaviors.

    2. Therapist assumes that family is a system and thus OP's behaviors must be the complement of what s/he has represented as behaviors of others.

    3. Therapist constructs a symbolic representation of the family system/interactional patterns by bringing together the two complements (adds 1 & 2 above).

from Gestalt therapy and, (4) use of chalkboard to sketch structural relationships.

In the case of David, after a therapeutic alliance had been established, the therapist inquired about David's perception of the problem in the family. David responded by complaining that he felt humiliated by his family. His mother treated him like a child, and his father was always down on him. He indicated that he had run away from home because he couldn't stand it anymore. "I felt asphyxiated. I couldn't breathe. I escaped and I didn't even look back."

Later in the session, the therapist discovered that what had precipitated David's running away was the way his parents treated him when they found out he had an older (18-year-old) Anglo girl friend. They would not let him stay out late with her or talk with her on the phone after 10 P.M. This information provided the therapist with some content around which to further track the family interactional patterns. Using an empty chair to represent mother, the therapist directed David to sit on the empty chair and say what mother would say if he stayed out too late with his girl friend, Patty. David said that she would say, "Mi niñito, eres muy niño para esas cosas" ("My little child, you are too young for these things.") David acted out how she would baby him while patting him on the head. The therapist then asked David to change chairs and say what his father would say. When David acted out his father's role, he shifted his style and manner. His father, he said, would get angry and accuse him of being "a no-good, lazy bum." The use of such techniques to facilitate enactment analogues helped to clarify the conflicting role relations that David played vis-à-vis both his parents, as had been diagnosed in the initial family assessment interview.

This enactment analogue confirmed the initial assessment, and enabled the therapist to "track" in the sense of "following" the family structure in sufficient detail to understand David's complementary role in the interactional structure, as well as the parents' role: David would accept each parent's definition of his role in the family and would allow himself to be placed in a position that detours through him the parental disagreements over his role in the family. Enactment thus encompasses both the OP's behavior and the family's behavior as they join in a repetitive, reinforcing pattern of sequential interactions. The enactment analogue also set the stage for the therapist to "track" in the sense of "moving through" the family process for the purpose of restructuring, as described in the next section.

Once the family pattern had been enacted and the therapist has identified the most *clearly* complementary behaviors between the OP and the rest of the family, the therapist is in a position to begin directing changes in the family through David. As will become clear later, the critical conceptual discovery that makes OPFT possible is found in *this* behavioral complementarity between the OP and the rest of the family.

Restructuring

Restructuring refers to the actual interventions that are designed to change family interactional patterns. In CFT, restructuring takes place through direct therapist interventions to alter dysfunctional interactional patterns. In OPFT, on the other hand, the therapist directs changes in dysfunctional interactional patterns by bringing about changes in the OP's complementary behaviors that maintain the dysfunctional interactions.

A basic assumption of structural systems therapy is that a change in family interactional patterns (i.e., at the interpersonal level) will effect an intrapersonal change (i.e., affect and cognition) in family members. The critical notion in this assumption is that change must occur at both levels, the interpersonal and the intrapersonal, and that the two co-vary. Thus, structural family therapy focuses on bringing about interpersonal change and assumes that intrapersonal change will follow. On the other hand, individual psychotherapies, in general, focus on intrapersonal change, with little attention to structural change in interactional patterns. OPFT, in contrast to structural family therapy and individual psychotherapy, focuses on both interpersonal and intrapersonal change. In OPFT, the therapist facilitates intrapersonal changes in the OP for the specific aim of bringing about changes in the OP's interpersonal behaviors, and more specifically, those behaviors that maintain familial dysfunctional interactions. The therapist then encourages, facilitates, or directs the OP to change her/his interpersonal behaviors that maintain these undesirable interactions. When the OP complies, the interactional patterns themselves are forced to change as one "cog in the systemic wheel" behaves differently. It is assumed that as other family members change behaviorally, intrapersonal changes will also occur in them.

INTRAPERSONAL RESTRUCTURING.   In the case of David, having used the enactment analogue to set the stage for tracking the family process, the therapist then began to restructure David's introjection of the family's interactional patterns. The stage was set when David reported each of his parent's behavior toward him, alternatively babying and denigrating him. The therapist "tracked" in the sense of "moving through" from the reported interactional pattern to David's (intrapersonal) introjected complementary behavior.

During the next session, the therapist used a Gestalt (fantasy) technique to move through by tracking David's complementary role in the family's interactional structure. The therapist had David experience one of his legs as portraying his response to the role in which his mother cast him, and then his other leg as portraying his response to the role in which his father cast him. The leg that symbolized his complementary behavior to his mother dragged slowly, as if it were handicapping him, or holding him back, representing a babyish role that he felt was restraining him or holding him back. The other leg was agitated, moved rapidly, and appeared out of control. This leg, David confessed, represented his life in the streets, as well as his life as his father represented it, because in fact, when he had run away he had been involved in a disturbed and dangerous life-style trafficking in drugs, thus fulfilling his father's expectations as "a no-good bum." David's habitual response to his parents has been one of allowing himself to be manipulated to the behavioral extremes that his parents expected of him in his role of IP. David, however, with the experiential understanding of his conflicting role behavior, now wished to reach a middle ground more suitable to his stage of life, that is, neither child nor adult, but adolescent. He wanted to feel, behave, and be treated like a person his age.

Through this Gestalt exercise, the therapist achieved sufficient intrapersonal restructuring to permit movement toward interpersonal restructuring. It should be noted that in OPFT, in contrast to most individual psychotherapies, the only intrapersonal changes sought are those changes that are required to permit restructuring of the corresponding interpersonal dysfunctions.

RESTRUCTURING AT THE INTERFACE OF INTRAPERSONAL AND INTERPERSONAL LEVELS. Once the therapist has accomplished some basic intrapersonal restructuring, the therapist is ready to begin the transition to interpersonal restructuring through the OP. But how? A method that has been useful in OPFT to restructure at the interface of the intrapersonal and interpersonal levels is to *split the OP's executive observant ego* from the OP as s/he usually functions (reactively and complementarily) in the family system. What does splitting of the ego involve? Let us consider the example of David.

For the sake of a simple illustration, let us use the example of David's relationship with his father. At the time of intake, David is cast in the IP role by a family in which the father continuously denigrates and devalues him. When his father badgers him with examples of David's flaws or faults, David withdraws. The therapist, through the enactment analogue, has identified clearly one repetitive sequence of behaviors in which father and David play a complementary role in labeling David as the IP (father actively IP's David, and David accepts father's accusations). The therapist is now ready to provide David with a perspective on his complementary role in maintaining this interaction. This is accomplished by having David "observe" the interactional sequence described above. The technique that allows David to "observe" the interactional sequence is the so-called "splitting of the executive observant ego." The therapist asks David to imagine seeing himself in the family context while the interaction is ongoing. Thus, David is asked to observe, together with the therapist, an imagined family interaction. The part of David that observes the interaction is David's executive observant ego, whereas the part of David that is imagined as taking part in the interaction is the David who has introjected a complementary role to the family system. As David observes the imagined family interaction, he is taught by the therapist how he contributes to the interaction that eventuates in his being labeled an IP by passively accepting that label and role.

Carrying out this process through imagery is somewhat arduous, but it does represent one method of creating awareness for the OP of her/his complementary role in a particular family interaction. It is easier to carry out this part of the therapy if a videotape of the family interaction is available. It can be used in place of imagery for teaching the OP her/his complementary role in family interactions.

In order for the OP to accept responsibility for her/his complementary role in family interactions, it is necessary to explore with the OP the extent to which, on the one hand, her/his role is perceived as essence (that's who I am) or, on the other hand, as reactive to family interactions (this is how I behave when...). A useful therapeutic tool to facilitate the OP's taking responsibility for her/his complementary behavior at this point is to *reframe* the OP's conceptualization of self from one in which s/he sees self in the role cast by the family as a matter of essence to a conceptualization of self as reacting to family interactions. This technique is useful because it is easier for a person to accept responsibility for problem behavior if it is perceived as peripheral rather than as essence. Moreover, it is easier for the OP to accept changing that behavior if it is perceived as not only problematic but peripheral.

The basic goal in reframing in this situation is to change the OP's acceptance of the narrative line or family script about a particular issue. For example, in the case of David, the therapist might reframe his position in the family in the following manner. Initially, both David and his family see him as the problem person. The therapist, however, perceives that David is allowing himself to be cast in the problem person or IP role. Thus, the therapist can reframe David's perception of himself from "I am a problem person" to "I am behaving in a way that allows my being cast in that role."

INTERPERSONAL RESTRUCTURING.   Once the OP clearly understands his/her complementary roles in the family, and has given up her/his desire to play these roles, the OP now has an investment in changing the family's dysfunctional patterns. In this respect, then, the OP and the therapist now have explicit common goals and they become therapeutic allies as they face the remainder of the family. The final step in the therapy is to carry out the actual interpersonal restructuring with the aid of the OP, and frequently through the OP.

A technique used to interrupt repetitive family interactions is to "coach" the OP to change her/his behaviors in the family. This change was referred to above under the BSFT section as creating "reversals."

The therapist, for example, might coach David to stand up to his father when his father begins to denigrate him. The way in which system change takes place is that when the OP changes her/his behavior, in effect, s/he has interrupted the repetitive and sequential flow of family interactions which casts her/him into the IP role. This is a clear example of how OPFT differs from many other psychotherapies. It does not stop at creating awareness, but rather uses awareness as a tool for redirecting the interpersonal behavior of the OP and thereby brings about system change.

In conjoint family therapy, the therapist could have caused this interruption of repetitive sequences around IPhood during family sessions, and hence the therapist can be present to support the change. In OPFT, however, the therapist must rely heavily on the OP's ability to change her/his own behavior and to maintain the change in the face of strong family pressure to return to the family's homeostatic balance. Hence, the OPFT therapist must rehearse with the OP his change in behavior, and it is particularly important to role play various alternative outcomes that could ensue from the OP's change. The purpose of rehearsal is to allow the therapist to identify resistances in the OP, to give the OP an experience of mastery, and to attempt to prevent possible family sabotage of the OP's new or changed behavior.

In OPFT, as in the conjoint modes of BSFT, homework tasks are important techniques for promoting generalization of new behaviors learned during therapy. In OPFT, however, homework tasks are the primary mechanisms through which the therapist directs interpersonal restructuring in the family through the OP. The homework tasks involve the OP's changing her/his behavior in a complementary role. There are several aspects of these tasks that deserve discussion. One is that prior to assigning a task as homework, considerable rehearsal should take place at the office, as already explained above. Second, the task must pertain to a behavioral pattern in which the OP plays a complementary role. For example, although it is possible for David to change his interaction with his father which casts him in the IP role, it is not possible to assign David a task that involves primarily an interaction between father and mother, because it would improperly triangulate David. Third, it should be noted that homework tasks must always interrupt or modify a *specific* interactional sequence (e.g., father IPs son—son accepts IP role). Finally, homework tasks must be concrete and direct a change in the OP's complementary behavior (e.g., David's passive behavior in response to his father's denigrations).

In the best of all worlds, when the OP changes, the family will accommodate itself to the change, thereby reinforcing the new behavior. In the real world, however, the response to the OP's changed behavior is family pressure to return to its previous homeostatic balance. The confrontation between the OP trying to create and maintain change, and the family's trying to prevent it will tend to produce a family outburst or overt crisis. At this point, families are often accessible to the therapists, and in fact, it is an ideal moment for the therapist to request and typically obtain a family therapy session.

These family sessions are an important adjunct to OPFT, but are conducted differently from sessions that are part of a conjoint family therapy program. The critical difference is that in conjoint family therapy, the therapist may restructure family patterns by changing alliances between the therapist and particular family members as appropriate. In a family therapy session of the OPFT variety, the therapist maintains a clear alliance with the OP, now turned therapeutic ally.

As is well recognized by family therapists, OP's reports may not accurately reflect their actual changes within the family. For this reason, too, it is desirable to obtain one or two family sessions. In these sessions, the therapist can observe the actual change that has taken place, and can capitalize on all the rehearsing that has gone on in OPFT to encourage stronger reversals by the OP while the therapist is present to support these changes.

A family session or two also provides an opportunity—albeit a limited one— for the therapist to intervene directly in family interactional patterns in which the OP is not complementary (e.g., in the case of David, the therapist may intervene in the marital relationship directly during a conjoint session). In one or two family sessions, however, it may not be possible to bring about major structural changes in these other family dysfunctional patterns. Rather, it is only possible to change those aspects of these "other" dysfunctional interactions as they affect the OP.

When Is OPFT the Treatment of Choice?

There are a variety of clinical situations in which OPFT may be more desirable or feasible than conjoint family therapy. OPFT can be a treatment of choice in those instances in which an adolescent has been identified as the family's IP, but the family is unwilling to come into treatment. In such cases, the family rigidly defines the singularity of the problem as lodged in the IP, and refuses to come into treatment. Yet, the etiology of the problems seems to be lodged in family dysfunction.

When a parent is the IP, it may be that a certain degree of privacy is desired, and yet family conflicts may be a critical component of the etiology. There are also those instances in which a family is too volatile to be able to work together, at least initially, as a family. On occasion, when the IP is a very young child, the therapist may choose not to bring the child into therapy to avoid further labeling of the child. In those instances, the therapist may prefer to work with a parent (usually the mother) as the OP.

OPFT might be the treatment of choice when a youth has been placed in a residential treatment program far away from home. In these instances, even if family dynamics are considered to be responsible for the youth's dysfunction, it is far too costly and difficult to have the family attend sessions regularly. It may then be possible to conduct the treatment partially through OPFT with the adolescent in the residential program and on occasion bring in the family for a conjoint session. Finally, there may be times when a therapist chooses treatment goals that clearly favor assisting one member rather than treating the whole family, as in the case of dysfunctional adolescents with highly disturbed parents. In these instances, the focus of treatment could still be family oriented, but the effort to assist is purposefully focused on the adolescent in treatment.

At the present state of development, OPFT is only intended to correct those family dynamics that are complementary to the OP. In those cases in which the therapist desires to treat the whole family pathology, conjoint family therapy, when possible, is the treatment of choice.

DISCUSSION AND CONCLUSION

This chapter has described an innovative application of structural family concepts for use in cases where families are not available. One Person Family Therapy consists of a clearly defined set of strategies and steps rooted in structural systems family therapy. This "one person" approach to family therapy is made possible by recognition of the relationship between introjection and family interaction patterns, that is, that each family member internalizes her/his complementary behavior which supports and maintains repetitive family interactional patterns. Thus, at the conceptual level, OPFT represents a contribution to our understanding of the interface of intrapersonal and interpersonal dynamics. At an applied level, OPFT makes a clinical contribution by extending the benefits of family therapy to populations and cases for which families are unavailable. Furthermore, results of the data from the research project where OPFT was first systematically examined, provide empirical evidence for the effectiveness of the approach (Szapocznik, 1983; Szapocznik, Kurtines, Foote, Perez-Vidal, 1983).

This chapter began with a discussion of several instances in which therapies target at the interface between a larger dysfunctional system and a symptom-bearer. Traditionally, individual therapy approaches have focused on changing the symptom-bearer. At the other end of the theoretical pole, systems theorists and therapists have operated on the premise that dysfunctional systems should be the target of intervention and not their symptom-bearers. This chapter offered an alternative to either the individual or the systems perspective. This new approach is firmly based on a systems perspective, both in understanding the problem and the change process. However, this new approach suggests that even though a symptom is seen as resulting from a dysfunction of a larger system, the change agent can strategically choose to change the dysfunctional system, on the one hand, or merely its impact on the symptom-bearer, on the other hand. Thus, although we recognize the greater value of treating larger dysfunctional systems, we also recognize that given limited resources or special circumstances, it may not always be possible to pursue the greater good.

This chapter provided techniques for intervening at the interface between a family member who is the symptom-bearer, and a family's dysfunctions as they affect the symptom-bearer. The approach lends itself either to assist the symptom-bearer in lessening the impact of the larger system's dysfunctions, or to treat the larger system through the symptom-bearer. At a conceptual level, the concepts proposed herein can be generalized beyond families to other systems and their symptom-bearers, and thus have implications for general systems therapy, and for conceptualizing systems change.

REFERENCES

Aponte, H.J. (1974) Psychotherapy for the poor: An ecostructural approach to treatment. *Delaware Medical Journal,* 1–7.

Bowen, M., Dysinger, R.H., & Basaminia, B. (1958) *The role of the father in families with a schizophrenia patient.* Paper presented at the annual meeting of the American Psychiatric Association.

Carter, E.A., & Orfanidis, M.M. (1976) Family therapy with one person and the family therapist's own family. In P.J. Guering (Ed.), *Family therapy: Theory and practice.* N.Y.: Halsted Press.

Coleman, S.B., & Davis, D.I. (1978) Family therapy and drug abuse: A national survey. *Family Process,* **17**(1), 21–29.

Haley, J. (1976) *Problem-solving therapy.* San Francisco: Jossey-Bass.

Kaufman, E., & Kaufman, P. (1979) Multiple family therapy with drug abusers. In E. Kaufman, & P. Kaufman (Eds.), *Family therapy of drug and alcohol abuse.* New York: Gardner.

Madanes, C. (1981) *Strategic family therapy.* San Francisco: Jossey-Bass.

Minuchin, S. (1974) *Families and family therapy.* Cambridge, Mass.: Harvard University Press.

Minuchin, S. (1976) Structural family therapy. In G. Caplan (Ed.), *American handbook of psychiatry,* (Vol. 2). New York: Basic Books.

Olson, D.H., Russell, C.S., & Sprenkle, D.H. (1980) Marital and family therapy: A decade review. *Journal of Marriage and the Family,* **42,** 973–994.

Scopetta, M.A., King, O.E., Szapocznik, J., & Tillman, W. (1977) *Ecological structural family therapy with Cuban immigrant families* (Technical report for the National Institute on Druge Abuse). Miami: University of Miami Spanish Family Guidance Center.

Stanton, M.D. (1979) Family treatment approaches to drug abuse problems: A review. *Family Process,* **18,** 251–280.

Szapocznik, J. Brief Strategic Family Therapy (1979–1983): A Final Report, National Institute of Drug Abuse Grant Number R18 DA 03224, 1983.

Szapocznik, J., Scopetta, M., Aranalde, M., & Kurtines, W. (1978) Cuban value structure: Treatment implications. *Journal of Consulting and Clinical Psychology,* **46,** 961–970.

Szapocznik, J. Kurtines, W.M., Foote, F., Perez-Vidal, A., & Hervis, O. Conjoint versus one person family therapy: Some evidence for the effectiveness of conducting family therapy through one person. *Journal of Consulting and Clinical Psychology,* 1983, **51,** 889–899.

Van Deusen, J.M., Stanton, M.D., Scott, S.M., & Todd, T.C. (1980) Engaging "resistant" families in treatment: I. Getting the drug addict to recruit his family members. *International Journal of the Addictions,* **15**(7), 1069–1089.

CHAPTER 16

Manifestations of Possession in Novel Ecological Contexts

GARY S. HURD AND E. MANSELL PATTISON

INTRODUCTION

The phenomenon of demon possession has been a historical curiosity and anthropological exotica. It would seem that "possession states" are indeed an extraordinary psychiatric symptom.

Our western views of health and illness, cause and effect, reality and fantasy, are the product of an evaluation of construction and explanation of reality determined largely by the empirical rationalism of experimental science, its adoption by medicine, and transmission to psychiatry. This western mode of thought and its attendant construction of reality has usually been the measure against which all other cultural constructions of reality are tested; whereas so-called primitive cultures were considered to be magical, irrational, simplistic, and naive. From this point of view, it seems absurd that sophisticated western people should evince interest, much less believe in magical, mystical, and metaphysical ideas that western culture has long since abandoned for more realistic views and explanations of the world. In particular, the belief in demons, possession, and exorcism seem especially atavistic.

Yet, there is widespread renewal of popular interest in the supernatural, mystical, magical, and "irrational" in contemporary western society. Consider the popularity of contemporary religious youth cults, the middle-class interest in religiously toned self-help, the intelligentsia fascination with holistic health and imported eastern mysticism, and the current mental health enthusiasm to identify and utilize indigenous cultural healers (Pattison, 1978). Even greater then is the dilemma of the mental health practitioner when confronted with a patient who attributes his or her difficulties to being possessed or due to spells, curses, or hex magic sent against the patient by malicious others. Not only might these attributions be independent of psychopathology but they will typically fall outside the cultural and personal experience of the clinician, who has been trained and even reared in an empirical, rationalistic tradition.

The phenomena of possession has been studied from the vantage of many different disciplines, and has produced a plethora of data and confounding theories. In studying the literature, one must be impressed by the insularity of much of the work, whether by psychiatrists, psychologists, sociologists, anthropologists, historians, or theologians. This has fragmented formulations of the issues at hand. What is needed as Kleinman (1977) points out, is a multidisciplinary and interdisciplinary integration. The strands of data need synthesis. Therefore, in this chapter we will not attempt to cite or review all of the extant literature (which is enormous), but will attempt a step conceptual integration, with the citation of particularly relevant and illustrative sources.

This history of possession is rooted in religion. Early history of religious possession is given by Russell (1979), medieval history by Knox (1950), renaissance history by Thomas (1971), and recent by Podmore (1963). The classic early review of possession states was written by Oesterreich (1966), followed by extensive anthropological analyses (Bourguignon, 1973, 1976; Douglas, 1970; Landy, 1977; Lewis, 1971; Mair, 1969; Rush, 1974). Empirical field and case studies have been published from a social science perspective (Crapanzano & Garrison, 1977; Goodman, et al., 1974; Loudon, 1976; Tiryakian, 1977), whereas psychiatrically oriented volumes have also appeared (Cox, 1973; Kiev, 1964; Prince, 1968; Yap, 1974). This substantial literature reflects the active scholarly and professional interest in a topic that is not so esoteric as it might first appear.

Our concern, then, with possession must extend beyond just exotic phenomena, to consider the following issues: (1) the worldwide distribution and manifestation of possession states, (2), the sociocultural and psychodynamic parameters of possession, (3) the clinical components of the phenomena, and (4) the sociocultural implications. As we shall see, the phenomena of possession is *not* extraordinary; in fact, it is both quite ordinary and an integral aspect of western psychiatry.

SOCIETAL DISTRIBUTION AND CONDITIONS

Bourguignon (1973) conducted the most extensive recent research on a variety of altered states of consciousness, including trance and possession trance. In both states one can observe the trance behavior and measure physiological changes associated with the altered states of consciousness. Both are culturally learned behavior. Trance, however, is an *intrapersonal* event, the content of which can only be learned through description provided by the person having the experience. The possession trance is an *interpersonal* event, in which there is impersonation of another being on an occasion when there are witnesses. As such, the context and meaning of the event are known to the community, for whom the possession trance embodies common social and cultural symbols. In a survey of 488 worldwide societies, Bourguignon found that 90% had institutionalized one or the other of these states.

In general, Bourguignon found that the more simple societies practice trance behavior, whereas more complex societies engage in possession trance. In North America, Bourguignon found that 92% of societies have trance, 25% have possession trance, and only 3% have neither! Thus, possession states are neither extraordinary nor unusual in the life of most people. Bourguignon (1976a) concludes:

> One might ask how to account for our findings. A number of comments as well as hypotheses might be suggested. One: societies which do not utilize these states clearly are historical exceptions which need to be explained rather than the vast majority of societies which do use these states. Two: the specific beliefs associated with altered states are cultural inventions…Three: the specific behavior of altered states and the beliefs with which they are linked may be said to reflect certain types of social realities…Four: the institution of one or another or both of our types of altered states of consciousness may be said to "do" something on the one hand for the participating individual, the trancer or possession trancer, and on the other hand to "do" something, to fulfill a function, for the society.

In summary, the more complex, socially symbolic and community oriented possession trance is found in societies where symbolic modes of expressing social communication are necessary; whereas in more simple face-to-face social structure we find simple trance states.

We now narrow our inquiry to the more specific social conditions in which the explicit forms of possession as demon possession and exorcism appear. Although, the *belief* in demon possession and exorcism is *widespread,* the actual *occurrence* of cases of demon possession and the practice of exorcism appear to be more *limited.* In particular, Bourguignon has reported that the eruption of demonology is coincident with social situations where there is: (1) an oppressive social structure, (2) a loss of trust in the efficacy of social institution, and (3) a seeming inability to cope with the evils of the social structure. When these particular social situations obtain, we see the *personification of social evil* in evil demons, the displacement of social protest in the form of accusations of possession and witchcraft, and personal experiences of possession. Being possessed of social evil is personified, whereas accused, accuser, and exorcist act out the symbolization of the social conflict in a safely displaced form, because active social protest and reform seem impossible. Thus, there is social conflict and social ambiguity of action (Uzzell, 1974; Wilson, 1967; Wilson, 1971).

With an understanding of the social conditions which give rise to demonology, we see that contemporary social conditions in the western world are ripe for the reemergence of supernaturalistic belief systems, and even demonology: society has been perceived as oppressive, trust in social institutions has disintegrated, and a mood of helpless impotence in social action has emerged. So it is not surprising that the evil society should again be personified and symbolized in contemporary western demonology.

But not all persons in such a social situation participate in the possession and exorcism. Usually, it is only those in the community who are most oppressed and for whom social protest reform least viable who turn to possession and exorcism to ameliorate their plight symbolically. (Carstairs & Kapur, 1976; Wijesinghe et al., 1976) Further, in certain cultures some reports indicate that different personality types are more likely to seek possession and exorcism (Yap, 1961; Kuba, 1973). Thus, it is the combination of social conditions, community status, and personality structure that intertwines to produce demonology in practice.

PSYCHODYNAMICS VERSUS PSYCHOPATHOLOGY

Earlier literature on possession usually interpreted it as a manifested of psychopathology. As a result, there were many attempts to determine the particular type of neurotic or psychotic personality that was prone to develop possession. The purely psychopathological approach is inadequate, however, on several counts. First, recent careful studies of ritual trance and ritual possession trance, in both shamans and laypersons reveal that although *some* participants may be either neurotic or psychotic, this is *not* the general case (Hoch, 1974; Hippler, 1976). Second, the widespread distribution of possession militates against the plausibility of explaining possession phenomena solely as psycho-pathology. Third, the psychodynamics of possession have been made abundantly clear, but it is reductionistic to conclude that the explication of psychodynamics means psychopathology.

One of the basic problems in dealing with the issue of psychopathology is the distinction between "emic" interpretations (as the culture interprets the behavior) and "etic" interpretation (universalized scientific interpretation). These differences can be distorted in either direction. From an "emic" perspective one can observe the structural and functional value of possession in a culture, and therefore conclude that the possession is not psychopathologic because it is meaningful within the culture. Or from the "etic" perspective one might conclude that the behavior was psychopathological because it appears abnormal in terms of expected western norms of behavior. But these are misinterpretations. It is possible to derive from ethnographic data the cultural emic distinction as to whether a specific behavior or condition is "culturally normal," unusual or deviant but acceptable, or abnormal and not culturally acceptable. In all three instances we deal with psychodynamics, but only in the last instances with psychopathology. Thus, we are dealing with both the analysis of personality structure and social adaption. The psychological anthropologist George DeVos (1976) summarizes this dual synthesis:

We must maintain a clear distinction between the internal structuring of personality related to a concept of adjustment and social-behavioral responses which can be seen as adaptive or maladaptive for the individual within his nexus...to understand the interrelationships of social structure, possession behavior, and personality one must use a dual level of analysis with a structural-functional distinction to delimit and interrelate the concept of adjustment to psychological structure on the one hand, and adaptation to social functioning on the other.

We may note that there are always general social conflicts in a culture. These conflicts are then symbolized and some degree of cultural conflict resolution achieved through a variety of ritual symbolic activities (Turner, 1969). To the degree that the conflicts of the culture are conflicts for the individual, the symbolizing rituals afford personal melioration of experiencing cultural conflict (Firth, 1967; Obeyesekere, 1969, 1970; Skultans, 1974). This, then, is a general sociopsychological dynamic for participation in ritual trance and possession trance for many "normal" persons.

But again, we return to the issue of psychodynamics versus psychopathology. Freud (1922) states the classic psychiatric formulation: "The states of possession correspond to our neuroses...the demons are bad and reprehensible wishes." But his interpretation reduced demonology to nothing but individual neurosis, for he concluded that the actors in the drama of demonology were just acting out neurotic conflicts—as his case study demonstrated. Following the lead of Freud, psychiatric historians subsequently have interpreted the demon possession of medievalism as evidence of neurosis or psychosis, and concluded that, until modern psychiatry, the western world interpreted mental illness as demon possession. This interpretation is incorrect on two major counts.

First, recent historical studies have revealed that Freud and the psychiatric historians following him based their conclusions on the study of neurotics, from which they generalized to interpret all demonology. The documents of pre-scientific western history reveal that from early medieval times onward many clear distinctions were made between mental illness and demonology (Kroll, 1977; Neugeauer, 1979). In his analysis of medieval demonology, the Spanish anthropologist Baroja (1964) notes that western rationalism ousted the belief in witchcraft from its place in the collective consciousness of man, to survive only in the marginal circles of cranks and neurotics. (These were the possessed whom Freud observed.)

Second, the appearance of demonology in historical perspective reveals broader sociocultural issues than cannot be accounted for solely in terms of individual neurosis. Thus, the eminent medical historian George Rosen (1968) observes:

Witch hunting expresses a disease of society, and is related to a social context....To be sure, some individuals involved in witch trials were mentally and emotionally disordered. Most of those involved were not. In part, their reactions were learned, in part, they conformed because of fear-producing pressures.

Similarly, the historian Russell (1972) concludes:

But it will not do to assume that the witches were, on the whole, mentally ill. They were responding to human needs more universal than those of individual fantasy; universal enough to be described in terms of myth.... The phenomenon of witchcraft, whether we are talking about the persecutors or the witches, was the result of fear, expressed in supernatural terms, and repressed by a society that was intolerant of spiritual dissent. In most respects, a variety, or at least an outgrowth of heresy, witchcraft was one manifestation of alienation.

INTRAPSYCHIC EXPERIENCE, DESCRIPTION, AND INTERPRETATION

Before continuing to the substantive material of this chapter we must first delineate, for purposes of analysis, three levels of experience.

First, consider the intrapsychic experience closely corresponding to the definition of trance used by Bourguignon. This level of experience is deeply personal and is marked as typically being difficult or even impossible to communicate to others. The second level of experience is the individual's description of intrapsychic experience. Two important features of this level are that it is necessarily social and its expression is through a shared symbol system. This is close to Bourguignon's definition of possession trance. The third level is that of explanation or interpretation of experience. This level may proceed as either personal or social efforts but always occurs with references to a social or cultural belief system that mediates and structures experiences into categories meaningful to the participants. It is interesting to note that this third level exists independent from a primary intrapsychic event. Thus, an observer may only attempt interpretation of experience that has been described or observed. This is the level of scientific theory and also that of magical or religious belief. The reliability and validity of interpretation, inasmuch as it is not based on primary or intrapsychic experience, is the central problem for the phenomenological philosophers.

Obviously all three levels of experience may co-occur simultaneously and with reference to the same events. An intrapsychic experience close to our topic, which is perhaps familiar to the reader, is the conversion experience. This is particularly true for the "born again" experience of the charismatic Christian churches. The profound nature of this intrapsychic experience is indicated by the weeping and not uncommon fainting observed at charismatic services. This experience is difficult to communicate, especially to those who have not in some way shared the experience. Indeed, at the level of description we have words used as "beautiful," "terrible," or "powerful," and rarely is there reference to the "publilc" features of the experience such as weeping. At the level of interpretation or explanation we commonly hear that the person was "being possessed (alternately, "touched") by the Holy Spirit." Here the independent nature of the explanation level becomes manifest. For an observer who subscribes to a belief system that does not admit possession or a Holy Spirit, the "born again" experience might appear as hysteria or perhaps as an affirmation of group membership. In fact, someone participating primarily at the interpretation level of experience is mainly concerned that his or her "experience" (actually their interpretation) becomes consistent with and nonthreatening to their established beliefs. By interpreting a difficult or unusual experience as part of an acceptable belief framework, the experience becomes nonthreatening. The prior existence of a belief framework often enables one to "explain away" problems or at least to make them tolerable.

This brief presentation will be of direct application in the following case histories by providing us with a schema to isolate the levels of experience at which different actors are participating. Also, the reader should note the nearly isomorphic relation between the levels of experience and the proposed categories of possession phenomena.

CATEGORIES OF POSSESSION PHENOMENA

The concepts of possession by "other forces" are both ancient and widespread. The level of abstraction, however, varies widely throughout time and culture. At the concrete end of the spectrum, there is a high degree of personification and specification. Thus, one may be possessed by a specific "spirit" of a specific person or animal, which produces specific behaviors in the "possessed" person. In the middle, there is possession by generalized spirits, ghosts, or supernatural beings, which may in turn produce specific acts or generalized sets of behaviors. And at the most abstract level, we have "possession" by thoughts, impulses, memories, or images. One may be possessed by either good objects or bad objects; and possession may produce either socially desirable or undesirable behavior (Lambert et al., 1959). Usually, however, possession involves bad objects that produce undesirable behavior.

The term *possession* is used to describe three rather separate categories phenomena:

1. *Possession States* (PB), which are extraordinary stereotyped patterns behaviors, recognized and defined in the culture as a "state of possession." This may be subdivided into two subsets: (a) possession state without altered state of consciousness (PS), and (b) possession state with altered consciousness, or *Possession Trance* (PT).
2. *Possession Behavior* (PB), which is recognized by the culture as disordered atypical, deviant, unusual, or extraordinary; whereas the behavior is ascribed to or interpreted as "possession."
3. *Possession Explanations* (PE), which are cultural beliefs about why certain everyday events such as accidents, illness, or misfortune occur.

The term *possession* has often been used for all, or one, or a combination of these definitions of possession. However, for further scientific research and discussion, that we must now use more precise terminologies. In turn, much of the confusion in the literature is due to this imprecise use of terminology. A further confusion arises from the fact that these three major categories at times overlap and interdigitate in actual life situations. For heuristic purposes, however, it is useful to consider each of these major categories separately.

TRANCE, POSSESSION TRANCE, AND POSSESSION STATES

These states of consciousness and associated behaviors have a number of points in common. They are not typical of the participants behavioral repertoire and rarely constitute daily routine. They are marked by a specific on set and termination which may generally be anticipated by the participant. Finally, these states of consciousness are highly stereotyped and patterned behaviors that satisfy criteria for appropriateness held by other significant participants or observers.

Trance and other similar altered states of consciousness are culturally prescribed practices that are performed primarily by individuals as *personal ritual* which have personal and private satisfactions. Most common of the trance states are those related to meditation and correspond to the intrapsychic level of experience. One should note that even the inwardly directed trance state occurs within a carefully prepared social context; the mantra of Transcendental Meditation or, as another example, the highly structured context of Zen Buddhism.

Trance is distinguished from possession trance as well as by the ascription of the participants' behavior to possession. Thus, possession trance corresponds to the description level of experience where both actor and observer are interacting to inform each other as to the nature of the experience. Indeed, it is not uncommon to find that the principal actor, the one possessed and participating at the intrapsychic level, to profess ignorance as to their behavior during the trance and to request this information from other participants.

Example 1.

Glossolalia or "speaking in tongues" is a form of possession trance of considerable antiquity. Modern manifestations of this behavior are linked to the biblical account of the apostles experience when they gathered to celebrate Pentecost:

Acts 2:4—"And they were all filled with the Holy Ghost, and began to speak with other tongues, as the Spirit gave them utterance."

The contemporary settings for "speaking in tongues" are typically fundamentalist Christian churches. During hymn singing following a sermon or while being exhorted to "let the Spirit in" some members of the congregation begin systematically swaying or shaking. Their body movements become more intense as they leave their seats and slowly move toward the center aisle or the area below the pulpit. Some may fall to the floor, but all begin to make rather strange utterances with no discernible pattern (not discernible to the author GSH). These utterances, the "tongues," are punctuated by shouted praises to

God as well as questions about which members of the congregation seek spiritual guidance. The utterances and body movements continue until several questions are "answered," usually by the minister or other member "interpreting" the meaning of the utterances. At the conclusion of the possession trance the more active participants are sent back to their places where they may inquire about the questions asked and the answers received. This may be repeated several times with each episode lasting from 1 to 20 minutes. (Observations by G.S. Hurd, see Griffith et al., 1980; Ness, 1980).

We find here participants at all three levels of experience, although the primary intrapsychic experience of the possession trance is felt by relatively few participants at one time. For these participants all of the indicators for possession trance are satisfied at an immediate level of abstraction.

In the following examples we find a simpler situation of a village dance in which one of the dancers becomes possessed by various animals. Example Two is a portion of a song performed during a possession trance.

Example Two:

The Fish does... HIP

The Bird does... VISS

The Marrot does... GNAN

I throw myself to the left

I throw myself to the right

I am the fish...

(Africa:Gabon Pygamy, Rothenberg, 1969)

A similar possession experience at the description level of experience with a high degree of specification is provided by Bleek (1936):

Example Three:

The Moon speaks with the side of his tongue. Therefore he speaks with his tongues' tip because he feels he is the Moon who tells his story, and he does so, because he feels that he is the Moon, he is not a person, who will speak nicely, for he is the Moon. Therefore, he tells the Moon's story, he does not tell a person's story, for he thus speaks, he thus tells the Moon's stories.

(Africa:lxam Bushmen quoted in Rothenberg, 1969)

In general, possession trance is practiced by shamen or healers as part of rituals of healing or divination and by community members as part of symbolic religious rituals that deal with conflicts in the local societal structure. Both instances may be used to symbolize societal conflict, and through the possession ritual effect social conflict resolution.

Possession state (PS) is distinguished from possession trance (PT) in that it is always related to a specific conflict situation, typically arising between the individual expressing ·PS and once or more of their socially significant alters. Like PT we note the highly stereotypic behavior that includes all those attributes which the appropriate reference community utilizes to indicate possession. There is generally a specific onset of the behavior; however, unlike PT, PS is more likely to invade all of the affected individuals behavior. Unlike PT and possession behavior discussed below, PS is merely an expression of conflict not a means of conflict resolution. Varying degrees of specifications occur in PS, from particular spirits to the most abstract such as in hex magic or root work (Wintrob, 1973). Although there are available examples with a high degree of specification from other cultures, the case that we present here is that of a Possession State induced by root work.

Example Four:

A black male was admitted to the Adult Psychiatric Inpatient Unit at the Medical College of Georgia on referal from the Augusta City Police Department. In his midthirties, the patient had been born and educated (through a third year of college) in South Carolina. On admission the patient complained of inability to sleep, stomach ache, and the feeling that "there are snakes under my skin." Indeed this last symptom was accompanied by or in reference to occasional, apparently involuntary, microtremors in the patient's extremities. The patient's neurological workup was normal and the only medical findings were related to hypertension and poor nourishment. Sensitive to the patient's possible involvement with hex magic, the attending psychiatrist, Dr. E.R. Bishop, asked him if he thought that someone may have "put roots on him." The patient was at first hesitant but when certain his doctor was not making fun of him, he responded with relief that yes, his problems were definitely due to root work. When asked about who might have been responsible, the patient drew the business card of an apparently well-known "root doctor" from his wallet! He told us that he was sure that this was the person who performed the magic. The next logical question was: Would the same root doctor remove the hex? The patient said that he had approached the root doctor about this, but had been refused. We then learned that for over four years the patient had been traveling from town to town through out the southeastern states trying to find another root doctor able to help him. It was noted that the business card looked very professional, so surely the root doctor had been paid by someone. The patient told us that "it couldn't have been my mother" but "for sure it had to be my wife's father." Exploring the conflict between the patient and his father-in-law, it was discovered that it stemmed from the promiscuous behavior of the patient's wife. Both men held the other responsible, leading to heated arguments resulting at least once in the exchange of gunshots. After the shooting, the father-in-law bought the aid of a root doctor.

The clinical goal in this case was the amelioration of the patient's symptoms related to the root work. However, no attempt was made to "cure" the patient of the hex nor from his belief in hex magic. The approach taken was to have the patient explore and express his feelings about his wife and his father-in-law. It was the power of these conflicts that gave power to the hex. When the patient became possessed by the root magic, the conflict was removed from the accessible world into the unaccessible world of magic. This served to internalize the negative emotional content such that the patient could not intervene on his own behalf, nor could he pursue the original conflict to any conclusion. It should be noted that being possessed in this instance provided the patient with a means to leave the original conflict situation, which also included leaving an unhappy marriage.

POSSESSION BEHAVIOR (PB)

Under this category we observe behaviors that are recognized by the community as aberrant, abnormal, or deviate from an individual's normal behavior. This is in contrast to possession trance or possession state, which are recognized as "different" but nonpathological. Within a given individual, the severity of the manifestation of PB may fluctuate over time, but the associated behavior becomes an overall component of their daily routine. We find that possession behavior is always related to a conflict situation, which might be marital, familial, or communal. What we have then is a set of culturally provided symbolized behaviors available to an individual through which they may express neurotic conflict. As such, possession behavior always occurs at the description level of experience, with the primary intrapsychic experience being that of the generating conflict.

There are numerous excellent ethnographic analyses of such behaviors which demonstrate how the possession behavior symbolizes a specific conflict, and how such conflict may be reduced, ameliorated, or resolved through the symbolism of possession itself, as well as through ritual possession exorcism (Chakraborty and Baneriji, 1975; Prince, 1974; Sangree, 1974; Shack, 1971; Uzzell, 1974; Watson & Watson-Franke, 1977; Young, 1975).

Example Five:

An eighteen year old Mayan girl was betrothed to an older man who was the close friend of her father and paternal uncle. A few months before the wedding her fiance was killed in an accident. This caused considerable upset to her father, who had lost a good friend, but seemingly had little impact on the young girl. Her lack of display at the funeral caused negative reactions from the deceased's family as well as her own. Within a few weeks of the funeral she complained of nightmares and then of conscious visitations of her fiance who sought to possess her. The father then reported similar experiences and an indigenous healer was consulted, who performed a ritual exorcism. This consisted of drawing a circle of "magical power" around the girl and her father, so that they could not become trapped by the fiance's spirit. The healer then entered Possession Trance so that he could talk to the spirit an effect a positive outcome for his clients. During a lengthy discussion with the ghost, with the clients present, the healer repeatedly emphasized the sadness and grief of their loss but that the fiance must learn to forget his living friends. Similarly they must learn to live without him. At the conclusion of the exorcism the fiance's spirit accepted the situation and promised not to return.

(G. Hurd and M. Migalski, 1982)

Here we see the classic psychodynamics of grief work carried out through both the symbolism and the explanation of the healer. The magic circle, like death, separates the fiance from the girl and her father, and the conflict is projected onto the ghost reaffirming the normalcy and health of the clients. What is most interesting here is that grief was not at issue for the young girl. Hurd had the opportunity to discuss the impending marriage with the girl some six months prior to the events described above. He found out that she was quite unhappy about the engagement but could not resist her father's desire that she marry his friend. So, although her father was most likely using possession behavior as a means of expressing grief, she was reacting to her guilt and ambivalence concerning the death. Also, her actions provided the sanctioning community with the public display related to the fiance's death, which had been lacking at the funeral. Thus we note that although the healer was entirely successful, his assessment of the case was slightly off base. The majority of the girl's problems were related to her way of resolving the initial conflicts, no longer due to the conflicts. This is a characteristic of possession behavior and neurotic difference in general.

We might also call possession behavior "neurotic possession," because the affected persons are *unable* to resolve conflict otherwise, and resort to possession as the "neurotic symptom expression." Just as in more familiar neurotic symptoms in western psychiatry, the possession symptoms mask the conflict from both the possessed person and those significant others with whom the conflict exists. Thus, possession behavior affords expression of the conflict and aids in the repression of the conflict from consciousness (Weidman & Sussex, 1971; Wittkower & Weidman, 1969; Hillard & Rockwell, 1978).

POSSESSION EXPLANATION

Naturally, not all events of possession are a matter of neurotic conflict. Perhaps the majority of the world's societies today ascribe to supernaturalistic cosmologies. Thus, at the third level of experience, possession is used as an explanataion of accidents, trauma, disease, and misfortune.

What the western mind rarely sees is that western science and its construction of reality is terribly fragmented (Ehrenwald, 1976; Galdston, 1963; Rosenthal, 1971). The naturalistic system of the western world, rooted in the particularistic rationalism of latter-day humanism, provides proximate and limited explanations of isolated fragments of human life. Further, without ontological grounding it does not provide a rationale, nor purpose, nor meaning to life. Consider the conclusion of psychoanalyst Allan Wheelis (1971):

At the beginning of the modern age science did, indeed, promise certainty. It does no longer. Where we now retain the conviction of certainty we do so on our own presumption, while the advancing edge of science warns that absolute truth is a fiction, is a longing of the heart, and not to be had by man... Our designations of evil are as fallible now as they were ten thousand years ago; we simply are better armed now to act on our fallible vision.

That western technology has achieved greater creature comforts and longevity of life is indisputable, but what of the quality, meaning, and value of life? At the same time we fail to recognize that the concept of supernaturalism is a *western* construct. As the anthropologist Saler (1977) has pointed out, it is western thought that has construed a separation between natural and supernatural.

Levi-Strauss (1966), in his book *The Savage Mind,* demonstrated so-called primitive constructions of reality provide a much more coherent, cohesive, and explanatory model of the world and human behavior than does the western scientific construction of the cosmos. Science does not provide a very comprehensive description and explanation of human behavior.

Foster (1976) has compared naturalistic with supernaturalistic systems of thought about health and illness. He finds that naturalistic systems (western) view misfortunes and illness in atomistic terms. Disease is unrelated to other misfortune; religion and magic are unrelated to illness; and the principal curers lack supernatural or magical powers, for their function is solely an instrumental task performance. On the other hand, supernaturalistic systems integrate the totality of all life events. Illness, religion, and magic are inseparable. The most powerful curers are astute diagnosticians who employ both technical and symbolic means of therapeusis.

Early students of supernaturalistic healing systems, such as Ackerknecht (1971) and Rivers (1924), emphasized the particular magical beliefs and rituals of shamen and other folk healers; but they overlooked the complex integrated view of nature and humanity, and complex, refined distinctions that were made between different kinds of accidents, misfortunes, illnesses, and diseases, together with their causes and cures. Loudon (1976) comments:

This reduces the study of health and disease to studies of witchcraft, sorcery, magic, and in general curative or socially readjustive ritual practices, with herbalists and empirically rational treatment and prophylaxis as residual categories.

In brief, supernaturalistic systems deal with the total spectrum of human life and behavior, which integrates man and nature. A variety of supernaturalistic explanations exist to deal with all varieties of situations in life. Careful ethnographic studies reveal two major conclusions:

1. Supernaturalistic cultures do make distinctions between accidents, distortions of natural process such as a malformed fetus, hazards such as snakebites or tornadoes, psychosomatic disorders, personal and interpersonal conflict that we would term neurosis, and existential-religious issues of life (Bahr et al., 1974).

2. There are similar distinctions made between types of healers and intervention healing strategies for different life problems. Although such interventions may range from physicalistic (such as herb remedies) to purely symbolic rituals, they all are encompassed under a supernaturalistic rubric. Yet, both the common people and the healers differentiate different levels of intervention. (Bilo, 1977; Lin et al., 1978; Woods, 1977)

In sum then, we must avoid a reductionistic interpretation of all supernaturalistic systems as simply magical spiritualism. Such systems are often quite sophisticated and complex. Because supernatural explanations are embedded in the whole of the system of health and healing, as well as the spectrum of behavior, we can treat the concept of "possession" as just one specific phenomenon. Rather, there is a wide range of possession beliefs which is related to sets of behavior ranging from ritual trance on the most specific end of the spectrum, to abstract notions of the nature of man as embodiments of spirit.

In contrast to the above observations of specificity, it must be noted that "possession explanation," at times, are *overinclusive* of several different classes of behavioral phenomena:

1. *Psychosis as possession:* Apart from the "cultural-bound psychoses," which are usually explained as specific types of possession, there are often cultural explanations of possession in the classic psychoses of schizophrenia and manic-depression. Although there is no stereotyped behavior, such as is exemplified in the culture-bound psychoses, the aberrant, deviant, and bizarre behavior of the florid psychotic is taken as evidence of possession. In this case, we have psychotic elaboration and use of symbolic language and behavior of the culture (Ahmed, 1978; Wintrob, 1968, 1970).

2. *Combined functional-organic syndromes as possession:* Here we have a common behavior pattern, such as seizures, which may be either a "neurotic conversion" or "organic epilepsy." In a study of Navajho seizure disorders by Neutra et al., (1977), they found the seizure behaviors were identical regardless of etiology, and thus, seizures were ipso facto explained as possession and treated as such. The differentiation between the two etiologies was only revealed by long-term follow-up. The neurotic seizures disappeared after appropriate exorcistic healing, whereas the organic epileptic seizures persisted.

3. *Organic illness as possession:* Common illnesses often are not ascribed to possession. An excellent example of this phenemenon occured in the New Guinea highlands in the 1950s. A slow-growing virus epidemic developed in a small tribe. The illness was unknown to the tribe. The symptoms were a gradual but inexhorable neurological deterioration without alternation of mental status. The tribe ascribed the illness to a specific possession and quickly developed an exorcist cult. After about 20 years when the epidemic had disappeared, the tribe similarly gave up that specific possession belief and the exorcist cult disappeared (Lindenbaum, 1979).

SUMMARY

This chapter has considered the rather specific phenomenon of demon possession. We have seen that beliefs in possession and exorcism are part of a larger set of supernaturalistic beliefs throughout cultures, including our own western culture, the difference being the degree of abstraction of the concept of possession. Similarly, the exorcist varies from the traditional shaman to the psychoanalyst. Our understanding of possession phenomena must include an analysis of the culture, the community, and the individual. Possession ranges from culturally normal ritual states through various degrees of psychopathology, to asymbolic organic states that are definitional possession. Similarly, our study of exorcism reveals a wide range of techniques practiced by both traditional and scientific healers. Although scientific universal principles of exorcism can be elucidated, the actual practice of all exorcisms is embedded within sociocultural mileaux. At present, in the United States, there is a wide range of subcultural groups who believe and practice possession and exorcism. This pluralism presents significant challenges for the future of both traditional and scientific psychotherapies. In conclusion, what started out as a study of the extraordinary has brought major conceptual and practical challenges to the future of psychiatry.

REFERENCES

Ackerknecht, E.H. (1971) *Medicine and ethnology: Selected essays,* Berne: Verlay Huber.

Ahmed, S.H. (1978) Cultural influences on delusion. *Psychiatric Clin.* 11, 1–9.

Bahr, D.M., Gregorio, J., Lopez, D.I., & Alvarez, A. (1974) *Piman shamanism and staying sickness,* Tucson: University of Arizona Press.

Baroja, J.C. (1964) *The world of the witches,* Chicago: University of Chicago Press.

Bourguignon, E. (1973) *Religion, altered states of consciousness, and social change,* Columbus: Ohio State University Press.

Bourguignon, E. (1976a) *Possession,* San Francisco: Chandler & Sharp.

Bourguignon, E. (1976b) The effectiveness of religious healing movements: A review of recent literature. *Transcultural Psychiatric Review,* **13,** 5–2.

Bilo, Y. (1980) *The Moroccan Demon in Israel: The Case of "Evil Spirit Disease." Ethos* **8:** 24–39.

Carstairs, G.M., & Kapur, R.L. (1976) *The Great Universe of Kota. Stress, Change and Mental Disorder in an Indian Village,* Berkeley: University of California Press.

Chakraborty, A., & Baneriji, G. (1975) Ritual, a culture specific neurosis, and obsessional states in Bengali culture. *Indian Journal of Psychiatry* **17,** 211–216.

Cox, R.H. (Ed.) (1973) *Religious Systems and Psychotherapy,* Springfield, Ill.: Thomas.

Crapanzano, V., & Garrison, V. (1977) *Case Studies in Spirit Possession,* New York: Wiley.

DeVos, G.A., (1976) The interrelationship of social and psychological structure in transcultural psychiatry. In *Culture-bound syndromes, ethnopsychiatry, and alternate therapies* (Ed. W.P. Lebra), pp. 278–298, Honolulu: University of Hawaii Press.

Douglas, M. (Ed.) (1970) Witchcraft Confessions and Accusations, London: Tavistock Publications.

Ehrenwald, J. (Ed.) (1976) *The history of psychotherapy: From healing magic to encounter.* New York: Jason Aronson.

Firth, R. (1967) Ritual and drama in Malaysia spirit mediumship. *Comparative Studies in Society and History,* **9** 190–207.

Foster, G.M. (1976) Disease etiologies in non-western medical systems. *American Anthropologist,* **78,** 773–782.

Freud, S. (1922) A seventeenth-century demonological neurosis. In *Collected Works* (1961), London: Hogarth Press.

Galdston, I. (1963) *Man's image in medicine and anthropology.* New York: International Universities Press.

Goodman, F., Henney, J.H., & Pressel, E. (1974) *Trance, Healing, and Hallucination: Three Field Studies in Religious Experience.* New York: Wiley.

Griffith, E.E.H., English, T., & Mayfield, V. (1980) Possession, prayer, and testimony: Therapeutic aspects of the Wednesday night meeting in a black church. *Psychiatry* **43,** 120–128.

Hillard, J.R., & Rockwell, J.K. (1978) Dysesthesia, witchcraft, and conversion reaction. *JAMA* **240,** 1724–1744.

Hippler, A.E. (1976) Ahamans, curers, and personality: suggestions toward a theoretical model. In W.P. Lebra (Ed.), *Culture-bound syndromes, ethnopsychiatry, and alternate therapies.* Honolulu: University of Hawaii Press. pp. 103–114.

Hoch, E.M., (1974) Pir, faqir, and psychotherapist. *The Human Context* **6,** 668–677.

Hurd, G.S., Migalski, M. (1982) *Mediation of Paradox: Aspects of Brujria.* Unpublished manuscript.

Kiev, A. (Ed.) (1964) *Magic, faith and healing.* New York: Free Press.

Kleinman, A.M., (1977) Explaining the efficacy of indigenous healers: the need for interdisciplinary research. *Culture, Medicine, and Psychiatry,* **1,** 133–134.

Knox, R.A. (1956) *Enthusiasm.* New York: Oxford Press.

Kroll, J. (1977) A reappraisal of psychiatry in the middle ages, *Arch. Gen. Psychiatry,* **29,** 276–283.

Kuba, M. (1973) A psychopathological and sociocultural psychiatric study of the possession syndrome. *Psychiatria et Neurologia Japonica,* **75,** 169–186.

Lambert, W., Triandes, L., & Wolf, M. (1959) Some correlates of beliefs in the malevolence and benevolence of supernatural beings: a cross-cultural study. *Journal of Abnormal and Social Psychology,* **58,** 162–168.

Landy, D. (1977) *Culture, disease, and healing: Studies in medical anthropology.* New York: Macmillan.

Levi-Strauss, C. (1966) *The savage mind.* Chicago: University of Chicago Press.

Lewis, I.M. (1971) *Ecstatic religion: An anthropological study of spirit possession and shamanism.* New York: Penguin Books.

Lin, T-Y, Tardiff, K., Donetz, G., & Goresky, W. (1978) Ethnicity and patterns of help-seeking. *Culture, Medicine and Psychiatry,* **2,** 4–13.

Lindenbaum, S. (1979) *Kura sorcery.* Palo Alto, Calif.: Mayfield Press.

London, P. (1964) *The modes and morals of psychotherapy.* New York: Holt, Rinehart, & Winston.

Loudon, J.B. (Ed.) (1976) *Social Anthropology and Medicine.* New York: Academic Press.

Mair, L. (1969) *Witchcraft,* New York: McGraw-Hill.

Ness, R.C. (1978) The old hag phenomenon as sleep paralysis: a biocultural interpretation. *Culture, Medicine and Psychiatry,* **2,** 15–39.

Ness, R.S. (1980) The impact of indigenus healing activity: An empirical study of two fundamental churches. *Social Science and Medicine,* **14B,** 167–180.

Neugebauer, R. (1979) Medieval and early modern theories of mental illness. *Arch. Gen Psychiatry,* **36,** 477–485.

Neutra, R., Levy, J.E., & Parker, D. (1977) Cultural expectations versus reality in Navajo seizure pattern and sick roles. *Culture, Medicine and Psychiatry,* **1,** 255–275.

Obeyesekere, G. (1969) The ritual drama of the Sanni demons: Collective representations of disease in Ceylon. *Comparative Studies in Society and History,* **11,** 174–216.

Obeyesekere, G. (1970) The idiom of demonic possession. *Social Science and Medicine,* **4,** 97–111.

Oesterreich, T.K. (1966) *Possession: Demoniacal and other among primitive races in antiquity, the middle ages, and modern times.* New York: New York University Press.

Pattison, E.M. (1978) Psychiatry and religion circa 1978: Analysis of a decade. *Pastoral Psychology,* **27,** 8–33, 119–141.

Podmore, F. (1963) *From Mesmer to Christian Science.* Hyde Park, N.Y.: University Books.

Prince, R. (Ed.) (1968) *Trance and Possession States.* Montreal: R.M. Bucke Society.

Prince, R. (1974) The problem of spirit possession as a treatment of psychiatric disorders. *Ethos,* **2,** 315–333.

Rivers, W.H.R. (1924) *Medicine, magic, and religion.* London: Kegan Paul.

Rosen, G. (1968) *Madness in society. Chapters in the historical sociology of mental illness.* Chicago: University of Chicago Press.

Rosenthal, B.G. (1971) *The images of man,* New York: Basic Books.

Rothenberg, J. (Ed.) (1969) All lives, all dances, & all is loud. *Technicians of the Sacred,* New York: Anchor Books, p. 38.

Rothenberg, J. (Ed.) (1969) *Technicians of the sacred,* New York: Anchor Books, p. 388.

Rush, J.A. (1974) *Witchcraft and sorcery: An anthropological perspective on the occult,* Springfield, Ill.: Thomas.

Russell, J.B. (1972) *Witchcraft in the Middle Ages.* Ithaca, N.Y.: Cornell University Press.

Russell, J.B. (1979) *The devil: Perceptions of evil from antiquity to primitive Christianity.* Bergenfield, N.J.: Meridian Press.

Saler, B. (1977) Supernatural as a western category. *Ethos,* **5,** 31–53.

Sangree, W.H. (1974) The Dodo cult, witchcraft, and secondary marriage in Irigwe, Nigeria. *Ethnology,* **13,** 261–278.

Shack, W. (1971) Hunger, anxiety, and ritual: deprivation and spirit possession among the Gurage of Ethiopia. *Man,* **6,** 30–43.

Skultans, V. (1974) *Intimacy and ritual: A study of spiritualism, mediums, and groups,* London: Routledge & Kegan Paul.

Thomas, K. (1971) *Religion and the Decline of Magic: Studies in Popular Beliefs in Sixteenth and Seventeenth Century England.* London: Weidenfield and Nicolson.

Tiryakian, E.A. (Ed.) (1977) *On the margin of the visible: Sociology the esoteric, and the occult.* New York: Wiley.

Turner, V.W. (1969) *The ritual process.* Chicago: Aldine.

Uzzell, D. (1974) Susto revisited: illness as a strategic role. *American Ethnologist* **1,** 369–378.

Watson, L.C., & Watson-Franke, M. (1977) Spirits, dreams and the resolution of conflict among urban Guajiro women. *Ethos,* **5,** 379–387.

Weidman, H.H., & Sussex, J.N. (1971) Cultural values and ego functioning in relation to the typical culture-bound reactive syndromes. *International Journal of Social Psychiatry,* **17,** 83–100.

Wheelis, A. (1971) *The end of the modern age.* New York: Basic Books.

Wijesinghe, C.P., Dissanayke, S.A.W., & Mendis, N. (1976) Possession in a semi-urban community in Sri Lanka. *Australian N.Z. Journal of Psychiatry,* **10,** 135–139.

Wilson, M. (1971) Witch beliefs and social structure. *American Journal of Sociology,* **56,** 307–313.

Wilson, P.J. (1967) Status ambiguity and spirit possession. *Man,* **2,** 366–379.

Wintrob, R.M. (1968) Sexual guilt and culturally sanctioned delusions in West Africa. *American Journal of Psychiatry,* **124,** 84–95.

Wintrob, R.M. (1970) Mammy water: folk beliefs and psychotic elaboration in Liberia. *Canadian Psychiatric Association Journal,* **15,** 143–157.

Wintrob, R.M. (1973) The influence of others: witchcraft and rootwork as explanations of disturbed behavior. *Journal of Nervous Mental Disorders,* **156,** 318–326.

Wittkower, E.D., & Weidman, H.H. (1969) Magic, witchcraft and sorcery in relation to mental health and mental disorder. *Social Psychiatry,* **8,** 169–184.

Woods, C.M. (1977) Alternative curing strategies in a changing medical situation. *Medical Anthropology,* **3,** 25–54.

Yap, P.M. (1961) The possession syndrome: A comparison of Hong Kong and French findings. *Journal of Mental Science,* **106,** 114–137.

Yap, P.M. (1974) *Comparative Psychiatry,* Toronto: University of Toronto Press.

Young, A. (1975) Why Amhara get Kureynya: Sickness and possession in an Ethiopian Zar cult. *American Ethnologist,* **2,** 567–584.

Epilogue

Therapist, client, and setting form a single and complementary unit; psychotherapy does not ordinarily occur without psychotherapist, without patient, or without an environment that they and other members of the culture recognize as therapy. And just as therapist and client play complementary roles, psychopathology and treatment are complementary functions in the total ecosystem in which they are embedded. Psychotherapy exists where psychopathology is expected to exist. Cultures that do not recognize psychopathology do not recognize a psychotherapist. In the final analysis, it is the interactive ecosystem as a whole that demands the presence of both pathology and treatment.

Where there are not adequate resources, niches may be generated that use few resources, such as the welfare system. Further, econiches may be created that are occupied by complementary role pairs requiring fewer total resources. Thus, illness occupies both doctor and client.

It is fascinating to observe, in the economics of state hospital systems, that the difference between the annual income of the patient population and the average income of the community served by the hospital produces a dollar figure approximately equal to the amount of wages paid to the staff. In what are undoubtedly oversimplified terms, state hospital systems provide an opportunity for the ecosystem to support both staff and patients for an amount no greater than that required to support either staff or patients alone. The distribution of decision-making, power, and competence demands is similarly disproportionate. In an ecosystems frame of reference, the term *human resources* has a dual meaning: Human resources are those utilized by human beings, but they may also be human themselves.

Energy resources are typically distributed in a pyramidal structure. That is, a typical organizational chart is small at the top and becomes larger at the bottom. This scheme allows organizations to become extremely complex, extremely effective, and extremely powerful; it allows the size of organizations to extend in an almost limitless fashion. But with increased size comes increased disparity in decision making. The effect may very well be that the role occupied by most inhabitants of the particular system—that is, the "normal" role—may be one that is extremely stressful for the individual. Further, the efficiency of the system demands that persons who cannot perform competently be excluded.

In both clinical and community mental health contexts, the practitioner attempts to minimize exclusion and stress. The probability of success is termed *prognosis,* a prediction of outcome based on symptoms. What the prognosis also indicates is the extent to which the culture will support changes in behavior for a person of a particular age, sex, socioeconomic level, symptom complex, and set of circumstances. When a client begins to dress differently, present himself differently, involve himself in different social networks, or join different social organizations, the message is sent to others about the client's "place" in the ecosystem: the therapist is attempting to reclassify the client in the "eyes" of the system.

What prevents the client from simply solving a problem or self-reclassifying is ambivalence. The client may enter therapy with alternative solutions in mind, but he is aware that a solution is also a risk in his acknowledged social context. The client has, after all, behaved in certain consistent ways and taken consistent positions with others; others may then demand a "reason" to change one's behavior or one's relationships. The therapeutic context itself allows the client to reject dysfunctional behaviors, attitudes, and commitments; but it also is understood by others in the client's life that therapy brings change. A change contract exists not only between therapist and client but also between a client and the ecosystem surrounding both client and therapy. For some people, a funeral may be a necessary context in which to express grief and loss and to gain support. For others, a depression and psychotherapy may be necessary to deal with loss or to begin demanding that relationships change and personal needs be met.

The client's ambivalence is traditionally described in such terms as "defenses" or "resistance." The words themselves are revealing of the processes. A person "defends" against attack; in the therapeutic process, the "defenses" of the client are protective not only of aspects of self that may be threatening but also protect against the destructive potential of an ecosystem in which personal needs may not be supported by social context. The process becomes "resistance" when the therapist "takes sides"—that is, begins to coerce the client on behalf of the system or force the client to act without recognizing the legitimate basis of defenses.

The problem or symptom that the client presents to the therapist in a therapeutic context is not the essential focus of the therapeutic process. The client could obtain expert suggestions or sensible alternatives from a number of sources, and the therapist rarely suggests solutions that could not be equally well obtained from persons already known to the patient. The task of the therapist is then to discover the client's solution and to create an environment in which it can occur.

For some therapists there is a second process based on the therapist's knowledge that the client is embedded in a total ecosystem and may be experiencing distress related not only to presenting complaints but also to what is not occurring in the total ecosystem. For example, the client may have interpersonal problems with the marital partner. But the client may be relatively inactive in stress-reducing recreational activities, may be experiencing significant stress related to an employment situation, and may be relatively unskilled at utilizing social protective mechanisms (insurance, savings, legal systems, health service, etc.). In one way or another, the experienced healer determines what is not occurring in the client's life by determining what the client ordinarily does 24 hours a day and 7 days a week, quite apart from the areas that the client can readily identify as sources of distress and that form the basis for formal diagnosis.

An intervention into this interactive ecosystem by the therapist entails an intentional attempt to alter the client's perception of the problem and his behavior in a complex ecosystem that he has failed to identify as a source of distress. Family therapy provides an obvious example of strategic intervention. For instance, the initial complaint may concern a family member who is experiencing difficulty in school. By the time the therapist's strategy has fully unfolded, the problem is defined as an interaction among all members of the family and may involve interactions between family members other than the original client.

Psychodrama provides another illustration. The protagonist and director select a critical event that represents a conflict area in the protagonist's life. The event is at first carefully reenacted so that it is as real as possible and includes as many of the original sensations and experiences as possible. Through doubling, role reversal, and other directors' maneuvers, the therapist or director begins to modify the client's perception and behavior in relation to the earlier event. By the time the psychodrama is concluded, the client views the earlier event differently, has behaved in that situation in different ways, and has generalized the event and its significance to his or her current situation. In the process of reorganization, the client may develop a new frame of reference with which to reinterpret his or her own relationship with his or her personal world. This, in turn, may affect behaviors and responses that the client is likely to make in day-to-day living. Thus, the stress/exclusion process and "prognosis" are modified as the client reclassifies self to others.

If there is no self-presented client and we attempt to modify stress/exclusion processes, then the preventive mental health intervention becomes more difficult for the practitioner to define. Communities, like clients, seem to be ambivalent: What is of value and how much human cost is acceptable? There may well be defensiveness, resistance, and reinterpretation in the process of change. Wallace (1959), based on his study of therapeutic process among the Iroquois, describes the process of becoming a healer as an instance of *mazeway resynthesis.* The term refers to a reorganization of one's mode of perceiving the world in an attempt to make sense of a highly anxiety-provoking environment. The healer is viewed as a person whose capacity for conflict resolution extends across a range that allows understanding of both dysfunctional persons and the norms of the community. Hall (1973) has characterized the functioning of the therapist as related to "out-of-awareness cultural systems." He suggests that a particular social system may lack the words, concepts, or symbols to describe a particular human behavior but may nonetheless attach particular importance to that behavior. People may then find themselves in a position of behaving without control or understanding. A discrepancy develops between the individual's sensations and experiences and his or her ability to deal with others in the social context. The role of the therapist, independent of the particular culture, is to bring such out-of-awareness behavior under the conscious control of the individual in a manner that is acceptable and compatible with the demands of the society.

This view essentially assumes that the therapist influences the client in such a way as to induce change in his or her interaction with the ecosystem. The intervention may, however, be focused more on the community than on the patient. Holland and Thorp (1964), and Gillen (1948), have described the healing processes in Mayan communities as focused on the community itself. The culture is organized largely on a kinship basis and is relatively homogenous. Illness is generally viewed as resulting from a lack of harmony in family, interpersonal, or spiritual relationships; it is therefore dealt with in the context of the total kinship community. The elaborate ceremonies of the healer include suggestions for modified behavior on the part of the client, but they appear to be largely effective because they achieve a consensus among the community with regard to the acceptable behavior of the client and the support with which the community will respond to behavioral changes. There are emerging models, a growing body of knowledge, a state of the art of practice, all of which point clearly to the integration of intervention and prevention; whether termed ecological or interactional or systematic or Mayan, they hold promise.

REFERENCES

Gillen, J. (1948) Magical fright. *Psychiatry,* **11,** 387–400.

Hall, E.T. (1973) Mental health research and out-of-awareness cultural systems. *Anthropological Studies,* **9**: *Cultural illness and mental health.* Washington, D.C.: American Anthropological Association, pp. 97–103.

Holland, W.R., & Thorp, G. (1964) Highland Maya psychotherapy. *American Anthropologist,* **66,** 41–52.

Wallace, A.F.C. (1959) The institutionalization of cathartic and control strategies in Iroquois religious psychotherapy. In M.K. Opler (Ed.), *Culture and mental health.* New York: Macmillan, pp. 63–96.

Author Index

Numbers in *italic* are pages on which the full references appear.

Subject Index